Hunters at
the Margin

The Nature | History | Society series is devoted to the publication of high-quality scholarship in environmental history and allied fields. Its broad compass is signalled by its title: nature because it takes the natural world seriously; history because it aims to foster work that has temporal depth; and society because its essential concern is with the interface between nature and society, broadly conceived. The series is avowedly interdisciplinary and is open to the work of anthropologists, ecologists, historians, geographers, literary scholars, political scientists, sociologists, and others whose interests resonate with its mandate. It offers a timely outlet for lively, innovative, and well-written work on the interaction of people and nature through time in North America.

General Editor: Graeme Wynn, University of British Columbia

Claire Elizabeth Campbell, *Shaped by the West Wind: Nature and History*

Tina Loo, *States of Nature: Conserving Canada's Wildlife in the Twentieth Century*

Jamie Benidickson, *The Culture of Flushing: A Social and Legal History of Sewage*

William J. Turkel, *The Archive of Place: Unearthing the Pasts of the Chilcotin Plateau*

James Murton, *Creating a Modern Countryside: Liberalism and Land Resettlement in British Columbia*

NATURE|HISTORY|SOCIETY

Hunters at the Margin

Native People and Wildlife Conservation in the Northwest Territories

JOHN SANDLOS

FOREWORD BY GRAEME WYNN

UBC Press • Vancouver • Toronto

16 15 14 13 12 11 10 09 08 07   5 4 3 2 1

Printed in Canada on ancient-forest-free paper (100% post-consumer recycled) that is processed chlorine- and acid-free, with vegetable-based inks.

Library and Archives Canada Cataloguing in Publication Data

Sandlos, John, 1970-
    Hunters at the margin : native people and wildlife conservation in the Northwest Territories / John Sandlos.

(Nature, history, society 1713-6687)
Includes bibliographical references and index.
ISBN 978-0-7748-1362-4

    1. Native peoples – Hunting – Northwest Territories – History – 20th century.
2. Wildlife conservation – Northwest Territories – History – 20th century.
3. Wildlife conservation – Government policy – Canada – History – 20th century.
Subsistence hunting – Northwest Territories – History – 20th century. 5. Big game hunting – Northwest Territories – History – 20th century. I. Title. II. Series.

QL84.26.N6S22 2007   333.95'96097192   C2006-906292-7

Canadä

UBC Press gratefully acknowledges the financial support for our publishing program of the Government of Canada through the Book Publishing Industry Development Program (BPIDP), and of the Canada Council for the Arts, and the British Columbia Arts Council.

This book has been published with the help of a grant from the Canadian Federation for the Humanities and Social Sciences, through the Aid to Scholarly Publications Programme, using funds provided by the Social Sciences and Humanities Research Council of Canada.

UBC Press
The University of British Columbia
2029 West Mall
Vancouver, BC V6T 1Z2
604-822-5959 / Fax: 604-822-6083
www.ubcpress.ca

To the memory of David Buller and Lily Buller

Resource agencies have been structured not so much to be responsive to new learning, but to maintain control over resources, information, and people.

– R. Edward Grumbine, 1997

Modern statecraft is largely a project of internal colonization, often glossed, as it is in imperial rhetoric, as a "civilizing mission." The builders of the modern nation-state do not merely describe, observe, and map; they strive to shape a people and landscape that will fit their techniques of observation.

– James C. Scott, 1998

Many wildlife professionals see themselves as custodians of a conservationist ethic that is above politics. This perspective sets them apart from those who manage resources such as timber, oil and gas, or minerals, although the promoter's view is not unknown in wildlife agencies when a particular resource appears to have great commercial possibilities.

– Peter Usher, 1994

Contents

viii · Contents

Maps, Tables, Figures

FOREWORD

The Enigmatic North

by Graeme Wynn

LTHOUGH PEOPLE OCCUPIED the northern circumpolar region thousands of years ago, notes Derek Hayes in his recent *Historical Atlas of the Arctic,* the area remained "a huge blank" on maps of the Western tradition until the end of the medieval period, "supporting nothing but theories as to what was there."[1] From a cartographic point of view, this implied veil of ignorance was drawn back slowly but successfully as Western explorers, whalers, and others traversed, named, described, and charted this mysterious, elemental, beautiful but forbidding territory, until its capes and bays, coastlines and mountains were brought to Cartesian order on modern-day maps.

This is only part of the story, of course. Indigenous peoples who had occupied these areas for thousands of years had intimate knowledge and finely developed understanding of the northern territories that were their homelands. Most of those who came from afar to draw the features of the land into European atlases and Western worldviews were translators as much as creators of information about these vast spaces. Few were as explicit about their borrowing and dependence as the English adventurer Warburton Pike, who embarked late in the nineteenth century, on a "shooting expedition" into the "unknown land" of the Barren Grounds (previously traversed, it should be noted, by Samuel Hearne, the overland Franklin expedition, and others). Pike's journey carried him "through a great deal of new country," where he "discovered, as we white men say when we are pointed out some geographical feature by an Indian who has been familiar with it since childhood" several lakes and streams that he attempted to mark on a rough map.[2]

Whatever the elisions and imprecision of newcomers' encounters with them, the Arctic and sub-Arctic continue to hold Western imaginations in thrall. They remain "lands beyond," unforgiving, sparsely inhabited and seldom travelled, expensive to cross, and at the same time fragile and vulnerable. Perhaps this helps to account for the surge of interest in ice-bound regions in recent years. Eric Wilson, who has both fostered and reflected upon this in *A Spiritual History of Ice*, observes that the *New York Times* reviewed five or six times as many books on polar subjects in the four years after 1997 as it did in the preceding six. Half a dozen years into the new millennium, evidence of rapid and extensive melting of the Arctic icecap and anxieties about the consequences of global warming have only heightened the "millennial disquiet" to which Wilson attributed the outpouring of polar meditations at the end of the twentieth century. Indeed, Wilson argues provocatively that ice (and by extension ice-bound regions) manifest "annihilation and restoration, horror and joy," and thus share many of the paradoxes that mark Western visions of apocalypse.[3]

Be such sweeping claims as they may, the Canadian North remains hard to understand. Frequently referred to, rarely engaged, and surprisingly mutable, it is even, puzzlingly, somewhat itinerant. The idea of the "true North strong and free" holds a central, mythological place in the Canadian imagination, but quite where this North begins and what references to it mean have shifted through time and space, a detail too often ignored in easy assertions of continuity in conceptions of "Canada-as-North." Typically such claims trace a smooth and unbroken arc from the voyages of polar explorers, through Robert Grant Haliburton's essay "Men of the North," to John Diefenbaker's new vision of Canada as a northern nation and the defence of Canada's claim to Arctic sovereignty late in the twentieth century. Thus English navigators such as Martin Frobisher and John Franklin are assimilated into a quintessentially Canadian story, and quite different imagined geographies are forced into a teleological historical narrative.[4]

In the second half of the nineteenth century, when enthusiasts for the new Dominion celebrated the invigorating properties of ozone-rich northern air and envisaged Canadians as "northmen of the New World," given to tossing pine trees about in their glee, they had their eyes and minds fixed on the southern edge of the pre-Cambrian Shield and the agricultural potential of the great Northwest that lay beyond. These were northern realms from the vantage point of Toronto and neighbouring American states, but in latitudinal terms, at least, large areas of the nineteenth century's storied "north woods," as well as the Ontario town of North Bay, are closer to the tropics than is Vancouver. Despite Confederation-era politician D'Arcy McGee's allegorical vision of Canada as a northern nation bounded by three oceans and thus rimmed by water like the shield of Achilles, the Arctic islands were not formally recognized as Canadian territory until 1880, and then the transfer took place in what one historian characterized as "a fit of absence of mind." As the Colonial Office had it, they were annexed "to prevent the United States from claiming them, and not from the likelihood of their proving of any value to Canada." Indeed, Janice Cavell has argued in the *Canadian Historical Review* that most nineteenth-century Canadians "did not see the Arctic as part of Canada at all"; in her view, an historical paradigm of east-west expansion and rural settlement – an agrarian rather than a northern myth – held sway among Canadians well into the twentieth century. By this account, proponents of northern development typically struggled against an "ingrained indifference to northern matters."[5]

Given the attention afforded the Far North in recent decades, and the spectacular way in which the Yukon and Alaska were thrust into public consciousness by the Klondike Gold Rush of 1898, this might seem surprising. But the geographical and imaginative remoteness of Arctic and sub-Arctic Canada in the 1890s should not be underestimated. At the beginning of that decade, George M. Dawson of the Geological Survey of Canada published a map "Showing the Larger Unexplored Areas" of the country. There were sixteen of them, all extensive, and they encompassed the entire country north of the fifty-fifth parallel, as well as substantial tracts south of this between Lake Winnipeg and the coast of Labrador. As Warburton Pike saw it, apart from a few Hudson's Bay Company trading posts and an occasional mission station, this "great northern country" was "entirely given up to what it was evidently intended for, a hunting-ground for the Indians."[6]

A few years later, the American sportsman Caspar Whitney, who headed north on snowshoes into "a country which seemed to hold naught for the traveller but hardship," began an account of his journey:

> Far to the northwest, beginning ten days' journey beyond Great Slave Lake and running down to the Arctic Ocean, with Hudson's Bay as its eastern and Great Bear Lake and the Coppermine River as its western boundaries, lies the most complete and extended desolation on earth. [This is] the Barren Grounds ... [a] timberless waste where ice-laden blasts blow with hurricane and ceaseless fury ... ; where rock and lichen and moss replace soil and trees and herbage; and where death by starvation or freezing dogs the footsteps of the explorer.[7]

In more muted tones, Elihu Stewart, the Chief Inspector of Timber and Forestry in the Dominion Forestry Branch, began an account of his journey down the Mackenzie River in 1906 with the observation that "perhaps no portion of America has received greater attention from the explorer during the last three centuries than the Sub-Arctic regions of Canada, and yet they remain practically unknown to the present day."[8] Enigma indeed. But it was journalist and historian Agnes Laut who best described the prevailing state of affairs when she echoed both Wilfrid Laurier's confidence in Canada's capacity to dominate the coming decades and Elihu Stewart's lament in the title of her article "The Twentieth Century Is Canada's: The Romantic Story of a People Just Discovering Their Own Country." Before the year was out the federal government joined the chorus with *Canada's Fertile Northland: A Glimpse of the Enormous Resources of Part of the Unexplored Regions of the Dominion.*[9]

"All Labrador, all Keewatin, all Mackenzie River, the most of the Peace river and Athabasca, nine-tenths of British Columbia, and the Yukon are still *terra incognita* for the prospector," wrote Laut enticingly in 1907. Yet northern development was slow to gain momentum. Until the 1930s Canadian government initiatives in the North were mainly defensive and strategic, in response to American, Danish, and Norwegian claims to the area. In 1939 there were twenty or so police posts and about 16,000 non-Native residents in the Yukon and Northwest territories. Trading and mission locations aside, a dozen mines, a small oil field near Norman Wells, a communications network in the Mackenzie Valley, and a few radio direction-finding stations on Hudson Bay pretty much made up the sum of non-indigenous activity in this area. When it came during and after the Second World War, however, "discovery" proceeded at an astonishing pace. Then a powerful tide of development swept through the North, floated on dreams of what might be, fuelled by demand for new resources and facilitated by improvements in the technologies of communication.[10]

Construction of the Alcan highway to Alaska in the 1940s hauled formerly remote places and people into the maelstrom of the mid-twentieth century, and development of the Distant Early Warning (DEW) Line radar stations brought outsiders, jobs, southern commodities, and cash into the Far North as never before. As early as 1949 photographer Richard Harrington marvelled that the Arctic was then "less than a day away from Edmonton." Every day a flight left the Alberta capital for Yellowknife, which it reached "in five hours ten minutes, including stopovers." Northward from Yellowknife, there was "a monthly flight ... to Coppermine, one hundred miles north of the Arctic Circle," that took "something like six hours, including a halt at Port Radium." This was a far cry indeed from the old days, when "it had taken months to cover that distance by canoe or dogsled." Yet such was the intractability of this vast territory that a contemporary map of the Arctic published by *The National Geographic* declared that "the Northlands" were only "gradually revealing their secrets to man." Indeed it is difficult, early in the twenty-first century, to appreciate just how haltingly and incompletely these northern territories were brought within the compass of a larger Canada.[11]

Half a century after Laut's article appeared in *World's Work,* the minister of northern affairs and national resources in the Diefenbaker government described the North as a "new world to conquer ... a great vault, holding in its recesses treasures to maintain and increase ... material living standards." A few years later a brief essay written in the excited style characteristic of the *Imperial Oil Review* caught the new commercial and technological realities of the area on the fly:

> Much of the time, it's frigid and forbidding ... But somewhere under those wan winter suns, those tree stunted forests ... somewhere deep under the permafrost ... there may be oil [– almost 50 billion barrels of it]. Imperial's assault on the Territories began in earnest in 1963 ... This past summer [1965] Imperial prospected ... by gravitymeter ... In less than four months [the survey crew] helicopter-hopped around five million acres of the company's territory.[12]

For a few short years it seemed that a cornucopia of Arctic resources made available by new knowledge and improved equipment would shape the future of Canada. Oil and mineral exploration proceeded apace. Academics planned for, promoters enthused about, and conference delegates considered the implications of northern development. Then the rising voice of indigenous northerners and growing public concern about environmental pollution changed the terms of public discourse. In 1977, the *Report* of the Mackenzie Valley Pipeline Inquiry, chaired by Justice Thomas Berger, cautioned against the untrammelled exploitation of northern resources. By this account, a fragile environment, the lives that depended on traditional economies likely to be undermined by development, and the obligation to address indigenous land claims warranted the respect and attention of Canadians. At the very least, growth should be slowed to allow due consideration of these issues.[13]

Against this backdrop, *Hunters at the Margin* reminds us that the past is forever (like Warburton Pike's Barren Grounds) new country, open to (re)discovery and novel mappings. John Sandlos is not the first historian to direct his gaze northward or to consider nature conservation or wildlife management in Canada. This book takes its place alongside other scholarly accounts of northern development, from Shelagh Grant's discussions of sovereignty and security issues to Morris Zaslow's two volumes on the opening of the North and the northward expansion of Canada. Others have written frequently and well of the bison and the muskox and of the caribou and the crisis that afflicted them in the 1950s. And there is no dodging the fact that efforts at wildlife management by Canadian civil servants have been ably documented in other works.[14]

But if other authors have marked many of the features found in these pages in their accounts, their stories differ quite markedly from the one offered here. Sandlos brings fresh eyes and new questions to his exploration of this territory and traces a fascinating, revealing set of inscriptions on his welcome map of the North. His efforts force readers to think again about the contours of development and the intentional and inadvertent consequences that flow from the extension of power and authority over subject peoples and distant territories. More broadly, they invite reflection on the difficult and multifaceted relationships entailed in colonialism.

From one perspective, *Hunters at the Margin* finds its centre in conflict. It is an account of the struggles between Native peoples (whose traditional hunting districts extended through much of the Northwest Territories, or present-day Nunavut) and wildlife conservation officials (employed by the federal government to administer the three most important big game species – caribou, muskox, and wood bison – of this area). It recounts how officials anxious to put modern and scientific principles of game management into practice looked with disfavour upon Native hunting practices and sought to restrict indigenous peoples' exploitation of wildlife by imposing regulations, excluding them from designated areas, and changing their traditional patterns of behaviour. And it points out that Dene, Cree, and Inuit, whose lives depended, in many ways, upon the animals that roamed the North, resisted such strategies by voicing dissent, ignoring instructions, and disregarding the law.

Abstracted from its particular setting, the main line of this story is relatively familiar. Since the 1970s, there have been many accounts of social discord arising from restriction of local access to game and other resources, as state authority extended its tentacles over formerly remote territories and the wisdom of scientific experts was elevated above traditional, local knowledge. English historian Edward Thompson drew attention to struggles over the restriction of hunting and foraging rights in eighteenth-century England. The abjuration of indigenous peoples' traditional rights by colonial forest authorities has been well documented in various parts of the Indian subcontinent, and recent studies have done much to illuminate local resistance to these initiatives. Similar patterns have been discerned in the establishment of southern African game parks. In the United States, a small library of impressive studies has traced the ways in which Indian dispossession has been associated with the creation of national parks and the strong conviction that wilderness must be uninhabited. And Canadians have their own accounts of parallel developments in Ontario's Algonquin Park and recently in Banff National Park.[15]

But *Hunters at the Margin* is not just another expansive Canadian example of a well-worn tale. Although Sandlos reaffirms what others have demonstrated in part, that the quickening of northern economic development in the late nineteenth and twentieth centuries posed a serious threat to northern wildlife, he extends and refines our understanding of how this happened and how it was perceived. He acknowledges that hunting pressures increased with the influx of people and that new markets for meat and hides encouraged Native hunters into new territories. Beyond this, however, he wants readers to understand that human impacts on northern environments precipitated ecological changes that cascaded through northern ecosystems and that these effects were poorly understood for several decades. If the "state of ecological unconsciousness" that some historians ascribe to those who planned the Alcan highway through Yukon territory in the 1940s was less marked east of the Rockies, the ecology of big game animals in this area was almost certainly less well understood than that of snowshoe hares (and other small mammals), which had been the focus of intensive investigation by the Oxford University animal ecologist Charles Elton.[16] Even in the 1950s, when the decline of caribou herds in some parts of the North came to be comprehended as a crisis, wildlife experts differed widely in their interpretation of the disaster. Many indicted the predatory behaviour of wolves, some lamented "orgies of killing" by Native peoples, and others simply attributed the problem to "a greatly increased [human] population over-burdening a depleted game population" (pp. 223, 222).

In these circumstances, it was relatively easy to conclude, as newcomers to the North and interested southerners were inclined to do, that efforts to protect northern wildlife were warranted. Sport hunters prized the game: Warburton Pike and Caspar Whitney were only two among dozens who set off across the northern prairies and into the mountains after muskox, wood bison, and other species. Many other factors converged to focus attention on the place and plight of wildlife in the North. New ideas about conservation and preservation were in the air at the turn of the twentieth century. In the United States, Gifford Pinchot and John Muir were spokespeople for and symbols of less spendthrift attitudes to North American nature, and the movements they helped to define quickly had influence across the forty-ninth parallel. Canadians borrowed from American national park legislation in establishing their own remote parks, albeit initially for tourism, sport hunting, and game conservation rather than wilderness protection. Inspired by "Pinchotism," they established the Commission of Conservation in 1909 to inventory and manage the "natural resources" of the country. In Canada between the wars, "Wild Goose" Jack Miner attained celebrity through his work in bird banding and conservation advocacy, while Ernest Thompson Seton, Charles G.D. Roberts, and Grey Owl produced dozens of immensely popular stories that made heroes of animals. South of the border, Aldo Leopold adapted and codified emerging ideas – about nature as a mechanistic system and Charles Elton's insights into population dynamics and carrying capacity – into a new field, identified by the eponymous title of his 1933 book *Game Management*.[17]

After 1945, as northern development quickened and the "northern vision" of Prime Minister John Diefenbaker gripped the imaginations of Canadians, new bureaucratic, scientific, and professional approaches to wildlife management based on Leopold's principles were added to the arsenal of schemes for the conservation of big game in the North. As the twentieth century ran its course, herds were surveyed, animal population counts were refined, enormous sanctuaries were established to protect muskox and caribou herds, indigenous hunting was monitored and restricted, and wolf eradication programs were implemented. Some of these measures pointed to and others were justified by reports of "slaughter" and "crisis." Together they painted a canvas against which the very survival of big game in the North seemed to be at stake. Common and largely uncritical assessments of those who led endeavours to preserve and conserve the herds understandably tended to represent them as enlightened heroes.

Yet those efforts were rarely unambiguous. Although those involved in protecting northern wildlife sometimes justified regulations, sanctuaries, and other interventions by proclaiming the intrinsic value of wild animals, they sought to manage herds and people for many reasons. Plains bison were brought to Alberta from Montana early in the twentieth century in an attempt to preserve a species decimated by commercial hunters, but their relocation to Wood Buffalo National Park led to hybridization of plains and wood buffalo and the spread of tuberculosis. By the 1960s, a "strict management, slaughter, inspection and processing programme" had been implemented. This yielded "exotic" meat for sale to southern Canadian consumers, and the program of intervention was defended with the argument that its profits would underwrite the costs of bison management and contribute to the national economy.[18] Free-ranging caribou were also regarded as potential organic machines, capable, under appropriate management, of turning tundra and boreal vegetation into valuable meat. From such views of wildlife, it was but a short step to the conviction that profit units had to be protected, even at the cost of undermining traditional Native hunting cultures. To this end, the government endeavoured to shift indigenous hunting to marine resources and to ease perceived pressure on caribou herds by relocating and retraining indigenous groups in ways intended to facilitate their adaptation to the modern economy.

Hunters at the Margin reveals these ancillary, perhaps even subliminal, agendas and offers the fullest, and perhaps the most impressive, account yet of the ways in which efforts to conserve animals were linked with broader colonial initiatives. It lays bare the intimate connections between wildlife management strategies and other modernizing initiatives such as commercial development and the extension of bureaucratic order over people and nature. In this reading, wildlife conservation becomes as much a form of "institutionalized social control over indigenous people" as a response to declining big game populations (p. 192).

All this helps us to refine and sharpen our still incomplete understanding of the enigmatic North, of the intentions of those charged with the administration and development of these Arctic and sub-Arctic regions and the challenges they faced, and of the changing lives of the indigenous peoples who were its most numerous inhabitants throughout these years. If, in the end, Sandlos complicates the story of this time and place, it is both because it has a much more nuanced past than many earlier accounts have acknowledged and because he refuses to reduce to a formula the variable and contradictory impulses that shaped the actions of those about whom he writes.

Wildlife conservation strategies had enormous influence on the lives of many indigenous northerners, but many of those who implemented them wrestled to reconcile antimodernist sentiments with a strong faith in bureaucratic management, or preservationist ideals with the pragmatic demands of political superiors, just as Native peoples responded in different ways to the challenges and opportunities of a growing southern presence in their traditional territories. If colonialism entails the occupation of hinterland territory and the subjugation of hinterland peoples by the apparatus of a distant state, Sandlos reminds us that it is often a messier and more variable process than the easy transformation of ecologies and societies by homogeneous and simplified management schemes that it is sometimes taken to be. Just as theorists often find the wayward world spilling beyond the grasp of their elegant constructs, so this thoroughly researched and closely detailed work reminds us that historians must use a broad palette in their analyses of societies replete with ambiguities and contradictions.

Preface

ANY WRITERS HAVE DESCRIBED THEIR CRAFT as a solitary act, and certainly many lonely hours have been spent drafting and redrafting these chapters. But the creation of a book is also a collective endeavour, a distillation of thoughts and advice from a supportive cast generous enough to comment on work while it is still in progress. Certainly this volume could not have been written without the incisive commentary of many within the broader academic community. My doctoral supervisor at York University, Anders Sandberg, helped this work evolve from its genesis as a graduate term paper to its first full incarnation as a doctoral dissertation. Anders provided crucial guidance to my research and pointed criticism when I needed it the most. The two other members of my doctoral committee also contributed greatly to the development of the ideas within these pages. Catriona Mortimer-Sandilands not only helped refine several key concepts in the early drafts of this work, she constantly pushed me to paint its story on a much broader canvas than I might otherwise have done. Viv Nelles was an enthusiastic supporter of the project and provided vital commentary from the very beginning. Stephen Bocking offered extremely helpful comments in his capacity as the external member of my dissertation examining committee. Several colleagues and friends have granted critical observations on all or part of what became this book at various stages, including Matthew Evenden, Liza Piper, Alan MacEachern, Tom Nudds, and three anonymous scholars who reviewed the manuscript for UBC Press. Throughout my graduate school career, I have been fortunate enough to have encountered colleagues – Sherilyn MacGregor, Dean

Bavington, Jenn Cypher, Adrian Ivakhiv, and Nick Garside – whose work and ideas have been inspirational, and whose friendship helped me survive the gruelling process of writing a dissertation. Randy Schmidt and Graeme Wynn both provided enthusiastic editorial support and key advice on the difficult process of turning a dissertation into a book. My editors at UBC Press, Camilla Blakeley and Sarah Wight, provided invaluable suggestions at the final stages of the project. Finally, Rajiv Rawat and Seth Loader produced the beautiful maps that appear in this book.

Several institutions provided crucial assistance for the research and writing of this book: the Social Science and Humanities Research Council, the Ontario Graduate Scholarship program, the Faculty of Arts at Memorial University of Newfoundland, the Graduate Environmental Studies Students Association of York University, and the Faculty of Environmental Studies at York University. The Aid to Scholarly Publications Programme of the Canadian Federation for the Humanities and Social Sciences generously provided a grant to support the publication of the book. The staff, archivists, and librarians at Library and Archives Canada, the Prince of Wales Northern Heritage Centre (Northwest Territories Archives), the Wood Buffalo National Park Library, and various university libraries also furnished a great deal of friendly assistance that was essential to the completion of this project.

I am extremely fortunate to have a family that has offered not only an enthusiastic reception for the ideas in this book but also tangible support for the project. My father, Hank, and my mother, Betty-Lou, have served as both audience and cheerleader for my academic work, and more recently they have provided indispensable child care. My mother-in-law, Coby Wiersma, also came faithfully once a week to spend time with her grandson and free precious hours to complete this manuscript. Other family members – Lisa, Karyn, Dave, Jude, Maya, and Zachary – have offered unwavering encouragement and a much-needed refuge from writing. My son, William, fell in love with books almost from the day he was born two years ago. Every time he pleaded for yet another reading of his favourite stories, he reminded me that a book should always be a gateway to wonder. Finally, I cannot begin to account for the ways in which my wife, Yolanda, has supported this project from its inception. Not only did she provide vital encouragement during some of the most difficult hours of writing and research, as an ecologist she also patiently advised me on the intricacies of bison population dynamics and predatory-prey relationships as a substitute for normal dinner conversation. She, more than anyone, helped to bring these pages to the light of day.

A NOTE ON TERMINOLOGY

The archival documents used as the basis for this study generally do not distinguish among the ethnic and linguistic groupings of northern Aboriginal people, referring to them only as "Indians" or "Eskimos." In keeping with contemporary convention, the Athapaskan-speaking people of the Mackenzie Valley are generally referred to in this work as the Dene, although the names of linguistic subgroups (e.g., Chipewyan, Dogrib, Gwich'in) are used when I am certain that the people being discussed are members of these particular groups. The hunting people of the High Arctic are referred to as the Inuit throughout the book. The Cree people of northern Alberta also enter this story in the early chapters.

Changes to the administrative structure surrounding wildlife conservation in the Northwest Territories were a frequent and complex phenomenon throughout the twentieth century. To further complicate matters, the federal government administered wildlife affairs through a variety of divisions and bureaus during the period (see Appendix 1 for a summary). These changes are highlighted in the text only when they bear upon the narrative. To avoid cluttering the story with needless detail and confusing the reader, I have often used such generic terms as "the northern administration," "the federal wildlife bureaucracy," and "the department."

CREDITS

A condensed version of Chapter 5 was published as "Landscaping Desire: Poetics, Politics and the Early Biological Surveys in the Canadian North," *Space and Culture* 6, 4 (2003): 394-414. Parts of Chapters 2 and 3 appeared in "Where the Scientists Roam: Ecology, Management and Bison in Northern Canada," *Journal of Canadian Studies* 37, 2 (2002): 93-129. This material has been used with permission from the respective publishers.

The photographs that open each of the main parts of the book are as follows: p. 22, a lone buffalo on a utility road in Wood Buffalo National Park, 25 August 1946, LAC C-148458; p. 110, muskox on Devon Island exhibiting typical protective circle behaviour, Percy Taverner, no date, LAC PA-48029; and p. 140, caribou on the south shore of Carey Lake, J.B. Tyrrell, 1893, LAC PA-37622.

Hunters at
the Margin

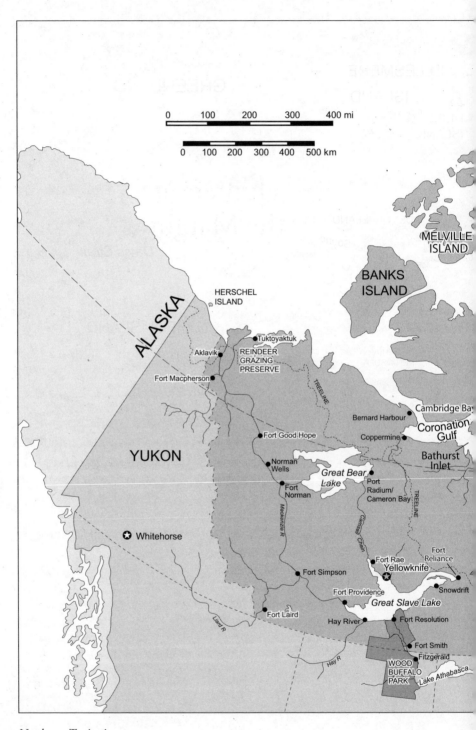

Northwest Territories, 1921-40

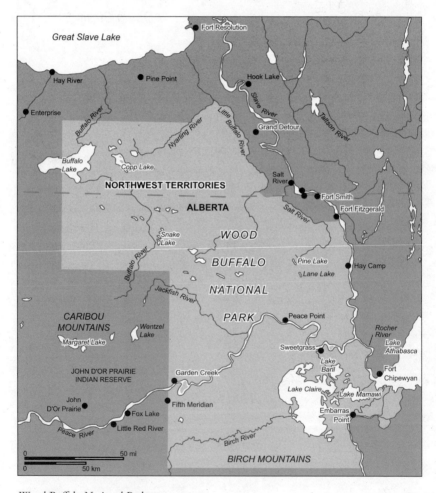

Great Slave Lake

Fort Resolution

Hay River

Pine Point

Hook Lake

Enterprise

Buffalo River

Slave River

Little Buffalo River

Nyarling River

Grand Detour

Teltson River

Buffalo Lake

Copp Lake

NORTHWEST TERRITORIES

Salt River

ALBERTA

Fort Smith

Salt River

Fort Fitzgerald

WOOD

Snake Lake

Buffalo River

BUFFALO

Pine Lake

Lane Lake

Hay Camp

NATIONAL

Jackfish River

PARK

Peace Point

CARIBOU MOUNTAINS

Wentzel Lake

Rocher River

Lake Athabasca

Margaret Lake

Sweetgrass

Lake Baril

JOHN D'OR PRAIRIE INDIAN RESERVE

Garden Creek

Lake Claire

Lake Mamawi

Fort Chipewyan

John D'Or Prairie

Fifth Meridian

Fox Lake

Peace River

Little Red River

Embarras Point

Birch River

BIRCH MOUNTAINS

0   50 mi
0   50 km

Wood Buffalo National Park

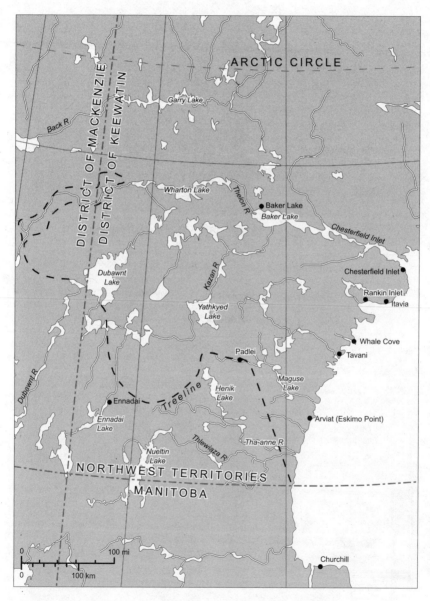

ARCTIC CIRCLE

Garry Lake

Back R

DISTRICT OF MACKENZIE

DISTRICT OF KEEWATIN

Wharton Lake

Thelon R

Baker Lake

Baker Lake

Chesterfield Inlet

Dubawnt
Lake

Kazan R

Chesterfield Inlet

Rankin Inlet

Itavia

Yathkyed
Lake

Whale Cove

Padlei

Tavani

Dubawnt R

Maguse
Lake

Treeline

Henik
Lake

Ennadai

Ennadai
Lake

Arviat (Eskimo Point)

Thlewiaza R

Tha-anne R

Nueltin
Lake

NORTHWEST TERRITORIES

MANITOBA

0   100 mi

0   100 km

Churchill

District of Keewatin

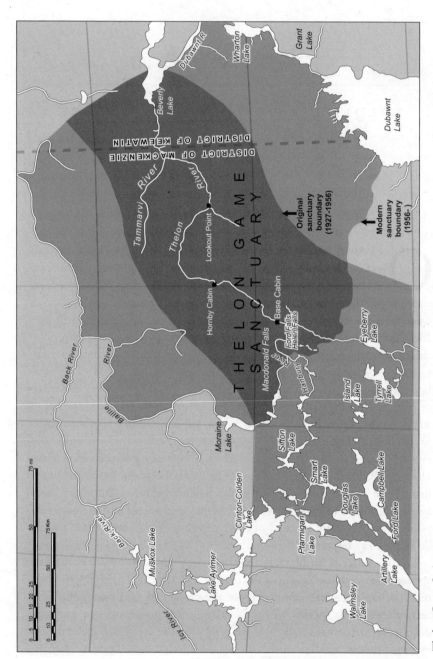

Thelon Game Sanctuary

Introduction

WILDLIFE AND CANADIAN HISTORY

O N 1 APRIL 1924, O.S. FINNIE WROTE A LETTER from the Canadian government to the "Indian people" of the Northwest Territories. As the director of the Department of the Interior's Northwest Territories and Yukon Branch, Finnie was responsible for the conservation of wildlife in the vast stretch of Canadian territory north of the sixtieth parallel. Accordingly, the letter (which was to be distributed as a pamphlet throughout the territories) provided a cautionary tale of a tribe "far away to the East" that was a "stupid people" because they had killed all the caribou they could until none remained, leaving their children hungry and without warm clothing. To avoid such a fate, Finnie offered several pieces of advice to the Native hunters of the North: kill only caribou that are needed for food and clothing, shoot only bull caribou, kill wolves on sight, and avoid hunting in the late spring and early summer when caribou hides were unsuitable for human clothing. The letter also warned that any hunting of the rare muskox would make federal wildlife authorities "very angry." Finnie nevertheless claimed that the government and the mounted police were the "true friends" of the Native hunter: "The Indians should do as they say because it is right."[1]

Finnie's letter is emblematic of the federal government's paternalistic approach to wildlife conservation in the Northwest Territories through much of the twentieth century. From the passage of the first wildlife protective legislation specific to the Northwest Territories in 1894 until the devolution of control over wildlife policy to the territorial government in 1970, federal wildlife authorities assumed that state control over the region's Aboriginal hunters was the only way to save big game populations such as the caribou, the muskox, and the wood bison.[2] There was no thought of implementing a co-operative approach to wildlife conservation during this period; the imposition of restrictive game laws, the enclosing of traditional hunting grounds within national parks and game sanctuaries, and the introduction of police and game wardens to the area were all part of a process whereby the federal state began to assert unconditional authority over the traditional hunting cultures of the Dene and Inuit, as well as the Cree inhabitants of Wood Buffalo National Park.[3] Native hunters were expected to submit to the remote authority of federal wildlife officials because, as Finnie's letter put it, the bureaucrats were "right." Indeed, the prevailing sentiment among conservationists in Canada through much of the twentieth century was that Native hunters in the Northwest Territories were incapable of conserving wildlife; only the rational intervention of the experts in the state bureaucracy could prevent the wholesale destruction of wildlife at the hands of northern Aboriginal people. Roy A. Gibson, the long-serving deputy commissioner of the Northwest Territories, summarized the attitude of federal wildlife officials in 1949 when he wrote, "Too often, I am afraid, the native mentality is left unconvinced by the logic of conservation and regards game laws as simply another of the white man's eccentricities."[4]

What Gibson dismissed as ignorance was more probably widespread political opposition to state conservation initiatives among Native hunters in the Northwest Territories. Dene and Inuit communities throughout the Northwest Territories, and also those Cree who hunted and trapped in Wood Buffalo National Park, formally resisted their marginalization from federal wildlife conservation programs through letters, petitions, and boycotts of treaty payments. Less formally, Native hunters simply refused to obey the game laws, hunting the animals they regarded as a birthright. In either case, many Native northerners bitterly resented the meddling of outsiders who purported to be managing northern wildlife in the best interest of local people. From the early twentieth century, the question of who rightfully controlled the wildlife of the Northwest Territories became one of the most intense sources of controversy between Native hunters and the Canadian federal government.

The historical antagonism between Native hunters and state officials in the Canadian North has much in common with the long international history of social conflict over local access to wildlife for the purpose of food and commodity production. Throughout the globe, the imposition of game regulations and other conservation measures in the rural periphery has engendered political discord: peasants versus wealthy landowners, local "squatters" versus elite sport hunters, indigenous people versus colonial authorities, and rural wildlife harvesters versus urban naturalists and wildlife enthusiasts. In England, conflict over access to game goes back to the Game Act of 1671, which designated hunting as the exclusive privilege of the landed gentry and marked the beginning of the "poaching wars" between the aristocracy and rural peasants that lasted for the better part of the next two centuries.[5] The essence of this dispute was exported to the rich big game areas of Africa and South Asia during the height of nineteenth-century European imperialism as increasing numbers of elite sport hunters travelled to the far-flung reaches of Empire in search of trophies. These hunters were generally contemptuous of local hunting customs, objecting both to the utilitarian nature of the hunt and to specific practices – particularly the use of traps and snares or firing into herds – that violated a sportsman's code founded on such sacrosanct principles as the careful stalking of the quarry and the use of only one bullet per animal. The sport hunting fraternity worked through lobby groups such as the Society for the Preservation of the Wild Fauna of Empire to convince the colonial authorities to impose game laws and establish wildlife preserves that would restrict local access to bush meat.[6] A rich vein of recent historical scholarship has suggested that sport hunters and nature enthusiasts in the United States practised a similar inequitable form of conservation in the late nineteenth and early twentieth centuries. This period witnessed the dawn of a conservation movement that imposed game laws to limit the hunting activities of rural "squatters" and expelled resident Native and non-Native people alike from lands that were enclosed as private game preserves or set aside by the federal government to preserve the fading wilderness landscape of a rapidly closing western frontier.[7] Legal instruments such as game regulations or the expropriation of land were thus as much an expression of political power over marginalized hinterland communities as they were the product of a practical wildlife conservation strategy.

The few major works on the history of wildlife conservation in Canada have tended to ignore the political conflicts surrounding state game protection initiatives, instead depicting the conservationist protagonists as wholly enlightened and heroic figures.[8] Although Tina Loo's recently released *States of Nature* and several regional studies from Atlantic and western Canada have begun to challenge this dominant narrative,[9] the classic account of the early wildlife conservation movement in Canada remains Janet Foster's *Working for Wildlife*, an unequivocally celebratory book first published in 1978 and now in its second edition. Foster's monograph was clearly influenced by several of the pioneering works of American environmental history published in the 1970s, books that tended to extol the virtues of wilderness activists such as John Muir and Aldo Leopold. Such people rejected the prevailing "doctrine of usefulness" associated with the progressive conservation movement in favour of a preservationist philosophy that advocated the strict protection of wilderness and wildlife in national parks and other nature preserves.[10] Foster contends, however, that preservationist thought in Canada did not originate with prophetic wilderness philosophers such as Muir and Leopold, but grew instead out of the heroic work of a few enlightened and dedicated federal government employees such as Dominion Entomologist C. Gordon Hewitt, Parks Commissioner James Harkin, and Maxwell Graham, chief of the Parks Branch's Animal Division. She describes Harkin, for instance, as a heroic figure whose efforts to advance the cause of wildlife conservation were fifty years ahead of his time. Graham, in turn, "helped to advance a policy of wildlife preservation throughout the Dominion," while Hewitt's tireless work made him "the most energetic and effective advocate of wildlife preservation within the Canadian civil service."[11] Written nearly two decades after Foster's volume, Michel Girard's history of the Commission of Conservation, *L'écologisme retrouvé*, also paints a largely celebratory picture of Hewitt's role promoting the protection of caribou, muskox, and migratory birds within the halls of the federal government.[12] In a more recent full-length study titled *A Passion for Wildlife*, J. Alexander Burnett heaps similar praise on the biologists who worked for the Canadian Wildlife Service (CWS) after its creation in 1947 as among "our unsung Canadian heroes."[13] Undoubtedly, the work of Foster, Girard, and Burnett has contributed significantly to our understanding of the broad achievements of federal wildlife officials over the past century. These authors are correct to assert that important conservation initiatives such as the International Treaty for the Protection of Migratory Birds of 1916, the protection of the last remaining free-roaming bison herds, the modest recovery of the whooping crane, and the establishment of the Committee on the Status of Endangered Wildlife in Canada would have been unthinkable without the energetic support of the wildlife conservationists within the CWS and the wider federal bureaucracy.

And yet the history of wildlife conservation in Canada is more complex than the overly laudatory interpretations of Foster, Girard, and Burnett allow. A close examination of the writings, policies, and actions of the federal government's conservation bureaucrats and biologists shows that they were not visionaries who sat outside of the political currents and eddies of their own historical period, but were instead adherents to many of the prevailing cultural and ideological influences that shaped the wider North American conservation movement. For example, Canada's early wildlife conservationists subscribed equally to Gifford Pinchot's mainstream progressive-era doctrine of conserving natural resources for their economic value and to Muir's more radical vision of preserving wilderness and wildlife for their intrinsic worth. Certainly many contemporary environmentalists would find little to admire in Maxwell Graham's frequent appeals to conserve the wood bison for their "valuable robe" and "first-class beef qualities."[14] James Harkin may have written eloquently of the aesthetic and sentimental reasons for protecting wildlife, but he also sat on a royal commission that advocated the domestication of barren ground caribou and muskox as livestock for a northern ranching industry.[15] Gordon Hewitt's sense of awe at the mysterious "lure of the wild" was tempered by his enthusiastic support for such initiatives as a caribou meat industry in northern Canada and the experimental cross-breeding of buffalo with cattle to create an ideal type of range animal.[16] The combination of such contradictory motivations within Canada's early conservation movement suggests that the philosophical dichotomy between "preservationist" and "conservationist" philosophies was not as rigid in the early twentieth century as some environmental historians have presumed.[17] Above all else, conservationists such as Harkin, Hewitt, and Graham were both practical administrators and idealists, willing to combine the lofty aesthetic associated with an emerging wilderness ethic and the more practical language of the commercial promoter in order to inspire public support or political action. Furthermore, nothing suggests that these conservationists understood these arguments as inconsistent or contradictory, or that they employed the strategy of "protective coloration" – adopting the rhetoric of managing wildlife in national parks and nature preserves for the purposes of state production while covertly attempting to implement more preservationist policies – that historian Doug Weiner has argued was the modus operandi for state wildlife bureaucrats in the Soviet Union during the early twentieth century.[18] Instead, the bureaucratic movement to protect wildlife in Canada was flexible enough to accommodate both the antimodernist desire to preserve wildlife as the most visible remnant of an authentic but fading wilderness and the modern faith in bureaucratic management as a means to cultivate and manage wildlife populations for recreational and commercial purposes.[19]

In either case, the subsistence hunting economies of Aboriginal people were excluded from the prevailing definitions of conservation adopted by the federal wildlife bureaucracy in the early twentieth century. Indeed, wildlife conservationists in Canada often held contemptuous views of Aboriginal hunting practices, a discourse that took on racist overtones as bureaucrats, naturalists, and biologists routinely interpreted reports of "wasteful" wildlife slaughters as the outgrowth of more general "primordial bloodlust" among Native hunters. Although the popular image of the primitive Native hunter as an environmental paragon living in harmony with the natural world had gained a degree of cultural currency throughout North America due to the rise of antimodern sentiment, promoters of this image such as the naturalist Ernest Thompson Seton, the author and painter Arthur Heming, and the Native poseur Grey Owl tended to reserve their idealized representations for the Natives of a distant past unsullied by contact with modern civilization.[20] Canadian wildlife conservationists often adapted this idea to their own political agenda, arguing that Native hunters who had been tainted by contact with guns, whisky, and unscrupulous traders had become incongruous in a wilderness landscape containing the continent's last pristine wildlife populations. But regardless of whether federal wildlife officials disparaged Aboriginal hunters as inherently destructive toward wildlife or as a fallen people whose harmonious relationship to wildlife had been destroyed by contact with whites, they reached an identical conclusion: the presence of unruly Native hunters in Canada's hinterland regions was inimical to the implementation of modern and scientific wildlife management intended to produce a usable surplus of wild game. The nearly universal denigration of Native hunting practices thus served an important legitimating function for federal wildlife officials; the assertion of state authority over people and wildlife at the periphery could be justified because the subsistence cultures were somehow deficient in their relationship to wildlife. By the account of most conservationists, both Aboriginal people and the animals they hunted needed the rational guidance of state wildlife managers in order to have any chance of survival.

The prevalence of such sentiments among Canada's early wildlife bureaucrats suggests a counternarrative to the overly laudatory historical interpretation of the conservation movement in this country: the introduction of federal wildlife programs to Canada's hinterland regions constituted an assertion of state authority over local people and wildlife populations, following a similar pattern to the colonial advance of state conservation initiatives in other parts of the globe. Of course, important distinctions can be drawn between colonial expansion in Canada and the establishment of European imperial holdings in Africa and Asia. Canada obviously never attained the status of an imperial power that was capable of imposing administrative rule over large indigenous populations on distant continents. It was instead a settler colony, one that, in the latter half of the nineteenth century, was intent on occupying the vast stretches of territory on the western plains and displacing the resident indigenous population within a reservation system.[21] At the dawn of the twentieth century, the colonization of the West had largely been completed and the federal government had begun to turn its gaze toward its northern territories, commissioning geologists, naturalists, and explorers to report on the potential for agricultural settlement in the region.[22] The first generation of conservation bureaucrats in Canada eagerly embraced and promoted colonization schemes in the northern territories, encouraging initiatives such as domestication and rational management of wildlife populations on vast ranches so that the North might be transformed from a homeland for hunters and trappers to a region bustling with settlement and industry. The colonial rhetoric surrounding such wildlife conservation initiatives received broad popular expression in the narratives of naturalists and sport hunters who paid tribute to the commercial potential of northern wildlife while condemning the region's indigenous hunting cultures as a wasteful and destructive element of the northern environment, a resident population that would therefore benefit greatly from the introduction of a European agricultural economy and a modern scientific approach to game management. Wildlife conservation was only one of several institutional agents of colonialism that brought profound changes to the Aboriginal cultures of northern Canada, most notably missionary education and later the introduction of wage employment associated with large-scale industrial resource exploitation. Moreover, the various institutions that asserted colonial authority over northern Aboriginal people rarely presented a unitary perspective on the issue of wildlife conservation. Roman Catholic missionaries and the Department of Indian Affairs tended, for example, to oppose restrictive game conservation measures, particularly if they harmed the material well-being of Native hunters and might lead to mounting relief bills.[23] Nonetheless, by the end of the 1920s, conservation had become a pervasive influence in the lives of many Native hunters, one of the main administrative instruments through which the state was able to reshape human relationships to local environments in large areas of the Canadian hinterland.

The bureaucratic enthusiasm for settling the North as a wildlife ranching area faded at the end of the 1930s for logistical and budgetary reasons, but the discourse surrounding northern wildlife conservation retained much of the colonial culture associated with the earlier expansionist movement.[24] The image of the Native hunter as a reckless killer of game remained the primary justification for wildlife conservation programs in the Far North through the interwar and postwar periods; federal wildlife officials responded to this stereotype with the gradual imposition of increasingly rigid forms of control over Aboriginal hunting activities in the region. This replacement of supposedly deficient local traditions and customs with a more appropriately modern approach to wildlife management took many forms (and it is here that one can observe the most obvious similarities with wildlife conservation programs in the colonized areas of Africa and South Asia). Regulatory restrictions on "excessive" hunting practices (often imposed by a territorial council consisting of appointed federal bureaucrats), the exclusion of local people from legislated wilderness areas, and coercive attempts to "educate" Native hunters about alternative resources such as fish and marine mammals all were common elements of federal conservation programs in northern Canada until the gradual devolution of authority over wildlife to the territorial government was completed in 1970. The result for many Native hunters was an erosion of sovereignty over wildlife and other local resources and the imposition of outside control over the most basic elements of their traditional subsistence cultures.

In terms of political boundaries, the landmass north of the sixtieth parallel that today consists of the Northwest Territories and Nunavut offers the most important regional setting in which to investigate the colonial nature of early federal wildlife conservation programs in Canada. Undoubtedly, many other areas of the country saw historical moments of conflict between local hunters and federal game authorities (particularly within the national parks), but the Northwest Territories is the only large contiguous landmass in Canada where the federal government retained constitutional authority over wildlife throughout much of the twentieth century. In addition, the Northwest Territories was one of the last regions of the continent to contain significant numbers of herd animals after the collapse of the plains bison in the late nineteenth century. Vast herds of migratory caribou still roamed the tundra and subarctic forests in numbers approaching the former glory of the bison herds, small herds of the exotic muskox still dotted the Arctic landscape, and the last free-ranging herds of bison in Canada wandered the region south of Great Slave Lake.[25] It is no wonder, then, that the Northwest Territories became a repository for many of the grandest ambitions of the federal government with respect to wildlife conservation.

The human geography of the Northwest Territories also contributed to the unique history of wildlife conservation in the region. The majority of people in this region have been, and continue to be, of Aboriginal descent, a population of relatively independent hunters and trappers who have never been displaced by the settlement rush that condemned so many Native people in the southern reaches of the continent to live on small reserves. Broadly speaking, the indigenous population of the region comprises two major linguistic groups. The Athapaskan speakers – now more commonly referred to as the Dene – who inhabit the subarctic regions near the tree-line include such linguistic subgroups as the Chipewyan, Dogrib, Slavey, Hare, Mountain Dene, Sahtu-Dene, and the Gwich'in. The Inuktitut-speaking Inuit hunters of the Far North live from the Arctic tundra interior to the vast Arctic Archipelago. Subgroups include the Inuvialuit and Copper Inuit of the western Arctic, the Iglulik and Baffinland Inuit of Baffin Island, and the Netsilik, Sallirmiut, and Caribou Inuit of the eastern Arctic.[26] Also spread throughout the subarctic region is a significant Métis population, some of whom arrived with the fur trade from the French-Métis settlements of Manitoba in the mid-eighteenth century, and others from a distinctive cultural group that arose through marriage between Dene women and European traders. Although many northern Métis were completely absorbed within the hunting and trapping economy and cultural life of the Dene, a unique social and economic life did emerge in the larger trading posts where many northern Métis served as economic and cultural middlemen in the fur trade. These northern Métis often maintained strong social ties with their Dene brethren but also adopted European social and cultural mores because of the distinctive roles they were granted at the large fur trading companies as guides, traders, clerks, and post managers.[27]

For many Native northerners, the federal government's efforts to restrict access to important game species represented a direct threat to their cultural life as hunters and fur harvesters. In the late nineteenth and early twentieth centuries, most Dene and Inuit in the Northwest Territories lived largely on the land in small and widely scattered hunting settlements, particularly during the winter trapping season, when the procurement of furs was integrated with a traditional seasonal round that included the taking of moose, muskox, wood bison, snowshoe hare, marine mammals, and fish (depending on regional availability). For many northern hunting groups, the large herds of barren ground caribou that migrated through the subarctic forests and Arctic tundra were an incalculably important source of food and raw material.[28] As late as the 1950s, certain Dene and Inuit groups were almost wholly reliant on caribou for food and clothing; even today the species provides a large portion of the fresh meat in many northern Aboriginal communities.[29] The hunting and gathering of food and fur were also fundamental to social and cultural life in most Dene and Inuit communities. The rhythms of daily and seasonal life were largely organized around such activities as running traplines, checking fish nets, tracking the movements of large game, preparing meat for storage, and manufacturing clothing from hides. Collective hunting and particularly the sharing of meat helped to structure and reinforce kinship ties and group solidarity in many Dene and Inuit bush settlements.[30] Game animals – particularly the caribou – also held a place of great importance within Dene and Inuit songs and stories.[31] Almost inevitably, the cultures of the Dene and Inuit came into conflict with the federal government's conservation programs: life on the land was impossible without access to animals.

The specific reactions of Native northerners to federal wildlife conservation policies are often difficult to discern from an archival record that overwhelmingly privileges the perspective of government officials. The barriers of language and literacy restricted the individual voices of northern Aboriginal people on issues of game conservation to a very few protest letters and petitions scattered within the voluminous official correspondence on wildlife issues. Oral history collections reveal much about the life that the Native elders lived on the land, but the tendency among participants to emphasize the practical and beneficial aspects of the independent bush life of past decades often obscures the history of conflict between Native hunters and wildlife officials in the Northwest Territories.[32] Nonetheless, a vivid impression of the anger directed at federal wildlife conservation programs emerges from the reports of government agents that lived in northern Aboriginal communities. Although one must be careful to read through the biases of outsiders living within an alien culture, the correspondence of Indian agents, the mounted police, game wardens, missionaries, and other local representatives provides an important record of organized political opposition to wildlife conservation in the form of treaty boycotts, the oral representations of Native leaders, and lobbying on behalf of those charged with offences against the game laws. It is also possible to interpret many recorded infractions of the game laws as a political reaction by Native hunters to the imposition of wildlife conservation. What federal wildlife officials dismissed as mere poaching or carelessness with campfires might also be understood as an attempt to reassert traditional patterns of hunting and burning on the landscape. Although the archival sources exclude much of the interior conversation among Native northerners on the issue of wildlife conservation, the existing records do provide an unambiguous picture of the hostile response Native hunters displayed toward federal wildlife conservation programs in the Northwest Territories.

In order to highlight the intensity of the historical conflict between conservationists and subsistence hunters in the Northwest Territories, this book has been written not as a detailed overview of federal wildlife policy but as an episodic account of disputes over access to three of the region's most important large game animals: wood bison, muskox, and caribou. Although access to small game and fur-bearers also sparked intense discord between Native hunters and conservationists, the charismatic big game species attracted the most attention from conservationists and in turn provoked the most embittered protests from Native hunters over restrictions on access to their basic food sources. Moreover, unlike moose, for instance, caribou, muskox, and wood bison were all believed to be threatened with endangerment or extinction, a circumstance that created a crisis atmosphere in the federal wildlife bureaucracy and prompted calls for action from conservationists outside of government.

The response of the federal government to these wildlife crises can be divided into four periods of vacillating interest in wildlife that were largely dependent on the general levels of bureaucratic interest in the northern territories. The first tentative demonstration of a desire to protect northern wildlife on the part of the federal government can be traced to a ban on all wood bison and muskox hunting by non-Native hunters established in 1894. Three years later, the federal government dispatched a small number of mounted police to the Northwest Territories to conduct an anti-poaching patrol on the bison ranges near Fort Smith. Despite this early enthusiasm, however, a regular patrol of game guardians was not established on the northern bison range until the Department of Forestry assigned two wardens to the area in 1912.

This period of relative indifference ended in 1917, when authority over wildlife in the northern territories was transferred to the Dominion Parks Branch, an administrative shuffle that granted wildlife enthusiasts such as James Harkin and Maxwell Graham broad power to form wildlife policy in the Northwest Territories. The end of the First World War also coincided with a growing fascination among federal officials with the idea of domesticating muskox and caribou (and also importing European reindeer) as an agricultural base for settlement of the North. Government interest in the economic opportunities associated with mineral and hydrocarbon development also resulted in the creation of the first administrative unit devoted exclusively to the region in 1921. Under its first and only director, O.S. Finnie, the Northwest Territories and Yukon Branch pursued an activist stance on issues such as health, education, and wildlife conservation. A rigid supporter of strict wildlife policies in the Northwest

Territories, Finnie was one of the first advocates of relocating Native hunters as a means of protecting local wildlife populations. This administrative enthusiasm for wildlife conservation had several important results: the passage of a more stringent Northwest Game Act in 1917 and again in 1929, the creation of Wood Buffalo National Park in 1922 and the Thelon Game Sanctuary in 1927, and the transfer of nearly seven thousand plains bison to the supposedly understocked northern bison ranges between 1925 and 1928.

This wildlife activism largely came to an end at the beginning of the 1930s, however, as reduced budgets for the Department of the Interior brought about the dissolution of the Northwest Territories and Yukon Branch in 1931 and an attendant reduction in the number of game wardens, police, and administrative staff in the Northwest Territories. Although this relative bureaucratic neglect of northern wildlife lasted through the Great Depression until the end of the Second World War, there were some innovations in conservation policy. Roy A. Gibson, the administrative chief of the Northwest Territories throughout much of this period, maintained a consistent interest in conservation and wildlife issues. Under his direction, northern field agents made the first attempts to divert Native hunters from caribou to alternative resources such as fish and marine mammals. Gibson was also among the first federal officials to articulate a policy of coercive relocation for hunters living near threatened wildlife populations. Between 1943 and 1947, Gibson and several Royal Canadian Mounted Police officers strongly advocated for the removal of several hunters from close proximity to the caribou herds of interior Baffin Island.

These new approaches to conserving northern wildlife laid the groundwork for a period of intense intervention in the lives of northern Native hunters between 1946 and 1970. The general postwar renewal of the federal bureaucracy allowed for a major increase in the number of federal field agents (police officers, game wardens, etc.) able to supervise the hunting activities of Native northerners. In addition, in 1947 the Canadian Wildlife Service was created, a government agency devoted exclusively to wildlife research and management in areas of federal jurisdiction. The wildlife service's biologists were deeply involved with many northern wildlife programs. Not only did the CWS conceive of a scheme to control the spread of tuberculosis in the northern bison herds by holding commercial slaughters in Wood Buffalo National Park, the agency also produced a flood of scientific reports pointing to an apparent massive decline in the mainland caribou herds that sparked an unprecedented flurry of conservation activism. At the urging of the CWS biologists, the northern administration strengthened the protective regulations for caribou, and federal wildlife officials also embarked on a program designed to alter fundamentally the subsistence hunting cultures of northern Aboriginal people. Through education campaigns and direct supervision, the federal government sought to "help" the Dene and Inuit abandon the caribou hunt by exploiting alternative food resources more efficiently or becoming wage labourers within the expanding northern industrial economy. In its most extreme manifestation, this new policy regime provided at least part of the rationale for one of the most autocratic program initiatives ever implemented by the northern administration: the relocation of Native hunters away from the caribou herds of the Arctic interior to coastal areas where they might be "rehabilitated" as fishers, whalers, or industrial workers. More than any other incident discussed in this book, this wide-ranging response to the postwar caribou crisis illustrates the extent to which wildlife conservation had an all-encompassing influence on the lives of many Native hunters, as the state attempted to manage and control the most basic elements of their traditional subsistence cultures.

Might the intervention of federal officials in the lives of the Dene, the Inuit, and the Cree hunters of Wood Buffalo National Park have been a just and necessary means of protecting northern wildlife populations that were on the brink of extinction? Certainly one cannot simply assume that the Aboriginal hunters of the Northwest Territories were living in a state of equilibrium with local wildlife populations. As the anthropologist Shepard Krech has argued so persuasively, the contemporary cultural stereotype of an "ecological Indian" living in a state of harmony with nature has tended to obscure the archaeological and historical evidence suggesting that some groups of Aboriginal hunters in North America exacted a devastating toll on local wildlife populations.[33] As in other parts of the continent, Native hunters in the Northwest Territories did at times overhunt certain wildlife populations, sometimes to devastating effect. The extirpation of the caribou from the Mackenzie Delta region in the late nineteenth century, in large measure due to the participation of Aboriginal people in the meat and hide trade on the Arctic coast, stands as a testament to this fact. But did the Native hunters of the Northwest Territories always kill wildlife to the point of excess, as many conservationists claimed? Much of the sentiment regarding the wanton hunting practices of Native people was built on a foundation of observer bias, racial stereotyping, and inaccurate second-hand reporting. Even in cases where the federal government's concerns over the impact of Native hunting on particular wildlife population were legitimate, one may still find more to admire in the intent of their action than in their paternalistic approach to conservation. As Krech himself argues, the fact that historical incidents of Aboriginal overkill did occur does not undermine the right or the ability of Native hunters to manage local wildlife populations in partnership with state experts, as in many of the recent co-management arrangements in the Canadian North.[34]

If Canada's early conservationists were blind to this option, perhaps the fundamental problem with their agenda rested not with its purpose but with its method. Until recent decades, the wildlife conservation movement in Canada was largely indifferent to the concerns of local people, often with dire consequences for the human and natural communities that lay in its path. Moreover, although the Canadian wildlife conservation movement may have been born out of a noble principle – the saving of that which is irreplaceable – its emphasis on domesticating northern wildlife populations for commercial purposes suggests that it did not always live up to this ideal. Writing in a broad context almost thirty years ago, the environmental philosopher John Livingston argued that wildlife conservationists failed to stem the swelling tide of species extinctions in the twentieth century because they embraced a managerial and scientific approach to their mission that valued living things only if they were useful to human beings.[35] Certainly Livingston's critique of an excessively human-centred approach to conservation can be readily applied to the proposals for northern wildlife ranches put forward by such early figures as Hewitt, Harkin, and Graham. It is likely, however, that the northern Aboriginal hunters who lost control over their subsistence hunting practices through the twentieth century held a differing view of conservation from Livingston. For them, the practice of wildlife conservation in Canada was not human centred enough.

PART I

BISON

A lone buffalo on a utility road in Wood Buffalo National Park, 25 August 1946,
LAC C-148458

I

Making Space for Wood Bison

O N 20 JANUARY 1898, A TRIAL WAS HELD in Fort Smith, a hamlet on
the Slave River just north of the present-day boundary between
Alberta and the Northwest Territories. A Chipewyan hunter named
François Byskie had been arrested and charged with killing two bison near
Lying Wood Mountain five weeks earlier. Although a federal law prohibiting all hunting of the elusive and rare herd of wood bison that inhabited
the range between the Slave and Peace Rivers south of Great Slave Lake
had been in place since 1894, the Byskie case marked the first conviction
of a Native hunter north of the sixtieth parallel for the crime of poaching
big game. In the course of the trial, Byskie readily admitted killing the
buffalo, but claimed the crime was justified because he was suffering from
starvation. The presiding justice of the peace, North-West Mounted Police
inspector W.H. Routledge, displayed little sympathy for this "excuse." He
concluded that, because two bison had been killed, a "spirit of mischief"
rather than acute hunger had motivated Byskie. Routledge confiscated the
two bison – one of which he noted would make a fine specimen for the
National Museum in Ottawa – and sentenced Byskie to a ten-dollar fine
or ten days' imprisonment with hard labour in lieu of payment. The police
officer reported that the local hunters took a great deal of interest in the
trial, because "Indians about the place were curious to know whether the
law could or would be carried out." Routledge concluded that the strict
application of the law had set an example that would prevent any further
illegal hunting of the wood bison: "Provided white men with evil intentions do not encourage the Indians to break the law, I think they will not

trouble buffalo, particularly in view of the Bysize [sic] case, and the fact
that a constable is stationed in the vicinity, and I may here say that Indians in the north have a wholesome dread of the police."[1]

Contrary to Routledge's prediction, the Byskie case was only the first of
several trials prosecuted against local hunters for poaching on the wood
bison range. Although there were very few documented cases of poaching
until after the designation of the northern bison range as Wood Buffalo
National Park in 1922, Native hunters actively protested the proposed
buffalo reserve until its creation, and afterwards continued to flout (or
resist) the federal game laws and assert their right to hunt on their traditional territories. At the core of the conflict between Native hunters and
federal wildlife officials were questions that had confronted the wilderness
and wildlife conservation movements in North America since their inception in the late nineteenth century: Who owns and governs access to
wildlife? How do state authorities establish untouched wilderness areas in
regions inhabited by human beings? Does the national interest in wildlife
and wilderness preservation supersede local subsistence needs?

The broad history of the federal government's early wildlife conservation programs suggests that these questions have been answered in a way
that favoured the imposition of absolute state authority over "pristine"
nature. Indeed, the late nineteenth and early twentieth centuries saw pronounced wilderness and wildlife activism in Canada. The federal government established twelve national parks between 1884 and 1920, instituted
the National Parks Branch in 1911, created the Advisory Board on Wildlife
Protection in 1916, and passed the Migratory Birds Convention Act in 1917,
a law that resulted from a treaty with the United States to protect waterfowl by creating uniform hunting seasons in both countries. These policy
initiatives had some profoundly negative consequences for Native hunters.
The Migratory Birds Convention Act, for example, effectively denied hunters
in northern Canada access to waterfowl by opening the hunting season on
1 September, well after most species had flown south for the winter.[2] Furthermore, as early as the 1880s the Canadian federal government was intent on establishing iconic western wilderness parks that would rival not
only the sublime mountain scenery but also the exclusionary policies associated with earlier US models. The creation of Rocky Mountains Park
in 1885 – which included the famous hot springs of present-day Banff
National Park – was intended almost entirely as an incentive for wealthy
eastern tourists to patronize the new intercontinental railroad.[3] The park
superintendent urged in his annual report for 1895 that a group of Stoney
Indians living near the boundary be permanently excluded from the park.

Following several boundary revisions, the issue was finally resolved when the Stoney band's hunting areas near the southern boundary of the park were made a game preserve in 1913.[4] Such expropriations of land for national parks from local Native and non-Native people alike remained common throughout southern Canada well into the 1970s.[5]

The circumstances surrounding the establishment of Wood Buffalo National Park suggest that the federal government was determined to create an exclusionary boundary in the South Slave region comparable to the national parks south of the sixtieth parallel. Shortly after the creation of the park in 1922, non-treaty Indians and Métis hunters were expelled from its boundaries. Treaty Indians who resided in the park were allowed to continue hunting and trapping, subject to strict monitoring and regulation by northern administrators and park wardens. Over time, the new game laws had a dramatic impact on Cree and Chipewyan hunters who lived near the northern bison range.[6] Decisions that had previously been made locally about what species to hunt and the best time of year to take particular game animals were now at least partly circumscribed by a formal legislative and regulatory framework that emanated from Ottawa. Those who violated these game laws, particularly those who killed buffalo, were subject to fines, prison terms, hard labour, and, worst of all, permanent expulsion from the park area.[7] Much like such iconic wilderness parks as Banff, Yellowstone, and Glacier, Wood Buffalo National Park was to become an object of displacement and resentment for Native people in the region, as the most obvious manifestation of a rigid conservation bureaucracy that had weakened their sovereignty over their traditional territory.

While the assertion of direct federal control over the traditional hunting activities of local Aboriginal people in the South Slave region implied a strong preservationist approach to saving the wood bison, the attempts to create a strict wildlife sanctuary in northern Canada also revealed the extent to which federal officials hoped to assert direct managerial control over the northern buffalo herds. Indeed, the earliest proposals for the sanctuary in 1912 articulated what was assumed to be a more rational and interventionist approach to the management and cultivation of the bison herds than had been practised by Native hunters. The new plans included the fenced enclosures and selective breeding programs to augment the numbers of bison and propagate quality breeding stock. In more general terms, then, federal wildlife officials readily combined the language of the wildlife preservationist with that of the utilitarian conservationist, arguing for the salvation of the bison based on the contradictory images of a wilderness and a semipastoral landscape. This hybrid of preservationist and conservationist philosophies may not have seemed at all contradictory to Native hunters in the South Slave region, however, as both were exclusionary discourses that implied the assertion of state power over a wildlife population that had been under the local control of Native hunters for generations.

SAVING THE WOOD BISON

The status of the wood bison herds in northern Canada began to alarm naturalists and government officials in the late 1880s. These animals constituted one of the last free-roaming buffalo herds in North America, and they were also thought to be a rare and unique subspecies of the southern plains bison due to their larger size, stockier build, darker coat, and more pronounced shoulder hump.[8] Among the first expressions of official concern over the fate of this elusive creature was a Senate report of 1888 postulating that a maximum of six hundred animals remained in the ranges of northern Alberta and the Northwest Territories.[9] Five years later, a Dominion land surveyor also noted the small wood bison numbers on the northern plains and recommended protective legislation in his report to the Department of the Interior.[10] In October 1893 the North-West Mounted Police commissioner, Lawrence W. Herchmer, estimated that the wood bison herd numbered only 150 animals in the land west of the Slave and north of the Peace rivers.[11] Among popular writers, the British hunter-naturalist Warburton Pike suggested in his account of a journey through the Fort Smith region in 1889 that the wood buffalo were so scarce as to be almost extinct, and the American hunter Caspar Whitney reported that only three hundred of the animals remained on the northern range in 1894.[12] All of these estimates must be treated with some scepticism, as none was the result of extensive or systematic survey work in the buffalo range. Most observers based their estimates of population declines solely on brief forays into the region immediately surrounding Fort Smith, a survey method that could not account for erratic herd movements or pockets of high population density. Moreover, the only baseline data against which to judge the apparent decline of the herds were the narratives of explorers such as Samuel Hearne and Alexander Mackenzie that described the wood buffalo as "very plentiful" near the end of the eighteenth century.[13]

Such imprecise information did not prevent the vast majority of witnesses from blaming local Native hunters for the apparent decline of the wood bison. Herchmer, for example, made abundantly clear his belief that

Native hunters were likely to eradicate the last of the wood bison. Deep snow in 1892 had restricted the mobility of the animals "and the Indians were thus able to slaughter a large number; from the best authorities I gather that over two hundred were thus killed, and I am personally aware that one trader named Secord alone secured over forty." Herchmer emphasized that these animals were the last free-roaming bison in the Dominion and requested passage of an order-in-council making it illegal to be found in possession of the hides or heads of the wood bison.[14] The following spring, Herchmer wrote again to his superiors in Ottawa citing anecdotal reports that a great number of wood bison had been killed near Great Slave Lake. He warned that only a very few animals would survive to the next spring, and that four officers using two dogsleds could "easily" enforce the necessary protective legislation, were it passed.[15] Herchmer's plea did not go unheeded. The first attempt of the Government of Canada to protect wildlife in the higher latitudes came in the form of the Unorganized Territories Game Preservation Act of 1894, which prohibited hunting wood bison throughout present-day Alberta and the Northwest Territories for three years.[16]

This legislation may have satisfied Herchmer and other critics of northern hunters, but it represented an incomplete understanding of the range of ecological influences that may have limited the wood bison population. The wood bison is a grazing animal that roams the open meadows and to a lesser extent the boreal forests of the northern plains in small herds that continually search out their preferred foods – sedges, grasses, willows, and lichen. Flooding, deep snow, and heavy freezing rain on significant grazing areas can cause sudden local population crashes due to mass drowning or restricted access to food. In fact, scattered anecdotal evidence suggests that one or all of these factors caused a major crash in the wood bison population in the late nineteenth century.[17] Recovery from such a population decline was, moreover, likely to be slow. Wood bison are not prolific breeders – the cows generally bear calves only two out of every three years – and the young animals are often subject to heavy wolf predation during the first vulnerable months of their lives.[18] Undoubtedly human hunters also took their toll on the wood bison throughout the nineteenth century. The movement of Chipewyan and Cree hunters closer to trading posts such as Fort Chipewyan at the end of the eighteenth century coincided with the introduction of a provision trade in wild game to supply the new settlement with food. Although the meat trade at Fort Chipewyan was local and therefore limited in size, the concentration of the region's human population near the post may have altered precontact patterns of anthropogenic burning in the region, causing at least some of the optimal meadow habitats of the wood bison to revert back to boreal forest.[19] But no factor can be isolated as the sole cause of the decline in the wood bison herds in the late nineteenth century. More likely, multiple factors – disease, severe weather, shifting human populations, and the commercial economy introduced by the fur trade – all played a role in reducing the wood bison to a remnant population confined to the relatively isolated forests and salt plains north of the Peace River.[20]

Regardless, the federal government focused on extending the "long arm of the law" further northwest at the end of the 1890s. The North-West Mounted Police began regular annual patrols to the northern buffalo range to enforce the new Game Act. On the first patrol in the winter of 1897, Inspector A.M. Jarvis levied several fines – mostly against white trappers – for the use of poison and for leaving campfires unattended. Recognizing that many Native hunters had not yet heard of the new laws, Jarvis did not stringently enforce the prohibition on buffalo but issued only stern warnings and posters urging them not to kill the wood bison. In one case, Jarvis managed to dissuade a hunting party led by the "well known" hunter Susa Beaulieu from embarking on a bison hunt near Smith's Landing.[21] This period of grace was short-lived: a police constable was stationed permanently at Fort Smith that summer to protect the buffalo, and by December he had gathered enough evidence of illegal bison hunting to bring François Byskie to trial. In January 1898, Inspector W.H. Routledge successfully prosecuted the first conviction of a Native hunter for bison poaching in the Fort Smith region.

The Byskie conviction may have highlighted the severity of the regulations associated with the new Game Act, but the federal government had made at least some attempt to address the needs of local hunters in the legislation. Although the Game Act imposed standardized hunting seasons on a host of game species over the vast territory that then constituted the Northwest Territories, Native hunters were exempt from all but the prohibitions on hunting bison. The exemption resulted largely from political pragmatism rather than a sincere effort by conservationists to recognize local Aboriginal hunting rights. During the debates over the Game Act, the minister of the interior, T.R. Daly, explained to the parliamentary opposition that "unfortunately, the inhabitants of the country are dependent upon the game for their food ... It is impossible to make the Bill more stringent unless we are prepared to feed these people."[22]

Although the Game Act did adopt some flexibility toward subsistence hunters in the North, the prerogative to restrict access to such "threatened"

northern wildlife species as wood bison now lay with the federal government. State officials assumed that standardized and easily enforceable regulations were the only scheme capable of saving the wood bison. To entrust the wood bison to the variable and informal decisions of the Native hunters who inhabited the northern range was unthinkable. The language of legal codes and schedules now governed access to northern wildlife; violations of the game regulations resulted in penalties ranging from fines to imprisonment.

For Native people in the region, the new game management system did not imply only an immediate loss of control over local resources; it was also accompanied by a formal loss of sovereignty over the local land base. The discovery of oil in the Athabasca River basin and the possibility of further gold strikes following the rush at Dawson prompted the federal government to organize a treaty commission in 1899 to secure cessions of land title from the Native communities between Lesser Slave and Great Slave lakes. The resulting Treaty 8 guaranteed signatories the right to engage in their "usual vocation" of hunting and trapping on surrendered lands, but these activities were now subject to government regulation and could be abrogated entirely on tracts "taken up from time to time" for settlement, industrial development, and "other purposes."[23] Testimony from witnesses to the treaty negotiations suggests that the guarantee of hunting and trapping rights was held out as a carrot during negotiations, while the provisions stipulating the surrender of land were not made clear to the Native signatories. According to oral recollections, concerns raised at the treaty talks in Fort Resolution during the summer of 1900 about the new hunting restrictions and the possibility that a preserve might exclude Native hunters permanently from the wood bison range were never adequately addressed.[24] The ambiguity attached to the resulting treaty – which apparently protected Native hunting rights while also providing for their dissolution at any moment – lay at the root of the political tensions over the sporadic federal attempts to create a wood bison sanctuary from 1912 to the actual creation of the park in 1922.

In the immediate aftermath of the treaty negotiations, however, federal efforts to protect the wood bison did not extend beyond the continuation of mounted police patrols on the buffalo range and the extension of the closed season on buffalo for three years in 1899 and for five more years in 1902.[25] Nonetheless, the combination of restrictive legislation, low bison numbers, and increased police patrols seems to have had at least some effect in curtailing any hunting that might have previously taken place. The reports and correspondence of the North-West Mounted Police from the years 1899 to 1907 suggest that, other than a few isolated incidents of buffalo "poaching" in which local hunters were either not notified or claimed to be unaware of extensions to the closed season, there was very little bison hunting in the South Slave region.[26] Indeed, the police reports tend overwhelmingly to blame wolf predation for the apparent decline in the bison herds. It is unclear whether this attitude represented an accurate assessment of the relative impacts of human and nonhuman hunting in the South Slave region or a tendency among the police to adopt the antipredator sentiments of the hunters they interacted with daily. For a short time, however, the debate over wood bison conservation turned not on controlling human hunting but on such issues as whether to institute a wolf bounty and whether to allow Native trappers to use poison to kill the wolves.[27]

The doubts surrounding the relationship between Native hunters and the wood bison were not permanently dispelled during this period, however. By the summer of 1907, a series of police reports and popular accounts of three expeditions along the Salt and Little Buffalo Rivers had returned Native hunting to the forefront of the debate over bison conservation in the Northwest Territories. The Royal North-West Mounted Police (RNWMP) inspector A.M. Jarvis was the leader of these forays into the bison range, accompanied at various times by the American naturalist Edward A. Preble and, most important, by the famous author-naturalist Ernest Thompson Seton. In his patrol reports, Jarvis firmly rejected the hypothesis that wolf predation was decimating the herds and revived the idea that "wasteful" Native hunters were exclusively responsible for the decline in the bison numbers. Jarvis believed that Native people were covertly killing bison because they often returned from their hunting expeditions with abundant pemmican but no moose hides. Jarvis assumed the hides had been disposed of in an effort to conceal incriminating evidence, and thus the meat *must* be bison. He also cited his difficulty finding backcountry guides at Smith Landing as proof that Native hunters were concealing evidence of wood bison slaughters throughout the surrounding country.[28] Asked to elaborate on his case against local hunters in a further report, Jarvis fell back on the racist assumption that Native people in general rather than a few individual hunters had a destructive relationship to wildlife: "The northern Indians are always in a chronic state of starvation, and when they do make a kill they never leave the pot till it is finished; they are improvident, they never look ahead. They can go out and kill a buffalo, and if they were caught could truthfully say they were starving. Now the nature of the Indian is to kill, and kill he will; even the smallest innocent singing bird he sees he will take up a stick or stone and endeavour to lay it out."[29] Jarvis asserted that Native hunters could not, by their very nature, be trusted near endangered wildlife. He recommended that a force of game guardians be assigned to the Fort Smith region, that heavy prison terms accompany poaching convictions, and that a national park be established as an "efficient and easy measure of protection [for] the whole area in question."[30]

Jarvis' contention that Native hunters represented a threat to the wood bison population reached a wide public audience through reports in *the Ottawa Free Press* and the *Edmonton Bulletin*. Here, the police inspector was reported to have said that wolf predation was a "mere excuse" meant to hide widespread bison poaching.[31] The 1911 publication of Ernest Thompson Seton's popular travelogue, *The Arctic Prairies,* provided a further public airing of the idea that Native people could not control their apparent primitive urge toward destructive hunting. Seton estimated that only three hundred animals remained in the northern wood bison herd (an assessment based on the fact that he saw very few bison on the first hunting trip, and little sign of the animals on the second two forays). He further cited Jarvis' contention that Native hunters were to blame for low wood bison numbers in the Fort Smith region. Seton quipped that "the Wolves are indeed playing havoc with the Buffalo, and the ravenous leaders of the pack are called Sousi, Kiya, Kirma, and Squirrel" – four local Chipewyans. He pointed to the same putative evidence that Jarvis presented about hunters who possessed pemmican that was "neither moose nor caribou" to argue that the numbers of bison were not increasing "chiefly because the Indians pursue them regularly for food."[32] In a more general reference that employed much of the same rhetoric as Jarvis' reports, Seton wrote, "The mania for killing that is seen in many white men is evidently a relic of savagery, for all of these Indians and half-breeds are full of it." He lamented that, for Native people, "it is nothing but kill, kill, kill every living thing they meet."[33]

In spite of Seton's claims, many of the mounted police who were responsible for protecting the wood bison disputed the idea that Native hunters were wanton killers of wildlife. Jarvis' and Seton's reports of an apparent Native hunting crisis on the northern bison range provoked more of a controversy than a call to action within the police force. Fred White, the comptroller of the RNWMP and the commissioner of the Northwest Territories, wrote to a colleague in November 1907 that the opinions of Jarvis "are merely a repetition of people who go through our North West by a particular route and form a general idea from what they see from the windows of a Pullman car or the buckboard or dogsled on which they are traveling." Days later, White wrote, "I am afraid Jarvis has laid the foundation for a lot of trouble for us when Mr. Thompson Seton gets down to the publication of his views (supported by an Officer of the Mounted Police)."[34] In response, White sent Major W.H. Routledge, now the district police superintendent, north to investigate Jarvis' claims and canvass the local opinions as to the causes of the decline in the wood bison herd. The vast majority of the testimony recorded by Routledge suggests that Native people were not guilty of widespread illegal hunting. A police sergeant recounted, for example, a conversation with Jerome, the oldest hunter in the Salt River Band, who claimed there was "no truth in that report [of Jarvis and Seton], because you would soon hear of it if that was the case, this I know to be a fact from my experience among the Indians."[35] Frank Pedley of the Indian Affairs Branch noted that "from information we have here it would appear that very little of this [poaching] is done and only in cases of extreme necessity. The Indians themselves, I believe, are as anxious as the government to see the buffalo let alone."[36] A local trader suggested that Jarvis' difficulty finding guides at Smith Landing was probably due to the reluctance of Native workers to abandon their guaranteed seasonal work loading barges during the busiest shipping months of June and July rather than a conspiracy to conceal evidence of bison slaughters.[37] A second trader claimed that a story from Seton's *The Arctic Prairies,* which told of a family living on buffalo tongues for the entire year in the community of Fort Resolution (near the mouth of the Slave River), was patently absurd. He speculated that Seton must have confused bison meat with caribou, because a buffalo had not been killed near the community since his arrival there in 1904.[38] Based on all of this testimony, Major Routledge finally reported to his superiors that he could find no indication of buffalo being killed near Fort Smith in the last two years. He further challenged Jarvis to produce evidence that would lead to the arrest of the "well known poachers" cited in his reports.[39]

Despite the tone of Major Routledge's report, over the next decade the Department of the Interior paid more attention to Seton's and Jarvis' proposals to address the supposed poaching problem through the creation of a game warden service and a buffalo reserve. As an initial step, in 1911 the department's Forestry Branch took over from the Royal North-West Mounted Police the responsibility for protecting the bison and established a regular game warden service operating out of Fort Smith.[40] A former biology student named George A. Mulloy and the trapper Peter McCallum were hired that summer as the first game wardens assigned specifically to protect the wood bison. The focus of their work was somewhat different, however, from the antipoaching patrols that Jarvis had envisioned.

The superintendent of forestry, Robert Campbell, instructed the men to devote the bulk of their efforts to trapping wolves; identifying other factors that might be reducing the wood bison population was a secondary concern.[41] Whatever the mandate, the initial patrols could hardly be described as a success on any level. In July 1912, a report from A.J. Bell, the government agent in Fort Smith, suggested that the two game wardens had experienced difficulty "getting in touch" with the wood bison herds in the vast ranges west of the Slave River.[42] The district inspector of forest reserves reported on a visit to Fort Smith in the summer of 1913 that McCallum had yet to kill a single wolf. To make matters worse, Mulloy and McCallum grew to dislike one another intensely: McCallum claimed that Mulloy's ill health hampered his trapping efforts, while Mulloy asserted that McCallum's age and poor eyesight prevented him from patrolling widely over the buffalo ranges.[43] The Forestry Department's half-hearted commitment to the game guardian program also hindered its effectiveness. When Mulloy resigned out of frustration in the winter of 1913, he was not replaced, leaving McCallum the lone patrolman for the entire wood bison range until a transfer of authority over northern wildlife to the Parks Branch in March 1917 resulted in the hiring of two additional game guardians.[44]

In spite of such handicaps, the game guardian program did produce the first specific proposals for a bison sanctuary in the region. In what was perhaps a reflection of their difficulty patrolling such a large area, McCallum, Mulloy, and their immediate supervisor, Bell, recommended that the wood bison be rounded up and protected in a 220-square-mile fenced compound near Fort Smith. The idea was not new: the famous game warden Buffalo Jones had enclosed a large herd of wild bison in Yellowstone National Park as a tourist attraction after his appointment in 1902, and when Buffalo National Park had been established near Wainwright, Alberta, in 1911, the entire park area was fenced so as to separate the plains bison from the cattle herds adjacent to the park.[45] The proposal for a fenced enclosure on the northern range stemmed from a similar pragmatic approach to conservation rather than a high-minded and idealistic attempt to save the world's last free-roaming herd of wood bison. Indeed, Bell argued that enclosing the herds was the only practical way to protect them effectively from wolves and any Native hunters who might suffer from the "great temptation" to shoot bison they encountered on the open range. This assertion was made despite Mulloy's reports that wolf predation on bison was insignificant and that Native hunters were not killing the wood bison due to their fear of the police and the abundance of moose. Even without a clear threat to the wood bison that could justify corralling the animals, Bell argued for administrative efficiency: "If it were possible to centralize these herds, the annual expenditure would be greatly reduced and more effective protection could be afforded them." He proposed an initial outlay of just over five thousand dollars for labour and fencing, part of which could be recovered by savings on the patrols and licence fees paid by sportsmen who travelled north to shoot selected old bulls for trophies.[46] Though the project was never approved, it marked the first of many proposals over the next fifty years to propagate the wood bison population through direct and intensive management of the herds themselves rather than of the Native hunters and wolves that inhabited their range.

The wood bison enclosure may have failed to inspire any enthusiasm from senior officials in the Department of the Interior because much more impassioned arguments for an open buffalo preserve had materialized within the department's Parks Branch. The primary author of these appeals was Maxwell Graham, chief of that branch's Animal Division, who began an administrative campaign in 1912 to wrest control of the wood bison from the Forestry Branch and create a large national park in the Slave-Athabasca region. Graham was a midlevel bureaucrat in a small administrative unit (with just three staff members) who used his relatively unregimented corner of the Parks Branch to lobby incessantly for new wildlife parks and tougher game laws. He had a remarkable ability to set a policy agenda from below, continually drafting lengthy and original proposals for wildlife projects to his superiors and pursuing them doggedly until they became departmental priorities. Graham's tireless promotion of the Nemiskam Antelope Preserve, for example, resulted in the creation of a park in 1915. He was also the first Canadian wildlife official to suggest that Canadian conservationists work with their American counterparts to create uniform migratory bird legislation, an initiative that resulted in the International Treaty for the Protection of Migratory Birds in 1916.[47] But arguably Graham's most important contribution to the wildlife conservation movement was his relentless, decade-long crusade to create a national park for the protection of the wood bison. Graham's compelling and forceful personality dominates the early history of Wood Buffalo National Park: no other individual shaped the early policies and local ecology of the park region to the same degree. The consequences of his managerial decisions have rippled down to the present.

Graham's campaign for a wood bison sanctuary began with a series of letters to his superior, Parks Commissioner James Harkin. In June 1912, Graham reported that McCallum's efforts to trap wolves had been ineffective and argued that the responsibility for protecting the wood bison should be transferred to the Parks Branch.[48] Graham then drafted a proposal for a wood bison preserve that contrasted sharply with the "administratively efficient" buffalo paddock envisioned by the Forestry Branch. He recommended to Harkin in December 1912 that a large national park be established north of the Peace River to encompass the entire wood bison range between the Caribou Mountains and the Slave River. The language Graham used suggests a strong affinity with the preservationist thinking that had so strongly shaped the wilderness protection movement in North America. He imagined transforming the hunting ground of the Chipewyan and Cree bands of the South Slave region into a federally controlled wilderness area, a national park where the wood bison could wander in a pristine state far removed from baneful human influence. Graham wrote of such wilderness preserves as if they were horns of plenty, spaces where wildlife could multiply and spill out over the surrounding landscape:

> The only way to continue in abundance and in individual vigour any species of game, is to establish proper sanctuaries, as thoroughly patrolled as the Rocky Mountains Parks and these must contain both summer and winter ranges. In such areas no hunting or trapping (excepting noxious animals) or dogs, should be allowed (excepting for transport purposes) and in them the game will then retain its native habits, and breed freely, while the overflow would populate the adjoining districts. This principle has been applied with brilliant success, where a protected strip of land on both sides of the Uganda railway is now absolutely swarming with game.[49]

Graham argued further that providing sanctuary to irreplaceable wildlife species such as the wood bison was a profound moral duty of national rather than purely local significance. "The interest of the entire people of this Dominion," he wrote to Harkin, "and to some extent that of the civilized world, is centred in the continued existence of the forms of animal life ... which have come down to us from an immense antiquity through the slow process of evolution."[50]

Although Graham's motives for establishing a buffalo park seem commendable, it would be misleading to imply that he was a visionary preservationist whose thinking was ahead of its time.[51] Graham certainly employed preservationist rhetoric to advance the cause of wildlife conservation, but in practice he was not a hands-off wildlife manager who was content to let the drama of evolution take its natural course. On the most basic level, he drew a sharp line between "useful" and "harmful" species of wildlife. He argued that the explicit purpose of the park was to protect "beneficial" game animals such as wood bison, caribou, moose, and deer; "injurious" animals such as wolves and lynx should be subjected to a bounty.[52] He was also not averse to applying intensive agricultural management techniques to wild herds of ungulates.[53] In fact, Graham initially thought the idea of a wood bison enclosure had some merit; he offered to provide several cows from Buffalo National Park in Wainwright to lure the northern bulls into the paddock.[54] He also felt some wood bison needed to be moved south to preserve the health and vigour of the plains bison at Wainwright. One of the chief arguments Graham concocted for transferring authority over the wood bison to the Parks Branch was that the 1,400 plains bison in Buffalo National Park had never been infused with "new blood" that was unrelated to the parent stock.[55] For Graham, wildlife conservation was thus not merely tantamount to setting aside large wilderness areas, but was also, to borrow from Aldo Leopold's early writings, "the art of making the land produce sustained annual crops of wild game."[56]

In this sense, Graham was very much a man of his time. In national parks throughout the continent attempts to preserve wilderness spaces were paradoxically combined with such intrusive management programs as predator control, wildlife feeding, experimental farms, and wildlife performances for park visitors. Prevailing images of the wilderness as a cornucopia for wildlife and a pleasure ground for people convinced bureaucrats such as Graham and Harkin that the "inviolate" wilderness needed managerial intervention to enhance the park environment for wildlife and human visitors. Tourism was not a large influence on the early proposals to create a buffalo preserve in remote northern Canada, but Graham promoted the sanctuary based on the idea that it was both a moral duty to save the bison and a prudent pragmatic gesture to improve the health and vigour of the herds.[57] For Graham, seemingly contradictory notions of preservation and conservation actually reinforced one another under a doctrine of improving nature according to the managerial dictates of the federal wildlife bureaucracy.

The early plans to manage wildlife in the projected wood bison sanctuary reinforced proposals to manage Native hunters in the region. For Graham, a prerequisite to asserting managerial control over the wood bison – rounding them up, transferring them, and protecting them in a wilderness park – was to discredit local systems of wildlife management practised by Cree and Chipewyan hunters. In one of his first letters recommending the creation of a wood bison sanctuary, Graham wrote to

Harkin that the records of the Forestry Branch and the Royal North-West Mounted Police proved that the slaughter of large game in the region was "enormous and wanton." The blame for this ongoing destruction of wildlife rested squarely with Native hunters who had been "tainted" by their contact with whites. In terms reminiscent of Inspector Jarvis' reports, Graham wrote, "An Indian with a gun will shoot any thing he sees until his ammunition is gone. They seem to be entirely devoid of any idea of economy in slaughtering, even though they must know they are certain to suffer from starvation, as a result of their indiscriminate waste of game."[58] In other words, contemporary Native hunters constituted an unpredictable, incongruous element in the local ecology of the wood bison; only the intervention of rational state wildlife managers could restrain the destructive impulses of a "fallen" race that apparently could no longer control itself. The most conspicuous theme in Graham's writings on the wood bison preserve was a profound antilocal sentiment that denied any parochial claim of an inherent right to access local resources. In a clear declaration of the federal government's authority over the northern wilderness, Graham wrote, "It is now generally conceded that the local inhabitants do not have the divine right to pollute streams with sawdust, or destroy forests with axe and fire, or slaughter every living thing; for game and forests belong to all the nation." Graham cited a precedent for removing the blemish of local hunters from the wood bison range: squatters had been persuaded to vacate Anticosti Island in the interests of game management. He suggested that "arrangements be made to induce the Indians to leave the particular district in question."[59] For Native hunters, Graham's attempts to protect and manage the northern bison both as a wilderness icon and as a semi-ranch animal entailed a dramatic displacement of local sovereignty over traditional territories and wildlife in the South Slave River region.

The evidence Graham presented for an overhunting crisis requiring the complete removal of Native hunters from the northern bison range was questionable at best. When pressed by Harkin, Graham relied almost entirely on the reports of the Seton and Jarvis expeditions from five years earlier. Despite an overwhelming number of reports from 1911 to 1916 suggesting that Native hunters were not killing the wood bison,[60] Graham argued continually that only the complete expropriation of the northern buffalo range for the purposes of a national park could save the remaining wood bison herds. In the spring and summer of 1916, Graham lobbied furiously for the designation of a buffalo sanctuary in the Peace River region. In April, he drafted a memo for Harkin to forward to the deputy minister urging the immediate creation of a strict wood bison preserve because of so-called incontestable evidence that Native hunters were killing the wood bison. He further argued that Treaty 8 provisions did not guarantee local Native people the right to hunt and trap in the region. The memo also recommended, for good measure, that Henry J. Bury, the inspector of timber for Indian Affairs, should "obtain a signed statement from the few Indians who hunt in the bison or buffalo country, in which statement they waive any fancied rights they may or may not think they possess to hunt and trap in the region."[61] Graham persistently urged his superiors to move quickly because no legal mechanism had been in place to protect the wood bison from Native hunters since the hunting ban had expired on 1 January 1912. Accordingly, in July Harkin presented a draft memo to the minister of the interior, W.J. Roche, which designated by order-in-council nine thousand square miles of the wood bison range north of the Peace River as the Caribou Mountains National Park.[62] Roche appears to have been cool to the park proposal, however, and directed Harkin to investigate the possibility of granting the commissioner of the Northwest Territories the authority to enact regulations to protect the wood bison. In August, the Department of Justice ruled that the commissioner had no legal authority to enact game laws. Harkin's assistant, F.H.H. Williamson, advised that the best possible way to protect the wood bison was to pursue the creation of the Caribou Mountains National Park. For reasons that are unknown – but probably because of wartime austerity – Harkin replied that the "matter has to stand." By the end of the year, Graham had enlisted in the armed forces as a recruiter. For the time being, his dream to create a national park for the protection of the wood bison lay dead on the order table.[63]

Graham's attempts to create a wood bison preserve were not entirely fruitless. Although the national park idea languished in bureaucratic limbo until after the war, responsibility for the wood bison and all other wildlife in the Northwest Territories was transferred to the Parks Branch in March 1917.[64] Graham had also been able to advance the premise among his colleagues that, in spite of all evidence to the contrary, the wood bison were threatened because of the reckless and wanton practices of local Native hunters. Like other attempts to impose state power over supposedly deficient local management systems at the rural periphery, Graham's campaign for a northern bison preserve was not just a noble or disinterested effort to save a species that was thought to be on the brink of extinction; it was also an attempt to redefine the local landscape and ecology according to the rational management schemes of the modern state.

SAVING NATIVE HUNTERS

However much Graham might have used his position in the Parks Branch to advocate strong federal control over wildlife in the Northwest Territories, his views did not represent a coherent federal wildlife policy regime. Graham's criticism of Native hunters and his advocacy for strict conservation measures emerged from a relatively small corner of the federal bureaucracy. While he invoked the rhetoric of state management as his conservation creed, there was seldom a unitary perspective on wildlife issues among representatives of the federal government in the Northwest Territories. The contradictory reports of the police indicate that the wider federal government had reached no clear consensus on the impact of Native hunters on the wood bison. The campaign to restrict Native hunting rights on the northern bison range may have blended the rhetoric of colonialism and conservation, but this particular "imperium" had distinct cracks.[65] In fact, the Parks Branch's first attempt to create a wood bison sanctuary produced tensions within the federal government over the so-called Native hunting problem that polarized the debate over the wildlife conservation in the Northwest Territories for the next half-century.

Opposition to the Parks Branch's rigid conservation agenda was particularly strong in the Department of Indian Affairs, where there was a growing sense that past policies emphasizing the assimilation of southern Native peoples as settled agriculturalists were unsuited to the hunting populations of the North. In areas beyond the agricultural frontier, where there would be no settlement rush and no push to transform a bush country into an agrarian landscape, the most viable – and the cheapest – policy was to encourage the hunting and fur-trapping economy that had dominated the region for two centuries. Indian Affairs officials therefore tended to endorse wildlife conservation only if it upheld hunting and trapping as the foundation of the Aboriginal economy in the North. Senior officials tended to champion legislation and wildlife preserves that protected fur and game from "outside" (i.e., white) hunters and trappers, but vigorously opposed those that restricted Aboriginal hunting activities. This defence of the traditional economy was not meant as a vindication of the importance of indigenous cultural survival. Instead, senior officials within Indian Affairs worried that dispossessed Native hunters might become expensive wards of the state.[66]

The tension between the Indian Affairs Department and wildlife conservationists was clearly evident at the National Conference on Conservation of Game, Fur-Bearing Animals and other Wild Life held in February

1919. In his opening address, Arthur Meighen, the superintendent general of Indian Affairs and minister of the interior, emphasized the absolute dependence of northern Native people on wildlife. He committed his department to helping Native people when wildlife was scarce, but he also emphasized that "such assistance can never take the place of that ability to help themselves which Indians alone can exercise if they are in the environment of wild life."[67] Meighen's emphasis on self-reliant Native hunters was echoed in a paper delivered by Duncan Campbell Scott, deputy superintendent general of Indian Affairs, titled "The Relation of Indians to Wild Life Conservation." Scott began by pointing out that Indian Affairs policy was to assist with the enforcement of provincial and federal game regulations, but he also stated that the dependence of Native northerners on game for their livelihood entitled them to a degree of sympathy. Thus the department must "endeavour also to mitigate the laws to meet any special conditions that surround the present mode of life of the natives."[68] This compromise position earned Scott a strong rejoinder from several of the conference delegates. In his own address, James Harkin argued that wildlife preserves prohibiting Native hunting activities were a critically important conservation tool because "even the Indians have a wholesome respect for park boundaries."[69] Similarly, the provincial game guardian from Saskatchewan, Fred Bradshaw, complained that the "wanton slaughter" of wildlife by Native people denied "law abiding" settlers and sport hunters access to game. Bradshaw stated, "The attitude of the Indian Department seems to be, that, while they are extremely sorry that such things [i.e., poaching] are happening – the poor Indian must be fed, and, presumably, in the cheapest possible manner. I venture to say, that the average Indian Agent encourages, rather than discourages, the illegal killing of big game. He feels it incumbent upon himself to keep expenses down to a minimum.[70]

The philosophical divide between Indian Affairs and the Parks Branch over the relationship between Native hunters and wildlife conservation had profoundly influenced Maxwell Graham's campaign to establish a wood bison sanctuary. After meeting with Graham in Ottawa to discuss the proposed wood bison sanctuary in July 1914, John McLean, the secretary of Indian Affairs, wrote an impassioned protest to Harkin. McLean reminded Harkin that Treaty 8 guaranteed Native hunters the right to pursue their "usual vocation" in the surrendered tract of land. Although McLean acknowledged that Treaty 8 allowed the government to designate tracts of land within the surrendered area for resource development and "other purposes," he also pointed out that the signatories had "scarcely contemplated" a wildlife preserve of such immense size on the hunting grounds near the Slave River. He requested that Harkin's branch take no further action until Indian Affairs could investigate the possibility of setting aside the Indian reserves that were promised in Treaty 8. Despite the assurance of more study, McLean concluded with a stinging indictment of the entire national park proposal: "It appears to be decidedly objectionable to have the tract set apart as proposed. It is the special hunting ground of the Fort Smith Indians and if it is closed they will be compelled to hunt on the Easterly side of the Slave River which is the hunting ground of other bands of Indians with whom there is certain to be trouble."[71] At a further meeting with Graham and Harkin three months later, Inspector Henry Conroy of Indian Affairs repeated many of McLean's objections. He argued fervently that the proposed buffalo reserve would interfere with the livelihood of approximately one hundred Native people who hunted and trapped in the area. The presence of these hunters, Conroy claimed, was actually a benefit to the wood bison because they frequently killed wolves. In a curious reversal of the common conservation policy with respect to Native people, Conroy suggested relocating the entire bison herd to a suitable habitat that would not interfere with the local hunters and trappers.[72] Although this proposal was never adopted as official policy, McLean's and Conroy's objections did successfully derail Graham's second proposal to the minister of the interior in June 1914 requesting the creation of a national park.[73]

Bureaucratic momentum to create a wood bison preserve was renewed, however, after the First World War. In June 1920, the Advisory Board on Wildlife Protection passed a resolution calling for the creation of a national park on the northern bison range.[74] In May, F.H. Kitto of the Natural Resources Intelligence Branch had been sent north to survey the natural resource potential of the Mackenzie District and identify a suitable boundary for a wood bison sanctuary. He spent two weeks on the wood bison range near the confluence of the Peace and Slave Rivers accompanied by Chief Pierre Squirrel, of the Fort Smith Chipewyan, and one of the buffalo rangers. Based on local testimony and his own observations, Kitto estimated that the bison in this area had increased to one thousand animals. The Catholic bishop Gabriel Breynat also suggested to Kitto that a second herd numbering close to one thousand animals ranged west of the Slave River between the sixtieth parallel and Great Slave Lake. Despite the apparent dramatic increase in the size of the herds, Kitto recommended the immediate creation of a national park to confirm federal control over the wood bison on the ranges between the Peace River and the sixtieth parallel. His concern was not the local Native hunters, but the fact that

the Alberta government was effectively claiming ownership over the southern herd of wood bison through the issue of hunting permits to hunters
and explorers such as John Hornby.[75] Although no immediate action was
taken on Kitto's national park proposal, Harkin did recommend to the
deputy minister of the interior in February 1921 the reservation of the
northern Alberta bison range from sale or disposal until a park boundary
could be established.[76] In the summer of 1922, Maxwell Graham (who was
now part of the Game Division in the newly created Northwest Territories and Yukon Branch) and the Dominion land surveyor, Fred Siebert,
were sent north to assess the size of the northern herd and permanently
settle the boundary issue. The two men confirmed the existence of a wood
bison herd numbering at least five hundred animals north of the sixtieth
parallel and recommended the creation of a park covering the entire buffalo
range from the Peace River to just south of Great Slave Lake.[77] Graham
characterized the need to protect the wood bison as "acute." Although he
claimed in his final report that treaty Indians had become "more amenable" over the years to the regulations prohibiting buffalo hunting, Graham alleged that "half-breeds and Indians from other districts ... are still
a menace."[78]

The treaty Indians of the South Slave region may have become "more
amenable" to the restrictions on bison hunting, but local opposition to a
bison sanctuary had magnified in the years since the Caribou Mountains
park proposal. Indeed, local objections to Graham's first park proposals
appear to have been relatively slight. In April 1916, Henry J. Bury had
reported that, after much discussion, the chiefs at Fort Chipewyan, Fort
Fitzgerald, Fort Smith, and Fond du Lac offered to move their hunting
and trapping areas from the intended Caribou Mountains National Park
without any compensation from the federal government.[79] But in the in-
tervening years a dispute over land distribution for a reserve had hardened
local attitudes against the bison preserve. For many years, the Fort Smith
band had been trying, in accordance with the provisions of Treaty 8, to
obtain a reserve at the mouth of the Salt River that could be used as a
hunting base and a site for small-scale agriculture. Chief Squirrel discussed
the matter with F.H. Kitto during his survey of the bison range in June
1920, declaring his support for wood bison protection so long as his
people were granted a place to hunt near the Salt River. Kitto endorsed
Squirrel's proposal, emphasizing that an influx of white prospectors and
trappers over the past two decades had spread such diseases as tuberculosis, whooping cough, and venereal disease among the Native population.
The creation of reserve areas separate from town sites such as Fort Smith

might, Kitto believed, offer some protection to a seriously weakened Native population.[80] Nonetheless, as part of its proposal to create a bison sanctuary, the Advisory Board on Wildlife Protection expressed concern that the intended reserve on the Salt River might be a strategic point from which Native hunters could pursue the wood bison.[81] Being simultaneously shut out of the nearby national park and shut in to a small agricultural plot set back from the Salt River was not a tantalizing prospect for Chief Squirrel. At treaty days in July 1922, he voiced his strong opposition to the bison preserve and sparked a long and antagonistic discussion between the assembled chiefs and the Indian agent, Gerald Card.[82] Although Card assured the chiefs that treaty rights to hunt and trap would be upheld, the bison preserve had clearly become a focal point for resentment over the expansion of federal game management initiatives in the Northwest Territories. In October 1922 the *Edmonton Bulletin* reported, "The Indians in the northern section of the province and the tribes on the Territories are much wrought up over the current rumour that a game sanctuary is to be established to the westward of the Slave River."[83] On the eve of its creation in December 1922, the proposed Wood Buffalo National Park had become a contested terrain.

Discord over the park proposal was not limited to local Native hunters; the proponents of the wood bison sanctuary also had to contend once again with critics within the Department of Indian Affairs. In the autumn of 1922, Indian Agent Card informed the press that local Native hunters had always obeyed the laws against buffalo hunting, that they felt pushed further back each year by encroaching white trappers, and that the creation of the buffalo reserve would be the "last straw" for them.[84] Nonetheless, senior officials within Indian Affairs had softened their blanket opposition to the park in the years since the first debate over the bison sanctuary. Rather than oppose the idea of a park outright, John McLean responded to the Advisory Board on Wildlife Protection's park resolution only with the suggestion that the proposed reserve at the Salt River should receive "sympathetic consideration" if the local Native people agreed to the creation of the bison sanctuary.[85]

At a meeting of the board held in April 1921 to discuss the findings of Kitto's survey, Henry Conroy and Gerald Card pointed out that the proposed park boundary would enclose the traditional Native hunting grounds. The two men did not suggest the abandonment of the park idea, but merely that the bison sanctuary should be restricted in size so the reserve could be set aside at the Salt River. They found an ally in Bishop Breynat, who suggested that the bison sanctuary be located in the Caribou Mountains, far from any of the settlements near the Slave River. Harkin, however, adopted the position that the proposed Salt River reserve would provide hunters with much too easy access to the buffalo range. He suggested pay- ing annual subsidies to the Indians to get them to forgo their hunting rights in the national park and move to another location. Although Card did express general support for a bison sanctuary, he warned that there would be "trouble with the Indians" if the buffalo sanctuary interfered with the hunting ranges of the Chipewyan hunters in Fort Smith and Fort Fitzgerald.[86] Card, Bishop Breynat, and Maxwell Graham eventually reached a compromise in the weeks leading up to the creation of the park: treaty Indians who had hunted and trapped in the park before its creation would retain these privileges, subject to game regulations that included a strict permanent ban on the buffalo hunt. All other hunters and trappers would be excluded from the area. According to Graham, this arrangement satis- fied both parties because the wood bison could be preserved in the wildlife sanctuary while the Native population were protected from the ongoing influx of "outside" trappers and traders.[87]

On 18 December 1922, Wood Buffalo National Park was designated as the first protected area in Canada to allow at least a portion of its resident population to retain their hunting and trapping privileges. But any illu- sions the authors of the legislation might have maintained of a harmo- nious George Catlin-like pleasure ground – a space where authentic (but pacified) Indians were preserved in conjunction with a representative assem- blage of Native wildlife – were quickly shattered. Conflict between federal wildlife conservationists and local hunters continued to shape the social and ecological landscape of this new wilderness area. Native people did not remain in the new park as the result of a spirit of conciliation between local harvesters and state officials. Rather, a bitter disagreement – among conservationists determined to save the last remaining wood bison, Native hunters committed to the protection of their treaty rights, and Indian Affairs officials for whom the preservation of the hunting and trapping economy was the only way to keep Native hunters off the dole – allowed for the retention of at least some hunting "privileges" within Wood Buffalo National Park. In the eyes of federal wildlife conservationists, Native hunters were a blemish on a landscape devoted to the preservation of the last of Canada's free-roaming bison. If they could not be relocated from the area for political reasons, then the game warden service needed to be enlarged. Indeed, one of Maxwell Graham's primary tasks when he sur- veyed the bison range in 1922 had been to reorganize and augment the game warden service.[88] Although the new warden service had to cover a vast territory on its patrols, Native hunting activities in the park would now be subject to the ongoing scrutiny and control of federal wildlife officers.

For Native hunters in the South Slave region, the establishment of a rigidly supervised game preserve on their traditional hunting grounds was the culmination of three decades in which the federal government had gradually eroded local sovereignty over land and wildlife. Before the late 1890s, no police officers, no game guardians, and no externally imposed legal codes governed the wildlife harvest in the Northwest Territories. Native hunters determined when to hunt and how many game animals to kill throughout their traditional territories. A quarter-century later, the creation of Wood Buffalo National Park dramatically increased the number of law enforcement and administrative personnel in the region. The federal government could now effectively administer a system of wildlife regulations that included such punitive measures as fines, jail terms, and hard labour for Native hunters who broke the law. While pressure from the Department of Indian Affairs had prevented the Cree and Chipewyan hunters who inhabited Wood Buffalo Park from being completely pushed aside by the new wilderness area, these hunters were now subject to a state system of wildlife management that was intent on controlling their traditional practices. This process of colonizing the local ecology and traditional livelihoods of Native hunters in the South Slave region was never complete, however, as local people continued to resist the recurring attempts of park managers to exclude them from the preserve and expand the scope of existing game regulations. In the coming years, Wood Buffalo National Park would come to be as emblematic of these conflicts as it was a symbolic monument to the last of the wood bison.

2

Control on the Range

IN May 1924, AN ARTICLE CELEBRATING the survival of the American bison in Canada appeared in the *Canadian Geographical Journal.* The author, F.H. Kitto, who had four years earlier conducted surveys of the wood bison range for the Department of the Interior, lauded the federal government's efforts to preserve the wild northern buffalo herds. "For over a quarter of a century the noble bison was mourned as lost," but with the creation of Wood Buffalo National Park in 1922, the Canadian government had taken a crucial step toward preserving this "monarch" of the Great Plains. Kitto wrote that the appointment of a resident park superintendent at Fort Smith and the hiring of experienced game wardens to patrol a newly built network of trails and cabins and enforce the prohibitions on buffalo hunting had made Canada the nation that had done more than any other to save the wild bison from complete extermination.[1]

In the view of several of Kitto's colleagues within the Department of the Interior, however, the conditions under which the new national park was established did not guarantee salvation for the wood bison. A lingering source of anxiety for federal wildlife conservationists was the presence of Cree and Chipewyan hunters and trappers within the park boundary. Although the park had been placed under the auspices of the newly created Northwest Territories and Yukon Branch for the sake of bureaucratic convenience, the first administrators of the new buffalo preserve were as staunchly in favour of strict conservation measures as their colleagues in the Parks Branch. Administrators at all levels in this new branch were just as likely to see Native hunters as pox to be removed from the wilderness

landscape south of Great Slave Lake. At the field level, the first park superintendent, John McDougal, suggested to his superiors in March 1926 that
Native hunters were probably killing buffalo, and "their departure from
the park would leave the buffalo unmolested except for wolves."[2] At the
midlevel of the northern administration, none other than Maxwell Graham was appointed in January 1922 to head the new branch's Game Division, where he continued to advocate for the removal of Native hunters
from the park he had worked so many years to create. And at the senior
level of the Northwest Territories and Yukon Branch, the idea that Wood
Buffalo National Park should be made a true game sanctuary found its
greatest advocate within the Department of the Interior. In January 1926,
the director of the new branch, O.S. Finnie, drafted a policy proposal
titled "Statement as to the Need for Eliminating Indians as Well as Other
Hunters and Trappers from the Wood Buffalo Park," which cited anecdotal reports obtained the previous year on a fact-finding mission to the
park. These reports suggested that Native hunters were consistently abus-
ing the game regulations (particularly the ban on bison hunting), building
permanent cabins in the park, and setting fires in the region. He concluded that a small amount of money should be used to buy off the treaty
Indians' hunting privileges in the park and that they should be subsequently removed to a reserve on the north side of Great Slave Lake.[3]

Finnie's proposal to expand federal control over the park area was part
of a general growth of the Canadian government's administrative presence
in the North during the early 1920s. The discovery of oil at Fort Norman
in 1920 renewed interest in the resource potential of the Northwest Territories. The federal government responded to the oil strike by dispatching
a treaty commission to the lower Mackenzie River Valley to extinguish
Aboriginal title to the region and thus open the door to further resource
exploration. The resulting Treaty 11 was signed in 1921.[4] In the same year,
the Northwest Territories and Yukon Branch established its first administrative office in the Northwest Territories at Fort Smith. The eleven civil
servants there were the front-line representatives for a wide range of branch
responsibilities: mineral exploration, the administration of the Northwest
Game Act, the regulation of trading posts, and the health and education
of the Native population. The historians Mark Dickerson and Shelagh
Grant have characterized the Northwest Territories and Yukon Branch
under Finnie's direction as a liberal and progressive administration, dedicated at least in part to protecting the interests of northern Aboriginal
people. Finnie did, for example, promote the expansion of medical services in the North (albeit with limited success).[5]

On the issue of Native hunting rights, however, Finnie maintained a hard line, arguing that federal wildlife policy should respond to national interests such as the preservation of rare species or the production of wildlife for commercial purposes rather than to purely parochial concerns. Although Finnie authorized the creation of three game preserves in 1923 near Yellowknife, the Slave River, and the Peel River where only treaty Indians were allowed to hunt and trap, he refused numerous requests from Dene groups to add lands to the preserve network as a measure of protection from the non-Native trappers who had begun to flood the region in 1919.[6] Finnie also argued continually in bureaucratic circles that, despite provisions in Treaties 8 and 11 guaranteeing Native people a right to pursue their "usual vocation" of hunting and trapping throughout the treaty areas, this right should be interpreted as only a privilege because of the clause in the treaties subjecting Native hunting activities to government regulation. On a much finer legal point, Finnie argued that the treaties also granted the federal government the authority to remove Native hunters from Wood Buffalo National Park through the provision allowing the expropriation of treaty lands "as may be required and taken up from time to time for settlement, mining, lumbering, trading or other purposes."[7]

Finnie's ongoing bureaucratic campaign to create an inviolate wilderness sanctuary out of Wood Buffalo National Park met continued opposition from the Department of Indian Affairs. When Finnie pressed for the removal of the remaining Native hunters from the park in the latter months of 1925, the proposal earned a strong rebuke from Duncan Campbell Scott, the deputy superintendent general of Indian affairs.[8] Scott wrote directly to Minister of the Interior Charles Stewart that a complete ban on Native hunting in the region was too sweeping a measure and would cause hardship among the local population. He allowed that those hunters who violated the game regulations, particularly the prohibition on buffalo hunting, should be dealt with severely, and promised to have his field agents issue "stern warnings" to hunters not to disturb the wood bison herds. Despite this concession, Scott wrote that "it is my view both official and personal, that the vital interests of the Indians should be paramount and should have precedence even over the protection of the wild life."[9] The standoff between Indian Affairs and the Northwest Territories and Yukon Branch appears to have forestalled any immediate effort to remove treaty Indians from Wood Buffalo National Park, as no authorization was ever issued by the federal cabinet or by senior administrators within the Department of the Interior.

Unlike treaty Indians, hunters and trappers of other ethnicities living within the park boundary were offered no clemency. One of the first priorities for federal officials after the establishment of Wood Buffalo National Park was to effect the complete removal of non-Native and Métis hunters and trappers from the park. Maxwell Graham had, in fact, already begun this work when he surveyed the bison range in the summer of 1922. Noting that the operations of the white trappers were "far more noisy" than those of Native people, Graham considered the relative newcomers an "absolutely undesirable" addition to the local population.[10] He also considered non-Native and Métis trappers a dire threat to the wood bison, citing an incident from the previous winter when a "Chipewyan half-breed" and a white man who "escaped to the United States" had together unlawfully killed two buffalo. In an effort to protect the winter range of the buffalo, Graham ordered that non-Native trapping operations should be restricted to within five miles of the Slave and Peace Rivers.[11] The following summer, notices were posted throughout the park that "it is unlawful for any person other than a bona fide native, being Treaty Indians, to hunt or trap."[12] This policy was strictly applied. When Finnie received a telegram from "the Olson Brothers" in June 1923 claiming squatters' rights because they had built a cabin and trapped in the park for four years, Finnie replied that no such rights would be granted and that the brothers no longer possessed trapping privileges within the park boundary.[13]

Exactly how many white trappers met the same fate as the Olson brothers is not recorded, but many were incensed at their exclusion from the park.[14] In July 1923 Finnie was informed that dislocated trappers had tried to "belittle" the park in the press with the unfounded claim that the wood bison were dying off due to the severe winter climate.[15] In August 1924, a group of seven white trappers met with Superintendent McDougal to protest their exclusion from the park. The group's spokesman, Louis Conibear, claimed that the Native trappers in the park were not harvesting fur-bearers to any great degree, and thus there was a substantial waste of animals that had died from natural causes.[16] A letter from the trader Col. J.K. Cornwall to Finnie summed up the frustration of white trappers who were forced to move their operations out of the park:

All of the hunters who have been trapping on this ground, who are not now eligible to trap there, are certainly very much riled up; they claim it is a vast area with comparatively few Buffalo on it; they have no desire to shoot the Buffalo, and have never shot any; there is plenty of fur and they are unable to understand why they are not permitted to trap ... I think they would have moved off with less resentment if they had been given a one year's notice, as

many of them had paid their License Fee to trap and were on their old trapping ground, and were ordered off in the middle of the season. Some of
these men have been occupying their trap-lines for some years. You can easily understand yourself how they would feel.[17]

The justice in the complaints of these displaced trappers is difficult to
evaluate. Many of the white trappers who flooded into the Northwest Territories in the 1920s were opportunists and profiteers hoping to "mine" as
much fur as possible and then leave the country.[18] Nonetheless it is too
simplistic to depict all the non-Native trappers in the Wood Buffalo Park
region as rapacious exploiters of wildlife whose primary purpose was to
make money and return south. In July 1923, an article in the *Edmonton
Bulletin* stated that most of the trappers who were to be evicted from
Wood Buffalo National Park had trapped in the area for "some years" and
were well known to the RCMP and the game wardens.[19] Louis Conibear,
for example, had moved his family to Fort Smith and opened a trading
post in 1912. The family did not pull up stakes after a short time but stayed
in the area. Louis' elder son, Frank, went on to relative fame as the inven-
tor of the Conibear trap for small animals, and his younger son, Kenneth,
became known as the "Kipling of the North" for his novels about the
Canadian sub-Arctic. Ironically enough, Conibear Lake, named in Kenneth's
honour, sits within Wood Buffalo National Park.[20] In addition to these
longer-term residents, many of the trappers who arrived in South Slave
region in the early 1920s were European immigrants and returned soldiers
searching for a new start after the devastation of the First World War.[21] In
the case of the former, a more generalized nativist sentiment may have
underlain the decision to exclude non-Native trappers from Wood Buffalo
National Park. Maxwell Graham, for instance, noted on his survey of the
park area in 1922 that one of the greatest threats to the local wildlife was
"the white trappers, many of whom are foreigners with no respect for
law."[22] Finnie displayed much the same disdain. When commenting on
McDougal's meeting with Louis Conibear and other non-Native trappers,
he noted derisively that all the trappers save one "appear from their names
to be of foreign extraction."[23]

Such derogatory attitudes suggest there was little hope for a rapproche-
ment between park administrators and local non-Native trappers in the
early 1920s. Indeed, Finnie rejected pleas of Conibear and others for access
to the park, arguing that it was in the best interest of white trappers to
vacate the area because the "unmolested" fur-bearers within the preserve
would thrive and overflow to the surrounding region.[24] Evidently, Finnie

would employ almost any argument to justify state control over the area: antiforeign sentiment, the apparent threat non-Native trappers presented to the wood bison, or the condescending logic that exclusion from the park actually served the interests of those who were forced from the area. Though wildlife populations in the early 1920s appeared healthy, park administrators adamantly refused to allow non-Native trappers to share in the available fur resources in Wood Buffalo National Park. Understandably, as Colonel Cornwall suggested, many of the expelled trappers were incensed at their removal from the park.

The reaction of the other ethnic group excluded from Wood Buffalo National Park – the Métis hunters – is difficult to discern from the available documents. As will be discussed later in this chapter, Métis trappers protested the expansion of the Wood Buffalo National Park south of the Peace River in 1926, often in concert with white trappers. Any Métis objections to the establishment of the original park boundary may have carried so little political weight that they went largely undocumented. It is equally possible that a majority of these trappers lived outside the original park and closer to the muskrat-rich delta country near Fort Chipewyan and thus expressed their disapproval only when the park was finally extended into this area. There is, however, some evidence that Métis objections to the establishment of the original park were registered at the local level. On 8 November 1923, Park Superintendent John McDougal brought forth a recommendation at a meeting of the Advisory Board on Wildlife Protection that "half-breeds" should be allowed to hunt and trap in the park. Because McDougal was generally a strict adherent to wildlife conservation orthodoxy, the motion was more likely a response to political pressure from discontented Métis hunters than the superintendent's own initiative.[25] The board rejected the proposal because of fears that any recognition of Métis rights in Wood Buffalo National Park might set an "undesirable precedent" for game management in the rest of the country. A more general anger among Métis hunters over their exclusion from former hunting and trapping grounds continued to simmer for at least a decade after the creation of the park. In September 1932, six Métis trappers who had been evicted from the park – Willie H. Heron, Fred Berens, Susie Beaulieu, Jean King Beaulieu, François King Beaulieu, Paul King Beaulieu, and Augustin Mecredi – forwarded a petition to the Department of the Interior complaining that they had been expelled into an area already overtrapped by whites and requesting a reinstatement of their trapping privileges. The chair of the Dominion Lands Board rejected this request, claiming that his department had "no power" to change the conditions governing access to the game and fur-bearing animals of Wood Buffalo National Park.[26]

The exclusion of non-Native and Métis trappers from Wood Buffalo Park did not create a hunter's paradise for the treaty Indians in the area. Indeed, the northern administration continued to argue that the presence of Native hunters was incompatible with the purpose of the national park. On an official visit to the park in September 1925, O.S. Finnie expressed concern that treaty Indians were hunting and trapping in the park more actively because of their monopoly on access. To his horror, Finnie also discovered that Indian Agent Gerald Card had informed local people that all Treaty 8 hunters – regardless of whether they had previously operated within the park boundary – were allowed to hunt and trap in the park without regard for any of the game regulations save the ban on hunting buffalo.[27] Taking all of these factors into account, Finnie concluded that the number of Native people hunting and trapping in the park both legally and illegally had reached crisis proportions. Although it had been thought that only thirty or forty Native people would be eligible to hunt and trap in the park, it was now apparent that over one hundred would claim the privilege. Finnie wrote to Roy A. Gibson, the assistant deputy minister of the interior, with a plea to remove the "excess" hunters on the buffalo range: "Unless we can keep them out of the Park, we will be in constant suspense regarding fires and the killing of buffalo, and the wildlife of course will seriously suffer."[28]

The evidence supporting many of Finnie's claims against Native hunters was highly suspect. One damning report he received from zoologist William Rowan concluded that Native hunters were "keeping down" the bison population based on the discovery of five adult buffalo skeletons on an expedition to the park in the late summer of 1925. If wolves had killed the bison, Rowan reasoned, they would have also left the calf bones. Therefore Native hunters had probably killed the bison and buried any calf bones because "a young buffalo would be far easier to dispose of than an adult and a shortage of calves would fit so admirably into the wolf story." Though this was a somewhat circular argument – to implicate the wolves one would, as Rowan suggested, have to leave the calf bones exposed – Rowan nonetheless concluded that he was "greatly tempted, with [Ernest Thompson] Seton, to trust the four-footed wolves a great deal further than those with two legs."[29] Similarly, Superintendent McDougal received a report of an illegally killed bison and, despite a lack of clear information, proceeded to blame Native hunters. He wrote, "as no white men or breeds are allowed in the park, circumstantial evidence would go to prove the killing was the work of Indians."[30] It is of course possible – perhaps even likely – that some undocumented cases of Native hunters poaching bison in the park occurred before the first conviction against a Native hunter was secured in 1926. But the superficial evidence used to tarnish Native hunters in the region suggests that park administrators were willing to exaggerate the dangers facing the bison population as a means to further their goal of establishing a "pure" wilderness park in the South Slave region.

In any event, continued bureaucratic pressure from the Department of Indian Affairs precluded the outright expulsion of Native hunters from the park area. The park administration therefore adopted a strategy of restricting access rights to the park on an individual basis. In December 1925, Finnie instructed Park Superintendent McDougal to grant hunting and trapping privileges only to those who were on the local treaty pay list and who could prove "to your satisfaction" that they had traditionally hunted and trapped in the park.[31] By placing the burden of proof squarely on the applicant, the park administration had granted itself a tremendous degree of latitude to exclude "undesirables" from hunting and trapping in the park area. Even before this order had been issued, the claim of the hunter Susie Marie was rejected, for example, not only because his name did not appear on the treaty list, but also because senior officials within Indian Affairs concluded that Marie was "probably a half-breed."[32] The park administration also cancelled the hunting and trapping privileges of Native hunters who violated game laws and park regulations. Finally, Finnie issued orders to McDougal that any person found guilty of starting fires or killing buffalo should have his or her permit to hunt in the park permanently revoked.[33] This policy of banishing lawbreakers from the park was sanctioned by Duncan Campbell Scott. Permanent expulsion from the park thus became a common punishment (in addition to a fine or imprisonment) for even the most minor infraction of the game regulations.[34]

Thus the game regulations per se did not represent the most significant change in the lives of Native hunters within Wood Buffalo National Park (in the earliest years of the park's existence, the northern administration had simply applied existing game regulations from Alberta and the Northwest Territories to the portions of the park within each jurisdiction). Instead, the combination of unique forms of punishment for infractions of the game laws – particularly expulsion from the park – and the increased capacity to enforce the law represented the most visible manifestation of state control over Native hunters in the park. The latter point cannot be emphasized enough. After the expansion of the park's game warden service in 1925, at least ten game wardens patrolled the area of the original park north of the Peace River.[35] While this force may not seem overly large for 10,500 square miles of rough terrain, only three game guardians had been assigned to protect the wood bison before the establishment of the park in 1922. Furthermore, the Wood Buffalo National Park warden service represented a far higher concentration of game officers than anywhere else in the Northwest Territories.[36] The park administration placed a heavy premium on building an effective force of game wardens to supervise the hunting and trapping activities of Native people within the park. In March 1926, Superintendent McDougal wrote to his superiors, "In order that the buffalo get proper protection from the Indians I recommend that the present warden service be increased to such an extent that every Indian in the park could be closely watched, no matter what place in the park he might be."[37]

The Cree and Chipewyan hunters of Wood Buffalo National Park clearly resented the intrusion of the game regulations, the park boundary, and the warden service. In January 1926 Finnie cited reports from Superintendent McDougal that "the Indians in this northern range are extremely hostile to the presence of our wardens."[38] Native hunters who were excluded from the buffalo range flouted the regulations prohibiting them from hunting and trapping in the park. In February 1925, Warden G.D. Murphy reported that he and Warden D'Arcy Arden suspected Native trappers of entering the park from Red River and killing beaver illegally near the headwaters of the Jackfish River.[39] John Baptiste, a chief of the Cree at Little Red River, complained to Warden Arden in March 1926 that his people could not obey the prohibitions on hunting and trapping in the park if they could not identify the arbitrary line that constituted the park boundary. In an almost playful critique of the haphazard designation of the park as a wilderness sanctuary, Baptiste argued that if the boundary was not visible (i.e., cut into the forest), then it was imaginary. He told Arden that "he had eight men of his tribe hunting in that country and he would tell them they could imagine they were outside the boundary."[40]

Despite such protests, the northern administration was in no mood to liberalize the regulations governing access to Wood Buffalo National Park. After all, controlling the hunting activities of the Native people within the park was seen as only a stopgap measure until sufficient political will emerged within the wider federal bureaucracy to remove the hunters once and for all. In April 1926, Finnie once again pleaded with Duncan Campbell Scott to allow the complete removal of Native hunters to a reserve north of Great Slave Lake, arguing that the "spillover effect" of abundant game and fur from a fully protected sanctuary would benefit all hunters in the area. Scott replied that he had noted Finnie's concern and that the matter should receive "careful consideration at a future date."[41] Nonetheless, a persistent dissonance between the interests of Native hunters and the northern administration continued to dominate the politics surrounding Wood Buffalo National Park. The effort to supervise and control Native hunters in the park took on an added urgency after 1925, when it was decided to stock the vast ranges of Wood Buffalo National Park with thousands of plains bison from southern Alberta. No longer was the purpose of the park to protect a rare and endangered population of wood bison; park administrators were now also intent on protecting an investment.

MANAGING WILDLIFE

The bureaucratic campaign to remove Aboriginal hunters from Wood Buffalo National Park may appear at first glance as an attempt to create a vast natural reservoir where bison and other wildlife might multiply free from human intrusion. But while federal wildlife officials envisioned a pristine landscape with no permanent human presence, they did not imagine a preserve devoid of all human influence. In keeping with the earliest proposals for a ranch-like northern buffalo preserve, the park administration quickly began to consider dramatic interventions in the nonhuman ecology of the park in order to increase the biological productivity of the bison herds. Within three years of the park's establishment, it was clear that the wood bison herds would not only serve as emblems of a fading western wilderness but also herald a new era when bureaucratic managers would dominate nonhuman as well as human lives in the South Slave region.

The practical origins of this new managerial ethos can be traced back almost two decades to the first attempt of the federal government to preserve the remnant plains bison herds. In 1907, the government had purchased one of the last herds of plains bison from Montana rancher Michael Pablo and, between 1909 and 1914, transferred them to the fenced-in range on the newly created Buffalo National Park near Wainwright, Alberta.[42] By the early 1920s, park managers faced the dilemma common to many enclosed buffalo parks on the southern plains: what to do with an erupting bison population in a park that was surrounded by land designated for agricultural purposes. When the issue of hunting licences and the provision of breeding stock for ranchers failed to reduce the bison population, the Parks Branch began in 1922 to slaughter the surplus animals. Immediate public opposition to the slaughters (particularly among humane societies) reached a peak in 1923 after several reports in major newspapers that a Holly-wood film company intended to make a movie of the annual kill using "authentic" costumed Native people to hunt down the animals from horse-back with spears. The negative publicity prompted federal wildlife officials to undertake a management scheme that forever tarnished their image as saviours of the bison and earned them the enmity of zoologists through-out North America.[43]

The impetus to find a humane alternative to the slaughter program at Buffalo National Park appears to have originated in the office of W.W. Cory, the deputy minister of the interior. In May 1923, he wrote to James Harkin that "instead of slaughtering [the surplus bison at Wainwright] it would be a good idea to transfer some of the healthy young stock to the Wood Bison Reserve administered by the Northwest Territories Branch."[44] On 30 May, Cory, Harkin, O.S. Finnie, Maxwell Graham, Dr. Frederick Tor-rance, the veterinary director general with the Department of Agriculture, and A.G. Smith, the superintendent of Buffalo National Park, all met to discuss the idea. In the days before the meeting, Graham had expressed concern to his superiors about the possible spread of tuberculosis from the infected Wainwright herd to the wood bison. He also hinted at possible objections from prominent wildlife conservationists: "It is a question whether the authorities, such as Doctor W.T. Hornaday, would approve of plains bison being introduced and interbred with the 'wood-buffalo.'"[45]

But Graham emerged from the meeting a convert to the transfer proposal. Possibly Torrance added sufficient scientific legitimacy to the scheme by suggesting that separating yearling animals from the main herd and testing them for tuberculosis before shipment would reduce the risk of disease transmission.[46] In any case, Graham became the most visible proponent of the transfer program both publicly and within the federal government. His tenacious – even narrow-minded – commitment to the transfer project left little room for compromise. Graham dismissed the opinions of leading zoologists and ignored expert advice from within the civil service. In one glaring example, he repeatedly cited Torrance's view that shipping young animals would reduce the risk of tuberculosis trans-mission to negligible levels but neglected to mention that a key condition for Torrance's approval of the transfer plan was the separation *and* testing of the animals for tuberculosis – and that these tests had been dispensed with due to potential cost overruns.[47] He also appealed to public senti-ment. In an article for the December 1924 issue of the *Canadian Field-Naturalist*, Graham claimed the transfer project was meant to "save for posterity the calf crop at the Wainwright Park for 1922-23, which other-wise cannot, apparently, be saved."[48]

Graham's public defence of the transfer proposal produced immediate objections from the wider scientific community. The respected naturalist W.E. Saunders wrote a letter to the editor of the *Canadian Field-Naturalist* calling for abandonment of the scheme, as did the Cornell zoologist Francis Harper, who challenged the Canadian government to refer the transfer scheme to a vote at the 1925 annual meeting of the American Society of Mammalogists.[49] At the same time, William Rowan, a zoologist at the University of Alberta, was organizing colleagues around Canada to oppose the bison transfer.[50] Rowan convinced scientists such as A.E. Cameron at the University of Saskatchewan, B.A. Bensley at the University of Toronto, and C. McLean Frazer at the University of British Columbia to write to the minister of the interior, Charles Stewart, and argue passionately that the wood bison subspecies (*Bison bison athabascae*) identified by Rhoads in 1898 would be lost to science forever if allowed to interbreed with the introduced plains bison (*Bison bison bison*). The zoologists' argument did not rest solely on the erudite taxonomic value of the wood bison; the intrinsic value of the species was also cited. Cameron wrote that the wood bison were "a natural asset in which all Canadians must be interested," and Rowan argued that "the proposed introduction is to be greatly regretted as it means the permanent loss to Canada and to the world of the largest known living bison." A second major concern was the risk that the Wainwright animals would infect the northern bison with tuberculosis. The zoologists urged a cautionary approach to the problem of overcrowding at Wainwright, and some were critical of the very idea of an intrusive managerial approach to wildlife ecology. Bensley, for example, wrote that "a policy of keeping the Wood bison under conditions where they would have a free practically unrestricted range, where they could propagate naturally, and be protected against contamination either as a result of hybridization or from disease would seem to be a sort of safety-first measure which would be based on common sense and doubtless would be supported by public sentiment. There is a sufficient record of failures to justify the wisdom of letting well alone."[51]

The zoologists' objections to the transfer proposal were part of a debate over the philosophy and practice of wildlife management that reverberated across North America in the early 1920s. On one side of the intellectual divide were university-based zoologists who were influenced by the ecologist Frederic Clements' idea that a "balance of nature" free from any overt human interference provided the highest degree of stability and permanence for natural ecosystems. On the other were bureaucratic wildlife managers who had traditionally manipulated ungulate populations in parks and protected areas to produce a usable surplus of game animals through

herd transfers, predator control, and feeding programs. For many zoologists, the irruption and subsequent collapse of the deer population on the
Kaibab Plateau above the Grand Canyon following several years of predator control operations had been a watershed event that proved human
meddling with balanced predator and prey populations was a disruptive
influence on stable ecosystems. The issue came to the fore at the 1924
meeting of the American Society of Mammalogists, where a fierce debate
erupted between zoologists who defended the vital role of predators in
natural ecosystems and government wildlife managers who argued that the
US Bureau of Biological Survey's predator control programs were ecologically pragmatic and economically indispensable.[52]

Graham's sympathies clearly lay with the managerial pole of this debate.
He responded to the criticisms of the transfer proposal by insinuating that
the zoologists who opposed the project were "ivory tower" critics who were
unaware of actual conditions in Wood Buffalo National Park. He repeatedly cited Charles Camsell's 1916 geological survey, Fred Siebert's 1922 boundary survey, and his own observations on the same journey with Siebert as
proof that there were two distinct herds in the park – one in the north near
the Salt River and one in the south near the Peace River – and that these
animals never intermingled because they were separated by a twenty-mile
band of muskeg. Since the Wainwright animals were to be released only
in the southern range, Graham reasoned that the wood bison in the northern part of the park would remain undisturbed. If this argument failed to
convince the sceptics (the muskeg was, after all, frozen much of the year),
Graham declared that the extinction of a species was not at issue because
the wood bison were distinct only due to geographic factors. As proof, he
claimed that the plains bison at Elk Island National Park had adopted
some of the characteristics of the wood bison (darker pelage, larger size,
etc.) after only ten years in a wooded environment. The plains bison introduced into the northern range would thus effectively become wood bison,
obviating the theoretical taxonomic concerns of zoologists.[53]

Graham also promoted the transfer as an eminently practical way to
maximize the resource potential of an underutilized wildlife range. From
the earliest days of Wood Buffalo Park's existence, Graham had combined
preservationist rhetoric with utilitarian arguments for conserving the wood
bison. He wrote in 1922, for example, that the northern bison deserved
protection in a national park simply because "they are the last of their
species living to-day under absolutely free and wild conditions." And he
simultaneously claimed the proposed bison preserve could contribute to
the nation's agricultural industries: "Looking to the future success of the

experimental cross-breeding between buffalo and domestic bovines, it is imperative that a reserve stock of pure blood bison of the highest potency should be kept in reserve, so that the ultimate fixed type of new range animal may continue to pass on to successive generations the potent qualities of the true bison, hardiness, thriftiness, a valuable robe, and first-class beef qualities."[54] In keeping with such sentiments, one of the key arguments Graham used to promote the transfer project was that "in the immediate future this project holds out the promise of re-stocking vast areas suitable for the propagation of bison at comparatively little cost." Once this was done, "the introduced plains bison, under the leadership and protection of the adult wild ones now in the southern range of the Wood Buffalo Park, should so multiply that a future source of food supply may be assured the Natives in the surrounding district."[55] For Graham, preservation and production were not mutually exclusive wildlife management objectives: the former demanded control over human hunters, while the latter required the manipulation of the bison population.

The emphasis on utility in Graham's comments suggests that the bison transfer was not, as Janet Foster has argued, merely a mistake made by a bureaucracy imbued with a philosophy of visionary preservationism.[56] The principles behind the transfer proposal were entirely consistent with the contradictory amalgamation of preservationist sentiment and quasi-agricultural approaches to wildlife management that dominated Canada's conservation bureaucracy during the 1920s. Federal wildlife officials routinely applied the principles of commercial agriculture to the bison conservation programs; even the few remaining herds of plains bison in Canada's national parks system were subject to experiments in agricultural breeding and domestication. In 1921, the Dominion entomologist and leading conservationist C. Gordon Hewitt wrote in his seminal volume on wildlife conservation that "the greatest value of the buffalo ... lies in the possibility of its domestication." He went on to praise recent experiments that attempted to cross "surplus" bison with domestic cattle and yaks at the Dominion Experimental Station in Scott, Saskatchewan, for their potential to add to the agricultural economy of the Great Plains.[57] Although such federal bureaucrats as Harrison Lewis, chief migratory bird officer, and Hoyes Lloyd, superintendent of wildlife protection, openly opposed the bison transfer, their objections were tied more to their respective positions as editor of the *Canadian Field-Naturalist* and president of the Ottawa Field-Naturalists (organizations that virulently opposed Graham's plan) than to any coherent preservationist philosophy dominating the federal bureaucracy. Indeed, when the Ottawa Field-Naturalists passed a motion opposing the transfer in February 1925, Lloyd and Lewis had to resign their positions within the club or face the prospect of losing their civil service jobs.[58] Clearly Graham's enthusiasm for managing the bison as both a symbolic marker of the wilderness and a potential commercial product lay at the core of the federal wildlife bureaucracy's approach to wildlife conservation during the early decades of the twentieth century.

Considering the disparate political, technical, and ethical positions of the rival factions in the debate over the transfer proposal, it is not surprising that the tensions between the two camps boiled over in the summer of 1925. In the days leading up to the first shipment of Wainwright bison, the project was denounced in a desperate and almost belligerent article in the *Canadian Forum*. Authored anonymously by "A Canadian Zoologist," the article strongly contested many of Graham's key arguments about the low-risk nature of the transfer. It stated that the risk of tuberculosis transmission was acute no matter what precautions were taken and that even if there were separate herds in the park, the introduction of large numbers of bison to the southern range would surely encourage a migration to the north in a search for food. The article concluded with a condemnation of the transfer project that might have unnerved a dedicated conservationist such as Graham: "Never before in the annals of conservation, as far as we are aware, have the last survivors of a unique race of animals been knowingly obliterated by a department of conservation."[59]

In the end, the arguments of the zoologists were not enough to sway a bureaucracy that was determined to manage the problem of overcrowding at Buffalo National Park by stocking a supposedly underutilized northern range. On 21 June 1925, the first shipment of 196 plains bison arrived by barge and were released at LaButte along the Slave River (two had died in transit). By the beginning of August, 1,926 plains bison had been relocated to Wood Buffalo National Park. Over the four summers from 1925 to 1928, a total of 6,673 bison were shipped by rail and barge to their new northern range.[60] At the time, many hailed the transfer project as a practical success. Laudatory press reports appeared in newspapers across North America, and even some former critics such as Edmund Seymour and M.S. Garretson, the president and secretary of the American Bison Society, and also the conservationist William T. Hornaday, were persuaded to soften their stance toward the program.[61] The vast majority of the bison survived the arduous transportation process, and the park wardens reported that the animals were responding well to their new environment.[62] Where there had once been hundreds of bison on the northern range, now there were thousands.

Any thoughts that local Native hunters might have harboured about a revival of the legal bison hunt were quickly dashed, however, as Finnie ordered a warden to accompany the first shipment and cautioned that "Treaty Indians and their dogs must be kept away from the introduced buffalo."[63] Over time, the question of how to manage the northern bison turned from how to save them from subsistence hunting to how to manage the surplus stock for commercial production. In turn, the presence of the "Wainwrights" provided new ground for conflict between federal officials and local hunters in the Wood Buffalo National Park region.

CONSOLIDATING CONTROL

The general atmosphere of distrust between local people and state officials that had emerged with the establishment of Wood Buffalo National Park was only heightened by a series of policy decisions in the wake of the bison transfer. One immediate point of contention was the fact that, shortly after their release, some of the Wainwright bison had wandered outside the southern boundary of the park onto the rich trapping grounds near the Peace-Athabasca Delta. The park wardens somewhat comically began to patrol the Peace River in canoes in a futile attempt to keep the new arrivals within the boundary; subsequent efforts to herd the recalcitrant migrants back across the Peace using horses were also largely unsuccessful. Warden Mike Dempsey reported in January 1926 that up to 350 bison had crossed over the park's southern boundary.[64] This sudden introduction of several hundred large grazing animals onto the trapping grounds north of Fort Chipewyan led to a series of ecological changes that severely reduced the ability of local Cree trappers to obtain fur. In March 1926, the Catholic bishop Célestine Joussard wrote to the Department of Indian Affairs to complain that the bison scattered around Lake Claire, Lake Mamawi, and Lake Baril were feeding on roots and herbs and thereby destroying muskrat houses in the region. The buffalo were also trampling, scattering, and breaking traps in the area. The bishop asked that a wire fence be strung along the Peace River (from its junction with the Slave River to Peace Point) to prevent further migrations of bison onto the trapping grounds near Fort Chipewyan.[65]

Despite initial efforts to contain the southward migration of the bison, the northern administration was attuned more to the grazing potential of this newly discovered bison range than to the concerns of local trappers. A report from the trader Thomas Woodman in November 1925 that the thousands of acres of range near Fort Chipewyan could accommodate the Wainwright bison "for years to come" created enthusiasm at the most senior levels of the Department of the Interior for extending the park boundary south of the Peace River.[66] When Superintendent McDougal surveyed the region in February 1926, he reported large herds of bison that were thriving on excellent feed. He estimated that the area around Lake Claire could hold two thousand bison and should be added to the park.[67]

The reaction of local residents to the proposed "park annex" was mixed. In March 1926, O.S. Finnie spoke on the telephone with Colonel Cornwall, who assured him that all northern residents were in sympathy with the idea of extending the park so long as their hunting and trapping privileges were not restricted.[68] That same month, McDougal claimed that he had received opinions from "leading residents" in Fort Chipewyan, and all but Bishop Joussard supported the park annex so long as the hunting and trapping rights of treaty Indians and "Half-Breeds" (i.e., Métis) were not abrogated.[69] But not all the residents of Fort Chipewyan – leading or otherwise – supported the park annex. In April, a petition was forwarded to Minister of the Interior Charles Stewart claiming that residents of the district had learned "with alarm" of the proposal. The petitioners argued that the area had been a Cree hunting ground since time immemorial, that whites and "half-breeds" in the area were voters with "well established rights," that restrictive hunting laws might increase the incidence of starvation, and finally, that extending the park "would give the impression that government cares more about the buffalo than the Indians."[70]

Finnie attempted to circumvent nascent opposition to the park annex by conforming to local sentiment and protecting the rights of all prior occupants (whites, Métis, and treaty Indians) to hunt and trap in the area. Although this allowed him to dismiss the concerns of the petitioners as "without any basis in fact," the extension of the park south of the Peace River clearly did not mean "business as usual" for local hunters and trappers.[71] Once again, the northern administration coupled the granting of privileges to hunt and trap in the park with broad and arbitrary rights to revoke those liberties on an individual basis. The September 1926 order-in-council that extended the park south to its present boundary required residents to obtain a licence to hunt and trap in the park. Another measure required people to obtain a permit – granted at the discretion of the park superintendent – just to enter the park.[72] According to the departmental solicitor the park superintendent could legally refuse these permits for any reason, such as a shortage of game, a family being too "well to do" to need game in the park, and the general "undesirability" of the individual.[73] Not only were permits required to enter the park, but movement within the boundaries were restricted by the division of the park into three hunting and trapping permit zones: "A" (the NWT section of the park), "B" (the Alberta section north of the Peace River), and "C" (the park annex south of the Peace River).[74] While the extension of the park was "sold" to the population around Fort Chipewyan as a measure designed merely to protect the Wainwright bison, the new permit regulations granted the park authorities arbitrary power over local hunting and trapping rights.

For those denied permits to the park annex, no formal process was implemented to appeal their expulsion. The onus was placed on the applicants to prove they had hunted and trapped in the area before its annexation by the park; those who objected could remove their hunting and trapping operations from the park area or violate the law. In March 1928, for example, Warden G.D. Murphy reported that a Native trapper named Ada had been denied a permit because he could not prove he hunted in the park annex before 1926. Ada and a party of trappers had decided to disregard the permit restrictions and enter the park near Deep Lake; Wardens Dempsey and Arden were dispatched to Fort Chipewyan immediately to investigate and lay charges if possible. Although they did not find Ada, they did investigate the case of Jeremy Burke, who had been found within the park boundary without a permit. When Dempsey discovered that the "Burke boy" had entered the park to visit his sick mother, he issued a temporary permit that did not include hunting and trapping rights. While this incident does suggest some flexibility in the system, it also reveals how the permit regulations could arbitrarily split families and kinship groups at the edge of the park boundary.[75]

On a much broader scale, the extension of the park and the new permit regulations appear to have created a split in the Peace-Athabasca Delta Chipewyan band between "park" hunters, who concentrated their efforts west of Fort Chipewyan, and the nonpark hunters who moved east toward Lake Athabasca. As a result of this division, the park Chipewyan decided in 1944 to formally change their ethnic allegiance and join the Cree band under Chief John Cowie in a political alliance that was intended to strengthen each group's claims to a reserve within the park.[76] The change in the park annex from a local hunting ground to a federally managed wilderness area thus transformed traditional kinship and ethnic allegiances in the region. The new park boundary was not simply the expanding geographical border of a federal wildlife preserve; it also came to represent the growing divisions and shifting alliances within the complex social landscapes of the South Slave region.

The expansion of the park boundary and the tougher permit regulations were accompanied by efforts to further extend the reach and effectiveness of the warden service. By the early 1930s, a network of patrol trails, overnight cabins, and phone lines had been built at strategic locations throughout the park. Reports for the winter of 1932 indicate that most wardens spent ten to nineteen days each month on backcountry patrols.[77] Although the dozen or so wardens who patrolled the park at this time had to cover a much greater area after the park expansion, their presence in the park annex ensured that charges for game offences presented a very real threat to the local population. Park administrators were clearly aware of this fact. When the wardens began randomly searching boats for illegal beaver pelts, McDougal commented that, although no evidence was uncovered pointing to contraband beaver shipments in the park, "the rumours of searches spreading throughout the country will have a good effect."[78] In keeping with this strategy of "sending a message" to Native hunters, the park wardens sometimes used intimidation as a law enforcement tactic. When, for instance, Simon Whiteknife refused to allow Warden Wylie to search his boat for illegal beaver pelts, Wylie informed Whiteknife that the refusal would constitute a tacit confession of guilt and that the park administration was likely to revoke his hunting permit.[79] Although the game wardens could not directly supervise the activities of each hunter in the park (as McDougal had hoped), the sporadic presence of law enforcement officers along the rivers and traplines in the park annex forced local people to accept that their former sovereignty over the wildlife commons had been usurped by a state authority intent on enforcing its own game laws.

CHALLENGING STATE AUTHORITY

On 28 June 1926, a large crowd of spectators gathered at Fort Chipewyan to witness the trial of Pierre Gibot and his father, Theophile. Three weeks earlier, Pierre had admitted to the game warden Hugh McDermott that, with the help of his father, he had killed two of the newly introduced Wainwright bison just south of the Peace River, in the area that was soon to be incorporated into Wood Buffalo National Park. In due course, McDermott arrested the two Cree hunters at Fort Chipewyan and arranged for their transfer aboard the *M.V. Ranger* to the park administrative office at Fort Fitzgerald. During the long journey down the Slave River, McDermott further interrogated the two men, who admitted they were not starving when they killed the buffalo, but hunted the animals because their supply of meat was running short.[80] The next day, Park Superintendent John McDougal formally charged Pierre Gibot with buffalo poaching and his father as an accessory to the crime. He then released the prisoners to their camp near Rocher River and arranged for a trial at the annual treaty gathering in Fort Chipewyan because he "thought the moral effect of having the trial held there at Treaty time would be beneficial."[81] Indeed, over two hundred Cree and Chipewyan people were on hand to watch the park superintendent (who presided over the trial as a justice of the peace) sentence Pierre to six months and Theophile to three months in the provincial jail at Fort Saskatchewan.[82] After reading the sentence, John McDougal lectured the audience on the gravity of the crime that had been committed; he further warned that anyone found killing buffalo in the future would lose their privilege to hunt and trap in the park.

The Gibot case was one of several similar poaching trials in the aftermath of the Wainwright transfer (see Table 2.1). Between 1926 and 1935, eleven people were convicted of bison poaching within Wood Buffalo National Park in five separate cases. Two additional cases, one involving rumours of a bison killed by the trapper Alex Watsuga in May 1934 and a confirmed bison kill near Little Buffalo River in September 1935, went unsolved.[83] Although these figures represent slightly more than one confirmed case every two years, the number of convictions does suggest some intensification of bison poaching given that it is double the number of cases prosecuted in the first three decades after the introduction of protective bison legislation.

What explains this escalation in the number of recorded bison poaching incidents within Wood Buffalo Park? One possible clue lies in the fact that all of the cases resulting in convictions occurred in or near the park annex. Not only did this area include the largest number of active park permit holders, but because so many of the plains bison transferred between 1925 and 1928 had migrated south of the Peace River, suddenly thousands more bison were available to hunters and trappers near Fort Chipewyan.[84] A second possible explanation is the increase in law enforcement personnel. Game wardens were a prerequisite for poaching convictions, and the rise in convictions may, to an extent, reflect only the increased ability of the park staff to monitor a practice that had previously remained largely unrecorded. Finally, the socioeconomic conditions facing northern hunters and trappers during this period may also have played a role. Global fur prices had recently collapsed after peaking in 1919. Intense competition, the influx of "outside" trappers, and the periodic dwindling of local wildlife populations ensured that the fur industry was in serious decline by the

TABLE 2.1   Convictions for killing bison or possessing bison meat in and near Wood Buffalo National Park, 1898-1944

Name	Trial date	Sentence
François Byskie	28 January 1898	Fined $10
Unknown	Winter 1921-22	Fined $300
Pierre Gibot	26 July 1926	Six months in jail
Theophile Gibot	26 July 1926	Three months in jail (accessory)
John "Mustus" Gladu	30 May 1930	Four months' hard labour; park permit revoked
Joseph Wakwan	10 July 1930	Six months' hard labour; park permit revoked
Joseph Pamatchakwew (Wandering Spirit)	10 July 1930	Three months' hard labour; park permit revoked (accessory)
Leo Pamatchakwew (Wandering Spirit)	10 July 1930	Three months' hard labour; park permit revoked (accessory)
Boniface Driscoll	4 June 1934	Three months' hard labour (no park permit)
Modeste Desjarlais	4 June 1934	Two months' hard labour (no park permit; accessory)
Joseph Desjarlais	4 June 1934	Fined $70 plus $6.75 costs (Desjarlais was a minor)
Aimable Pamatchakwew	4 June 1934	Six months' hard labour; park permit revoked
Leonard Peckham	23 June 1935	Three months' hard labour
David (King) Beaulieu	11 June 1941	Fined $100; plus three months' hard labour
Jean (King) Beaulieu	11 June 1941	Fined $50; plus thirty days' hard labour (accessory)
Fred Gibot	12 June 1942	Fined $30 for possession of buffalo meat; park permit revoked
Fred Gibot	16 February 1944	Thirty days' hard labour (charged with possession of buffalo meat)

NOTE: Most of those jailed for killing buffalo were given the option of paying fines ranging from $300 to $600. The records for buffalo convictions are scattered among files at Library and Archives Canada (LAC), and it is thus impossible to know if this record is complete. Each of these cases did, however, result in a flurry of letters, many of which appear in several different files.

SOURCES: W.H. Routledge, Patrol Report, Fort Saskatchewan to Fort Simpson, in "Report of the Royal Northwest Mounted Police," *Sessional Papers* 15 (1899), RG 85, vol. 769, file 5222, pt. 1-2, LAC; Maxwell Graham, *Canada's Wild Buffalo: Observation in the Wood Buffalo Park* (Ottawa: Department of the Interior, 1923), 11; RG 10, vol. 8409, file 191/20-14-1, pt. 1, LAC; RG 85, vol. 1214, file 400-2-3, pt. 3, LAC.

early years of the Great Depression.[85] For hunters and trappers on the edge of privation, killing the suddenly abundant plains bison was a practical response to hunger.

When, for instance, the Cree hunters Joseph Wakwan, Leo Pamatchakwew, Aimable Pamatchakwew, and Joseph Pamatchakwew were charged in July 1930 for killing five bison, Warden Dempsey noted that their settlement at the mouth of the Peace River was always in need of destitute rations (because, he concluded, they spent too much time holding tea dances). At the trial, Wakwan testified that the spoils of the bison hunt had been distributed among many of the people in the small settlement. When Dempsey asked Wakwan why his hunting party had not taken moose, he replied that moose did not last as long as the much larger bison. At the end of the proceedings, the local Cree chief stood before the audience of sixty to complain that the federal government had not distributed enough rations to his community, putting hunters in a position where they needed to break the law simply to feed their families.[86] In a similar case that spring, the Métis hunter John Gladu was convicted of killing a bison near Egg Lake that he claimed had charged him. When asked why he had not reported the incident to the wardens, he admitted candidly that he thought the killing would go unnoticed and that he needed the meat.[87] In both of these cases, the claim that bison poaching was necessary due to local food shortages was treated with little sympathy; all the hunters except Aimable Pamatchakwew (for whom there was insufficient evidence) were sentenced to three to six months of hard labour and permanent expulsion from the park.

The incidents of poaching within Wood Buffalo National Park were not merely an opportunistic response to the increased bison population, however; nor did they stem solely from poverty. Bison poaching also allowed the Native community to express collective dissent against the arbitrary application of state power over traditional hunting rights in the region. The public trials of the hunters who had been charged with bison poaching became a flashpoint for Native hunters protesting the game regulations. At the Gibot trial, the discussion after the verdict was dominated by complaints about the new federal game laws that had been imposed on Native hunters. Local chiefs seized the occasion to recall the broken promises of previous treaty meetings, where hunters had been assured they would be given permission to kill one buffalo per family each hunting season if they agreed to four consecutive years of strict protective measures. The chiefs emphasized the difficulty of getting fresh meat in certain seasons and argued they should be allowed to kill buffalo in times of hunger. When McDougal hinted that something "might" be done to allow Native people to secure buffalo meat if the herd increased to a large size as a result of protective measures, they stated bluntly that they did not believe him. McDougal wrote that the chiefs "had often heard sweet words at other meetings, but it did not prevent their hunting rights being affected from time to time, and they consider this Country their Country, as they were here before the Whitemen and they never asked the Whitemen to come and give them Treaty. They also claimed the Buffalo were here before the Whitemen and this was their Country also."[88] Similarly, at the Wakwan and Pamatchak-wew trial, the Cree chief not only objected to the shortage of government rations but also argued that the prairie buffalo were fair game because the government did not advise local Native groups at the time Treaty 8 was signed that these animals would be transported to their hunting grounds.[89]

Individual hunters who were punished for killing bison also understood their plight in political terms. The Métis hunter John Gladu and the Cree hunter Joseph Wakwan saw their permanent expulsion from the park as a particularly unreasonable disciplinary measure, and both men conducted lengthy letter-writing campaigns to have their hunting and trapping rights in the park reinstated. Although their letters emphasize the material hardships they faced and at times adopt a deferential tone (often stating that the authors now realized that killing bison was a mistake), they also make the political assertion of a pre-existing hereditary right for Aboriginal people to hunt and trap within Wood Buffalo National Park. Both men argued that the park included the country in which they had been born and spent most of their lives. Gladu stressed this point at length in a letter to Superintendent McDougal on 10 June 1932:

> Through the cancellation of my permit, I have been permanently expelled from my home country, "the Quatre Fourches" where I was born and raised, and where my father, mother, and other relatives are still living. I was obliged to break a trail on the hunting ground of the Half-Breeds of Fort Chipewyan Settlement, on the North shore of Athabaska Lake; in this country quite new to me, and already covered with numerous trap lines, I barely escaped starvation last winter along with my family. In the Spring, looking for a better place of living, I moved over with the wife and children to the Delta of the Athabaska River; but here again I find myself in a very precarious position, as most of this hunting ground is going to be made into a reserve for the Chipewyan Indians of Jackfish Lake, and so I will not be allowed to hunt and trap there either.
>
> In consideration of the great difficulties I am working under, especially in the present time of great depression in the price of fur, I earnestly beg

your Department to allow me again to live and trap in my home country, the Buffalo Park, promising you to observe very carefully all the Park Regulations, as far as I may be aware of them.[90]

Nearly two years later, Gladu further emphasized his roots within the park: "I was born in this Park and my Mother is still living in this Park, my Father having died last year. I have been living in this Park all my life before this trouble. I think I have atoned for any offense I have committed and I spoke to Sergt. Bryant [RCMP], being non-treaty, about getting back into the Park and [he] asked me to write to you about it, as it has been so hard for me to make a living outside this Park, as I always also spent my summers with my relatives in the Park where there were lots of fish and I knew that country so well."[91]

In July 1937, Wakwan made a similar plea to the park superintendent for reinstatement of his permit:

I wish to beg for a favour please; if you can do something for me, that is to say that I wish to get back in the old Buffalo Park if I can where I was born and raised. I used to hunt in the old Park for years, until, I am sorry to say that I made a mistake by killing a wood buffalo a long time ago and since then I am out of the Buffalo Park, while, a few other men that made the same kind of mistakes are allowed to go in the old Park to trap and hunt, therefore, would you be good enough to put this application before the Department at Ottawa. I wish to state also, that mistakes will occur no more from me.[92]

These letters imply that for Native hunters the reinstatement of park hunting and trapping privileges carried a much deeper significance than the satisfaction of immediate material needs. The offenders' campaign was tantamount to the assertion of an inherent or customary right to hunt on the land that they and their families had occupied in the past. In a sense, poaching, punishment, and political resistance went hand in hand in Wood Buffalo Park; to disobey the law and refute assigned penalties was to undermine the legitimacy of a set of game regulations that had been imposed by outsiders.

Indeed, the discontent surrounding the bison poaching cases spilled over into broader opposition to any attempt to regulate hunting and trapping activities within the park boundary. Networks of resistance to the regulations, for instance, had clearly spread throughout the park by the beginning of the 1930s. The game wardens in particular noted the difficulty of securing convictions against local hunters when word of the wardens' presence leaked out everywhere before their arrival. In June 1931, Warden De Courcy Ireland noted that "under present conditions it is very hard for Wardens to suppress the illegal taking of beaver. They wait until all Wardens called in on their unavoidable summer assignments, and as beaver pelts are saleable until June 15th, they have lots of time to operate. That Indians have an almost uncanny means of receiving information, through underground channels, was evidenced by the fact that they obviously expected to be searched."[93]

Similarly, the park wardens and the RCMP met a wall of silence when they attempted to investigate the killing of a bison near Little Buffalo River in 1935. Although wardens suspected the Begayeur family because they were the only group camped near the dead buffalo, efforts to elicit information from residents of Salt River, the nearby settlement, met with repeated denials of any knowledge about the case. Of course, local residents may not have known who killed the buffalo, but it is equally conceivable that the community had closed ranks when faced with the common irritant of the game laws. The RCMP constable who wrote the final report on the case suspected as much: "Undoubtedly one or all of them know who killed the Buffalo but I am of the opinion, that they knowing that the last man convicted of killing a Buffalo was a White man who was sentenced to three months I.H.L. [hard labour] ... they therefore made up their minds to know and say nothing if questioned."[94]

More direct forms of protest against the park regulations were practised as well. A major catalyst for dissent among local hunters was the creation of a uniform set of game regulations for the park in 1933. Two years earlier, the Northwest Territories and Yukon Branch had been dissolved and the park placed under the auspices of the Dominion Lands Board. Although the administrative reorganization did end Finnie's hard-line leadership of the northern administration, the change did not liberalize the application of game laws within the park. On 14 December 1933, an order-in-council applied the Northwest Territories game regulations to the entire park area. More important, the minister of the interior acquired the authority to establish closed seasons and bag limits that were specific to Wood Buffalo National Park.[95] Local hunters were wary of the new regulations. In July 1935, the Indian agent at Fort Resolution reported that the Native trappers in the area had complained during the annual treaty payments that the bag limit for beaver was not generous enough and that park permit holders should be allowed to fill their quota outside the park boundary.[96] On a trip to Hay River the following spring, Warden Dempsey heard many of the same objections from Chief Lamalice, who said that his people had hunted beaver for ages and they were still as plentiful as in the past. Although Dempsey reported that the Hay River band was in good humour when he left, tensions over the beaver regulations were part of a more general frustration with the levels of control and supervision exacted upon the lives of Native hunters and trappers in the park. Dempsey wrote that the warden permanently stationed at Hay River "has had to be very patient and tactful as the Indians appear to bitterly resent any supervision of their hunting and trapping as unwarranted interference."[97] Chief Seypekaham from Little Red River appeared to confirm this sentiment when he wrote to the new park superintendent, MacKay Meikle, to demand a quota of ten beavers each for the single men of his band: "I would like to repeat that we don't want the game laws to be changed in any way in the future."[98]

At the same time local hunters were expressing their disdain for new game regulations, renewed efforts to limit access to the park fuelled hostility toward the park administration. By the summer of 1933, senior administrators within the Dominion Lands Board had expressed concern that nearly 190 permits had been issued to hunt and trap in the park annex. In an effort to reduce the number of permit holders, the park regulations were amended in October 1935. Applicants had to prove that they were "bona fide" residents of the park before 1926 and also that they were dependent on the park wildlife for their livelihood.[99] This directive was given a strict interpretation, and local hunters were denied permits for almost any imaginable reason. Most commonly, hunters who had moved out of the park before 1926 and were now hoping to regain access to their old traplines were deemed to be no longer dependent on the park wildlife.[100] From 1934 to 1939, at least thirty-nine local people had their hunting and trapping privileges in Wood Buffalo National Park revoked.[101]

These measures outraged local hunters. Dempsey alluded to this anger in February 1937 when he reported that "it is very difficult to get some of the Indians to understand the regulations governing the issue of permits to hunt and trap in the park. They seem to have the fixed idea that if at any time during their life they have made a hunting or trapping trip in what is now the park that they are eligible for a permit."[102] Large numbers of protest letters were sent to park administrators demanding the reinstatement of hunting and trapping rights within the park. For example, in 1936 Joseph Tuckaroo wrote, "My father died when I was small and I have been living with my Mother at Jackfish Lake and Trapping around Grey Wavey Creek. There are so many trappers around there now that I would like to obtain my rights to trap on the Wood Buffalo Park."[103] In July

1940, the Fort Chipewyan trapper Alfred Benoit forwarded a similar request based on the fact that he had recently been granted status as a treaty Indian:

> I am writing to ask you to try and procure for me my rights to trap in the Old Park.
>
> Eighteen years ago, I was trapping there, but when they made the division, as I was a halfbreed, I was told by the Park Warden – Lucas by name – that I would have to move out.
>
> As I am now a Treaty Indian, I would like to be reinstated in my old trapping grounds, as I find it hard to make a living for my family, where I now am trapping. My family as you know is quite large, and I would be very grateful to you if you would make an effort on my behalf, to get me back in the Old Park, where fur is much more plentiful.
>
> If you make enquiries of the Councillor Isidore Simpson, he will tell you, that I was with him trapping at the time I speak of, eighteen years ago, and I am sure that he will be able to tell you, that I broke no laws while I was trapping there.
>
> Thanking you and hoping you will be able to do something.[104]

Many permit applicants also complained that the regulations prevented family members who had moved away for extended periods from rejoining relatives who hunted and trapped within the park. Thomas Loutit, a park permit holder living in Fort Chipewyan, waged a long letter-writing campaign to have his sons Walter and Richard granted permits so they could help their aging father with his trapping operations. Despite persistent lobbying from 1936 to 1949, Loutit was never able to work his traplines with his sons because park officials concluded that the two young men had lived away from the park for too long to be considered dependent on the game.[105] In a similar case, a Native trapper from Fort Chipewyan, William St. Cyr, wrote to the acting park superintendent, Dr. J.A. Urquhart, requesting a permit so he could live in the park with a family that had informally adopted him. He concluded with the following desperate plea:

> So in fall I stayed with Firmin Powder, but his is in the park. He is at 8 miles from Chipewyan, along side of Athabasca River. I got chase out of there because I had no Lisence for the park. And today I'm writing you to ask you if I can get a park permit. You know doctor, I'm a poor orphan, no mother, no dad, no sisters, and no brothers, I am just alone on this poor earth. I've got no home, "My home should be in heaven, where my mama is." And

Firmin told me he will be glad to keep [me] as his own boy because he hasn't a boy to help him. He's got a boy but [he] is half dead, poor boy! I say from my part that Firmin is like my real dad, doctor, and his wife is like a real mama. So I'd like very much to stay with them for all my life doc because they are good peoples and I'm very fond of them. It's the first good family that I've found to stay with. But they are in the park. I'd like very much to know if I can go in the park with them. In waiting for the answer doctor, I am staying here in Chipewyan. Please write me as soon as possible so as I'll know what to do. I'd like very much to stay with the Powder family.[106]

Of course, St. Cyr's letter could be interpreted as a ploy to gain access to the park's game resources, but the many letters sent to park officials decrying the new permit regulations for severing family ties at the park boundary suggest a deep anger at this aspect of the policy initiative.

Of all of the letters condemning the injustice of the permit regulations, perhaps none match the forcefulness and conviction of those written by Adam Boucher and his wife, Victoire. Boucher was chief of the Fort McKay Chipewyan band, located just south of the park annex on the Athabasca River. Victoire and her mother, Sophie Ratfat, lived in a cabin along the Birch River in Wood Buffalo Park, and both women held permits to hunt and trap there. When Victoire and Adam Boucher married in 1928, she was forced to leave her mother's cabin because he did not hold a park permit. Although Boucher was granted special permission to visit his wife's relatives in 1928, he was determined to gain hunting and trapping privileges within the park. In 1934 he applied to the Indian agent for a permit, but when no answer was immediately forthcoming he moved his family into the park annex in March 1935. Boucher's permit application was rejected a month later; the district agent noted that "owing to his gambling tendencies he would not be an acquisition to the Wood Buffalo Park."[107] The Bouchers were subsequently evicted from the park, which both felt to be a violation of their hereditary rights. Victoire wrote to the park superintendent in February 1936 asking him in no uncertain terms to "please send me my list to go my place – my house is there again. Because is so poor here to stay here if. I go there I could makes my live. My parent are there all altime to see them, I don't have nobody with me We are alone my boy too that all 3 three of us. Please send me again hurry I want it. My parent too want me there altime again. I gut list from Buffalo park My name is was Victoire Ratfat. Before is name is I ben there a stay I was born there too."[108]

In a separate letter, Adam Boucher also emphasized his deep roots in the local landscape: "I been trapping already two year ago and my wife want to trapping in the park. Batilime Bird he go in. Park is not his own place. Why is that I am from there. You can put me in. My place it was. I was born there and those is not from there, how is that. Isidore Simpson and ... Louis Bouchie ... if you don't keep out from there I am going too. If you don't keep out those I see the head man and or a letter. I spend lots of money down ... Please send me back a letter. Hurry." Boucher finally warned that he would "go in" no matter what the decision.[109] He made good on this threat after his permit application was again rejected in March 1937. In the spring of 1939, Boucher was caught within the park passing seven illegally trapped beaver to his mother-in-law, Sophie Ratfat, so she could get them stamped for legal export under her beaver permit. He was fined twenty-five dollars.[110] Regardless of the outcome of the case, Boucher's actions can be seen as a form of political protest aimed at the arbitrary nature of the park regulations that separated his wife from her family. He did not, after all, try to hunt secretly near the edge of the park boundary; instead he proclaimed his intention to hunt and trap in the park, inviting close surveillance from the park wardens.[111]

Were all of the individual acts of lawbreaking, letter writing, and petitioning to local officials in the first decade after the creation of Wood Buffalo National Park indicative of a more widespread protest movement against the game regulations? Recent historical works by such authors as Karl Jacoby and Ramachandra Guha have interpreted poaching and arson as a form of political resistance to state control over local customary use rights in hinterland regions. Guha has noted that, in spite of the tendency among Marxist intellectuals to dismiss peasant protests as spontaneous, disorganized, and nonideological, protest movements in India were a creative and sophisticated defence of local economic interests and cultural values.[112] Guha's description of the peasants in northern India who revolted against colonial forest policy in the early twentieth century has a parallel to the rebelliousness of the hunters and trappers of Wood Buffalo Park during the same period, in that the movements contained elements of both political expression and pragmatic materialism. On the one hand, local people protested state-imposed regulations because they interfered with the traditional material basis of their livelihood; on the other, they articulated a set of cultural and political values rooted in the notion of customary use rights, hereditary land title, and, in the case of Wood Buffalo Park, a treaty guarantee of the right to hunt and trap.

The dynamic character of the protest movement in Wood Buffalo National Park was in part a product of the far-reaching nature of the regulatory mechanisms that the federal government had imposed on Native

Look at
next page too -
omg!

No ranches,
but sports hunter

people in the region. The assertion of state authority over wildlife in Wood Buffalo National Park was not limited to restrictions on Native hunting and trapping activities, but also caused dramatic changes to community, kinship, and cultural relationships among the Cree and Chipewyan communities in the region. Native hunters thus framed their response to the expanding regulatory authority of the park administration in terms of both the material and cultural survival of Aboriginal communities in the region. The protest letters sent to park officials routinely vacillated between these two poles, pleading dire hardship and privation as a reason for liberalizing access to the park, while also asserting the inherent right of Aboriginal people to live as hunter-gatherers on traditional lands. Poaching incidents evoked these two seemingly disparate themes: killing game illegally meant cash income or food for empty bellies, but such acts were also a form of civil disobedience, an expression of discontent with the disruption of community life that had accompanied the creation of a national park and its attendant alien system of game laws. To ignore the game regulations was, in a sense, an act of political restoration, an attempt to return to the time before an arbitrary and largely impersonal state bureaucracy mediated the relationship between humans and nature in the region.

Perhaps the local hunters in the park region also recognized inconsistencies in the policy regime governing Wood Buffalo National Park. By the mid-1930s, estimates of the post-transfer bison population ranged from 7,500 to 12,000 animals (see Figure 2.1).[113] Clearly the survival of the species was no longer in question, but rather than afford local people the opportunity to hunt bison for food, the government maintained a strict ban on bison hunting for decades after the Wainwright transfer. Meanwhile, many government wildlife "preservationists" were also hoping to realize the commercial potential of the expanding buffalo herds. In May 1927, Superintendent McDougal recommended that sport hunters be allowed to kill "useless" old bulls for a fee of five hundred dollars, with the meat going to feed the park wardens. O.S. Finnie, who had been so intent on removing Native people from the park to protect the bison, also recommended selling premium bison licences to sport hunters, noting that "this should bring in good revenue and in addition there would be the revenue from the sale of meat." He also suggested constructing an abattoir as a source of revenue for the park.[114] The idea was taken up by Finnie's successor, H.E. Hume, in the winter of 1931, when he instructed J. Dewey Soper, the first biologist to conduct an extensive survey of the bison population, to report on the advisability of establishing an abattoir in the park to produce buffalo meat for relief purposes and for sale to white settlers and mining communities.[115]

Almost two decades passed before an abattoir was constructed in Wood Buffalo National Park, but a small annual bison slaughter was authorized in the winter of 1929 to distribute relief meat through the Indian Affairs Branch and the local missions. Since Native hunters could not, in the view of park officials, be trusted to hunt the surplus bison, then the park wardens would kill buffalo to provide cheap meat to the people who had been forbidden to hunt them a generation earlier. A memo penned by the deputy minister of the interior in February 1932 argued that "it would be extremely unwise to permit the Indian families to visit the Park and shoot buffalo even under the supervision of a Warden." Slaughtering the buffalo was, nevertheless, acceptable so long as the government officials conducted the operation according to the principles of rational herd management: "As we see it, the first thing to ascertain each year is how many animals are needed and then the Wardens can kill the outcast bulls and old cows."[116]

At the root of the conflict between local hunters and park administrators was not only a preservationist philosophy that opposed any human presence in the park, but also two different approaches to managing and utilizing wildlife resources. Efficient and controlled exploitation had become the rationale of the bison management programs proposed by park administrators. The decentralized wildlife management practised by local

2.1   An aerial photo of a buffalo herd taken during a population survey, 17 July 1946. LAC C-148456

hunters – which according to park officials only encouraged random and impulsive depredations on the park's wildlife – had no place in modern herd management. Managing human activity and managing wildlife went hand in hand in Wood Buffalo National Park. By the 1930s park wardens often hunted for bison one day and patrolled for Native buffalo poachers the next.[117]

This contradictory approach to bison management was difficult for Native hunters to accept, and many attempted to challenge the expanding authority of the state over local wildlife. A striking example of widespread dissent occurred after a request from the community of Fort Resolution for permission to kill one bison per family was refused in February 1937. That summer, there was an open revolt over the issue when Native hunters from the surrounding region refused to take treaty payments. In an apparent attempt to defuse the boycott, the presiding RCMP officer, Sergeant Makinson, explained that even if local hunters wanted to take bison only in cases of starvation, "this request could not be granted, for the privilege would be abused, as some would think that they were in a starving condition very quickly." Makinson went on to argue that "the Government was preserving the buffalo for the Indians' own good, and that any of the old buffalo that were killed the meat [sic] is sent to the Indian schools and hospitals."[118]

This comment is a fitting epitaph for the first two decades of bison management in Wood Buffalo National Park, a period that witnessed an erosion of local sovereignty among Native hunters as the state adopted an increasingly assertive managerial stance toward people and wildlife. By the late 1930s, the region had been subject to a strict set of game regulations, a warden service, jail terms for infractions of the game laws, the expulsion from the park area of many people, and the introduction of thousands of plains bison that remained strictly inaccessible to Native hunters. In a general critique of the wilderness idea, the philosopher Thomas Birch has argued that designated wilderness spaces such as national parks allow the state to incarcerate and control wildness within heavily regulated "prison-like" environments.[119] The early history of Wood Buffalo Park provides compelling support for the notion that parks could function as prisons not only for wildlife but also, in effect, for people. The expansion of game laws and permit restrictions in the park and the first attempts to intensively manage the park's bison herds meant that both local people and local wildlife were enclosed in a federal space devoted to the intense regulation and supervision of their lives. No longer were local hunters permitted to decide even how best to feed themselves; only government officials could manage the bison through a controlled cull and distribute the spoils in a manner they thought best served the interests of the local population. From the perspective of local people, it is hard to see what benefits – despite Sgt. Makinson's assurances – had accompanied the creation of the park. Only a generation earlier, hunters had been largely free to manage the wood bison and other wildlife according to their own cultural values and traditional sources of knowledge. Now they had come face to face with the autocratic tendencies of a modern administrative state that attempted to control the human relationship to nature within the boundaries of Wood Buffalo National Park.

3

Pastoral Dreams

I N APRIL 1940, A POSTER TITLED "Notice to all Indians: Protect the Muskrats and Beaver" was distributed throughout Wood Buffalo National
Park. The notice, drafted by Park Superintendent J.A. Urquhart, warned
local trappers that "it would be foolish to permit trapping these animals
until they have increased to a large number." Urquhart did, however, promise that "the Government men are doing all they can to increase the number of muskrat and beaver in the Wood Buffalo Park." He described dam
projects the government had initiated to raise the water levels in sections
of the Peace-Athabasca Delta to increase fur production and informed
local people that trapping within these "fur restoration" areas was forbidden. "Before trapping in the Park," Urquhart warned, "Indians must get
their trapping permits from the Game Warden who will tell them what
they must do." He finally assured the Native trappers that these new restrictions were in their own best interest: "If the Indians work with the
Government men and help to stop trapping in these places for a few years,
there will then be plenty of fur for all."[1]

The content of this notice marked a subtle shift in the focus of wildlife
policy within Wood Buffalo National Park. Since the creation of the park,
the attention of federal wildlife managers had been devoted almost exclusively to the protection and propagation of the northern bison herds. But
internal memos and published reports throughout the 1930s and 1940s
asserted that the "post-transfer" bison population – now estimated to be
nearly twelve thousand animals – was so large that it was spilling over
the southern boundary of the park. Federal government biologists such as

J. Dewey Soper and C.H.D. Clarke declared the dramatic expansion of
the range and size of the herds a conservation success story. The imminent
extinction of the northern bison had been averted; there was thus little
justification for maintaining the crisis atmosphere that had dominated
bison management in the region over the past five decades.[2]

Nonetheless, several new wildlife crises attracted the attention of park
administrators at the end of the 1930s. The steep decline of muskrat in the
Peace-Athabasca Delta after 1935 presented a particularly acute problem
for the park's wildlife managers and the local Indian agents because the
species was a mainstay of the local trapping economy. Reductions in the
harvest of beaver and moose in the early 1940s, coupled with reports of a
shortage of game and fur animals throughout northern Canada, led to the
perception that, save for the bison, wildlife populations within Wood Buffalo
National Park were in a general state of decline.[3] Consequently, for the
first time in nearly half a century, species other than the buffalo received
the close scrutiny of park administrators.

In addition to the new focus on a wider range of fauna, a new approach
emerged to managing wildlife within the park. Park officials continued to
underscore the role of human hunting and trapping as a primary limiting
factor on wildlife populations, but they also began to accept that changes
in the nonhuman ecology of the park might also be having a dramatic impact. A particularly strong influence on federal wildlife officials during this
period was the research of Charles Elton, who theorized that individual
wildlife species did not inevitably move toward steady and optimal population levels but were subject to periodic fluctuations in abundance.[4] Humans
were only one of many influences on this process of dynamic change: disease, predation, prey availability, and habitat changes could all contribute
to dramatic variations in wildlife populations. Furthermore, the high and
low populations of many species oscillated in regular cycles that were,
according to Elton, constant and predictable. The implications for wildlife managers were staggering: if the extremes of the population cycle
for economically important wildlife could be predicted accurately, then
interventions ranging from reduced quotas to habitat enhancement could
immediately respond to any severe downturn in the population of economically important wildlife species. Elton promoted this idea directly
to Canadian wildlife officials. In September 1938, he attended a meeting
of the federal Advisory Board on Wildlife Protection, where he suggested
that a research program on population cycles would enable the federal
government to predict future downturns in the northern trapping economy with a high degree of accuracy. He further advised the board that his

research on Hudson's Bay Company records dating back to the eighteenth century indicated that trapping had had little impact on the fur-bearer population in northern Canada. Instead, environmental factors provided the key to understanding the root causes of crashes in fur populations.[5]

For federal wildlife officials, the idea that natural causes might underlie fur shortages (and the consequent economic hardship for Native northerners) prompted immediate research into the possibility of mitigating dramatic crashes in wildlife populations within Wood Buffalo Park. Officials in the Indian Affairs Branch and the Department of Mines and Resources appointed J.L. Grew, a fur farmer from Ontario, to survey the Peace-Athabasca Delta region for suitable dam sites in the summer of 1938. His report characterized the fur situation in the delta as dire. Water levels had fallen to as much as three feet below normal in many parts of the delta, and the reeds, lilies, and cattails that were the preferred food of the muskrat had been overrun with weedy brush in many places. The consequent lack of fur in that winter's trapping season had left the Native population at Fort Chipewyan in desperate economic circumstances. The fur situation was so bad, Grew reported, that traders no longer offered credit to local trappers; only those "exceptional" and "thrifty" individuals who had planted a vegetable garden that summer were able to "assist themselves to a more comfortable living."[6] As a remedial measure, Grew proposed the construction of dams across at least four of the myriad small creeks in the Peace-Athabasca Delta. The following summer, he was hired to supervise the construction of small dams across the Boots Snye and the Murdock, Dempsey, and Savard creeks in the southeast corner of the park.

The pilot fur restoration project was hardly a success. The construction was completed on schedule in the summer of 1939, but engineering problems resulted in cracking, sagging, and large breaches in the dams. Although muskrat became notably more abundant up to 1942, the dams were not maintained after 1941 due to cost overruns and wartime austerity. Faced with further drying in the delta region in the summer of 1943, Park Superintendent MacKay Meikle was left only to hope that large ice jams and widespread flooding the following spring might counter the drying trend. The water levels in the delta continued to fall the next summer, however, and the muskrat harvest subsequently dropped from roughly 40,000 animals per year between 1938 and 1943 to a mere 8,884 in the 1944-45 winter trapping season.[7]

The failure of the dam projects led park administrators to reconsider the idea that habitat improvements were enough to address the decline in the park's fur-bearer population. A report on the fur conservation projects drafted in April 1940 did emphasize the impact of habitat loss on the muskrat, but went on to state, "The game and fur has been depleted to such an extent that stringent conservation measures were necessary in order to conserve the remaining wildlife supply."[8] In the winter of 1942, park officials moved the closing date for the muskrat season back from 15 May to 2 May, limiting the number of days available to shoot animals in open water.[9] The restrictions on beaver hunting and trapping were even more severe. In August 1943, a reduction in the bag limit from fifteen to ten beaver was approved for all of the Northwest Territories, including Wood Buffalo Park. Nevertheless, the biologist J. Dewey Soper reported in May 1945 that many lakes in the park were "nearly depopulated" of the animals. Soper believed that the low water table was the root cause of the shortage but also that Native trappers had severely reduced the population as they shifted their efforts to beaver from the declining muskrat. Although he recognized that further trapping restrictions might render many Native hunters and trappers dependent on relief, Soper recommended a year-round closed season on beaver in the park.[10]

The reactions of local hunters and trappers to the emerging fur crisis and the new regulations were varied. Local leaders understood the gravity of the situation and had begun to develop their own strategies to address the decline in game populations. At the annual treaty celebrations held in Fort Chipewyan in July 1942, Band Councillor Isidore Simpson requested that the federal government institute a closed season on marten for five years so the country could be restocked with the species. Simpson also recommended limiting the number of muskrat traps to thirty per trapper so animals were not lost due to neglect by those with excessively long trap-lines.[11] Yet while local leaders advocated specific conservation strategies to protect fur populations, they also firmly rejected many of the conservation measures imposed on them by federal wildlife officials. At the same treaty meeting, Councillor Benjamin Marcel complained that the new closing date of 2 May for the muskrat season was too early and should be extended closer to the middle of the month to allow at least some hunting after spring breakup. Indian Agent J. Melling reported that most trappers from the region appeared to agree with Marcel, including many that "bear in mind the need for, and essential principles of, fur conservation."[12] At the north end of the park, Indian Agent J.H. Riopel reported in September 1944 that trappers from Fort Resolution and Hay River objected to both the closed season on marten and the reduced bag limit for beaver.[13] Native hunters also steadfastly opposed the recommendations of a special panel that had been appointed to investigate the fur conservation problem in Wood Buffalo National Park. In the summer of 1945, the committee, made up of Soper, J.L. Grew, Superintendent Meikle, and Warden Mike Dempsey, held five meetings in the settlements surrounding the park to canvass local opinion on its proposals to create designated group trapping areas and implement a year-round closure of the beaver season. The results of the meetings were unequivocal: the hunters who attended overwhelmingly objected to any proposal that would limit the beaver harvest or restrict the movement of trappers to registered areas. The panel concluded, "It is very apparent the majority of the Park Indians and half-breeds are not favourably inclined toward any changes in the present regulations or beaver trapping practice."[14]

This local opposition appears to have had little impact on senior policy makers. A complete ban on beaver hunting in Wood Buffalo Park was instituted at a meeting of the Northwest Territories Council in September 1945. And a system of registered group trapping areas was introduced in 1949, with a new set of game regulations specific to the park.[15] Despite the agreement among park administrators and Native hunters as to the gravity of the local fur situation and the need for at least some conservation measures, there was an intense conflict over the precise methods used to conserve wildlife, and implicitly, over which of the park's constituent groups – harvesters or managers – was best positioned to make decisions about the trapping of particular fur species. The chief of the Cree band at Fort Chipewyan, John Cowie, summed up the position of local hunters when he wrote to the acting park superintendent, A.H. Gibson, in February 1946 to plead for an end to the closed season on beaver. Cowie promised that if the season were open his hunters could help the wardens obtain an accurate count of the beaver: "You will be supprized when this count is taken at the number of Beaver which is really there."[16]

As in the previous two decades, more direct forms of resistance accompanied the official objections of the park's hunters and trappers to the fur conservation measures. Although the scant records of convictions for game law violations render it impossible to draw a comprehensive picture of the political context surrounding criminal activities in the park, at least some infractions probably constituted a confrontation of the federal government's attempts to criminalize subsistence practices during this period. Throughout the 1940s, Aboriginal hunters were convicted for a range of crimes such as exceeding newly imposed bag limits, violating increasingly lengthy closed seasons, and setting snares, after this common practice was banned throughout the Northwest Territories in 1936 to protect "trapwise" animals who would otherwise survive the winter.[17] Native trappers in the Peace-Athabasca Delta also objected to a ban on the customary practice of setting traps within muskrat houses because they believed the wreckage caused by breaking open the much smaller pushups, or air holes, was nearly impossible to remedy and inevitably resulted in the freezing of the air chamber. A report tabled in October 1940 by a fur specialist with the Indian Affairs Branch pointed to a broad popular opposition to a regulation that had redefined a traditional practice as a crime: "The regulations for trapping muskrat at the present time, leaves [sic] a very bad and detrimental impression on the people as well as lack of confidence in those administrating the area."[18]

The ongoing ban on setting forest fires also remained ineffective against the weight of tradition. Warden reports and memoranda from senior civil servants in the 1940s note the preponderance of brush fires throughout the park, which they attributed to Indian "carelessness" with campfires. More likely, these fires continued the traditional practice of deliberately burning off meadows to create optimum bison and moose habitat. Native people also burned sloughs or creek bed areas in the spring to stimulate the growth of reeds and grasses for muskrat.[19] The official concern about fires was so great that Roy A. Gibson, deputy commissioner of the Northwest Territories, patronizingly considered purchasing the film *Bambi* to educate hunters about the evils of forest fires, but he balked at the price of this commercial film.[20]

Although the willingness of Native hunters to disobey the park regulations clearly challenged federal authority in the region, the political nature of these lawbreaking activities should not be overstated. On a very basic level, it is difficult to determine the extent to which the crime reports in the archival record represented a more general flouting of the park regulations. From 1938 until 1946 the number of wardens patrolling a park area the size of many European countries fell to between five and seven officers, so many violations of the regulations may have gone unnoticed. Thus a small number of convictions for a particular offence may represent a more extensive pattern of lawbreaking.[21] But any widespread movement to break the game laws in Wood Buffalo Park during the 1940s may have been associated more with pragmatism than with politics, because Native trappers faced bleak economic conditions over the course of the decade. The severe decline in the take of muskrat in the park and the closing of the beaver season in 1945 had, in fact, thrown many Native trappers below the subsistence threshold.[22] To make matters worse, the Advisory Board on Wildlife Protection approved amendments to the Northwest Territories and Wood Buffalo Park Game Regulations in January 1946 limiting the annual moose harvest to one bull per hunter.[23] The Hudson's Bay Company manager at the Fifth Meridian post described grim conditions in 1946: "This year is the worst I have ever seen for fur in my short period with the Company. If it wasn't for squirrel and family allowance, these Indians would be practically starving to death. As it is, they can just barely feed the dogs and themselves, with the dogs running a poor second. This is the one year the beaver should be open at least to help these Indians out because God alone knows what they will do this summer."[24] Chief John Cowie echoed this sentiment when he made an "urgent appeal" to Park Superintendent A.H. Gibson to reconsider the closing of the beaver season because it was a "hard year" for the people of his community.[25] Given the increasingly dismal economic situation facing Native hunters, the increase in fur poaching incidents in the mid-1940s can be attributed in part to the attempts of local people to feed themselves.

Nonetheless, lawbreaking activities in the "fur crisis" years occurred within the context of an ongoing political effort by Native hunters to divest themselves of federal game restrictions and reassert some of their former sovereignty over land and wildlife in the Wood Buffalo Park region. In the early 1940s, Native leaders had initiated several formal challenges to the legitimacy of federal authority over the park region. In February 1943, Indian Agent Melling held a meeting with leaders of the Cree band at Fort Chipewyan regarding the much-reviled restrictions on movement between the "A" (NWT section), "B" (north of the Peace River), and "C" (south of the Peace) areas of the park that had been imposed in 1926. Cree leaders such as Chief John Cowie and "Headman" Ambel objected to the area restrictions partly because of the disunity the system had sowed in the local Cree population, but also because at times even close relatives were prevented from visiting one another.[26] To the likely astonishment of Native leaders, federal officials did relent on this issue in May 1943 after a legal ruling from the departmental solicitor that the park's enabling legislation did not authorize the confinement of Aboriginal hunting and trapping "privileges" to one area of the park.[27]

This rare affirmation of a legislative right to hunt and trap in all areas of the park occurred simultaneously with a second and more overt attempt to undermine the hegemony of the northern administration over wildlife policy. In the early 1940s, the Cree band at Fort Chipewyan had begun to press for a reserve in the southern portion of the park at Peace Point. The proposal was partly meant to fulfill the long-standing promise of reserves included in Treaty 8, but it was also a means to elude many of the most grievous consequences of the game laws. Many of the Cree band's appeals for a reserve highlighted the fact that Alberta had recently adopted a system of registered trapping areas, leaving hunters who were expelled from Wood Buffalo Park for violating the game regulations with nowhere to pursue their trade.[28] In May 1944, Chief Cowie wrote to the inspector of Indian agencies to argue that a reserve would end the hardships faced by hunters expelled from the park, particularly if the Cree band was afforded sovereignty over wildlife on reserve lands. Given a reserve, the band could also stave off the worst effects of the fur shortage by building permanent houses, planting gardens, and raising livestock on their land.[29] MacKay Meikle, the park superintendent, recommended against the idea in June 1945 due to concerns about the protection of the buffalo in the area and because lawbreakers with cancelled permits might be able to hunt in the reserve section of the park. Meikle made the astonishing claim that the Cree hunters did not need their own reserve because "the park is a wonderful game reserve for them and they have good hunting and trapping privileges."[30]

In spite of Meikle's assurances, Native hunters and trappers did not regard their hunting and trapping privileges in Wood Buffalo National Park as sufficient to maintain their livelihoods. The decline of fur populations in the park and the consequent imposition of much stricter game regulations in the late 1930s and early 1940s had affected almost every aspect of Cree and Chipewyan material culture in the region. Species that had been mainstays of the trapping economy now carried shortened hunting seasons, reduced bag limits, or were completely off limits. Local anger over federal game laws found expression in the campaign among the Cree of Fort Chipewyan for a reserve, the protests over park regulations, and the periodic violations of the game regulations. More than anything else, the punitive consequences of game law violations, particularly expulsion from the park, had convinced Cree leaders of the need to assert sovereignty over their own territory and throw off their paternalistic relationship with the park administration. The widening net of game regulations associated with the fur crisis of the 1940s had thus galvanized the Cree leadership in the Peace-Athabasca Delta region not only to try to ease the worst effects of the fur shortage and its attendant game laws, but also to question the political legitimacy of federal authority over their traditional hunting territories.

The intense controversy over access to fur in Wood Buffalo National Park dissipated somewhat in the late 1940s and early 1950s as a series of scientific reports recorded a reversal of the drying trend in the Peace-Athabasca Delta and a subsequent dramatic increase in the beaver and muskrat populations.[31] A new set of game laws drafted under the authority of

the National Parks Act in 1949 marked the beginning of a general relax-
ation of the strict fur regulations imposed nearly a decade earlier. Most
important, the new regulations removed some of the most onerous restrictions on key fur-bearing species by establishing a second winter muskrat
season in the month of December. An open season for beaver north of the
Peace River was established in January 1952 and subsequently extended
through the entire park in October of the same year.[32]

The conclusion of the fur crisis did not mark an end, however, to the
efforts of federal wildlife officials to intensively manage both people and
wildlife in Wood Buffalo National Park. As enthusiasm for developing the
resources of the Canadian North began to build in the 1950s, federal officials revived the idea that the northern bison herds might be cultivated
and managed as a profitable natural resource rather than simply an aesthetic wilderness showpiece. The conflict over access to wildlife in Wood
Buffalo Park thus evolved from a dispute between local harvesters and a
federal bureaucracy intent on removing all human presence from the wilderness park into a struggle between Native hunters determined to regain
access to wildlife for subsistence and a northern administration determined to exploit the park's namesake for commercial purposes.

BISON FOR SALE

Amid the fur crisis, park managers displayed only a limited interest in
Wood Buffalo National Park's bison herds in the years before and during
the Second World War. Small annual slaughters of twenty to thirty animals were conducted for relief purposes, but other than a casual survey of
the buffalo in 1944 by B.I. Love, the superintendent of Elk Island National
Park, there was no scientific study of the bison and no management program for the species.[33] Antipoaching patrols did continue through the
1940s, but usually in the form of dogsled patrols on existing trapping
trails, which was an effective means of identifying fur violations but less
helpful in determining the health and numbers of the widely dispersed
bison herds.[34] More generally, reports from J. Dewey Soper, on a return
visit to the park in 1945, and from the district forest officer in 1949 suggested that the park as a whole had been neglected; overgrown roads,
downed telephone lines, and collapsing warden cabins illustrated a serious
decline in the park's law enforcement and patrol capabilities.[35]

While park officials were less than attentive to bison management during the 1940s, access to the herds did not fade from the political agenda of

Native hunters in the region. In the winter of 1947, the new park super-intendent, Eugene Oldham, noted that many hunters had become "queru-lous" as to whether they would derive any benefit from the expanding bison herds.[36] The closed season on buffalo – now in its fifth decade – was a long-standing grievance among local hunters, but their renewed pressure for access to buffalo meat was also tied to the shortage and consequent strict regulation of other big game species in the region. Not only had the aforementioned decline in the park's moose population led to a limit of one bull moose per hunter in 1946, but the barren ground caribou migra-tion had largely bypassed Fort Resolution and Fort Smith in the winters of 1944 to 1946.[37] The extreme game shortages do not appear to have pro-voked increased incidences of bison poaching, as there are no records of convictions for killing bison in the relevant park files after 1941. It is un-clear whether the lack of prosecutions reflected a real decline in illegal bison hunting or simply a shift in law enforcement priorities toward fur protection. But Native hunters in the park region continued to press for an opening of the bison season through more formal avenues of political protest. In February 1947, for example, MacKay Meikle (now chief of the Mackenzie Division within the northern administration) reported that hunters in Fort Smith and Fort Chipewyan had pressured the Indian agent at several past annual treaty gatherings to convince the government to allow buffalo hunting for food.[38]

The park administration was not completely indifferent to the plight of Native hunters and trappers. In response to repeated requests for access to bison meat in the 1940s, park administrators increased the annual relief slaughter of bison for distribution through the Indian Affairs Branch and the mission schools and hospitals. Since its inception in 1929, the official park slaughter of bison had resulted in an annual kill of roughly thirty ani-mals (Figures 3.1 and 3.2). After 1942 the number of bison taken annually for relief purposes increased steadily to approximately fifty in the mid-1940s and to one hundred by the end of the decade.[39] But while park officials were willing to increase the amount of government-slaughtered bison meat available for local consumption, under no circumstances were they willing to lift the closed season on bison or cede control over the herds to local hunters. In his annual report for 1947-48, Park Superintendent Oldham recommended that one buffalo should be allotted to each Native family in the region, but only if the wardens did the killing and the families were left responsible for butchering and transport.[40]

Oldham's recommendations were the product of an emerging belief among federal wildlife scientists that expanding the controlled and supervised bison slaughter might both help the local population and allow for the selective culling of the buffalo herds. The biologist C.H.D. Clarke argued unequivocally against an open season in 1944 because it would be "very difficult to regulate the total kill and to confine it to areas where it would be justified." In areas where bison herds were well established, however, Clarke maintained that an expanded slaughter of young bulls would limit range destruction, prevent overcrowding and the spread of disease, and help to preserve the pure wood bison population that was now, in the wake of the bison transfer, inevitably composed mostly of older breeding stock. In sum, a controlled slaughter would allow park officials to manage the herds for optimum production. An open season, Clarke reasoned, might preclude the careful selection of animals to be culled as part of a modern herd management program.[41]

The movement towards an expanded scientific culling program was linked to a broader international shift in the philosophy and practice of wildlife ecology during the 1940s and 1950s. By the beginning of the Second World War, the noninterventionist ethos that had produced so much opposition to the Wainwright transfer two decades earlier had given way to a more intrusive approach among wildlife scientists. According to Donald Worster,

3.1 Two young buffalo killed during the 1948 bison slaughter in Wood Buffalo National Park. LAC C-148899

ecologists in the 1930s had already begun to reject the organic holism associated with Frederic Clements' "balance of nature" school in favour of a
mechanistic model more amenable to production-oriented and managerial interests. Led by such luminaries as Arthur Tansley, Eugene Odum,
and the previously mentioned Charles Elton, the new ecology emphasized
the importance of "bio-economic" concepts: production, consumption,
population cycles, and energy flows. By revealing the complex workings of
these phenomena, the new ecology implied that natural processes could
be manipulated and readily improved upon in carefully managed resource
production programs.[42] No longer would the scientific community oppose
the efforts of government bureaucrats to intensively manipulate wildlife
populations as a boon to sport hunters or for agricultural purposes. Beginning in the interwar period in North America, the stamp of scientific
approval was readily accorded to all manner of interventionist wildlife
management programs, particularly those designed to optimize available
food supplies by stocking underutilized parks and preserves with wildlife
or by culling surplus animals from apparently overcrowded ranges. Maintaining an appropriate balance in the relationship between wildlife populations and their habitat could no longer, it seemed, be entrusted to the

3.2   Hunters skin a bison as part of the 1948 slaughter, Wood Buffalo National Park.
LAC C-148901

vagaries of either nature or local hunters; instead, the authoritative guidance of natural scientists was required to tinker with the organic machine.

The postwar development of a more intensive managerial approach to wildlife conservation in Canada can also be attributed to an important institutional change in the federal bureaucracy: the creation of the Dominion Wildlife Service (later the Canadian Wildlife Service, or CWS) in 1947. The most important and immediate result of the agency's establishment was an increased capacity to conduct wildlife research within national parks. Some sites such as Wood Buffalo National Park were even assigned a "resident" CWS biologist to conduct ongoing surveys of significant wildlife populations. The growth and centralization of Canada's wildlife research infrastructure within the federal government (and the paucity of university-based wildlife scientists in the postwar period) signalled a conspicuous integration of pure research and applied management programs in the national parks.[43] Indeed, from the beginning it was apparent that the CWS would not function as a pure research body but would attempt to combine bureaucratic priorities such as revenue generation with an intensive approach to wildlife management. In a paper presented to the Dominion-Provincial Wildlife Conference in 1945, Dr. Harrison Lewis, who was to become the first director of the CWS, emphasized the importance of "cropping" surplus wildlife to prevent disease, overcrowding, excess grazing, and damage to commercial interests. Citing the necessity of an annual buffalo slaughter on such fenced ranges as Elk Island National Park, Lewis argued that culled animals should be fully utilized to prevent waste and, if possible, to produce income for the federal government. In more general terms, Lewis remarked, "We must realize the importance of Canada's wildlife resources in the post-war development of the country. Ninety percent of the area of Canada supports wildlife and on two-thirds of the area it is the most important permanent crop."[44]

This comment seemed prophetic as the bison slaughter in Wood Buffalo National Park expanded rapidly to become a full-scale industrial operation in the 1950s. Between 1951 and 1967, the federal government culled over four thousand bison in Wood Buffalo National Park as part of a herd management program (Figure 3.3). In the process, park officials produced a so-called by-product of close to two million pounds of meat for relief purposes, local retailers, and the emerging commercial market for wild game in southern Canada.[45] Although bison slaughters were common in fenced national parks with no predators such as Elk Island and Buffalo National Park (which was closed in 1939), Wood Buffalo National Park was the first protected area in Canada where large-scale bison slaughters were conducted on a large open range that showed little evidence of excessive grazing or overcrowding. Today, the incongruity of large round-ups, mass slaughters, and the construction of abattoirs in one of Canada's largest and most remote national parks raises the question of how a meat production industry arose in a supposed wildlife sanctuary where the bison had been protected from Native hunters for decades

In a very brief analysis of the "slaughter period," the anthropologist Patricia McCormack has argued that the commercialization of the northern bison resulted from the simultaneous desire of federal biologists and northern bureaucrats to increase the region's resource potential as part of the postwar northern development paradigm, and to reduce disease through "herd sanitation" programs.[46] Certainly the Northern Administration Branch applied the northern development mantra to Wood Buffalo National Park with great enthusiasm in the 1950s as it issued leases for timber berths near the Peace River and licences for commercial fishing on Lake Claire. Many senior branch officials also considered returning a portion of the park to the Province of Alberta in the 1960s to allow mining and petroleum exploration.[47] In addition, the slaughter program was accorded a degree of scientific legitimacy as a wildlife management project designed to control disease. In 1944, B.I. Love, the superintendent of Elk Island National Park, conducted a biological survey of the northern bison herds and confirmed that tuberculosis had spread from the Wainwright bison to the wood bison.[48] In January 1950, the CWS biologist Ward Stevens concluded from a sample of forty animals that 18 to 26 percent of the park bison were

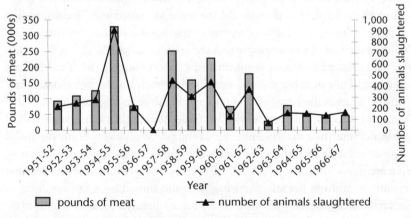

3.3   Bison slaughters in Wood Buffalo National Park, 1951-67
SOURCE: RG 84, vol. 2239, WB299, pt. 2, Library and Archives Canada.

infected with tuberculosis and that the highest risk for disease trans-
mission occurred when the animals were concentrated on their winter range.
Stevens recommended herd reduction as "the most logical method of [dis-
ease] control."[49] After the park's resident CWS mammalogist, William Fuller,
estimated from aerial surveys conducted in 1949 and 1951 that the bison in
the park numbered 12,000, a consensus began to emerge among federal
wildlife scientists that a large number of the animals could be removed
without harming the overall population.[50] Harrison Lewis suggested that
up to 500 "surplus" animals could be killed annually; his CWS colleague
John Kelsall estimated that the herds could withstand an annual slaughter
of 750 animals.[51] The taint of disease therefore became one of the most
important pretexts for asserting further state control over the animals in
the form of intensive herd management and commercial meat production.
Maxwell Graham's dream that the bison might one day produce a usable
surplus of ranch animals was finally realized, but only in response to the
worst effects of the intensive wildlife management program he had initiated nearly three decades earlier.

Although disease control and commercialization provided much of its
impetus, the slaughter program was also intimately tied to the federal government's attempts to control and marginalize human hunters in the park.
At the forefront of the arguments for a controlled bison slaughter in a
newly constructed park abattoir were the long-standing idea that the random depredations of Native hunters were incompatible with the scientific
management of bison to reduce disease and maximize biological production.
When Native hunters were hired in the late 1940s to assist the park wardens with the annual slaughter, the park field staff was immediately critical of their hunting techniques. One warden complained in November
1948 that the Native hunters routinely stalked the buffalo for five to ten
miles, then wasted their effort by rushing at them "haphazardly" and wound-
ing many animals.[52] Senior wildlife officials also noted that the hunting
crew could not pick out the older diseased animals under the random conditions associated with a field slaughter.[53] Some of the commentary on the
hunt contains a strong hint of racism. Chief Warden E.H. Essex noted, for
example, that "to a man used to the sanitation of packing plants, the spec-
tacle of a bunch of Indians hacking up a carcass must be shocking, as it is
to a layman."[54] Finally, when Dr. F.E. Graesser, veterinary inspector of the
Health of Animals Branch, participated in the annual hunt of 1950, he was
so appalled at the conditions that he recommended an end to the field
hunt and the construction of an abattoir to improve cleanliness and
butchering techniques.[55] A field slaughter employing Native hunters had

become, it seems, an anachronism, a backward local mode of production that was to be modernized through current technology and scientific expertise. Only a highly regulated slaughter using modern abattoir facilities could accomplish the careful and selective culling program that the northern administration envisioned for the park's bison herds.

Accordingly, the annual bison slaughter in Wood Buffalo National Park was transformed into a full-scale industrial operation by the winter of 1952-53. A modern abattoir, corrals, and drift fences were constructed at Hay Camp so that the random killing associated with the field slaughter could be replaced by a more precise test and slaughter program implemented to identify and destroy tuberculin reactors (Figures 3.4 to 3.7).[56] In an effort to recover construction and operational costs, buffalo meat was to be sold to the missions, the Indian Affairs Branch, and to northern retailers as a low-cost food supply for the local population.[57] A senior conservation official in the northern administration described the program in the following terms: "Through sound management practices in connection with the care of this herd and the utilization of the meat therefrom, within a period from five to six years, sufficient revenue could be obtained annually from the sale of meat products, etc., to balance this cost of maintaining the Wood Buffalo Park."[58] This approach to the slaughter provided the conceptual basis for official bison management policy in Wood Buffalo National Park throughout the 1950s and 1960s. In a 1954 report, the CWS biologist Ward Stevens articulated four policy goals that governed the bison slaughter program for much of its existence: to preserve the herds, to keep the population within the capacity of the range, to reduce the incidence of diseases such as tuberculosis (and later brucellosis and anthrax), and to provide "a cheap source of meat for the resident population of the Northwest Territories and Wood Buffalo Park."[59]

Although the last provision of Stevens' policy can be interpreted as a pragmatic and benevolent attempt to improve the diets of Native northerners with local country food, it was also meant to bolster other elements of the wildlife conservation agenda. From the earliest years of the expanded slaughter, senior wildlife officials hoped that bison meat from Wood Buffalo National Park would reduce hunting pressure on wildlife in other parts of the Northwest Territories. At a meeting of the Advisory Board on Wildlife Protection held on 31 January 1951, Harrison Lewis raised the possibility of distributing increased amounts of bison meat to relieve hunting pressure on the barren ground caribou population, thought to be in a state of sharp decline throughout the Mackenzie Valley region.[60] When concern over caribou peaked in 1955 with the declaration of a "caribou crisis" in

northern Canada (see Chapter 7), F.J.G. Cunningham, director of the Northern Administration and Lands Branch, wrote a long position paper directed
at the commissioner of the Northwest Territories calling for a dramatic
increase in the distribution of buffalo meat from the park and reindeer
meat from the Mackenzie Delta ranch. Cunningham argued that alternative
meat sources could help to constrain the "indiscriminate" Native slaughter of caribou. In other words, the handout of government-slaughtered
wildlife might encourage northern hunting cultures to curtail or abandon
their traditional subsistence activities.[61] In addition, centralized control
over the distribution of bison meat was considered an appropriately inexpensive way to provide relief in kind rather than in cash that might be
wasted on frivolous luxuries. The bison cull within Wood Buffalo National
Park was thus tied not only to such pillars of the modernist state as scientific expertise and bureaucratic management, but also to more paternalistic aspects of the emerging welfare state and its relationship to Native
hunters in the North.

The goal of providing an inexpensive meat supply to northern residents
eventually had to compete with the federal government's desire to develop
the commercial potential of the bison herds. As early as the summer of
1954, Fred Fraser, the director of the Territorial Division, suggested to the

3.4   The Hay Camp Abattoir in 1952. LAC C-148893

deputy minister that the principle of supplying cheap buffalo meat for local markets might have to be abandoned because the Hudson's Bay Company had been unable to sell much meat from the 1953 slaughters. Unless export markets were developed with southern meatpackers, Fraser warned, there might be no place to sell the surplus bison from the annual slaughters.[62] The department therefore made arrangements with P. Burns and Co. of Edmonton to sell five hundred buffalo carcasses from the 1954-55 slaughter. When Canada Packers (which had supplied a butcher for the first large slaughters) objected, an agreement was reached to allot each company three hundred animals.[63] To meet these new obligations in southern Canada as well as the ongoing commitment to the Hudson's Bay Company, the missions, and Indian Affairs, over nine hundred bison were killed at Hay Camp that winter. The packing companies were sold the best cuts of meat for the developing southern markets at rates lower than the Hudson's Bay Company paid; local people were left with the tough meat of the older bulls and higher prices in the local grocers. The affront was too much for the Catholic missionary at Aklavik, who issued a cutting indictment of the program in a local newspaper:

> Even buffalo meat could have been shipped from Smith and sold for less than the local reindeer if the price was anywhere near the 5 cents per pound

3.5   Bulldozing a carcass toward the Hay Camp Abattoir, 1952. LAC C-148893

price this meat was sold for to Canada Packers and Burns and Co. last season. Natives, however, were being charged 55 cents per pound for inferior
meat. Of the 904 buffalo killed last January at the Hay Camp, the commercial companies with their own butchers on the spot took the calves and
the choice meat, leaving the rest for the hospitals and the natives of the
country. In other words, the meat rejected by the Outside Companies was
later sold to the natives of the country for ten times the price! The Packers
got 75 cents per pound in Montreal for this meat.[64]

In addition to such local criticisms of the program, Canadian Wildlife
Service biologists worried that the newly commercial focus of the slaughter might undermine the scientific legitimacy of the disease control program. This apprehension was well founded: many senior officials within
the Department of Northern Affairs were willing to disregard the objective of disease control if it interfered with the development of viable commercial markets. In 1954, for instance, the Hay Camp slaughter facilities
proved to be too small to allow for tuberculin testing of the nine hundred
animals needed to meet the needs of the packing houses. Fred Fraser, one

3.6   Dr. F.E. Graesser inspects
a bison carcass at the Hay
Camp abattoir, 1952.
LAC C-148895

of the leading proponents of the commercial slaughter, blithely noted, "No doubt ... we will be killing off a number of tubercular free animals, which we should be conserving. However, it will give us the opportunity of making a trial shipment to a packing house, and may induce the packing house people to give consideration to purchasing larger quantities of meat commencing next year."[65] No testing was conducted again the following year when over two hundred animals were slaughtered at a partially constructed abattoir facility in the Lake Claire area. In protest, Ward Stevens, the author of the original bison management policy, wrote to F.J.G. Cunningham with a stinging rebuke of the entire program: "As I remember the view which was taken when this project was drawn up, the primary reason for constructing the abattoir was to process buffalo which showed positive reaction to tuberculin testing ... A slaughter merely to provide meat for local or other consumption loses sight of the integrated programme which we had drawn up previously wherein this would be one of several aims propounded."[66] The objection was enough to halt the slaughter program for one year until the Sweetgrass abattoir near Lake Claire was completed in the summer of 1957. A full testing and slaughter program was inaugurated in the winter of 1957-58, and 451 animals were killed.[67]

Commercial considerations nevertheless continued to dominate the bison management program. In 1961, the northern administration's Industrial

3.7   Bison meat ready for shipping from Hay Camp, 1952. LAC C-148897

Division took direct control over the marketing of buffalo meat and related products such as hides, heads, and horns. Its promotional campaign was intended primarily to develop a market for bison meat as a specialty product in southern hotels and restaurants, along with a broad array of other exotic northern delicacies and curiosities such as Arctic char, whale, and seal.[68] The campaign included newspaper and radio ads, press releases, and a hospitality suite at the 1962 Canadian Restaurant Association convention in Toronto's Royal York Hotel.[69] In the summer of 1967, a large portion of the 162 bison slaughtered in Wood Buffalo National Park the previous autumn went to supply the Canadian Pavilion at Expo with ground meat for quintessentially Canadian buffalo burgers.[70]

The park's field staff and biologists continued to raise concerns that the demands of the Industrial Division for a steady supply of buffalo meat might lead to the destruction of animals just to serve the southern commercial market. A report produced by CWS biologist Nick Novakowski in February 1961 maintained that the slaughters, combined with severe flooding in 1960, had "decimated" the bison population. He criticized the bison management program for a lack of focus, stating that "at present no policy exists."[71] Novakowski's superiors quickly advised him that his comments were "ill-considered," and a full test and slaughter program proceeded in September 1961, when approximately four hundred bison were killed.[72] Widespread flooding the following year rendered the abattoir at Hay Camp unusable and further reduced the number of bison around the Sweetgrass site. The Industrial Division nevertheless requested 50,000-100,000 pounds of meat for the southern specialty market. Park Superintendent B.E. Olson noted that a kill of that size would require the slaughter of prime breeding stock, and "to do so would not be management, or herd reduction, but sheer mass murder." Olson cautioned, "We have here a fundamental conflict between a scientific and practical management policy of the buffalo herds in the park and the production of first class meat for the sophisticated 'outside market.' In a normal year there need not be a dangerous conflict between these two but in a year such as this the conflict is irreconcilable."[73]

The emerging debate over the contradictory objectives of the buffalo management program was interrupted by the outbreak of anthrax in 1962 in the bison herds just outside the northeastern park boundary, in the Grand Detour and Hook Lake areas.[74] The disease spread to the park herds in 1964 and 1967, and the perceived crisis meant that criticism of the mass slaughter program quickly subsided. Indeed, the anthrax outbreak justified an even more intrusive bison management program, as CWS biologists and the park staff took drastic steps to contain the disease. In the

summer of 1964, a multiagency anthrax committee recommended depop-
ulating the herds in the Grand Detour area to create a buffer zone between
the infectious area and the park bison (the disease is transmitted to bovine
species through localized pockets of infectious spores in soil and plants).
Attempts to herd buffalo by helicopter had only limited success, as animals from outlying areas dispersed into the infectious area. Hence the
wholesale eradication of the Grand Detour herd was attempted in November 1964 and again in March 1965. Just over 550 bison were killed during the operation, and close to eighty-two thousand pounds of meat were
salvaged for human consumption in local communities. Buffalo herds within
the park were further "thinned" and attempts were made to inoculate as
many animals as possible in massive round-ups at the Sweetgrass and Hay
Camp abattoirs.[75]

The consensus and single-minded resolve produced by the anthrax control program was not simply a momentary response to a passing crisis. The
advocates of disease control and commercialization of the northern buffalo
herds may have differed on the relative weight the bison management program accorded to each priority, but they agreed on the need for a controlled slaughter. As Olson pointed out, the disparity between the two camps
did not produce a "dangerous conflict" under normal circumstances. Indeed,
the narrow focus on disease control as the raison d'être for bison conservation through the mid-1960s was still firmly tied to the economics of sustained yield bison management that the federal government had promoted at least since Maxwell Graham's day. In a major study of the park's
bison herds published in 1962, the park's resident biologist, William Fuller,
echoed earlier managers such as Graham and O.S. Finnie by attempting
to reconcile the goals of profit and preservation. Fuller argued that the aesthetic and historical value of the bison might best be preserved with a
"hands off" management program in much of the park but that in areas
such as Lake Claire and Hay Camp, where the bison population was heavily concentrated, management to reduce disease might profitably produce
a saleable annual crop of meat so that "the industry could operate without
cost to the taxpayer."[76] Six years later, L.P.E. Choquette and Nick Novakowski authored a report that similarly aligned the disease control program
with the interests of pragmatic resource production. The two biologists
lamented that, by their estimate, the northern bison range could hold
fourteen thousand animals but was at present "understocked" with only
ten thousand animals. The mere preservation of the bison was not the key
issue: "The low productivity, caused chiefly by brucellosis and malnutri-
tion, and the high mortality do not significantly endanger the population,

but at the same time, there is a substantial waste of a resource." Choquette
and Novakowski recommended a five-year disease eradication program involving fencing bison herds at various points in the park, testing and
slaughtering all reactors for tuberculosis and brucellosis within the con
fined areas, and eradicating all the buffalo in the surrounding area.[77]

Choquette and Novakowski's management plan was never implemented,
primarily due to apprehension about the costs and possible negative public reaction to the mass slaughter of the bison herds.[78] But the philosophy
behind their proposal – combining scientific and commercial goals within
an apparently seamless policy agenda – remained central to the slaughter
program throughout much of its existence. Moreover, in political terms,
ecological crises such as disease outbreaks and local game shortages provided wildlife biologists and park administrators with the impetus and
justification for managerial actions that further asserted the state's ownership of the bison herds. The intensive management of the bison through
herding, disease testing, and slaughter was only one facet of this interventionist philosophy. Wolves, for example, were subject to eradication programs to protect the Sweetgrass product long after predator control had
been abandoned in other national parks.[79] And although Native hunters
in the Northwest Territories were permitted to hunt bison outside the park
after 1955, the prohibition on hunting bison within the park continued to
be enforced, in part due to pragmatic concerns about the possible spread
of tuberculosis to the human population, but also because park officials
thought "uncontrolled" hunting pressure from human or canine predators
might interfere with the principles of the regulated bison management
program.[80]

By the late 1950s, park officials had, in fact, changed their defence of the
ban on hunting buffalo in the park from an appeal to save an endangered
species to a contention that the buffalo must be exposed only to certain
kinds of regulated butchery. In 1958, Ben Sivertz, the director of the Northern Administration Branch, recommended against a request from Indian
Affairs to allow trappers in Wood Buffalo Park to kill one buffalo per family because such a hunt might interfere with the controlled slaughter program. Granting such a request might also, Sivertz reasoned, be the "thin
edge of the wedge" for unrestricted hunting rights within the park.[81] In
February 1961, the park superintendent, B.E. Olson, rejected a similar
petition from Chief Seypekaham of the Little Red River band because
Native hunters would inevitably kill younger and healthier bison, in con-
travention of a management program that supposedly focused on older,
crippled, and diseased animals.[82] That same winter, Olson raised concerns

with his superiors about Native hunters near Fort Chipewyan who had apparently "decimated" the bison that had strayed south of the park boundary. The fact that these animals were part of the same Sweetgrass herd that had been subject to large government-sponsored slaughters since 1957 was not lost on federal officials, who petitioned the Alberta government to introduce protective measures on bison so a continued Native hunt would not interfere with the park's disease control and commercial slaughter operations.[83]

The combination of strict hunting prohibitions and export-driven commercial slaughters in Wood Buffalo National Park could scarcely have appeared to Native hunters as anything less than a blatant appropriation – or even theft – of local wildlife resources by state authorities. Undoubtedly, the contradictory policies surrounding the bison slaughter forced many Native hunters to further question the legitimacy of federal authority over the wildlife in the South Slave region. Referring directly to the long history of small- and large-scale slaughters dating back to 1928, a park conservation plan authored in 1988 noted that "the inconsistent history of bison protection and exploitation has likely encouraged the illegal hunting of bison from the earliest years of protection."[84] Although specific documentation of the Native reaction to the slaughter program is scant, the political leadership of local Native groups had become extremely critical of the park's interventionist approach to bison management by the end of the 1960s. In January 1969, the Deninoo Association, an advocacy group based at Fort Resolution, delivered a brief to the Northwest Territories Council expressing its unequivocal opposition to enclosing the bison herds outside the northeast boundary of the park and slaughtering much of the remaining wild population (as proposed in Novakowski and Choquette's disease containment program). The association stated, "Besides being an important part of our history and culture, the buffalo is a vital source of our food." The brief pointed out that maintenance of the local trapping economy would become even more difficult if hunters were not able to kill bison along their traplines. Framing access to the bison as an issue of fundamental justice for Native people rather than a question of necessity, the association argued that unfettered access to wildlife in the Northwest Territories had always been the exclusive right of Native hunters, and therefore "the government has no right whatsoever to make plans regarding these animals without first consulting with us and the other people of the North. Without doing so they are breaking the Treaty." The association concluded with the demand that, if the enclosure of the bison herds was inevitable, the people of Fort Resolution should be given their own herd to manage.[85] In a similar brief, the Thebacha Association, an Aboriginal community development organization in Fort Smith, went one step further. After expressing "great consternation" at the proposal to enclose the bison herds due to the "inane waste of our most vital food supply," the group followed the federal government's lead by demanding that four thousand buffalo be turned over to them for management on an enclosed commercial ranch. Although one could interpret these protests as an attempt to create local business opportunities and not a defence of traditional hunting rights, the Native leadership maintained that local control over wildlife was intimately connected to the assertion of political sovereignty for their people: "We know that each member on our Council is not only interested in economic development but feels the deep needs for emancipation of our indigenous people and their contribution to progressive development in conjunction with conserving something very close to our hearts, our wildlife and homeland, protected as near as possible in its natural state."[86]

Although Native people were willing to adopt the federal government's intensive agricultural approach to managing the buffalo herds, senior wildlife officials were reluctant to relinquish control over the northern bison. Alan Loughrey, the deputy director of the Canadian Wildlife Service, argued in no uncertain terms that local Native people were not suited to the task of managing the buffalo and that the proposed disease control program should remain under the exclusive control of the scientists who had produced many years of dedicated research on the bison. Loughrey also framed his objections to the ranching proposals in racist terms, arguing that Native people were at far too "primitive" a stage in their cultural development to adapt to the life of a modern rancher. "We doubt very sincerely," Loughrey wrote to his superiors, "that a major undertaking such as proposed by the Thebacha Association is within the capability of any group not acculturated by tradition or training to an agrarian occupation. The modern technology required for an undertaking of this magnitude is beyond the comprehension of any average layman."[87]

Such a response indicates that bison management in and around Wood Buffalo National Park was tied as much to the politics of state control over wildlife and northern people as it was to "saving" the bison from disease and human hunters. Even if local Native groups were willing to forgo their "reckless" traditional hunting practices and exploit the northern bison according to modern herd management principles, the authority of the federal officials over local wildlife in and around the park remained sacrosanct. According to wildlife officials such as Loughrey, Native people were by their very nature antithetical to the enlightened practice of wild-life conservation: they were as much in need of management as the ani-mals they hunted. The postwar expansion of an intensive and technocratic approach to conservation programs such as the fur enhancement project and the bison slaughter only reinforced the idea that backward Native hunters had little to contribute to the management of wildlife in Wood Buffalo National Park. Conversely, the consolidation of state control over wildlife in the South Slave was anathema to local Native groups, who re-peatedly emphasized their moral claim to sovereignty over land and wild-life as a source of their political and cultural identity.[88] For the time being, however, federal wildlife officials were determined to maintain a rigid dis-tinction between the managers and the users of wildlife in Wood Buffalo National Park; such terms as "co-management" and "local consultation" did not enter the wildlife conservation discourse in the North for at least a decade after the end of the commercial bison slaughter in 1967. In the end, the bison slaughter program was cancelled not because of local Native objections but because of cost overruns, equipment problems, and ongo-ing difficulties finding suitable markets for buffalo meat.[89]

Even the gradual transfer of the park from the administrative auspices of the Northern Administration Branch to the National and Historic Parks Branch from 1965 to 1969 – which slowly moved the park's management priorities away from resource production and toward a more "hands off" preservationist philosophy – did not immediately alter the rigid approach federal officials had adopted toward the regulation of Native wildlife har-vesting in the park.[90] Indeed, the gradual resurgence of preservationist sentiment among officials within the Parks Branch led to the revival of a very old policy idea: the removal of traditional hunting and trapping activ-ities from Wood Buffalo National Park. In October 1967, Superintendent Olson informed his new superiors in the Parks Branch that the number of legitimate claims of hereditary hunting privileges in the park had increased to over four hundred. Although Olson acknowledged that many of these people had become wage earners and were not actively hunting and trap-ping, he maintained that "while the issuing of General Hunting Licences was suitable in the past it does not lend itself to present day management and also the policies and concepts of a National Park. Tradition and hered-itary rights are in direct conflict with game management as a sound man-agement program cannot be put into effect."[91] For much of the next year, senior park officials discussed the legal implications of revoking heredit-ary Native hunting privileges in Wood Buffalo National Park. Echoing pol-icy discussions from a half-century earlier, the department's legal advisor subsequently argued that Treaty 8 did not prevent the federal government from revoking the existing hereditary hunting privileges and over time excluding Native harvesting activities from Wood Buffalo National Park.[92]

AFTER THE SLAUGHTER ERA

For reasons that are not entirely clear, the administrative push to exclude Native hunters from Wood Buffalo National Park in the late 1960s was not successful. But conservation policy in the park had come full circle. For over fifty years, Native people living in and near the park had been press- ing for maintenance of their traditional control over local wildlife, with little more result than a revival of earlier proposals to expel them from this first northern wilderness sanctuary. Between these historical bookends lies a narrative inscribed with the attempts of the federal government to enact a wildlife policy devoted to the regulation of both people and animals in the South Slave region. Some may object to this assessment of the Canad- ian government's motives, arguing that the imposition of state-controlled conservation in the region was a matter of ecological necessity rather than a blunt assertion of power over local hunters. Indeed, given the crisis at- mosphere surrounding the collapse of the bison in the late nineteenth cen- tury, the early attempts to protect a remnant herd of the animals were both necessary and responsible courses of action on the part of the federal government (however exaggerated the threat from Native hunters may have been). Many of the most dramatic federal interventions in the human ecology of the South Slave region, however – the creation of the park annex, the effective enforcement of the game laws, and the cancellation of permits – occurred only after the introduction of thousands of plains bison to the park had removed any doubt as to the survival of the north- ern herds. In the end, many of the federal government's control measures seem to have remained in place for the sake of control itself. Strict prohi- bitions on Native hunting in the park persisted even after the federal gov- ernment had begun to slaughter the bison in large numbers.

The history of wildlife conservation in Wood Buffalo National Park thus has a colonial tinge. Indeed, Native hunters of the South Slave region had much in common with the rural subsistence hunters and gatherers in other parts of the globe who have been afflicted with "ecological imperi- alism" of one form or another. Like the conservation reserves established by European imperial powers in South Asia and Africa to enclose local forests and wildlife for the purposes of state production, Wood Buffalo

National Park served to extend federal power over local wildlife resources and marginalize the Aboriginal hunters who had hunted in the region for centuries. The combination of strict prohibitions on local bison hunting with a commercial slaughter of the same nominally protected animals was one of the most visible and contradictory manifestations of this power; so too was the presence of an angry and dissident local population along the park boundary line that demarcated federal authority in the region.

The expansion of state power that accompanied the creation of Wood Buffalo National Park was alike in kind if not absolute severity to the more overtly oppressive moments in the global history of wildlife conservation. The meting out of relatively small fines and brief jail terms for game law violations may appear benign when compared with, for example, the application of the death penalty to deer poachers in eighteenth-century England.[93] Yet the frequent expulsion of Native people from their traditional hunting grounds for the most minor offences against the Wood Buffalo Park game regulations – a policy that condemned many people to poverty and hunger – suggests that conservation policy in Canada could be similarly inhumane.

Much has changed in the four decades since the last bison slaughter in Wood Buffalo National Park. The ongoing political activism of Native northerners throughout the 1970s and 1980s, the formal affirmation of Aboriginal treaty rights in the Canadian courts, the growing acceptance among biologists of traditional environmental knowledge as an important wildlife management tool, and the slow evolution of federal wildlife policy toward the co-management of national parks and wildlife with Native governments have all profoundly changed the relationship between Native hunters and the Wood Buffalo Park administration.[94] In 1986, the Fort Chipewyan Cree, now named the Mikisew First Nation, won a land entitlement settlement arising out of the unfulfilled terms of Treaty 8. The agreement guaranteed perpetual hunting, trapping, and fishing rights on three million acres (12,141 square kilometres) of land defined as the "tradition area" (nearly nine thousand square kilometres of which lies within Wood Buffalo National Park). The agreement also provided the Cree with a broad array of new powers to influence wildlife policy in the park: majority representation on a Wildlife Advisory Board, the authority to determine the eligibility criteria for hunting and trapping permits, the power to decide how many permits will be issued for the traditional area in any given year, and finally, the creation of a reserve in the park at Peace Point.[95] In a more recent, high-profile case, the Mikisew band was able to stop a proposal to build a winter road across the park from Garden Creek in the west to Fort Smith in the east. The Cree successfully argued before a federal court in December 2001 that a two-hundred-metre buffer prohibiting firearms use around the road, combined with potential environmental impacts such as erosion and habitat fragmentation, violated the band's treaty right to hunt and trap on their traditional lands. The federal government then successfully appealed the ruling, but in November 2005 Canada's Supreme Court cancelled the road permit because Parks Canada had failed to consult the Mikisew Cree about the possible impact on hunting and trapping rights guaranteed under Treaty 8.[96] The legal authority – and perhaps the moral weight – accorded to treaty provisions guaranteeing the right to hunt and trap in Wood Buffalo Park has increased dramatically since the days when federal bureaucrats characterized Native harvesting as a "privilege" that was tolerated out of necessity. Though not as sweeping as the provisions of the Cree settlement, agreements have also been reached with the Smith's Landing First Nation (in Fort Smith and Fort Fitzgerald) in May 2000, and the Salt River First Nation in November 2001, over their long-standing claims to reserve lands in Wood Buffalo National Park under the terms of Treaty 8.[97]

As significant as these developments are, the wildlife policy regime governing Wood Buffalo National Park still contains vestiges of the colonial relationship between the federal government and Native people. In a broad sense, the principle of joint management of park resources was not enshrined in the National Parks Act passed in December 2000. Under the terms of the legislation, the federal cabinet retains ultimate authority to create the game regulations for the park, and the exercise of all the "powers" granted to the Wildlife Advisory Board are subject to cabinet approval.[98] A cursory glance at the most recent version of the park's game regulations reveals that some of the most reviled provisions of an earlier era persist: the closed season on buffalo, the issue of park permits at the discretion of the park superintendent, and the authority of park officials to revoke permits of those who violate the game laws.[99] While Native hunters and trappers in the Wood Buffalo National Park region have been accorded certain rights to hunt and trap in accordance with treaty guarantees, few of these rights fundamentally obstruct the constitutional prerogative of the Canadian government to regulate wildlife harvests on federal lands. Indeed, the regulatory authority of Native people in the park remains largely advisory in nature; the absolute power of the state to regulate the Native harvest remains intact.

Despite such inequity, the conservation successes associated with the park's wildlife policy have garnered international acclaim. In 1983, the United

Nations Educational, Scientific and Cultural Organization named Wood Buffalo National Park a World Heritage Site because it held the world's largest free-roaming bison herd and the summer nesting grounds of the endangered whooping crane. The UNESCO designation celebrated the unique natural history of Wood Buffalo National Park while ignoring the park's more ambiguous human heritage: the litany of injustice inflicted on local Cree and Chipewyan people as they lost their political autonomy to the federal government's wildlife conservation program.

PART 2

MUSKOX

Muskox on Devon Island exhibiting typical protective circle behaviour, Percy Taverner, no date, LAC PA-48029

4

The Polar Ox

IN HIS EXPANSIVE 1921 MONOGRAPH ON wildlife conservation, Dominion entomologist C. Gordon Hewitt issued a passionate plea for the protection of the muskox. He described this exotic Arctic animal as among the "most interesting" of Canada's native fauna, a creature whose biological features – long curved horns, a shaggy coat, and a short tail – displayed a certain affinity with wild species such as the American bison and domesticates such as Scotch cattle and sheep. According to Hewitt, the once abundant *Ovibos moschatus* had been reduced over the past half-century to a few remnant herds on the Arctic mainland and a small number of larger herds on the Arctic islands. He argued that the causes of this dramatic decline were many and varied: an international trade in muskox robes that had been pursued vigorously since the 1860s, the numerous sport hunting expeditions that had sought out this exotic animal since the late nineteenth century, the thousands of animals that had been killed to feed exploration efforts in the High Arctic, and finally the apparent "recklessness" of Native hunters. Hewitt therefore advocated passionately for the preservation of these animals, claiming that the muskox were in need of "absolute protection," and that their extermination "is only a matter of a few years, unless proper and adequate steps are taken to put an end to the killing of the animal for the sake of its skin."[1]

Hewitt's concern for the fate of the muskox was not solely a sentimental interest in preserving a unique and exotic North American big game animal. He was also enthusiastic about the possibility of domesticating at least some of the remaining muskox herds as commercial livestock in

Canada's northern territories. Citing numerous reports from promoters of northern development, Hewitt reasoned that muskox might provide both a secure source of meat and milk for northern people and a supply of wool for international markets. The success of William T. Hornaday's experiments raising muskox in the more southerly climate of the New York Zoological Park indicated to Hewitt that breeding stock could be imported for use as domestic range animals in temperate latitudes. If further experimentation proved that muskox could not be raised in milder climates, Hewitt was convinced that domesticating the animals of northern Canada could "furnish a factor of inestimable economic importance in the agricultural development of large tracts of our northern regions which are at present producing only furs."[2]

To the contemporary reader, Hewitt's aggressive promotion of a new commercial ranching industry using wild animals might seem strange in a volume whose main purpose was to promote the philosophy and practice of wildlife conservation. Yet as in the case of the wood bison, Hewitt's contradictory emphasis on both production and protection was shared by his colleagues in the federal wildlife bureaucracy. On the one hand, federal wildlife officials adopted a preservationist approach toward the remaining muskox herds, establishing an absolute ban on hunting the animals in 1924 and creating the rigidly protectionist Thelon Game Sanctuary three years later. On the other hand, wildlife conservationists within the federal bureaucracy put forward wholly utilitarian rationales for muskox conservation, arguing that the herds should be saved from the "improvident" depredations of Native hunters so they could become the basis for a new northern ranching industry. Although the previous chapters on the wood bison demonstrate that ambitious schemes to develop the commercial potential of northern wildlife were not unique to the muskox conservation programs in the Northwest Territories, the "polar ox" offers perhaps the most startling historical example of convergence between the ideals of the wildlife preservationist and the industrial promoter in Canada. For federal wildlife conservationists, the muskox became both an exotic emblem of northern Canada's wilderness character and a symbol of its future economic potential.

In either case, the material requirements and hunting rights of northern Aboriginal people were often ignored. Federal wildlife officials set about replacing the supposedly indiscriminate hunting economy of the Dene and Inuit with a putatively more ordered system of exploiting the herds based, as Hewitt explained it, on "our modern knowledge of animal husbandry and veterinary science."[3] Indeed, Hewitt's evocation of themes such as the conversion of Aboriginal hunters into agriculturalists, the replacement of wild fauna with domesticates, and the introduction of scientific animal husbandry links muskox conservation to a colonial discourse on the inevitable northward expansion of Canada. More than any other species, the muskox inspired federal officials to associate their conservation efforts with the expansionist dream of establishing a new northern ranching frontier rather than the more modest goal of preserving a unique form of Arctic wildlife.

THE DECLINE OF THE MUSKOX

The Canadian government first took an interest in the muskox after reports of a severe decline in the range and numbers of the species appeared in the 1910s and 1920s. In a scientific monograph published in 1913, J.A. Allen, a naturalist with the American Museum of Natural History, cited a variety of anecdotal reports suggesting that the muskox had become "much fewer" over the past hundred years and had been extirpated from large areas on the west coast of Hudson Bay and from a vast stretch of western Arctic coast between Coronation Gulf and the Bering Sea in Alaska.[4] In his classic work *The Lives of Game Animals,* Ernest Thompson Seton made the extraordinary claim that the muskox had declined from a population of one million at the time of contact to a mere fifty thousand animals in the late 1920s.[5] W.H.B. Hoare, a special investigator with the Department of the Interior who travelled to the Thelon Game sanctuary in 1928, cited a wide variety of exploration narratives to suggest a dramatic reduction of the muskox population in the Northwest Territories to only nine or ten thousand animals.[6] In an appendix to Hoare's report, Rudolph M. Anderson, the chief biologist with the National Museum of Canada, roundly criticized Seton's numbers. He claimed that the bare rock and glaciers that covered much of the High Arctic tundra could not provide forage for one million large grazing animals and that even the late-nineteenth-century trade in muskox robes was not extensive enough to have killed off so many thousands of animals. Anderson's population estimate for the Arctic muskox herds did not paint a much more hopeful picture than Seton's, however. He used police reports and exploration narratives to conclude that a mere five hundred animals remained on the Arctic mainland and thirteen thousand on the Arctic islands.[7]

The severe decline in the muskox herds was the consequence of a series of profound changes to the social and economic landscape of the Canadian

Arctic during the latter half of the nineteenth century. By far the greatest impact on the herds during this period was an expansion of the muskox robe trade. Prices rose dramatically after the supply of bison robes from the southern plains began to diminish, and the arrival of American whalers in the western Arctic in the 1880s provided ample opportunities for Native hunters to trade muskox skins. Over the six years of intense exploitation from 1890 to 1895, 7,534 muskox were killed on the Arctic mainland ranges to provide robes to the Hudson's Bay Company, a figure that does not include the muskox Native hunters may have killed to provide flesh and robes for rival trading outfits along the Arctic coast.[8] The completion of the transcontinental railroad in the late nineteenth century also brought British and American sportsmen to the Arctic by making it possible to mount an expedition from Calgary.[9] Although the mortality due to such sport hunting expeditions was relatively low, many of these forays coincided with the peak of the hide hunt in the early 1890s and thus contributed to the cumulative impact during this intense period of human predation on the muskox herds. A greater source of muskox mortality than sport hunting was the intense Arctic and polar exploration that began in the late nineteenth century. In a broad analysis of the available published sources, the geographer William Barr has estimated that the total kill of muskox by exploration parties in the High Arctic from 1875 to 1917 amounted to 1,252 animals.[10] Spread over forty years, this number does not suggest that northern explorers caused any broad collapse in the Arctic island or mainland muskox herds. But the tendency of explorers such as Robert Peary and Donald MacMillan to slaughter entire herds in support of their expeditions may have led to the severe decline or extirpation of local muskox populations on the Arctic Archipelago.[11]

The behavioural characteristics and ecology of the muskox also probably played a role in the decline of the species. Muskox offer a particularly easy target for hunters armed with rifles because of their habit of forming a stationary defensive circle in response to wolves or the advances of untied hunting dogs. And high mortality rates inflicted by human hunters are not easily restored because the rate of reproduction in muskox herds is generally low. Cows may conceive beginning as young as two years old if their preferred food of willow and sedge is abundant, but more commonly start at four years of age. They give birth to single calves annually but bear calves only in alternate years when nutrition levels are low. These young animals face a precarious existence, because wolves prey on muskox calves preferentially and can be a major cause of mortality within the herds. Severe climatic events such as deep or crusted snow and ice cover on the ground may also increase adult muskox mortality by impeding their grazing and restricting herd movements. Although the introduction of the robe trade and other external hunting pressures in the late nineteenth century was the primary cause of the muskox's general decline during this period, this increase in human predation may have worked in tandem with increased pressure from other sources of mortality to cause the extirpation or severe decline of the species in some regions.[12]

The earliest proposals to establish formal protective legislation for the muskox came, ironically enough, from several of the sport hunters who travelled north to obtain a trophy of the species in the late nineteenth century. Although many of these hunters were enthralled by the act of killing the animals – even the conservation-minded naturalist Ernest Thompson Seton described his party's successful muskox hunt as the "supreme moment" of his journey north in 1907 – others wondered whether the animal was a suitable target for a true "sporting" gentleman.[13] In a hunting narrative published in 1898, Frank Russell described killing a herd of muskox that had been forced by dogs into a defensive formation as a "simple act of butchery." He urged sport hunters to stay out of the muskox country, for killing such hapless animals carried none of the "triumphant exhilaration" associated with the moose or the wapiti. In keeping with such sentiments, the geologist James Williams Tyrrell recommended in 1901 the creation of a strict game sanctuary between the Thelon and Back Rivers in order to preserve the remaining muskox herds of the Arctic interior. The hunter David Hanbury also urged protective measures, particularly a legislated ban on the trade in muskox skins, in the account of his travels published in 1904.[14] Thus the idea that some sort of protective legislation was needed if herds were to survive began to filter through the popular literature on the North.

It was not the sport hunting narratives, however, but the incessant lobbying of the famous Arctic explorer Vilhjalmur Stefansson through the 1910s that finally persuaded the Canadian government to take notice of the plight facing the muskox. An eccentric wanderer who was enthralled with the Arctic and the traditional Inuit methods of survival in the region, Stefansson became obsessed with the idea of conserving the muskox as the basis of a future Arctic ranching economy. He led major expeditions along the Arctic coast from 1908 to 1911 for the New York Museum of Natural History, and, under the auspices of the Canadian government, led the Canadian Arctic Expedition from 1913 to 1918.[15] The primary focus of Stefansson's early career, however, was to conserve the remaining muskox and caribou herds as a supply of country food for the Inuit. In January 1914,

Impact of game laws on non-Natives + Métis really botd throughout.

Stefansson wrote to Prime Minister Robert Borden to warn that the trade in muskox robes might cause the extirpation of the species west of the Back River in less than ten years.[16] One month later, the explorer again wrote to Borden and also to Clifford Sifton, chair of the Commission of Conservation, to caution that the extirpation of the caribou from the Mackenzie Delta region had resulted in a general impoverishment of the Native people in that region. In contrast to these "fallen" people, the Inuit in the Coronation Gulf region still lived in a state of primitive affluence because the introduction of guns had not yet destroyed the local wildlife supply and the introduction of disease had not yet decimated the human population. The situation was nevertheless swiftly becoming desperate, according to Stefansson, because an American trading schooner, the *Teddy Bear*, had arrived in the region in 1911 to distribute rifles and trade for caribou and muskox hides. In order to conserve the muskox herds, Stefansson recommended an absolute ban on the robe trade, a measure he felt would create a de facto sanctuary for the species in the interior tundra region by removing the incentive for Inuit to hunt inland from their coastal settlements.[17]

Stefansson's reports of a dwindling muskox population created a great deal of anxiety among federal wildlife officials. In March 1914, Maxwell Graham, who was chief of the Parks Branch's Animal Division at this time, responded to the sentiments in Stefansson's first letter to Borden with the advice that protective legislation for the muskox was a far greater priority than formulating a conservation policy for the still abundant caribou. Graham proposed the creation of a game sanctuary on Victoria Island and in the Coronation Gulf region where only the Inuit would be permitted to hunt. He also suggested distributing wolf traps among the Inuit to reduce the impact of these predators on the caribou and muskox herds.[18] Three months later, Graham produced a report on the muskox at the behest of the minister of the interior. Aside from extensive material on the biology of the species, it discussed the possible reasons for the dramatic decline in the muskox herds. For the most part, Graham blamed the robe trade, but he also highlighted the more recent lucrative trade in live muskox calves for zoos, particularly the "wicked and criminally wasteful" practice of killing an entire herd just to obtain their young. He recommended several conservation measures to address these issues: a closed season for all but Native hunters and travellers who were in need of food, a permanent ban on hunting muskox with dogs, a restriction on the selling of skins to only those traders who possessed an approved government tag, and the creation of absolute sanctuaries where the muskox might multiply and "overflow" into the surrounding districts.[19] Henry J. Bury, the inspector of timber for Indian Affairs, expressed similar sentiments in his report on game conditions in the Northwest Territories issued in November 1915. Like Graham, Bury laid much of the blame for the decline in the muskox at the feet of the robe trade, particularly the demand the traders had created for the soft fur of unborn calves. Although Bury had held strong reservations about the feasibility of enforcing game regulations in the vast tundra regions, he recommended that a closed season be implemented "as soon as an organized scheme of administration in matters pertaining to the Northwest Territories is placed in motion."[20]

Perhaps the most remarkable feature of Graham's and Bury's reports is the lack of any explicit condemnation of Native hunters for any role in the decline of the muskox. In contrast to the prevailing conservation discourse, which tended to blame northern Aboriginal hunters for the decline in the wood bison and admonish their allegedly wanton methods of slaughtering caribou, federal officials generally followed Stefansson's lead and blamed external forces such as the fur trade and Arctic exploration for the decline in the muskox herds. In some cases, the overt racism that was common in the early conservation movement did enter the discussions over the fate of the muskox. In 1914, the American naturalist J.A. Allen wrote that "the Eskimos and muskoxen can never live together, owing to the improvident ways of the Eskimos, who are unable to resist the temptation to destroy every animal of a muskox herd they chance to meet, regardless of the waste of life and resources thus incurred."[21] Yet perhaps because of the abundant written records pointing to very specific sources of increased muskox mortality, senior wildlife officials apportioned much of the responsibility for the decline of the muskox to forces that were largely outside the control of Native hunters.

The focus on the hide trade as the primary cause of the muskox's decline seems to have struck a chord with members of the newly created Advisory Board on Wildlife Protection when they were charged with drafting the Northwest Game Act. When the legislation was passed in June 1917, it included a complete ban on the trade in muskox robes and a year-round closed season on the species. The latter provision nevertheless exempted all Indians, Eskimos, and "half-breeds" who were "actually in need of the meat."[22] Rather than reflecting concern for the material needs of Dene and Inuit hunters on the part of the board's wildlife conservationists, this "starvation clause" may have stemmed from the resolve of the Department of Indian Affairs, and particularly its representative on the Advisory Board, Duncan Campbell Scott, to prevent Native northerners from becoming dependent on relief issues.[23] Nonetheless, the subsistence hunters of the northern tundra could use the muskox as an emergency food supply if the caribou migration failed to appear. This hunting privilege was soon compromised, however, when the federal government began to consider an apparently more judicious means of exploiting the muskox herds in the years following the First World War.

ARCTIC RANCHING

The idea of domesticating the muskox as a source of meat and wool has a fairly long history in North America. French officer Nicholas Jérémie, who was in charge of Fort Bourbon on the west coast of Hudson Bay from 1697 to 1714, sent muskox wool to France as early as 1709 so it could be manufactured into fine stockings.[24] In 1784, the noted British naturalist Thomas Pennant made the first explicit proposal to domesticate the muskox for the purposes of commercial wool production: "Beneath every part of the [muskox's] hair grows in great plenty, and often in flocks, an ash-coloured wool, most exquisitely fine, superior, I think to any I have seen and which might be very useful in manufactures if sufficient could be procured." Although a few promoters continued to extol the commercial potential of muskox ranching, no attempt was made to domesticate the species until 1899.[25] A.G. Nathorst, a Swedish university professor interested in the economic opportunities offered by muskox, shipped four experimental calves from Greenland to his native country, but all died from diseases shortly after their arrival in Europe.[26]

This early interest in the commercial possibilities of the muskox paled in comparison to the dedication and enthusiasm with which Vilhjalmur Stefansson pursued the dream of domesticating the species. By his own account, Stefansson was converted to the idea of muskox ranching in 1916, when he and his party of sixteen men spent a year living in "intimate association" with the species on Melville Island, consuming the meat and fat of the animals, making candles with the tallow, and building shelter with the hides. Despite the frequent killing of the muskox by Stefansson's party, the explorer noted that there were "numerous herds still peacefully grazing about the camp."[27] Based on this experience, Stefansson's initial interest in conserving the muskox primarily for the use of Aboriginal hunters expanded into a persistent international campaign to promote the ranching of the species as a harbinger of economic expansion into the Far North. In 1917, Stefansson drafted a report titled "Possible New Domestic Animals for Cold Countries" for the high commissioner for Canada in London,

Sir Richard McBride, copies of which were circulated to C. Gordon Hewitt and the parks commissioner, James Harkin, in November 1918. The document argued that the muskox was far superior to the reindeer for the purposes of a northern ranching industry. muskox produced three to four times the meat and milk, they were much easier to herd, they were not susceptible to wolf attacks or stampeding in the vicinity of dogs, and they could furnish large amounts of wool without having to be killed. Stefansson believed that the domestication of the muskox would create an agricultural base for a settled and industrious "Polar Mediterranean," founding a whole new economic order in Arctic Canada: "If the rate of increase of muskoxen is similar to that of sheep under domestication, or even similar to that of cattle and if – as seems certain – ther [sic] proves a commercial market for their wool, a hundred thousand square miles of the continental and island part of Arctic Canada could eventually be converted into as profitable pasture land as large as sections of Australia, to say the least. Should mines and other industries develop, that would only increase the value of the muskox as a local source of meat and milk."[28]

Stefansson also promoted his scheme for a muskox ranching industry among the politically powerful and moneyed classes. In 1917, he sent samples of muskox wool to Prime Minister Borden and to Edmund Walker, president of the Canadian Bank of Commerce. On Armistice Day, Stefansson addressed the Empire Club at Massey Hall in Toronto, where he impressed upon the city's financial and social elites the idea that civilization could be brought to the North only if large herds of domesticated reindeer and muskox were established as an agricultural base. Stefansson also obtained the support of one of North America's most famous sport hunters and wildlife conservationists, Theodore Roosevelt, who responded to the explorer's entreaties in March 1918 with the assertion that "it is a capital misfortune that the muskox has not been tamed. To tame it would mean possibilities of civilization in northernmost America which are now utterly lacking."[29] Though it may seem strange that such an ardent sport hunter preferred to see the muskox become a ranch animal rather than remain in its wild state, Stefansson's vision of an expanding northern civilization held an irresistible lure for imperialists such as Roosevelt, as well as for the political and business elites who turned their gaze toward a last frontier in Canada's Northwest Territories.

Stefansson's Arctic utopianism did nevertheless contain an element of crass commercialism. One of the more bizarre aspects of Stefansson's promotional endeavours was his campaign to change the name of the muskox in order to overcome the persistent rumour that the meat had an unpleasant "musky" odour. In the fall of 1920, Stefansson attempted to convince James Harkin that a new name – polar oxen, Canada Ox, woolox, or simply ovibos – might enhance the commercial potential of the animals. The proposal received harsh criticism from the Advisory Board on Wildlife Protection in November 1920 and was ultimately abandoned. Nonetheless, the incident suggests that Stefansson played the part of both the charlatan and the visionary, willing to mix his dream of a northern Mediterranean with the more prosaic concerns of a salesperson.[30]

If Stefansson's penchant for publicity encouraged some scepticism within the federal bureaucracy, he was nevertheless able to inspire a general enthusiasm among senior wildlife officials for his proposal to domesticate the muskox. In February 1919, the members of the Advisory Board on Wildlife Protection, including Harkin, Hewitt, Anderson, and the assistant chair of the Commission of Conservation, James White, met the deputy minister of naval services and the chief of the US Biological Survey to discuss the possibility of co-operating with the Americans to implement Stefansson's proposals. The board concluded that it was both possible and desirable to transfer muskox from Ellesmere Island to experimental ranches at Chesterfield Inlet on the west coast of Hudson Bay and St. Michael's Island in Alaska, with costs to be shared evenly by both governments.[31] In April, Hewitt and White met with the explorer Donald MacMillan in Boston to secure his services capturing muskox calves on Ellesmere Island.[32] Although the project was never carried out, the board members had thoroughly embraced Stefansson's intention to transform the seemingly barren Arctic tundra into a landscape rich with commercial wildlife ranches. With only limited knowledge of the muskox, and without any scientific appraisal of whether the species could actually be domesticated, Canada's leading wildlife conservationists had rushed to endorse the idea of conserving the "woolox" for its use value as a farm animal.

Most important for Stefansson, his grandiose scheme also received enthusiastic support from the senior political wing of the Canadian government. In the early months of 1919, Stefansson gained a powerful ally when he managed to favourably impress the minister of the interior, Arthur Meighen, with his vision for northern development. Meighen began to promote the muskox proposal throughout the corridors of Parliament, finally arranging for Stefansson to address a joint session of the Senate and the House of Commons on 6 May 1919. The speech was a remarkable success, embodying the heady optimism associated with the end of the war years: Stefansson's evocation of the northern tundra as a future meat and wool-producing region of unparalleled potential captured the collective imagination of the assembled legislators. Two weeks later, Meighen convinced his cabinet colleagues to authorize a royal commission to examine the possible development of reindeer and muskox industries in the Far North.[33] The commission comprised a railway commissioner, John Gunion Rutherford, a manager at Harris-Abattoir Co., James McLean, the parks commissioner, James Harkin, and of course Vilhjalmur Stefansson, who later resigned because of a potential conflict of interest over his application for a grazing licence on southern Baffin Island.[34] The commission held a series of hearings in Ottawa from January to May 1920. No hearings were held in the Northwest Territories, and Dene and Inuit hunters were conspicuously absent from the proceedings. The commissioners instead relied on the testimony of several "expert witnesses," mainly missionaries, fur traders, and members of the Geological Survey of Canada who had travelled extensively in the Northwest Territories. In some respects, however, these informants failed to provide the unqualified support for domesticating the muskox that Stefansson and his supporters had hoped for. Several witnesses described the meat as superior to beef, but others found it unpalatable, with the hunter and explorer Henry Toke Munn attesting to the rankness and "muskiness" of meat from the older bulls.[35] Perhaps the most damaging evidence for Stefansson and his supporters came in a letter to the commission from William Hornaday, a leading American conservationist and curator of the New York Zoological Gardens, stating that combing the wool out of the thick hairy overcoat of the muskox held in the zoo was an extremely tedious process. Moreover, an animal who was subjected to this experiment at the zoological gardens died of pneumonia one month later. Consequently, Hornaday doubted if muskox wool could be produced on a commercial scale, a sentiment the commissioners shared in their final recommendations.[36]

Harkin, Rutherford, and McLean did nevertheless agree with Stefansson that the muskox should be exploited as a domesticated ranch animal. Based largely on Hornaday's limited experience handling muskox in New York, they concluded that the muskox were suitable livestock for the development of a domestic meat industry in the Far North. Their final report recommended the creation of a research station on one of the Arctic islands where small herds of muskox could be domesticated for experimental purposes. If the project proved successful, then "considerable numbers" of muskox could be brought further south to more accessible areas such as the coast of Hudson Bay, where "their development from a national economic standpoint may be carried on and extended."[37]

While the commission advocated a cautious and experimental approach to the actual process of taming the wild muskox, it did not consider the social impact the transformation of local economies to industrial-scale muskox production might have on local Native people. Although some of the commission's witnesses mentioned that Native hunters and trappers might have difficulty immediately transforming themselves to herders, none contemplated how they might react to the possible enclosure of vast tracts of their traditional hunting and trapping lands for grazing purposes. Indeed, to the Dene and Inuit, the final report of the royal commission probably appeared to be less a visionary development scheme and more overt colonialism, a demand by the state authorities that they give up their "bush life" to take part in a more modern agricultural economy as herders or general labourers. The potential cultural conflict between Native hunters and the agricultural promoters within the federal bureaucracy never materialized, however, as logistical problems with transportation prevented even small-scale projects to domesticate the muskox until after the Second World War.[38] Nonetheless, the Dene and Inuit hunters of the Northwest Territories experienced increasing regulation and surveillance of their hunting activities in the years immediately following the royal commission's report, when the federal government protected the muskox as a prospective source of wealth for the entire nation.

PROVIDENCE, PROFIT, AND CONSERVATION

The first sign that the federal wildlife officials had adopted a tougher approach to the enforcement of the game laws preventing muskox hunting came even before the work of the royal commission was completed. In May 1919, Captain George Comer wrote to Stefansson that Inuit hunters from Etah, Greenland, were intent on hunting muskox on Ellesmere Island because they found the crossing to be easier than they had formerly supposed. Furthermore, Comer reported that Donald MacMillan, the explorer who had previously killed hundreds of muskox on the Arctic islands, was heading north to set up a trading post on Ellesmere Island.[39] In July, the deputy minister of the interior, W.W. Cory, requested that the Royal North-West Mounted Police set up a post on Ellesmere to deter any potential mass slaughter of the muskox herds. The mounted police comptroller replied that it would be too costly to establish a post in such remote territory. The best he could do was to ask his officers at the Chesterfield Inlet and Herschel Island posts to warn all traders and Inuit hunters not to infringe on the provisions of the Northwest Game Act.[40]

Lacking the ability to enforce its own game laws in the High Arctic, the federal government turned to diplomatic channels in an effort to conserve the muskox. On 31 July 1919, the Canadian government sent an official request to Denmark for decisive action to prevent the Greenland Inuit from killing the muskox on Ellesmere Island.[41] The reply from Denmark, which was not forthcoming until April 1920, included a letter from Knud Rasmussen, an explorer and businessman who had recently set up the Thule trading post in Greenland. The letter argued unequivocally that muskox skins were absolutely essential to the Greenland Inuit for clothing and bedding; to deny them this material good would have "disastrous consequences" for these particular "esquimaux." Rasmussen also insisted that the muskox herds on Ellesmere were large enough that "the danger of extermination can scarcely be described as imminent." Finally, and most provocatively for Canadian officials, Rasmussen contended that "the territory of the polar esquimaux falls within the region designated as 'no man's land' and there is therefore no authority in the district except that which I exercise through my station."[42] Based on this reasoning, the Danish government rejected the Canadian government's concerns over the muskox hunt, stating that it concurred entirely with Rasmussen's views.[43]

The Canadian response to the Danish position was predictably negative. Rasmussen's letter represented a threat not only to Canada's claim of sovereignty over the Arctic Archipelago but also to its emerging plans to domesticate the muskox. Indeed, the hearings of the reindeer and muskox commission were nearing an end just as the Danish position became known in official circles. Perhaps reflecting the weight the federal government accorded to muskox conservation, James Harkin was appointed in 1919 to a technical advisory board composed of senior civil servants charged with the task of asserting the Canadian government's sovereign claim over the Arctic Archipelago. Sovereignty became something of a preoccupation for Harkin. Throughout the spring and summer of 1920, he corresponded frequently with senior departmental officials on the issue and also consulted Vilhjalmur Stefansson a great deal for "expert" advice. In May 1920, Stefansson provided Harkin with a lengthy refutation of Rasmussen's arguments. According to Stefansson, the Danish trader and explorer had practised some deception in claiming that muskox skins were indispensable for life in the Arctic, when in fact they were used only for bedding. He also urged Harkin to convince the senior levels of government to assert Canada's sovereign authority in the Arctic and take steps to prohibit the hunting activities of the Greenland Inuit.[44] One month later, Harkin reiterated Stefansson's comments in a long memo to W.W. Cory, deputy minister of the interior. Above all else, Harkin argued that the sovereign right of Canada to enforce its game laws in the Arctic islands must be respected. As long as domestic laws prevented Inuit hunters in Canada from hunting muskox except in cases of starvation, it was hardly fair for hunters from Greenland to kill the animals merely for their skins. Fair treatment of Inuit hunters living in Canada was not Harkin's only concern, however. He also pleaded for firm diplomatic action "on account of the probable steps to be taken for the development and domestication of muskox." If the muskox herds were ever to serve as an agricultural resource, it was "of the utmost importance to Canada that the last remaining herds of muskox – those on Ellesmere land – and contiguous territory – should be conserved."[45]

In November, a report of the technical advisory board emphasized the broader cornucopia of natural resources on the Arctic islands. Aside from herds of muskox that could supply ranches with seed stock, coal deposits were reported on Axel Heiberg Island, and Ellesmere Island's Precambrian rock formations held the promise of iron, nickel, gold, and radium. To protect these valuable resources, the committee recommended the establishment of police posts on Ellesmere, Bylot, and Devon islands and the relocation of Inuit families from more southerly points to effectively occupy the High Arctic.[46] While the latter proposal was not carried out until the 1950s, the two police posts that were established on Ellesmere at Craig Harbour and Pond Inlet in 1922 provided federal wildlife officials with at least some means to supervise the hunting activities of the Greenland Inuit and enforce Canada's game laws.[47] In the wake of Stefansson's campaign for muskox domestication and the royal commission's findings, the federal government was determined to project its authority toward even the most remote Arctic locations to protect the muskox as a potential domesticated ranch animal.

The northern administration was also intent on adopting severe measures to protect the muskox herds of the Arctic mainland by the mid-1920s. The report of the royal commission set much of the tone for this new conservation campaign, arguing that Inuit hunters represented the most severe threat to the survival and future commercial viability of the mainland muskox herds. In their final report, the commissioners wrote, "Witnesses agree that the Esquimaux, like the Indian, is naturally improvident in the matter of food supply, and that he will, when opportunity offers, destroy an entire herd [of muskox] without regard to possible future requirements."[48] In November 1923, the biologist and northern explorer Rudolph M. Anderson added specificity to this charge when he warned Maxwell

Graham that Native hunters had nearly killed off the muskox herds near Bathurst Inlet. Graham in turn advised his immediate superior, O.S. Finnie, that the plight of the muskox should be brought before the Advisory Board on Wildlife Protection. On 20 November, Finnie informed the board's secretary, Hoyes Lloyd, that the status of the mainland muskox had become precarious, in all likelihood because the Inuit were travelling large distances inland to kill the animals "without the excuse of hunger and starvation."[49] On 14 January 1924, the board recommended a complete ban on muskox hunting in the Northwest Territories. Three months later, a federal cabinet decree removed the "starvation clause" from the regulations governing the muskox hunt, prohibiting Native hunters from legally hunting the animals under any circumstance. The basis for the cabinet decree included reports that Native hunters had taken "undue advantage" of the starvation clause, organizing hunting parties to the interior while packing large amounts of food from their coastal camps.[50]

The new absolute restriction on muskox hunting met an extremely favourable reaction in the press, with many reports noting the potential for Canada's muskox to supply food to world markets if they received proper protection.[51] Nonetheless, the degree to which the new regulations should be enforced among the "primitive" Inuit along the Arctic coast provoked a heated debate within the federal bureaucracy. The controversy stemmed from a report that W.H.B. Hoare forwarded to Finnie in the summer of 1925. Hoare was an Anglican lay missionary and experienced Arctic traveller who had been sent to the Far North the previous spring by the Department of the Interior to assess the size of the caribou herds and to preach the gospel of wildlife conservation among the Inuit. He reported that Inuit hunters who wintered near Bernard Harbour had killed up to thirty-five muskox northwest of Great Bear Lake in the late summer of 1924. After learning of the hunt from a local trader, Hoare met with the Inuit at Bernard Harbour and informed them they had broken the law and "displeased" the government. The assembled hunters dismissed Hoare's threats of prosecution with the suggestion that a prison term on Herschel Island would bring good food on a regular basis.[52] Rather than interpreting such comments as an indication of the desperate material conditions facing Inuit communities, many federal officials were offended by this apparent contempt for the game regulations. Inspector T.B. Caulkin, the commanding officer for the RCMP in the Arctic, promoted tougher sentencing for muskox poaching, including hard labour in the guardroom at Aklavik, so the Inuit "would change their opinion of the past treatment they have been accorded, and the ease with which they apparently view the same."[53] Both Finnie and Anderson supported Caulkin's assertion that "drastic action" was needed to halt the illegal killing of muskox.[54] Parks Commissioner James Harkin nevertheless objected to such an uncompromising position on the basis that it was unjust to punish a "primitive" people when they possessed only a limited ability to understand a "white man's" system of crime and punishment.[55]

Although Harkin's comments seem patronizing, they did prompt the Advisory Board on Wildlife Protection to consult several "expert" witnesses on the problem of enforcing the prohibition against killing muskox. At its meetings in late 1925, the trader Charles Klengenberg claimed that shortages of caribou in the western Arctic had forced the Inuit to kill muskox out of need. He argued that diplomacy among the Inuit was preferable to strict enforcement of the game regulations. The prevailing sentiment among other witnesses was less sympathetic. The explorer John Hornby, who had spent the previous winter observing the muskox herds at the north end of Artillery Lake, testified that diplomacy would not stop the killing of muskox and that "fairly drastic" actions such as the prohibition of trading posts near the interior muskox ranges and the creation of a muskox sanctuary in the Thelon River region were needed to save the herds. The trader William Duval suggested prison, hard labour, and a diet of bread and water, so those convicted of killing muskox might "feel the penalty" more readily.[56]

The advisory board resolved the issue with a compromise. On 16 December, Finnie informed RCMP Commissioner Cortlandt Starnes that police should ensure Inuit hunters were aware of the game laws before laying charges. In cases of repeat offences or failure to heed police warnings, hunters "should then be arrested and punishment commensurate with the offence then be meted out to such natives." Finnie reminded Starnes that strong enforcement of the game regulations was ultimately for the good of local people, in part because "it is hoped some day to domesticate the musk-ox so that they can be of real benefit to the natives through their wool and milk."[57] According to Finnie's logic, Native hunters who exploited a traditional source of food in the present must be punished so that the same animal could be exploited as a domestic livestock in the future. A project that had always been promoted as a development scheme for the benefit of the national economy was now assumed to have inherent benefits for local people, even as these same Dene and Inuit hunters bore the brunt of the regulations protecting the seed stock of this future northern ranching economy.

The Thelon Game Sanctuary

The Thelon Game Sanctuary today evokes a range of images associated with Canada's luminous Arctic wilderness. Although not as widely known as such iconic wilderness spaces as Banff and Jasper national parks, the game sanctuary has achieved almost legendary status among wilderness enthusiasts in Canada and throughout the world. A canoe trip through the sanctuary passes through the heart of the northern tundra. At the confluence of the Thelon and Hanbury rivers, a wooded "Thelon oasis" contains a rich assemblage of rare wildlife such as the muskox and the barren ground grizzly bear. Since the pioneering canoeist Eric Morse completed the first recreational trip down the Thelon River in 1962, many other adventurers and wilderness tourists seeking the solitude of the "pure" wilderness have followed.[58] Some have written extensively of the rapture they experienced in the Thelon region. The wilderness writer M.T. Kelly described the Thelon region as a landscape that is "capable of love," while the canoeist David Pelly described his trip down the Thelon River as "a feeling of having awoken from a dream, to find yourself within a beautiful, peaceful sanctum."[59]

For all the contemporary superlatives bestowed upon the Thelon region, few people are aware that the designation of this "loving" landscape as an official wilderness area gave rise to a vehement conflict between federal conservation officials and the trappers who worked this landscape for their living. The first official recommendation to set aside an area between the Thelon and Back Rivers to preserve the remaining mainland muskox herds came in 1901 in a report from the geologist James Williams Tyrrell on the region northeast of Great Slave Lake.[60] No action was taken, however, until John Hornby proposed a game preserve to protect the muskox in a report presented to the Advisory Board on Wildlife Protection in November 1925. Hornby had spent much of 1924 and 1925 exploring northeast of Great Slave Lake with fellow adventurer J.C. Critchell-Bullock; both men confirmed that a large number of muskox survived in an uninhabited area near the confluence of the Thelon and Hanbury rivers. Hornby recommended the extension of the Back River Game Preserve southward to protect the muskox, a move that would have excluded non-Native hunters and trappers from the area.[61] The advisory board went one step further, passing a resolution on 28 May 1926 calling for the creation of a game sanctuary that would exclude all hunting and trapping activities within its borders.[62] Although the sanctuary was conceived as an emergency measure to save one of the last viable herds of muskox on the Arctic mainland, commercial considerations were also used to justify this new protected area. An article from the *Natural Resources Canada* newsletter published by the Department of the Interior claimed that the Thelon Game Sanctuary would do much to conserve a species that was easily domesticated and valuable for its meat and robe: "Canada's effort to save [the muskox] is not actuated by sentimentality but by business prudence. The Dominion government must care for the big game for the sake of the Indian and Eskimo inhabitant, both from humanitarian motives and as a means of maintaining a vigorous native population, without which development of the various resources of the north would be impossible."[63]

While the conservation of the muskox in the Thelon Game Sanctuary was thought of as a contribution to the development of the North, federal officials failed to take into account the impact of the new protected area on the existing hunting and trapping economy in the region. In a letter to Hoyes Lloyd, the advisory board secretary, O.S. Finnie justified the exclusion of both Native and non-Native hunters and trappers from the sanctuary with the claim that "no person or persons are trapping in this area and there are no trading posts. The creation of the sanctuary, if it is done at once, would not interfere with the rights of anyone."[64] But when twenty-four thousand square kilometres of Arctic tundra were finally set aside as the Thelon Game Sanctuary by cabinet decree on 15 June 1927, it immediately became apparent that several people did maintain cabins and traplines in the area, all of which were now unusable in light of the absolute ban on killing fur-bearers and game within the sanctuary. The loudest protests came from the non-Native trappers, many of whom already felt grievously wronged by the setting aside of the Arctic Archipelago the previous summer as a game preserve restricted only to Native hunters. In July 1927, several newspapers reported that the trappers Malcolm and Allen Stewart, J.W. Cooley, F.L. "Bearcat" Buckley, and Fred Lind were extremely upset to find that the new game sanctuary had enclosed many of their trapping areas. These men complained bitterly to the media that the sanctuary represented a grave injustice, particularly since they had not seen a single muskox near their traplines for years. In one interview, Cooley said that "he and all the trappers from the Far North now in the city do resent the way in which departmental 'experts' at Ottawa have coolly sliced off a large area without consulting the trappers concerned."[65] In a similar tone, Malcolm Stewart declared,

It is just a case of someone no nearer than Ottawa taking out a map and blocking out a district and naming it as a preserve without knowing whether the animals it is desired to preserve are in that district or not ... The government charges us $75 a year for a trappers' license and after we have gone in there and done all the heavy spade work necessary and made considerable financial outlay, someone in Ottawa draws a pencil around a district on the map, calls it a sanctuary, and we are driven out of the country.[66]

With only two to five years of experience as trappers, these relative newcomers might appear to have a somewhat tenuous claim to an inherent right to exploit the wildlife of the region. Yet their criticisms of federal officials for failing to conduct more than a rudimentary biological survey before the creation of the sanctuary are apt. Other than the observations contained in Tyrrell's report on his travels through the region in 1900 and Hornby's account of his trip down the Thelon in 1924-25 – both of which emphasized that the muskox were concentrated near the confluence of the Hanbury and Thelon rivers – little was known of those portions of the sanctuary far from the common canoe routes. Large areas of the sanctuary were in fact situated well south and west of the main muskox range; the original boundary did indeed look like a line drawn haphazardly on a map in an Ottawa office building.

The arbitrary nature of the sanctuary's establishment did not impact only outsiders who had gravitated to the Thelon region in their search for fur. Although there are fewer records of protest from the affected Dene trappers than from their non-Native counterparts, the sanctuary's Aboriginal residents resented the complete ban on their hunting and trapping activities. In the winter of 1932, Bishop Gabriel Breynat appeared before the Advisory Board on Wildlife Protection and the Northwest Territories Council to plead the case of several Dene hunters from the east end of Great Slave Lake who had been expelled from the southwestern end of the Thelon Game Sanctuary. Breynat's appeals on behalf of the excluded hunters were dismissed at the 3 February meeting of the Northwest Territories Council.[67] Perhaps for strategic reasons, Breynat framed his proposed resolution of the issue to the advisory board in terms of expedience rather than justice. According to Breynat, no muskox were known to inhabit the western portion of the sanctuary; reopening it to Native trappers might therefore alleviate the severe hardships resulting from a poor game and fur year without compromising the federal government's conservation objectives. But Breynat's petition did not receive a sympathetic hearing from the board. Both James Harkin and Rudolph Anderson countered that the sanctuary was intended not simply to preserve the muskox but also to serve more generally as a breeding reservoir for all types of fur and game animals so that they might spill over into the surrounding landscape. After much discussion, Breynat's proposal was consigned to the administrative purgatory of further consideration at a later date.[68]

Such indifference to local grievances in the Thelon region was typical of senior wildlife officials in the years immediately following the creation of the sanctuary. Rather than adjust the game regulations or boundaries of the sanctuary according to local knowledge of the location and abundance of the muskox, Finnie's Northwest Territories and Yukon Branch moved quickly after 1927 to establish more direct control over Native hunters in the area. In January 1928, W.H.B. Hoare was sent north once again on Finnie's orders as a special investigator for the Department of the Interior. His mission was to identify the most appropriate sites within the sanctuary for warden cabins, an administrative headquarters, and antipoaching patrol routes. He was also instructed to provide information on hunting activity in the region "to enable the Department to formulate regulations for the control and management of the sanctuary." In addition, Hoare was again ordered to preach the virtues of conservation to the local population, advising "all whites, Indians, or Eskimos that it is unlawful to kill or molest any wild life in the Sanctuary."[69] Hoare and his assistant, A.J. Knox, a warden from Wood Buffalo National Park, spent nineteen months on a remarkable journey by dogsled and canoe that traversed hundreds of kilometres of tundra and subarctic forest between Fort McMurray, Alberta, and Chesterfield Inlet on the west coast of Hudson Bay. Due to the harsh climate and the real danger of starvation, Hoare and Knox devoted a great deal of time to securing their own survival, relaying huge amounts of supplies from camp to camp, building rudimentary shelters, and in one extraordinary episode, building a canoe almost from scratch to enable their escape down the Thelon River.

The two men did nevertheless have the occasion to confront Native people they found hunting and trapping within the sanctuary. On 5 May 1928, Hoare discovered a trail with caribou remains scattered along its length that led inland from the western boundary of the sanctuary at Artillery Lake. That evening, Hoare crossed the lake to remonstrate with the ten Dene families that lived in a hunting encampment there, warning them that hunting caribou in the sanctuary was an offence that could lead to fines or imprisonment.[70] Also in the western portion of the sanctuary, on 20 March 1929, Hoare encountered two Dene hunters named Nezra and Wezo with caribou meat and a white fox killed so recently that it was still warm. Hoare confiscated the fox as evidence that the two men were hunting illegally and ordered them to leave the sanctuary. While Hoare does not record the two hunters' reaction, the Dene assembled at Artillery Lake had rejected Hoare's reprimand and displayed a distinct bitterness toward the sanctuary. The hunters in the group claimed that they "did not want any area closed to them as, in times of scarcity, when hard pressed for food they considered it their right to hunt anywhere." Hoare dismissed such concerns with the paternalistic suggestion that the creation of the sanctuary was in the Natives' best interest. He advised this particular group that protection of game within the sanctuary would lead to better hunting and trapping in adjacent areas, and thus the "chances of hard times would be greater if there was no sanctuary."[71]

Hoare concluded from his encounters with Native hunters, and from the frequent signs of campsites, trails, and caribou remains along his route, that poaching was common within the Thelon Game Sanctuary. He believed, however, that Native hunters were for the most part killing white fox for fur and caribou for food and hides. Hoare did find one cache of rotted muskox meat near the eastern boundary of the sanctuary in July 1929, but there was little evidence that Native people hunted these animals to any great extent.[72] The Anglican missionary nevertheless concluded that a greater law enforcement presence was necessary to preserve the wildlife within the Thelon Game Sanctuary. According to his reckoning, the muskox population in the sanctuary was critically endangered, with only two hundred and fifty animals remaining.[73] Hoare therefore sent Knox back to Artillery Lake to set up a warden station shortly after the two arrived at Baker Lake. With Finnie's authorization, Hoare also hired the trapper Hjalmur Nelson to guide Knox upriver and an Inuk named Telirhuk to assist the game warden in his efforts to guard the southwestern portion of the sanctuary against Native poachers.[74] Hoare then travelled to Ottawa to report on his findings, but he returned to the Arctic in the summer of 1930 to build a warden cabin at the eastern end of the sanctuary where the Thelon River drains into Beverly Lake. Although the cabin was completed in the summer of 1931, no game warden was ever assigned to the site. By 1932, Knox had also left his "western" warden station on Artillery Lake empty. The sanctuary was left to the distant and infrequent supervision of the RCMP detachments at Fort Reliance and Baker Lake.[75]

It is not entirely clear why the plan to establish a warden service in the Thelon Game Sanctuary was abandoned. At a meeting of the Northwest Territories Council in April 1938, Roy Gibson suggested that the small force was deemed ineffective given the vast territory to be patrolled and because the rough terrain prevented travel on all but the larger waterways.[76] In addition, the dissolution of the Northwest Territories and Yukon

Branch in 1931 and the subsequent departure of its director, O.S. Finnie, one of the most ardent conservationists within the civil service, may have dampened the administrative enthusiasm for a larger and more effective law enforcement agency in such a remote location. Budgetary restraint was also probably a factor in the decision not to enlarge the warden service. Considering the reductions imposed on the warden service in Wood Buffalo National Park during the early years of the Depression, funds were probably not available for an entirely new and even more remote warden service. Nonetheless, Hoare's call for stricter conservation within the Thelon Game Sanctuary was not completely ignored. In November 1929, the northern administration responded to the reports that Native people were hunting in the sanctuary, and also to an incident wherein a prospecting crew had shot a muskox while travelling through the sanctuary, by amending the game regulations to make it illegal for any person to enter or pass through the Thelon Game Sanctuary without the written permission of the Department of the Interior.[77] Although federal officials lacked a comprehensive means to enforce the new measure, this exclusionary policy was one of the most radical conservation measures ever introduced in Canada. For the first time, a wilderness area had been set aside that allowed no humans to set foot within its boundaries, not even the people who had lived and hunted in the region for centuries.

It is difficult to determine how Native hunters reacted to this new restriction on both their hunting activities and their movements within such a large area of the Arctic interior. Hoare's encounter with the ten Dene families on Artillery Lake suggests that at least some Native hunters were willing to defy the restrictions in the new sanctuary because they saw them as a violation of their traditional rights. Yet the absence of an active warden service or RCMP patrols in the sanctuary means there is little evidence as to whether illegal hunting and travel within the Thelon region were widespread. There are, however, some indications of broad discontent among local trappers. The reports of Harry Snyder and his companion F.M. Steel, whom the Northwest Territories Council granted permission to enter the Thelon River region in April 1935 to take photographs and films of the muskox herds, offers at least some insight into the attitudes among Dene hunters toward the sanctuary. In the starkest terms imaginable, Steel's report stated that both Native and non-Native trappers "seem to be badly disposed towards the Thelon Game Sanctuary." His informants reiterated the long-standing complaint that the southern and western portions of the game sanctuary contained no muskox but had withdrawn a substantial portion of good white fox country from their traplines. Steel quoted local Natives as stating, "Apparently the Government thinks more of the survival of the musk-oxen than they do of our welfare."[78] Snyder elaborated on these objections, saying Native hunters "resent the formation of the Thelon Game Sanctuary" because the enclosure of the south ern portion had left them bereft of an important hunting ground for the migrating barren ground caribou herds: "The natives feel that since this country south of the Thelon-Hanbury Junction is the natural early spring and later fall range of the caribou, the Government have deprived them of their normal supply of clothing and food without benefiting the other animals. Therefore they take it, and so express themselves, that the muskoxen have become their enemy."[79]

Did the exclusion of hunters from a large expanse of their own local environment create such an intense feeling of alienation that some began to see muskox as an enemy to be destroyed? Certainly such a phenomenon has precedents in other parts of the globe. Ramachandra Guha has argued that the imposition of restrictive conservation policies by the colonial forest authorities in northern India during the late nineteenth and early twentieth centuries caused rural peasants to intentionally degrade the environment, because ecosystems controlled by state and commercial interests became spaces that were at odds with the subsistence needs of local people.[80] The creation of the Thelon Game Sanctuary – though perhaps not as overtly tied to economic interests as a commercial forest reserve – nevertheless represented a similar imposition of a colonial conservation authority over the traditional hunting grounds of the Dene and Inuit. If Snyder's perception of local sentiment is accurate, then the creation of the sanctuary may have done more to produce local animosity toward the muskox than to secure protection for the species. Indeed, both Snyder and Steel concluded from the frequent occurrence of temporary hunting camps and the skittishness of the muskox herds that poaching was rampant in the sanctuary. Although the two men paradoxically suggested the expansion of the sanctuary to the Back River in order to protect the muskox herds outside the northern boundary, they also recommended the deletion of the area south of the Thelon and Hanbury rivers, which Snyder felt "would go far to remove from the Indians' minds the feeling of hostility toward the muskoxen."[81]

Snyder's and Steel's anecdotal evidence of local anger toward the muskox must nevertheless be treated with caution. The Snyder expedition found no muskox carcasses. Furthermore, the RCMP deemed allegations of muskox poaching made the following year by the expedition's Métis guide, E.G. Jones, to be false after further investigation.[82] The biologist

C.H.D. Clarke, who was studying the wildlife in the sanctuary throughout the summers of 1936 and 1937, concluded that Jones had concocted
the rumours because he had opposed the creation of the sanctuary and
wished to discredit the northern administration. Yet Clarke also concluded
from clear physical and oral evidence that Inuit hunters who travelled up
the Thelon River each summer to gather wood were frequently killing
muskox in the remote northern section of the sanctuary. The biologist
claimed that the Inuit hunters were "blissfully ignorant of any wrongdoing" and freely admitted their "crimes" because they thought they were
engaged in a legitimate subsistence strategy.[83] If these Inuit were not being
evasive in an effort to avoid prosecution, then poaching in this part of the
sanctuary was certainly not a form of conscious political protest.

Snyder's description of the local resentment directed at the muskox may
still be accurate, despite the scant evidence that Dene hunters were poaching muskox within the sanctuary. The Dene hunters living near the east
arm of Great Slave Lake tended to concentrate their illegal hunting and
trapping in the southwest portion of the sanctuary, where muskox were
extremely rare. As the experiences of W.H.B. Hoare and John Hornby
attest, a journey inland from Fort Reliance to hunt the herds near the Hanbury and Thelon rivers entailed considerable hardship and risk. A widespread poaching campaign to destroy the muskox as a means to discredit
the raison d'être of the sanctuary thus may not have been practical or even
possible for Native hunters. Yet dissatisfaction with the sanctuary clearly
remained at the forefront of the popular political discourse in local Dene
communities through the late 1930s. According to Hoare, who was again
travelling through the region as an assistant to Clarke's scientific study in
the summer of 1936, a rumour had recently spread among local Native people that Snyder had been given permission to kill muskox in the sanctuary.[84] The unfounded story proved to be a catalyst for the expression of a
more general anger at the loss of hunting grounds within the game sanctuary. In September 1936, the RCMP constable at Fort Reliance, W.J.G.
Stewart, reported that the "Snyder rumour" had caused a great deal of general discontent that summer among the Dene at Snowdrift and Artillery
Lake, who claimed they had more entitlement to kill muskox than any
white man. At the annual treaty gathering that summer, the assembled
Native people rejected Stewart's warnings not to enter the sanctuary because, as far as they were concerned, the southwest corner was now open
and they could enter whenever they pleased.[85] The animosity toward the
sanctuary had thus grown to the point where Native people were willing to
reject outright the laws that federal wildlife officials had imposed on them.

The circulation of the results of C.H.D. Clarke's biological investigation in 1937 excluded the possibility that restrictions on hunting and human movements within the sanctuary might be lifted in the near future. The biologist estimated that the total muskox population in the sanctuary had increased only marginally to 300 over Hoare's appraisal of 250 in 1929.[86] In light of these disappointing numbers and the allegations of extensive poaching within the sanctuary, the northern administration began to pressure the RCMP to enforce the game regulations. In July 1937, the commissioner of the Northwest Territories, Charles Camsell, informed the RCMP commissioner, S.T. Wood, of Clarke's hypothesis that Native hunters and trappers were illegally operating within the southern boundary of the Thelon Game Sanctuary. Camsell asked Wood if he could "please instruct [his] officers to give special attention to this problem as opportunity permits."[87] Wood reported to the Northwest Territories Council in April 1938 that there was no money to establish a police detachment near the sanctuary. Instead, he ordered a regular patrol of the sanctuary from Fort Reliance and hoped the force might soon have a plane with which to supervise the muskox herds from the air.[88] Six months later Commissioner Wood reported that the RCMP detachment at Port Harrison, Quebec, was to be moved to Baker Lake in order to allow closer surveillance of Thelon Game Sanctuary.[89] Perhaps as a consequence of these plans for more rigorous police supervision in the Thelon region, there was scant discussion in official circles or among biologists of muskox poaching or "problem" Natives within the sanctuary after 1937.[90] Indeed, the biologist John Tener concluded after a series of studies in the early 1950s that Native hunters had not been killing the muskox in the Thelon Game Sanctuary to any great extent.[91] The records of the northern administration indicate that muskox poaching did occur outside the sanctuary from time to time; most of these killings were described as a response to local food shortages rather than a form of organized protest.[92]

The Thelon Game Sanctuary was, however, a focal point for conflict between Native hunters and the federal government's muskox conservation program in the first decade after its creation. The radical preservationist policy pursued by the northern administration in the Thelon region created both alienation and disaffection among the resident Native population. One might argue that such a strict policy was necessary to preserve one of the last remnant herds of muskox on the mainland Northwest Territories, but the heavy-handed approach to this otherwise worthy goal created a profound local animosity toward the sanctuary, and might have actually caused an increase in muskox poaching.

One of the great contradictions associated with the history of the Thelon Game Sanctuary is that the preservationist principles that so severely restricted access to local game and fur were somewhat more pliable when economic interests were at stake. In 1956, the northern administration finally removed the contentious southwest corner of the sanctuary, not to conciliate Native hunters but in response to pressure from mining companies who wanted the area opened for mineral exploration.[93] Such willingness to accommodate the development of commercial enterprises within a strict wildlife preserve suggests that the history of the Thelon Game Sanctuary is equally a testament to the indifference of federal wildlife officials toward the Aboriginal people who depended on the area for fur and game as a visionary conservation initiative that saved an animal on the brink of extinction.

On a broader scale, the federal government's attempts to both preserve and manage the muskox are perhaps the least noteworthy of the efforts to conserve big game in the Northwest Territories. For many Native hunters, the muskox were no more than a casual or emergency source of meat and thus the attempts to conserve the species did not engender the same kind of widespread hostility and conflict as the efforts to conserve the caribou. Despite eruptions of local conflict over the federal government's approach to muskox conservation in the region of the Thelon Game Sanctuary in the late 1920s and early 1930s, the lack of a superintendent or a game warden service precluded the kind of sustained conflict between Native hunters and federal officials that was such a prominent feature of the social landscape of Wood Buffalo National Park. Constrained by budgetary austerity and the remoteness of the animals themselves, the federal government's muskox conservation program remained more of an ideal than a coherent policy initiative.

Yet for all of its pragmatic shortcomings, this attempt to conserve the muskox provides the clearest illustration of the contradictory philosophical principles that lay behind the federal government's approach to wildlife conservation in the Northwest Territories. In no other instance did federal wildlife officials so readily combine the passion of preservationist rhetoric with the pragmatism of progressive-era utilitarianism. Federal wildlife officials thought of the muskox both as an exotic creature that was emblematic of Canada's vast northern wilderness and as a potential farm animal that could provide meat, milk, and wool as a basis for a new Arctic ranching economy. To a large extent, the federal government's interest in muskox conservation after the First World War resulted from Vilhjalmur Stefansson's singular talent as a promoter of Arctic development in the halls of power. But Stefansson's ideas also fit perfectly with the prevailing philosophy of wildlife conservation in Canada, which valued the preservation of a species in direct proportion to its potential utility for human enterprise. The goal of domesticating the muskox never faded completely from the conservationist agenda in Canada, even after Stefansson had fallen out of favour with the federal government in the early 1920s.[94] In 1951, the Advisory Board on Wildlife Protection gave John J. Teal, a research associate at McGill University, permission to take eight muskox from Ellesmere Island for the purposes of domesticating the creatures at the Vermont Animal Research Foundation in Huntington.[95] The project was modest in scale – only seven calves in total were captured in the Thelon River region and shipped south in the summers of 1954 and 1955 – but Teal was no less enthusiastic about the commercial potential of qiviut (muskox wool) than Stefansson had been.[96] Teal argued publicly that "the quest for qiviut, the golden fleece of the arctic, may be the means by which we will open up the north for permanent settlement, and will achieve that greater wisdom, the happy adjustment of economy and environment."[97] But Teal's project was, in the end, only moderately successful. He proved that muskox could reproduce under open farm conditions and the wool could be gathered easily after the animals had shed their undercoat, but his efforts resulted in the creation of only a few small muskox ranches in the Arctic rather than the radical transformation of the northern economy that he and other promoters of muskox ranching had envisioned.[98]

Teal's project shows that the broader dream of building a northern civilization around an agricultural base of muskox ranching had survived for more than three decades since Stefansson had first began to promote the idea. During this period, federal wildlife officials did not limit their plans for conserving muskox to the usual legislative tools such as closed seasons or the creation of game sanctuaries. They also hoped that shifting the Arctic economy from the apparent vagaries of hunting and trapping toward the certainty of farming might save the muskox from annihilation. Canada's early wildlife conservationists had thus tied their effort to a novel form of ecological imperialism. Federal officials recognized that the harsh climate of the Northwest Territories would prevent conventional settlers and their attendant Old World domesticated animals from causing the kind of radical changes to the northern ecology that had so brutally displaced more southern Aboriginal people during the early period of European colonization in North America.[99] Instead, the promoters of muskox domestication believed that agrarian civilization could be imposed on northern Aboriginal people using a species that was already native to the region.

Conventional restrictions on the hunting activities of the Dene and Inuit were thus not intended merely to save a species on the brink of extinction; they were also a prelude to an entirely new way of life in the region. The history of muskox conservation thus suggests that the federal wildlife bureaucracy functioned as a colonial instrument meant to facilitate the rapid expansion of southern agricultural settlement and industrial activity in northern Canada. For Canada's early wildlife conservationists, it was not wildness that held hope for the preservation of the world. Rather, the wholesale domestication of the "polar ox" offered the best opportunity for the progress and salvation of Canada's northern frontier.

Part 3
Caribou

Caribou on the south shore of Carey Lake, J.B. Tyrrell, 1893, LAC PA-37622

5

La Foule! La Foule!

BEFORE THE ADVENT OF AIR TRAVEL in the Far North of Canada, the east arm of Great Slave Lake served as a key gateway to the tundra regions of the Northwest Territories. Beginning in the late nineteenth century, an assortment of hunters, naturalists, and geologists – most of whom travelled north via the Peace, Athabasca, and Slave river waterways – used this narrow eastern section of Great Slave Lake to reach the treeless Arctic prairies either by crossing over to its north shore or travelling to its farthest eastern extremity and traversing the portage to Artillery Lake. The place names on modern maps or nautical charts of the area show the traces of these men. Seton Island, Blanchet Island, Preble Island, Hornby Channel: much of the geography of the region is named for the naturalists who first came to record, identify, and catalogue its flora and fauna.

The impact of these naturalists on public perceptions of the northern landscape was much more significant, however, than their contributions to taxonomic science or the canonization of their names on a map. In the broadest sense, the Victorian passion for natural history in Canada – the organized effort to comprehend the apparent unity of nature by naming, mapping, and classifying all aspects of the natural world – was a critical influence on the emerging idea of a transcontinental nation.[1] With the acquisition of Rupert's Land and other northern territory outside the Hudson Bay drainage basin from the Hudson's Bay Company in 1870, the federal government gained dominion over the enormous landmass west of the Ontario-Manitoba border. Many of the naturalists who travelled to the Canadian North during this period thus saw themselves at the vanguard of an expanding federal power base at the farthest reaches of the nation. Several of the expeditions were, in fact, sponsored by such government institutions as the federal Senate and the Geological Survey of Canada; their primary purpose was to faithfully catalogue the resource potential of Canada's "fertile northland."[2] In many ways, the early practice of natural history in the North was, as Carl Berger has argued for Canada as a whole, "born of wonder and nurtured by greed," an expression of awe in the face of God's creation but also an assertion of sovereignty over that creation.[3]

The early attempts by natural historians to lay claim to the North's natural resources were not restricted to classic staple products such as minerals, oil, and timber. The dedicated amateurs who practised natural history in northern Canada were also concerned with the habits, life history, and population dynamics of wildlife. In addition to the geologists who searched for minerals and hydrocarbons, many voyeuristic and independent American and British hunter-naturalists engaged in a romantic quest for rare wildlife. Their unbridled longing to behold northern wildlife in a pristine state was tied to a larger "back to nature" movement that had captured the attention of the elite classes in Europe and North America during the late Victorian era. This period was the heyday of such legendary big game hunters as Theodore Roosevelt and Frederick Selous, who produced widely popular travelogues detailing their adventures in the imperial hinterlands of southern Africa and South Asia. These narratives lauded the purity of the unadulterated wilderness and extolled the virtues of the manly sport hunter's chase as the antidote to an overly regulated and effeminate urban society.[4] In North America, the advance of agrarian settlement and the collapse of wildlife populations on the western plains in the late nineteenth century led such hunter-naturalists as Ernest Thompson Seton, Warburton Pike, and Caspar Whitney to seek out the far northern landscape as a last pristine wilderness and hunter's paradise that encapsulated the primitive values of a bygone era. Although the unsettled regions of western Canada and the Atlantic forests remained popular hunting destinations well into the twentieth century, the travelogues and hunting narratives set in the Far North were in many respects the most visible manifestations of a nascent romantic attraction to the primitive wilderness.[5] The big game animals of northern Canada were intimately tied to this vision of the North as a last "pure" wilderness. By the late nineteenth century, the Far North was the last region of North America where large herd animals existed in any significant numbers; their presence in the landscape denoted a symbolic boundary where the domestic realm of civilization ended and the wilderness began. For many hunter-naturalists, vast herds of caribou or rare and exotic bison and muskox gave authenticity to their depictions of the North as a wilderness Eden, untouched by the corrupting influence of civilization.[6]

The naturalists who explored the Far North at the turn of the century were also devoted to very modern perspectives on northern wildlife. The hunter-naturalists in particular adhered to a "sportsmen's code" that defined the gentlemanly values appropriate to the upper-class origins of their sporting fraternity. This code included several fundamental ethical principles: the use of a single bullet for a single animal (as opposed to "snap shooting"), the selective killing of game animals according to their age and sex (killing females was absolutely forbidden), the fair chase of the quarry, and especially judicious hunting to avoid waste. Implicit in this sporting code was the idea that wilderness and wildlife could be appreciated appropriately only by a particular group of people. The conservator of sporting values was also almost inevitably an exemplar of white, upper-class, masculine virtues; women and non-Anglo-Saxons were excluded from this idealized wilderness space.[7]

The lobbying efforts and political connections of the sport hunting fraternity ensured that the central tenets of their code were increasingly identified as the key principles of rational and scientific wildlife management in Canada and the United States. Beginning in the late nineteenth century, the influence of sport hunting groups resulted in legislative controls on much-reviled "game hogs" throughout the North American countryside. Bag limits, closed seasons, and buck laws were among the most common means by which state wildlife bureaucracies asserted authority over game animals in the rural hinterland.[8] These new game laws were often aimed directly at the apparently wasteful practices of rural subsistence hunters and market shooters, frequently the very people with whom the sport hunters competed for access to game. The fervent lobbying of sport hunting groups for legislative controls on "game hogs" was often accompanied by public denigration of the hunting practices of other social groups and the consequent exaltation of the genteel etiquette surrounding the sport hunters' own approach to killing game.[9]

The earliest hunting books and popular articles inspired by the northern Canadian wilderness echoed these sentiments. Almost without exception, the sport hunters and naturalists who travelled to the Far North were sharply critical of Dene and Inuit hunting methods. Many accused Native hunters of conducting vast, uncontrolled slaughters of game and concluded that all Native hunters were, by their very nature, wanton killers of wildlife. Cultural biases were at the root of this scorn; Native people spearing large

numbers of caribou at river crossings to put up a winter's supply of meat
and clothing violated the sport hunter's sacrosanct ethos of the manly chase.
Furthermore, the image of the northern Native hunter as a destructive killer
desecrating a premodern wilderness furnished Canadian wildlife officials
with a powerful impetus to impose state authority and control over the vast
wildlife herds in the region. As in other parts of North America, the hunter-
naturalists' depictions of customary northern hunting methods as rudimentary and deficient provided an essential philosophical basis for what
federal officials believed was a more rational approach to managing wildlife.

    The far northern sport hunting narratives were not the only driving force
behind the expansion of state-controlled wildlife conservation above the sixtieth parallel. Although the big game herds of the Northwest Territories were
idealized as an unparalleled quarry for hunters, the difficulty and cost of
travel to the region limited the development of a recreational tourism industry for sport hunters. Accordingly, the first naturalists and geologists who
travelled north under the auspices of the federal government in the late
nineteenth and twentieth centuries – men such as the Tyrrell brothers, Guy
H. Blanchet, and, most famously, Vilhjalmur Stefansson – developed a different vision for the future of Canada's northern wildlife herds. These government emissaries envisioned an Arctic that was less a verdant hunter's
paradise than a fertile plain, where not only muskox but domesticated caribou and European reindeer might flourish as part of a northern ranching
industry. The official reports and popular narratives by these men did share
the sport hunters' sense of awe at the sheer size of the caribou herds and their
acute revulsion at the hunting practices of Native people. In addition to
advocating legislative controls on seemingly random and uncontrollable
Native hunting practices, many of the government-sponsored naturalists
promoted the replacement of the Native hunting economy with a rational
and efficient herd management program designed to exploit caribou as a
useful addition to the national food supply. These early proposals to fully
modernize the production of wildlife "resources" in northern Canada had
a profound influence on federal officials, who readily mixed the anterior
imagery of a last northern wilderness with a progressive vision of industrial
enterprises that would replace the "backward" hunting economy of local
Native people. Wildlife conservation and production were accorded equal
weight in this vision of the last wilderness frontier. If northern wildlife was
to be saved from the supposedly excessive depredations of Native hunters,
local conceptions of wildlife would need to be displaced by models of nature
that fit more readily into the economic agenda of the modern state.

Dominion entomologist C. Gordon Hewitt accentuated this point in his influential 1921 book, *The Conservation of the Wild Life of Canada*. Sounding a note of optimism, he wrote, "The advance of civilization into the more remote sections of Canada does not imply the total destruction of the wild life, but that civilization in its true sense signifies the elimination of the spirit of barbarism and the introduction of an enlightened attitude." In the same volume, Hewitt also promoted the domestication and rationalization of the northern caribou as a supply of meat and clothing for the entire nation: "Under proper protection and adequate supervision, there is no reason why we should not in the future develop a caribou meat industry, and export frozen caribou from the north."[10] At issue here was not merely a general idealism for saving wild game species from the supposed depredations of Native hunters; the early conservationists within the federal government also hoped to exploit wildlife to serve the economic needs of the Dominion. The natural history narratives that first described northern fauna and Native people in detail provided these officials with an interpretation of the northern social and ecological landscape they could use to shape a new commercial and managerial relationship over humans and wildlife in the region. These works were thus both an objective and scientific attempt to describe vegetation and fauna and a provisional form of surveillance, control, and supervision that represented a first tentative projection of state power into the region.

One of the first hunter-naturalists to travel to the Northwest Territories was the British adventurer Warburton Pike. A vehement critic of urban life, Pike journeyed northward from Edmonton in 1889 with the goal of travelling as far as possible from the corrupt influence of civilization. "A dweller in cities," he wrote, "is too wrapped up in the works of man to have much respect for the works of God, and to him the loneliness of forest and mountain, lake and river, must ever appear a weary desolation. But there are many sportsmen who love to be alone with Nature and the animals far from their fellow-men."[11] The reward for his journey was the opportunity to encounter and perhaps kill exotic wildlife such as the rare wood bison near Fort Smith and the muskox of the tundra plains. Despite his obvious delight in pursuing such large game animals, Pike reserved his most reverent commentary for the vast herds of caribou that migrated annually across the northern plains. When he encountered a large herd of caribou moving toward the tree line near MacKay Lake, he was enthralled by the immense throng of animals:

La foule had really come, and during its passage of six days I was able to realise what an extraordinary number of these animals still roam in the Barren Ground. From the ridge we had a splendid view of the migration; all the south side of MacKay Lake was alive with moving beasts, while the ice seemed to be dotted all over with black islands, and still away on the north shore, with the aid of the glasses, we could see them coming like regiments on the march. In every direction we could hear the grunting noise that the caribou always make when travelling; the snow was broken into broad roads, and I found it useless to try to estimate the number that passed within a few miles of our encampment.

While this description of the caribou may have been a somewhat overstated attempt to captivate his urbane readers, Pike believed that he had experienced an unsurpassed moment of rare beauty in the natural world: "This passage of caribou is the most remarkable thing that I have ever seen in the course of many expeditions among the big game of America."[12]

The naturalists who followed in Pike's footsteps over the next two decades echoed his astonishment and rapture at the sight of so many caribou. In the spring of 1893, the Geological Survey of Canada sent Joseph Burr Tyrrell and his brother, James Williams Tyrrell, to survey the region between Lake Athabasca and Hudson Bay. On 28 July, the brothers encountered a large herd of "reindeer" near Carey Lake in the Northwest Territories. In a popular narrative published five years later, James described seeing the caribou herd from his canoe in terms that recall Pike's astonishment at the vast number of animals in the herds: "Drawing nearer, we found that there was not only one band, but that there were many great bands, literally covering the country over wide areas. The valleys and hillsides for miles appeared to be moving masses of reindeer. To estimate their numbers would be impossible."[13] Some of these animals were killed for food, but the Tyrrells focused much of their energy on "hunting" the caribou with their camera; they gently approached the animals and took thirty-seven close-up photographs of the measureless herds in their natural habitat.[14] Similarly, the hunter-naturalist Frank Russell cited reports of an "unbroken line" of caribou that passed Fort Rae in 1877 over fourteen days, with herds so thick that daylight could not be seen through the advancing multitudes.[15] The British hunter-naturalist David Hanbury also noted on his expedition west of Hudson Bay in the summer of 1899 that the caribou "exist in hundreds of thousands; it is safe to say millions."[16]

Perhaps the most widely cited account of the caribou from this period came from the pen of Ernest Thompson Seton. In the summer of 1907,

Seton travelled with the American naturalist Edward A. Preble by York boat and canoe over the portage at the eastern extremity of Great Slave Lake to survey the country near Artillery Lake and the Casba River. He saw many scattered herds of caribou at the river and wrote, "From this time on we were nearly always in sight of Caribou, small bands or scattering groups; on and on and on, unlimited space with unlimited wild herds." To emphasize the enormity of the herds, Seton cited reports from the well-known hunter and naturalist Buffalo Jones, who had seen an "army" of millions of caribou at Clinton-Colden Lake in October 1897 while on an expedition to capture muskox calves. He also referred to a discussion with the hunter Henry Toke Munn, who claimed to have seen two million caribou at Artillery Lake in July 1894.[17] Much later, Munn described the caribou herds as "the greatest gathering of wild animals of one species in the world. There is nothing else like it to be seen anywhere to-day."[18] Certainly, such expansive herds of wildlife left a lasting impression on Seton, who wrote much later in his career of the "deep and blessed satisfaction" and the "sense of joy" that he experienced when observing wild caribou on the tundra.[19]

In some respects, the writings of the early northern naturalists offer a reliable description of barren ground caribou behaviour and ecology. The caribou is an extremely gregarious animal that wanders the northern boreal forest and Arctic tundra for much of the year in small herds that are almost continually searching for their preferred foods of lichen, willow, birch, grass, and sedges. In the late winter the barren ground caribou begin to mass in the thousands for their annual migration to calving grounds near the Arctic coast. In the autumn they gather once more for the return trip to their lichen-rich wintering grounds in the taiga forests of northern Saskatchewan and Manitoba, the Yukon, and the Northwest Territories. This migratory behaviour has many possible explanations: the caribou may be searching for lightly grazed pasture, moving to remote calving grounds as a means to elude predators, or taking advantage of windy coastlines to avoid biting summer insects.[20] Regardless, for one fortunate enough to be stationed along the ever-shifting migratory paths of the caribou, such a sizeable assemblage of large ungulates would almost certainly produce the feelings of awe and rapture experienced by Seton and his fellow naturalists. The large migrating caribou herds – with their attendant predators and parasites such as wolves, grizzly bears, golden eagles, and thousands of biting insects – constitute by far the richest pageant of life to be witnessed in northern Canada.

Nonetheless, it is likely that the swarming caribou herds numbering in the millions rather than the thousands that are so ubiquitous in early population assessments of the species resulted from observer bias grounded in wishful thinking. The caribou were, after all, the last herd animal of any significant numbers in North America. The naturalists who described them may have been overwhelmed by their own first glimpses of free-roaming herd animals crossing the tundra plains en masse. They may also have overstated the numbers to emphasize the exotic wonder of the northern landscape for their readers. John Gunion Rutherford, the chair of the royal commission investigating the feasibility of reindeer and muskox industries in the Northwest Territories, alluded to this possibility when he argued before the public hearings in May 1920 that the scattered reports over the past several decades of millions of caribou were a product of both second-hand reporting and "the tendency of the human mind and eye to exaggerate."[21] Whatever the veracity of the early reports of numberless caribou, estimating the population of wild ungulates was hardly an exact science during this period. Seton, for example, produced an extraordinary estimate of thirty million caribou in the northern barren ground region using the cattle density of Illinois as his reference point.[22]

Despite such imprecision, the image of immense caribou herds migrating across the open tundra became a profound symbolic marker of the northern landscape. Just as the buffalo had become inseparable from the archetypal western landscape, the seasonal migration of the caribou from their winter range in the subarctic forests to their calving grounds in the Arctic tundra came to encapsulate the North. Indeed, the symbolic importance of the massive armies of caribou was heightened for naturalists and conservationists precisely because the plains bison were a mere shadow of their former numbers by the end of the nineteenth century. When the first rhapsodic descriptions of caribou were published in the 1890s, the consequences of agrarian settlement and a domestic cattle economy on Canada's western plains had become abundantly clear to wildlife enthusiasts. The only open space in North America where wildlife remained in their primitive abundance was the Canadian North. Seton emphasized this point in the preface to *The Arctic Prairies*, where he asked rhetorically whether there was a man anywhere in North America who would not want to "roll backward the scroll of time" and experience the "romantic bygone days of the Wild West." Seton claimed there was still a place for such men, a landscape where "there is hoofed game by the million to be found [and] where the Saxon is as seldom seen as on the Missouri in the times of Lewis and Clarke. *Only* we must seek it all, not in the West, but in the far Northwest."[23] A new romanticism was thus ascribed to the North. The land that had been characterized as harsh and unforgiving in the wake of the disastrous Franklin expeditions in the early decades of the nineteenth century acquired a sentimental appeal as a landscape of plenty, teeming with herds of wildlife.[24]

As a consequence, the naturalists who followed in the path of the sport hunters in subsequent decades repeatedly described the caribou as the most important and magnificent visible feature on the tundra plains. Guy H. Blanchet published a striking example of this sentiment in the caption to a photograph that accompanied the popular record of exploration work he conducted in the Arctic for the Topographical Survey of Canada in 1924: "The Caribou gives life to the somewhat monotonous plains of the North, and in travelling in the country one finds himself most of the time watching a caribou or looking for one." Blanchet later described a gorge at the discharge point of the Coppermine River on Lac de Gras as "charming" and wrote that "animation was given to the scene by the constant and rather aimless travel of band after band of caribou, crossing and recrossing the river, feeding in the valley, and disappearing over the hills."[25] Explorer John Hornby described the caribou herds in similar terms. An eccentric wanderer popularly known as the "Hermit of the Arctic," Hornby wrote rhapsodically of the caribou in a series of notes he took while investigating the Thelon River area for the Department of the Interior in 1924-25: "No animal of the Northern Regions are so famed as the Barren Ground Caribou, even the wolves about which such fantastic stories are so often weaved, are dwarfed into insignificance when the talk is of the mighty herds of migrating Caribou." For Hornby, a northern landscape without the migratory herds was unthinkable. He wrote, "Without the Caribou the charm of the Barrens would disappear."[26]

SLAUGHTERING THE CARIBOU

Hornby's juxtaposition of the image of thronging caribou herds with its antithesis – a lifeless Arctic plain – was no mere rhetorical gesture. Although endlessly abundant caribou herds had been a common theme in northern natural history literature since the late 1890s, there was also a prevailing fear among the naturalists that the caribou might someday be hunted to near extinction like the plains bison. This concern was often expressed in conjunction with an absolute disdain for "excessive" Aboriginal hunting practices. Although wolves received a share of the criticism for their depredations on the caribou herds, Native hunters commonly endured the most severe reproach for their apparently wanton hunts. Dene and Inuit hunting practices, particularly the customary spearing of large numbers of migrating caribou at water crossings, seemingly disturbed the hunter-naturalists' notion of the undefiled and picturesque herds. Warburton Pike, for example, described a Dene caribou hunt in the following terms: "The best swimming-places are known and carefully watched, and woe betide a herd of caribou if once surrounded in a lake by the small hunting-canoes. One thrust of the spear, high up in the loins and ranging forward, does the work. There is no idea of sparing life, no matter what the age or sex of the victim may be."[27]

Pike's condescension toward Aboriginal hunting practices was a familiar trope in Victorian hunting narratives. Frank Russell noted, for example, the "thousands" of caribou speared in the back while crossing narrow lakes. He also suggested that firearms had vastly expanded the capacity of Inuit and Dene hunters to slaughter wildlife, with "disastrous results" for the caribou.[28] Although David Hanbury was somewhat sympathetic toward the Inuit hunters he encountered in the Arctic, noting the lack of waste and the careful planning and skill associated with each hunting expedition, he also described in vivid detail the "unsportsmanlike" nature of the slaughter at narrow water crossings.[29] The American hunter Caspar Whitney reserved particularly sharp criticism for the "wanton destruction" visited upon the caribou at river and lake crossings on his trip to the Northwest Territories in 1895. He was so "disgusted" by the sight of his Native guides chasing down bands of caribou that he refused to hunt with them. For the rest of his trip, Whitney wandered off alone whenever caribou were in sight, adhering to the principle of the fair chase as he stalked stragglers that had strayed from the main body of the herds. Finally, after witnessing his guides charge a herd of caribou on dogsleds, the American hunter "sat down and pondered why God in His wisdom had made these men, whose very existence depends on their hunting, so wanting in skill and judgement."[30] Both Pike and Whitney recorded that Native hunters wasted little meat, but their abhorrence of group hunting and large slaughters led them to speculate on the eventual fate of the caribou. Anticipating the concerns of later conservationists, Pike mused that "surely this [slaughter] should exterminate the game," and Whitney asserted, "That their numbers have been largely decreased is undoubtedly true, for the annual slaughter visited upon them by the Indians in the summer-time is as deadly as it is incredible."[31]

Such condemnation can, in part, be attributed to the complex relationship between the sport hunter and his Native guides: the expedition leader

often felt it necessary to affirm his superiority and assert his authority over
the men on whom he was absolutely dependent for direction and, in many
cases, sustenance. The sport hunting books from this period are thus replete
with disapproving comments on the general laziness or ill temper of guides.[32]
The most intense criticism was reserved, however, for cultural practices
that conflicted with the sportsman's ideal of the clean hunt. Vivid descriptions of Native people engaging in a wasteful slaughter of caribou, or hunting such rare species as wood bison and muskox to the point of extinction,
served to hide the fact that the sport hunter was also killing these animals,
in some cases with abandon and in others merely for a trophy. The cen-
sure of one set of traditions thus served to accentuate the nobility of the
sport hunter's own enterprise; shooting endangered species was morally
acceptable so long as the white hunter conducted a "careful" slaughter.

To underscore this point, many hunter-naturalists conflated their critique of Native methods of hunting caribou with the politics of racial dis-
tinction, identifying "wanton" and "improvident" hunting practices as an
innate characteristic of the Dene and Inuit. According to many northern
sport hunters, the "Indian" or "Esquimaux" hunter was, by his very nature,
a destructive killer of wildlife. Upon his return from a brief foray into the
tundra, Pike noted, for example, that the Native guides waiting at his base
camp had, in his absence, conducted a "stupid slaughter of caribou." The
British hunter concluded that "the love of killing seems deeply rooted in
the nature of most men, but the Yellow Knives have it more fully developed than other people."[33] Whitney used much the same language when
he alleged that "the [caribou] calves are killed for no other reason than to
gratify the northland Indian's love of destruction."[34] The obvious racism
manifest in such meditations on the difference between an innately "sav-
age" and a more consciously "civilized" approach to big game hunting suggests that reports of wantonly destructive Native hunters were as much the
product of observer bias as of the objective circumstances.

This is not to suggest that naturalists such as Whitney, Pike, and Hanbury simply fabricated their stories of mass caribou hunts. Overwhelming
historical and archaeological evidence shows that both Inuit and Dene
hunters traditionally conducted large seasonal slaughters of migrating caribou, often killing the animals en masse with spears after they had bunched
together at water crossings or been herded along drift fences into pounds.[35]
In some cases, these slaughters *were* wasteful according to prevailing European and North American definitions of the concept. In the late summer,
for example, Dene and Inuit hunters living close to the caribou herds
commonly killed large numbers of the animals primarily for use as winter

clothing. Caribou skins were at their prime during August; in autumn the skins were too thick to work with, and by late winter the warble fly larvae that reside beneath (and make holes in) the skins rendered them all but useless for clothing. Because the caribou were extremely lean in the summer (tongues and bone marrow provided the only significant source of the fat essential to the northern hunter's diet), and also in part because the downed caribou were difficult to preserve and transport in the warm season, much of the meat was frequently left to rot during the summer hunts.[36] The Europeans who first observed the summer slaughter reserved some of their harshest criticisms of Native hunters for the apparent wastefulness of this customary practice. For example, the chief factor of the Hudson's Bay Company, Roderick MacFarlane, described the summer hunts at Fort Anderson in the 1860s in the most severe terms: "The northern Indians were accustomed ... to slaughter thousands of reindeer annually, chiefly for their skins and tongues, and too often for the sheer love of killing."[37] Pike also wrote of the summer hunt as an orgy of waste, a vast slaughter of caribou in which "fully one-half are thrown away as not fat enough to be eaten by men who may be starving in a month."[38]

While such descriptions did not necessarily distort the outcome of the caribou slaughters, understanding the hunt as wasteful and improvident was a questionable interpretation of Dene and Inuit hunting practices. Indeed, to analyze the hunting cultures of northern Canada according to the Protestant ideals of thrift and economy overestimates the degree of choice available to people who were almost wholly dependent on the caribou for food and clothing. As the anthropologist Shepherd Krech has observed, defining the abandoned parts of the caribou as "waste" when other parts of the animals were vital for human survival may reflect a particularly acute form of ethnocentrism.[39] Given that the late-summer caribou were the only available source of skins for winter clothing, an item that was absolutely essential to the survival of Native northerners, is it defensible to characterize a hunt for those skins as wasteful?

The issue is certainly complicated by the fact that one of the most immediate concerns for wildlife conservationists at the beginning of the twentieth century was the decline of caribou near the western Arctic coast, an area where Inuit hunters had participated in a skin and provision trade with American whalers since the late 1880s.[40] But even if Native hunters did at times slaughter game in excess of their subsistence needs to exploit new economic opportunities, it is hardly plausible to conclude that Native hunters were inherently wasteful or compelled by a primordial instinct to massacre wildlife. Recent anthropological research suggests that Dene caribou hunts in both the precontact and modern eras were often highly organized and deliberate events.[41] The Dogrib, for example, designated certain hunters as captains who determined the scale and location of the hunt and directed post-hunt activities such as the production of dried meat.[42] Several anthropologists have also argued that the introduction of European technologies such as firearms did not, as many contemporary observers claimed, encourage Dene and Inuit hunting bands to kill as many caribou as was humanly possible.[43] Moreover, a wide body of co-operative research by biologists, anthropologists, and Native people has revealed an intimate local knowledge of the immediate and long-term trends in regional populations of barren ground caribou herds, which hunters used to effectively manage their harvest levels.[44]

The possibility that local systems of ecological knowledge might have actually aided caribou conservation efforts was not widely acknowledged in the earliest "outside" interpretations of northern caribou hunts. Instead, the naturalists who were so revolted by the hunting practices of Dene and Inuit people provided the basis upon which federal policy makers and the general public understood the relationship between people and wildlife in northern Canada. The federal government did not take any steps in the late nineteenth century to formally protect the caribou due to concerns about the possibility of starvation and destitution in the North. Indeed, the Unorganized Territories Game Preservation Act of 1894 exempted Native hunters who were "bona fide" residents of the Northwest Territories from the closed season on caribou. But the natural history narratives of the time had nevertheless firmly established among federal policy makers the idea that the Native hunter was improvident and destructive toward the caribou population.

In the early decades of the twentieth century, the popular discourse that cast Native hunters as wanton killers of caribou came to permeate the federal government's scientific and ethnological reports on the people and wildlife of northern Canada. A gradual growth in the number of government agents in the Far North and in the direct federal sponsorship of research in the region produced a broad array of popular and official literature concerning the impact of Native hunters on the barren ground caribou.[45] Meanwhile, the transfer of authority over wildlife in the Northwest Territories from the Forestry Branch to the Parks Branch in 1917 (an administrative change that brought wildlife enthusiasts such as Parks Commissioner James Harkin and the chief of the branch's Animal Division, Maxwell Graham, into positions of direct authority) ensured a receptive audience for the notion that the destructive hunting practices of Dene and

Inuit hunters necessitated legislative control to protect northern wildlife. No matter how amateurish their efforts at wildlife ecology and anthropology might appear today, the northern natural historians were in a position to have a much more direct influence over wildlife policy in the Northwest Territories than their Victorian predecessors.

As in the case of the muskox, no individual inspired federal wildlife officials on the matter of caribou conservation more than Vilhjalmur Stefansson. Indeed, many of the same pieces of correspondence that Stefansson forwarded to senior government officials on the issue of muskox conservation (discussed in Chapter 4) also contained urgent appeals for federal action to conserve the caribou. Stefansson's letter to Prime Minister Borden in January 1914 urged that the caribou be protected as a means to "conserve" the traditional Inuit hunting economy and the economic benefits associated with the northern fur trade. He proposed a closed season on caribou from October to April and an absolute ban on the skin trade in the coastal region east of the Mackenzie River.[46] His subsequent letter to Clifford Sifton, chair of the federal government's Commission of Conservation, outlined several reasons for the decimation of the caribou population in the Mackenzie Delta region and along the Arctic coast of Alaska after the first whaling ships arrived at Herschel Island in 1889. Inuit hunters were, according to Stefansson, fully implicated in this destruction of the caribou. He wrote, "Eskimos, and even white men, would frequently in traveling shoot a whole band when they knew that they would have to abandon everything to the wolves but a single carcass or a portion of one. At other times bands of Eskimos would shoot down hundreds from the large herds they met, and never touch an animal after it fell."[47]

Stefansson obviously abhorred the caribou slaughter in the western Arctic, but his analysis of Inuit hunting practices did differ somewhat from that of the earlier hunter-naturalists. An admirer of Inuit culture, and particularly the ability to survive in the Arctic environment, Stefansson blamed the profound economic and technical changes introduced to Inuit society by American whalers for the decline of the caribou rather than an innate propensity to slaughter wildlife. According to Stefansson, the Mackenzie Delta and Alaskan coastal caribou (today known as the Porcupine, Central Arctic, and Western Arctic herds) had been destroyed by the combined effect of the introduction of guns to the "Eskimo" by white traders (an argument that does imply the Inuit would kill as many caribou as possible given the technical means to do so), the creation of a market for wild meat to supply the whaling ships, and the intensification of the summer hide hunt at the behest of the fur traders. Stefansson warned

Sifton that the arrival of traders in Coronation Gulf meant that the caribou and the Inuit of that region faced a similar fate if the federal government did not take immediate action. He reported that only a few antiquated guns had entered the region as of 1911 but that the "comparatively inefficient" bows and arrows that limited the Inuit to a small caribou kill in the summer months would soon be replaced by high-powered rifles if the activities of the traders were not curtailed. Stefansson pleaded with Sifton to protect the caribou with "a wise interposition of the law" in the Arctic coast region, including Stefansson's earlier proposals for a closed season outside the summer months and a ban on the skin trade, as well as legalization of the use of poison to kill wolves and instituting severe penalties for killing caribou that were not absolutely needed for food purposes. Although Stefansson eventually devoted much of his public energy to the idea that domesticated muskox and European reindeer held the best hope for Inuit survival in the Arctic, in 1914 he clearly still believed that efforts to preserve the wild caribou and the "Eskimos" were one and the same.

Stefansson's analysis of the apparent crisis facing the caribou along the Arctic coast inspired a lengthy discussion among federal officials over the precise conservation measures necessary to protect the barren ground caribou. One of the most immediate and enthusiastic supporters of Stefansson's advocacy for reforms to the Northwest Game Act of 1906 – a law that had not been substantively altered since its previous incarnation as the Unorganized Territories Game Preservation Act of 1894 save for periodic extensions of the closed season on wood bison – was the Dominion entomologist, C. Gordon Hewitt. In the summer of 1914, Hewitt engaged in a series of discussions with Laurence Fortescue, comptroller of the Royal North-West Mounted Police, and Dr. H.W. Henshaw, chief of the US Bureau of Biological Survey, on possible revisions to the Game Act. Based on these deliberations, Hewitt drafted an official memorandum that included protective measures for the caribou: a ban on the killing of female and yearling caribou, a licensing system for the export of caribou skins (with a limit of two hides per trader), and the appointment of a separate force of game guardians to augment the existing police detachments.[48] Because the administration of the Northwest Game Act fell to the Department of the Interior, Sifton forwarded both Stefansson's letter and Hewitt's memorandum to W.W. Cory, the deputy minister of the department, urging immediate action to protect the caribou in the Coronation Gulf region. In spite of the fact that Cory's department had delegated responsibility for administering the Northwest Game Act to its Forestry Branch, Cory referred the entire matter to the "expert opinion" of Maxwell

Graham, chief of the Parks Branch's Animals Division. In September, Graham responded with a characteristically lengthy summary of the existing population estimates for barren ground caribou and a passionate plea for more stringent legislative protection. Using extensive quotations from naturalists such as Pike, Seton, Frank Russell, and A.J. Stone (who studied the caribou of the northern Mackenzie Valley in 1898-99), Graham argued that although the caribou population as a whole was not facing an imminent collapse, the tendency of Native hunters to slaughter large amounts of game had caused the extirpation of caribou populations near Fort Rae and in the Mackenzie Delta. To prevent such regional shortages, Graham enthusiastically supported Hewitt's proposed controls on the skin trade and the year-round closed season on female caribou and their calves.[49]

Despite this growing bureaucratic momentum for the proposed reforms to the Northwest Game Act, they did not become part of the legislative agenda in the autumn of 1914. It is likely that the government's preoccupation with the war in Europe overshadowed any attempt to reform the game laws. The case for tighter game regulations in the North was strengthened, however, by continuing reports of "reckless" caribou slaughters and the rapidly declining population of the herds along the Arctic coast. In 1915, Henry J. Bury, the inspector of timber for Indian Affairs, claimed in a general report on game conditions in the Northwest Territories that the caribou were subject to localized extinction due to hunting by Native people living along the pathways of the annual migration. In terms reminiscent of the earlier sport hunting narratives, Bury issued a graphic and scathing indictment of Native hunting practices on the caribou range:

> At the first approach of fall, [the caribou] congregate in enormous herds, sometimes 500,000 head, and follow some blind instinct which prompts them to migrate north, south, east and west on a never-ending search for food. This is their undoing, for, upon the approach of the caribou herds, the Indian hunters make elaborate preparations for wholesale slaughter, and it has frequently been found that, carried away by a certain amount of primordial instinct, they not only kill sufficient for food, but do not stop when that point is reached, and continue slaughtering right and left, merely depriving the carcasses of their tongues and hides.[50]

Bury's suggested policy measures to protect the caribou were vague: he recommended more study of their numbers and habits so that an adequate conservation policy might be enacted at a later date. His report was widely circulated among federal officials, however, reaching the desks of Graham,

Harkin, and Hewitt by the end of December 1915.[51] At the annual meeting of the Commission of Conservation in 1916, Hewitt presented the case for a revised Game Act and won strong backing in the form of a formal resolution supporting his proposals.[52] To press the point further, Hewitt forwarded a copy of Bury's report to the assistant chair of the Commission of Conservation, James White, in November 1916; Clifford Sifton also brought the issue directly to the attention of Prime Minister Borden. The minister of the interior, William Roche, assigned the task of drafting the new Game Act to the newly created Advisory Board on Wildlife Protection. After nearly six months of deliberations, Roche presented a revised Northwest Game Act to the House of Commons on 20 June 1917, and it received royal assent on 20 September.[53]

The early records of the advisory board do not contain a clear documentary record of the debate on the game laws for the Northwest Territories, but the final legislation suggests that some form of compromise was reached during the weeks of deliberation leading up to the passage of the new Game Act. The advisory board's original membership included some of the most passionate wildlife conservationists within the federal government, such as James Harkin, Gordon Hewitt, James White, and Rudolph M. Anderson. But the superintendent general of Indian Affairs, Duncan Campbell Scott, was also a member of the advisory board, and his presence almost certainly ensured that the economic self-reliance of subsistence hunting cultures in the Far North was taken into consideration in the legislation. The final Northwest Game Act had all the markings of a middle course between the interests of the staunch wildlife conservationists on the advisory board and Scott's tendency to resist any drastic infringement on the traditional Native economy. Hewitt's suggested ban on the killing of female caribou and their calves was abandoned, and "bona fide" resident Native hunters were exempt from the new licensing system governing all other hunters, trappers, and traders in the Northwest Territories.

Despite such concessions, the conservationists on the board did win the authority and flexibility to implement a broad range of conservation measures in the Northwest Territories. In order to avoid the cumbersome process of amending the legislation in Parliament each time federal wildlife officials proposed changes to the game laws, the federal cabinet was granted authority over many provisions of the Game Act: the issue of hunting and trapping licences, bag limits for individual species of birds and mammals, the appointment of game officers, the designation of seasonal and geographic restrictions on the hunting of elk and muskox, and the enactment of any other regulation "deemed expedient" for achieving the stated goals of the legislation.[54] The most dramatic change, however, was the reversal of a policy that had exempted Native hunters from the closed seasons on all game animals except for the muskox and the wood bison. Not only were Native trappers now subject to previously unheard-of closed seasons on most fur-bearing animals, but caribou hunting was prohibited during a closed season in October and November and from the beginning of April to the end of July. Native hunters, explorers, and "bona fide" residents of the Northwest Territories could take caribou during the closed season only to prevent starvation.[55] Native hunters in the Northwest Territories were thus subject for the first time to discretionary arrest and legal sanction for hunting their main source of subsistence. To those born early enough to have hunted before even the passage of the first Unorganized Territories Game Preservation Act in 1894, the introduction of legal codes to govern the caribou hunt in 1917 – even as closed seasons on waterfowl were imposed that year by the implementation of the Migratory Birds Convention Act – must have seemed a profound change in the social and political life of their communities. Other than the closed seasons on muskox and wood buffalo established in 1894, there had been no wildlife regulations to control the annual subsistence cycle of Native northerners before 1917.

The lack of a significant law enforcement presence anywhere in the Northwest Territories during this period probably diminished the effects of the new legislation on Aboriginal hunters. In 1918 there were only sixteen mounted police officers spread over five detachments in the Northwest Territories, prompting Commissioner A. Bowen Perry to report that "if [the new game laws] are to be progressively effective, our detachments will have to be increased." Although Harkin claimed in his report for 1920 that the new game laws were being enforced with "gratifying results," there were only four convictions under the Northwest Game Act between 1918 and 1921 (Table 5.1).[56] But the legislation made it clear that Native hunters were increasingly subject to the decisions of remote policy makers in Ottawa and their agents in the field. Although the available archival evidence contains few traces of Aboriginal voices from the period, one incident suggests that Native hunters actively resisted the loss of sovereignty over wildlife resources implied by the new game laws. On 15 July 1920, the Chipewyan, Slavey, and Dogrib people who gathered for treaty days at Fort Resolution went into open revolt over the new regulations and refused to take payments. F.H. Kitto, who was visiting the village while surveying the Northwest Territories for the Natural Resources Intelligence Branch, reported that the root of the protest was a litany of objections to the new game regulations: "Much complaint was heard about the North-west Game Act and the Migratory Birds Convention Act. It is claimed that the open season is too late in the fall as the birds have gone south before it comes into effect. It was also pointed out that fresh meat, other than game, cannot be obtained so far north and that the lack of it would seriously injure the health of the people. Further it was claimed that if strictly enforced these Acts would cause actual starvation among the natives."[57] According to oral reports gathered by Father René Fumoleau, the Native hunters felt that the new regulations violated the terms of Treaty 8 and demanded a new agreement. The impasse was only resolved when the chief of the Dogrib band, Susie Drygeese, signed an agreement with Bishop Gabriel Breynat and the Indian agent Gerald Card that provided for a large hunting preserve north of Great Slave Lake where game laws would not apply to Native hunters – a promise that was never fulfilled.[58]

Despite such protests, wildlife conservationists within the federal bureaucracy were intent on mobilizing the administrative and legal power of the modern state to protect the northern caribou from the supposedly reckless and corrupt hunting practices of the region's indigenous people. Although the practical results of the government's lawmaking and enforcement initiatives were tentative at best, federal officials were determined to circumscribe local decision-making power through the imposition of game regulations that standardized seasonal subsistence activities in the Northwest Territories. Three decades of alarming reports on the condition of wildlife in the Northwest Territories had finally produced a comprehensive legal framework for controlling the activities of Native and "outside" hunters in the region. The federal government could now turn its efforts to asserting direct control over the wildlife of northern Canada.

TABLE 5.1   Investigations and convictions under the Northwest Game Act, 1919-24

Year	Cases investigated	Convictions
1919-20	3	3
1920-21	1	1
1921-22	15	12
1922-23	12	8
1923-24	2	1

SOURCES: Royal Canadian Mounted Police, Commissioner's Reports, *Sessional Papers* (1920-25).

An Arctic Pastoral

Some might be tempted to argue at this point that the colonial discourse surrounding the imposition of the game laws in the Northwest Territories was incidental rather than fundamental to Canada's early conservation movement. The imposition of state authority over Native hunters was, one might contend, a product of necessity, not a driving force behind the effort to protect northern wildlife. Indeed, the efforts of Hewitt, Harkin, and Graham to expose the extant dangers to the barren ground caribou before a catastrophic collapse in the population seem, at first glance, to arise from a valiant attempt to save a species that was an irreplaceable part of the northern wilderness. In a very general sense, the incipient preservationist philosophy among leading figures in the conservation movement was a critical influence on the momentous reforms to Canada's federal game laws and the attendant expansion of the federal wildlife bureaucracy in the first two decades of the twentieth century. When leading conservationists such as Gordon Hewitt proclaimed that "it lies within our power to preserve for ourselves, but more particularly for posterity for whom we hold it in trust, the wild life of this country," his words seem a harbinger of a more recent discourse on preserving the natural world for its intrinsic value.[59]

But as with the previous examples of the wood bison and the muskox, the early caribou conservation discourse readily combined the language of preservationism with the cherished utilitarian tenets of the progressive-era conservation movement.[60] Hewitt may have quoted extensively from Warburton Pike, for example, to praise the magnificence of the vast multitudes of barren ground caribou, but he also argued for "the desirability of developing so important a natural resource for the benefit of the Dominion as a whole, inasmuch as it would provide a source of meat of incalculable value, and skins that could be utilized in the manufacture of many items of commerce and clothing."[61] Maxwell Graham also framed his arguments for caribou conservation in utilitarian terms, arguing for stricter game laws to protect the economic value of the caribou:

> Canada possesses to-day tens of millions of dollars of Barren Ground caribou meat and hides. These animals would, as before pointed out by me, be quite useless for transportation purposes, but of their value as furnishing nourishing meat there can be no question. Through their means, the Government, in my opinion, has now a great opportunity to reduce the cost of living; the immense herds on these Barren Grounds are transmuting otherwise worthless moss into palatable and nourishing meat, and, excepting where

these great herds or a portion of them, impinge on sparsely inhabited out-lying districts, their meat is being used to maintain and swell the ferocious hordes of Arctic and Barren Ground wolves.[62]

Such comments suggest that the colonial disposition of Canada's early wildlife conservation movement did not originate only with attempts to impose legislative controls on the "backward" customs of northern Native hunters and prevent the decline of the majestic caribou herds. It also grew out of a utilitarian ethos that advocated the appropriation and intensive management of wildlife for the purposes of commercial production.

Early proposals to domesticate the caribou as ranch animals were heav-ily influenced by the writings of the very naturalists and government field officers who had first expressed awe at the vastness of the herds and denounced Native hunters for slaughtering them. Federal officials often cited the estimates of million-strong caribou herds produced by Seton, Tyrrell, Pike, Russell, and Henry Toke Munn as proof that the caribou herds could withstand a commercial slaughter.[63] Furthermore, several natu-ralists and government agents – particularly those that followed in the wake of the late-nineteenth-century sport hunters – proposed their own schemes for the commercial production of caribou. Ernest Thompson Seton may have been moved by sighting so many wild caribou on the tun-dra, for instance, but he also advocated the domestication of the animals and the importation of Old World reindeer to occupy some of their range.[64] Henry Bury wrote in his report on northern wildlife that "it would appear judicious and wise policy to initiate an investigation into the numbers, habits, haunts and utilitarian uses of the caribou, so that steps may be taken to conserve and realize this valuable asset of the northern section of Canada."[65] At least some of the naturalists and government agents who travelled to northern Canada near the turn of the century were enthused about the possibility of transforming "Arctic Prairies" into a pastoral land-scape devoted to newly domesticated commercial livestock.

The heavy demands of the wartime economy provided a catalyst for plans to exploit the caribou as a domestic meat supply. By the latter stages of the First World War, senior wildlife officials in the Canadian govern-ment tended to use war-related arguments as a justification for their con-servation initiatives. One of the most significant arguments advanced in favour of the International Treaty for the Protection of Migratory Birds, for example, was that insectivorous birds helped protect the North Amer-ican food supply from agricultural pests.[66] On a broader scale, the histo-rian Edmund Russell has argued that the modern nation-state must not only muster armies and augment its domestic industrial capacity to engage in armed conflict, but must also fully "mobilize" the natural world as a material base for the pursuit of total war.[67] Cognizant of the comprehensive nature of modern warfare, Canada's senior wildlife bureaucrats considered the direct exploitation of the nation's wildlife – particularly the barren ground caribou – in support of the larger war effort. In October 1914, for example, Harkin's assistant, F.H.H. Williamson, wrote to Deputy Minister W.W. Cory with the suggestion that the hollow hair of the caribou might be fashioned into waterproof flotation suits for Allied sailors.[68] Three years later, an impending food shortage among the Allied nations and a ban on the domestic consumption of Canadian beef added weight to the idea that the barren ground caribou could augment the wartime food supply. In October 1917, Maxwell Graham wrote a lengthy memorandum to James Harkin about the precipitous decline in the livestock production of Europe and North America since the beginning of the war, which had left the Allies desperately short of meat. "The food problem," Graham wrote, "is now the paramount issue in this war," in part due to the increased food needs of an active military and civilian population. According to Graham, a foot soldier required a pound of meat per day if he was to endure ten to twelve hours of toil in the trenches. And the millions of civilian women who had been "drawn into physical labour" required more food than under normal conditions. To address this disparity between supply and demand, Graham recommended an investigation into the possibility of slaughtering twenty-five thousand of the "literally millions" of caribou roaming the barren grounds between Hudson Bay and Lake Athabasca.[69] After six months of research into the feasibility of the project, Graham concluded that airplanes could be used to herd the caribou toward Churchill, Manitoba. Native hunters could then slaughter the required number of animals, and the meat could be hauled by tractor along the coast to the head of the railroad. Not only would the caribou meat help to relieve the food shortage, Graham reasoned, but the hooves could be used for fertilizer, the antlers to make case-hardened steel, and, as Williamson had suggested, the hollow hairs could be used to fill life preservers.[70] The project was never carried out because providing the necessary labour, transportation, and storage facilities was logistically complicated, while the meat situation was deemed not serious enough to warrant immediate action. Harkin remained hopeful, however, that caribou might one day contribute to the nation's food supply. In his annual report for 1917 he assured his readers that "the caribou to-day constitute a great meat reserve for the country which can be made available if food conditions should continue to grow worse."[71]

In the absence of wartime supply pressures, however, Harkin rejected in its entirety a proposal from a private citizen, W.H.P. Jarvis, to set up an air training facility at Churchill where the pilots could herd caribou toward slaughter pens and also practise target shooting as they machine-gunned wolves that were travelling with the herds.[72] Harkin replied to Jarvis that the caribou probably would have been slaughtered for meat and other products had the war continued and also that it was desirable for the caribou to some day be used "conservatively" as part of a meat production program, but the cost of transporting the meat from the Far North remained prohibitively expensive.[73] Nonetheless, the enthusiasm of both Harkin and Graham for the proposed wartime "mobilization" of the caribou indicates that both men regarded the mass slaughter of caribou as acceptable resource exploitation, as long as the killing was conducted under federal authority to serve the national purpose.

The wartime food shortage produced only the first of several official proposals to manage the caribou as a commercial meat supply. The royal commission established in 1919 to examine the potential of muskox and reindeer industries in the Northwest Territories devoted considerable attention to the biological status and economic possibilities of the barren ground caribou. In their final recommendations, the commissioners advised that "special attention be given to the enforcement of such regulations as will effectively prevent the wasteful or useless slaughter of the wild caribou, either by natives or others." The caribou herds were to be saved because they were "a very valuable national asset, and one the value of which could be greatly enhanced under a definite policy of conservation and development." The commissioners therefore recommended that "provision be made for the domestication along intelligent lines, of such numbers of young wild caribou as may be conveniently handled with the [imported] reindeer herd."[74] Once again, a federal policy-making body was pressing for conservation measures intended to protect the caribou as potential commercial livestock rather than as part of a high-minded campaign meant to preserve the animals for the sake of posterity. As in other cases, the introduction of an ordered system of production under the rational guidance of the state was seen as a partial antidote to the wastefulness and uncertainty associated with Dene and Inuit hunting practices.

The association of the caribou herds with northern resource development received public support in the popular writings of naturalists who travelled to the Far North in the 1920s. The geologist Guy H. Blanchet, who had described the northern landscape as a verdant wilderness deserving protection, also wrote, "Viewing the so-called 'Barren Lands' in August, with their plains and undulating hills stretching on all sides to the horizon, enlivened by the colours of its vegetation and animated by the roving bands of caribou, it seems incredible that the country is destined to remain an unproductive waste."[75] Perhaps the most vivid image of an Arctic ranching economy in this period came from Capt. J.C. Critchell-Bullock in a lengthy serial describing his journey to the Arctic with John Hornby in 1924-25. The series of articles contains wide-ranging observations on the Arctic, including a detailed proposal for caribou ranching as an economic alternative to the supposedly random and destructive hunting of Native people. According to Critchell-Bullock, it was "apparently impossible to educate natives ... so that they will conduct their hunts in an orderly manner, for one thing they are so spread our over so vast a country, individually and by single families, that it is impossible to administer them."[76] If the game laws and the mounted police could not control the wide-open caribou hunt, then he believed the solution was to centralize and domesticate both the herds and Native people to better serve the purposes of conservation. When his party reached the picturesque site of Fort Reliance in August 1924, Critchell-Bullock envisioned a subarctic ranch that would promote the Progressive ideals of efficient resource conservation, economic productivity, animal welfare, public health promotion, and the back to nature movement:

> I pictured the place as a great sanitorium [sic], to which men with hope could come, and in a year leave with all their one-time strength and health. I fancied I saw a great caribou ranch on Artillery Lake, the barren lands about it their summer home, the edge of the timber the natural retreat of the bulls in winter. The patients living in shacks about Charlton Harbour, leading men's lives, assisting with the herding, fishing, and living off the superb flesh of the early Fall bull. A great industry, yet running sweetly because of the leavening touch of philanthropic endeavour concerned with it. White fox farms would come into their own, the torture of the steel trap, so unenviably associated with such a pleasant district, could be prohibited, and the Indians within the sphere of activities could be induced to lead lives of less ambiguity.[77]

This proposal – the domestication of the caribou as a means to impose social order on the economic and cultural life of the Native hunter – effectively sums up many of the central principles of conservation as practised by Canada's fledgling wildlife bureaucracy. Indeed, Critchell-Bullock's vision for his northern ranch stands as one of the most eloquent testaments to the federal government's initial attempts to redefine the relationship between people and wildlife in northern Canada according to a rational practice of wildlife management. At the root of this philosophy was the idea that both the wild caribou herds and the improvident Native hunter must be subject to judicious regulation – even some form of domestication. At the vanguard of this movement were the sportsmen and naturalists who wrote so vividly about the northern landscape in the late nineteenth and early twentieth centuries. Their descriptions of a northern wilderness populated by numberless caribou herds, their pragmatic proposals to domesticate the caribou as part of a northern pastoral economy, and finally their denigration of the Native hunter as irrational and destructive provided much of the impetus for wildlife conservation programs in northern Canada. The profound antilocal sentiment in the northern natural history literature accorded perfectly with a federal conservation bureaucracy that was anxious to accelerate efforts both to protect northern wildlife from the apparently idiosyncratic hunting practices of Dene and Inuit people and also to establish wildlife industries that might benefit the Canadian public as a whole. The denigration of local knowledge systems thus became the common language of natural historians and federal wildlife officials during this period and provided a necessary precursor to the consolidation of bureaucratic power over wildlife and people in northern Canada. Such initiatives as the imposition of a standardized caribou hunting season on all hunters in the Northwest Territories and the proposed domestication of the caribou were linked to a broader effort to supplant the unique and variable local systems of resource management (however limited the practical results of these programs may have been). Early caribou conservation measures in the Northwest Territories were thus as much an autocratic attempt to assert state power over humans and nature in the Canadian hinterland as a benign attempt to save a threatened wildlife population.

6

To Save the Wild Caribou

T HE PROTECTIVE MEASURES IN THE Northwest Game Act of 1917 did little to allay fears that the barren ground caribou might some day go the way of the plains bison. The writings of some naturalists and explorers who subsequently travelled to the region continued to stir up fears among federal wildlife officials of a crash in the caribou population. But the increasing numbers of police, government agents, and non-Native trappers who entered the region beginning in the 1920s were the wildlife bureaucracy's most important source of information about the impact of Native hunting on the caribou. Speculation and conjecture were the hallmarks of these reports: estimates of the total barren ground caribou population were often based on wildly hypothetical assumptions derived from reports of "scarce" or "plentiful" caribou within a particular region. Reports of mass caribou slaughters – particularly those forwarded to the police by the non-Native trappers who were in direct competition with Native northerners for game – were often based on rumour, hearsay, and second-hand evidence that turned out to be suspect upon further investigation.

In spite of such imprecision, many federal officials began to campaign for the imposition of further restrictions on northern caribou hunters in the early 1920s. Although the government has been characterized as indifferent toward northern Canada in the interwar years because it starved the Northwest Territories and Yukon Branch of funds and personnel to the point at which it became a "shackled administration," the case of caribou management suggests that the federal government did maintain a consistent and unwavering commitment to the development of an interventionist wildlife conservation policy in the North.[1] The interdepartmental Advisory Board on Wildlife Protection devoted an overwhelming amount of attention to northern wildlife during this period.[2] More important, the evolving structure of governance in the Northwest Territories allowed federal civil servants a more direct hand in the development of wildlife policy for the region. After the membership of the Northwest Territories Council was expanded in 1921 to consist of six federal civil servants, such staunch supporters of restrictive conservation policies as O.S. Finnie, Deputy Minister of the Interior W.W. Cory, and his assistant, Roy A. Gibson, gained a powerful voice within this governing body.[3] Although game ordinances were subject to the approval of the federal cabinet and limited by the statutory authority of Parliament, a large measure of the legislative and executive power to enact and administer game laws in the Northwest Territories rested with this small body of civil servants based in Ottawa.

While such an administrative framework allowed for frequent revision of the game regulations in response to ambiguous allegations of impending wildlife crises, it was also a thoroughly colonial instrument, responsive only to the "outsiders" who furnished reports on game conditions in the Northwest Territories and wholly unaccountable to the Aboriginal people on whose behalf northern wildlife was apparently being protected. Indeed, the steady stream of reports alleging mass wildlife slaughters conducted by Dene and Inuit hunters served to reinforce the notion that increased state management was the only possible way to save the barren ground caribou from annihilation. Federal wildlife officials therefore waged a consistent campaign to limit access to the caribou herds by adjusting closed seasons, prohibiting mass slaughters, limiting the sale of skins and meat, establishing outright hunting bans, and prosecuting some violations of the game regulations to the fullest extent of the law. By the 1930s, the northern administration had also begun to assert tentative control over the subsistence cycle of Native people, promoting increased fishing and limits on the number of sled dogs within education programs meant to alleviate hunting pressure on the caribou. Although federal officials had little evidence to suggest an impending collapse in the caribou population other than the contradictory reports of non-Native trappers and their own field agents, a dire sense of urgency nevertheless continued to provoke the northern administration in the interwar years to expand its influence and authority over people and wildlife in northern Canada.

THE WANTON SLAUGHTER OF THE CARIBOU

Among the many reports of Aboriginal overkill of northern wildlife that appeared in the 1920s, the most expansive and detailed was the first government-sponsored study of the barren ground caribou, organized by Finnie in May 1924. The survey was rudimentary by current standards: Finnie appointed a single amateur naturalist, the Anglican lay missionary W.H.B. Hoare, to conduct an expansive investigation of the range, numbers, and migration routes of the caribou population in the central Arctic over a two-year period. Hoare was also instructed to "personally disseminate propaganda regarding the conservation of Caribou among the Eskimos," particularly the regulation prohibiting hunting in the spring and summer calving season.[4] Although Hoare lacked the specific scientific training for a study of the caribou, he did not lack enthusiasm: he travelled an astonishing distance of over ten thousand miles from August 1924 to July 1926 by schooner, canoe, and dogsled along the Arctic coast as far east as Bathurst Inlet, and inland to the community of Rae on the north arm of Great Slave Lake.

Hoare concluded that the most dire threats to the caribou stemmed from the abandonment by the coastal Inuit of a "superstition" that had formerly prevented them from going inland to hunt caribou until the late summer and from the introduction of rifles in the late nineteenth century. Inuit hunters were now leaving their sealing and fishing camps earlier each spring to engage in the comparatively easy hunt of the caribou herds migrating northward to their calving grounds (see Figure 6.1).[5] Hoare claimed that the inland hunting, combined with the pervasive coal and oil smoke from the increasing number of trading posts along the Arctic coast, was diverting the caribou from their traditional spring migration to Victoria Island and other High Arctic islands, forcing them onto smaller calving grounds each year and exposing the concentrated herds more readily to human hunters. The missionary therefore took every opportunity "to teach and instruct [the Inuit] to save the caribou," pleading with them to obey the game regulations and remain on the coast eating fish from local lakes and streams until the late spring or early summer.[6]

Hoare did claim some success in his efforts. He reported in August 1925 that he had convinced many Inuit that the principles of caribou conservation were "nearer to the truth than their own wild ideas," and that he had persuaded half the Inuit population in the Coronation Gulf region to remain on the coast until summer.[7] He nevertheless concluded that the proliferation of trading posts and continued human hunting had created a desperate situation for the caribou herds that summered in the central Arctic. In a section of his report titled "To Remedy the Evils," Hoare urged the government to limit the number and location of trading posts along the Arctic coast and on the islands to the north, educate Native hunters against wanton slaughter, and create a caribou sanctuary on the Arctic Archipelago from the 90th to the 125th degrees of longitude. Hoare was also an early advocate of the development of alternative resources and economic opportunities among the Inuit (such as fishing, white fox farming, and reindeer herding) in order to conserve the caribou.[8] One of the most important means by which the state could impose discipline on "unruly" Native hunters was to fundamentally change the indigenous modes of production that he thought wrought so much destruction on the caribou herds.

Although Hoare's caribou study was a remarkable accomplishment in terms of the vast territory covered and the range of his observations, his final report stretched the bounds of scientific certitude in many respects. In general, Hoare's assertion of an impending caribou crisis was compromised by his relatively small experience in the Arctic and his consequent lack of historical baseline data against which to judge the present status of the caribou herds. For example, Hoare misinterpreted the concentration of migrating caribou herds on relatively small calving grounds in the spring

6.1   Inuit hunters returning from a caribou hunt, no date. LAC PA-42129

as the recent product of Native hunting pressure when in fact he was observing the traditional yearly spring aggregation of the Bathurst and Bluenose caribou herds south and east of the Coronation Gulf region. Furthermore, Hoare's contention that the migration of the mainland caribou herds from their "former fawning grounds" on "Victoria Land" and the other Arctic islands had been severely curtailed by smoke and Native hunters – an observation based partly on the fact he saw only thirteen caribou tracks while crossing Coronation Gulf in May 1925 where he had seen innumerable tracks six years previously – was also probably exaggerated. It is likely he was observing traces of the migration of caribou indigenous to the Arctic Archipelago between their winter range on the Arctic coast and their summer ranges on Victoria and King William islands.[9] Finally, Hoare's claim that the caribou had declined to one-tenth of their former strength because of human exploitation rested on a few first-hand observations of rotting carcasses in Inuit hunting camps and the testimony of traders at Rae that the caribou had previously been more plentiful in that region. He went on to cite the reports of once-numberless caribou herds that had been circulating in the natural history literature for five decades – particularly Ernest Thompson Seton's wildly speculative estimate of thirty million animals – as a standard against which to judge the present status of the herds.[10] To conclude from such unreliable numbers that "in a very short time the story of the barren ground caribou will coincide with that of the plains bison" seems almost extraordinary in retrospect, but Hoare may have felt the need to provide a particularly acute description of a wildlife crisis to spur government action on his recommendations for a more rigorous caribou conservation program in the Northwest Territories.[11]

The basic theme of a declining caribou population was repeated throughout the 1920s in informal reports to senior wildlife officials of the federal government. One particularly important source of information used to assess the impact of Native hunters on the caribou herds was correspondence from the newly established RCMP detachments along the Arctic coast. At a meeting of the Advisory Board on Wildlife Protection held on 2 November 1926, a report from RCMP Sergeant Barnes claimed, for example, that it was "hard to stop" Inuit hunters when they began to kill caribou because "they do not believe in the white man's version of a caribou slaughter."[12] A large number of explorers and fur traders were also called before the advisory board between 1924 and 1926 to testify on the possible threats facing the caribou herds. In March 1925, the sport hunter Henry Toke Munn claimed that the export of hundreds of caribou skins from Baffin Island to Hudson's Bay Company posts in Labrador and the

Mackenzie Delta were severely depleting the herds. He recommended a ban on the traffic in caribou hides and the creation of a game preserve on the Arctic islands.[13] At an advisory board meeting held in November 1925, John Hornby and the Independent fur trader Charles Klengenberg (who had lived near Coronation Gulf since 1888) cited the establishment of new trading posts as one major factor depleting the muskox and the caribou. Although he may have been slandering his competitor, Klengenberg claimed that the Hudson's Bay Company routinely killed caribou around its trading posts so that Native people would become dependent on the traders for provisions. He also referred to the effects of coal smoke on the caribou population and recommended a ban on trading posts in isthmuses where caribou formerly travelled between the Arctic islands and the mainland.[14] Three months later, the geologist Guy H. Blanchet told the advisory board there was a surplus of bull caribou in the Northwest Territories, a situation he attributed to the preference among Native hunters for the hides of the females and the young to manufacture clothing. He strongly endorsed proposals that had been circulating among federal officials to find some sort of industrial occupation for the Inuit, such as white fox farming, the tanning of seal skins, or the production of ivory, to relieve the strain on the caribou and muskox herds.[15]

Perhaps no informant on the question of barren ground caribou conservation influenced federal wildlife officials more than the Danish explorer Knud Rasmussen. From 1921 to 1924, Rasmussen had led the Fifth Thule Expedition, an archaeological and anthropological study of Inuit society across the Arctic. He appeared before a series of special advisory board meetings in late April and early May of 1925 to answer questions on the material and social life of the Inuit. His testimony clearly contradicted the "friendly" Arctic that Vilhjalmur Stefansson had been promoting in the public arena for several years. Rasmussen cited the yearly occurrence of starvation among the inland Caribou Inuit near Yathkyed Lake, the common practice of infanticide among the Inuit, and the general misunderstanding of "white man's" laws against murder as evidence that the cultural norms of Inuit were as harsh as the local climate.[16] With respect to the caribou, Rasmussen repeated the familiar charge that Native hunters engaged in wasteful slaughters at water crossings. Furthermore, the introduction of firearms and coal smoke along the Arctic coast was having such a severe impact on the caribou that Rasmussen predicted none would be left in ten years. Although the Danish explorer recommended the close regulation of caribou hunting at lake and river crossings and restrictions on the establishment of trading posts, he generally favoured modification

of the Inuit economy as the most pragmatic approach to caribou conservation. Rasmussen recommended, for example, the distribution of fish nets
to communities near lakes or the coast to prevent starvation and divert
hunting pressure from the caribou. He was most emphatic, however, in
his claim that the Inuit would become more "economical" and less wasteful if they abandoned caribou hunting for reindeer herding.[17] In general,
Rasmussen preferred acculturation through missionary education rather
than law enforcement as the best means to erase the social "pathologies"
(infanticide, murder, indiscriminate hunting, etc.) he associated with traditional Inuit culture. His was an entirely colonial vision of conservation,
requiring a dramatic transformation of Inuit social and material life.[18]

In keeping with Rasmussen's recommendations, federal officials proposed a series of reforms to the game laws and several changes to the material culture of northern Native people throughout the latter part of the
1920s. In March 1925, the Advisory Board on Wildlife Protection passed a
resolution calling for more research on wildlife conditions in the Canadian Arctic and the education of the Native population "along industrial
lines" to divert hunting pressure from the caribou herds. The resolution
also suggested conservation education among Native hunters to reduce
the wasteful exploitation of a valuable natural resource.[19] In addition, the
advisory board took action to limit the impact of the trading posts along
the Arctic coast and on the Arctic Archipelago, unanimously recommending in March 1926 the extension of the Back River Game Preserve east and
north to include the islands.[20] When this Arctic Islands Game Preserve was
created in July, hunting, trapping, and trading privileges were extended
only to Dene, Inuit, and "half-breed" hunters who were pursuing their
traditional livelihood. The order-in-council that established the preserve
also granted the commissioner of the Northwest Territories power to regulate the establishment of new trading posts throughout the area under his
jurisdiction.[21] Moreover, the advisory board condemned the export trade
in caribou skins with an informal call for a ban on the practice on 15 January 1925. No clear action was taken on the issue until July 1926, when the
advisory board approved a draft memo to the Northwest Territories Council requesting a ban on the traffic in caribou meat and skins, over the
strong objections of the Hudson's Bay Company.[22] The NWT Council
quickly approved the proposed amendment to the game regulations, and
in August an order-in-council banned the export of caribou hides or meat
from anywhere in the Northwest Territories.[23] Finally, Finnie took the first
step toward transforming the Inuit economy from hunting and gathering
to pastoral herding. In April 1926, he appointed the botanist Alf Porsild to

conduct a study of possible pasture areas near the Mackenzie Delta and Great Bear Lake for the development of a domestic reindeer industry in the Northwest Territories. Three years later, the federal government bought from an Alaskan company 3,400 reindeer, which were then herded, over a remarkable five-year period, to a grazing area east of the Mackenzie River. The project was never much of a success: problems with animals straying and grazing on unsuitable lands ensured that the herds did not increase to the point where they were anything but a local supplement to the diet of the Inuit in the Aklavik area.[24]

Taken together, these reforms represented a resolute attempt on the part of federal officials to address the concerns that had been brought before the advisory board. Many of the regulations, particularly those meant to control the establishment of new trading posts and hunting and trapping by non-Native outsiders, were intended to protect the interests of the Native population as well as limit the "outside" commercial exploitation of caribou herds. Other policy initiatives, however, such as the promotion of conservation education and the monumental task of herding reindeer all the way from Alaska, suggest that federal officials sought more direct forms of control over the local economy and material culture of Dene and Inuit hunters in order to protect the caribou population.[25]

Of all the proposed changes to the game laws in the 1920s, perhaps none inspired as much enthusiasm among federal wildlife officials as the plan to regulate what many considered the most disturbing aspect of the crisis facing the barren ground caribou: the wasteful slaughters that Native hunters were reportedly inflicting on the herds. In addition to the previously mentioned reports of mass slaughters conducted by the Inuit of the Arctic regions, officials had been deluged with reports concerning wildlife massacres in the subarctic regions inhabited by Dene hunters. Many of these reports came from the itinerant non-Native trappers who flooded into the region after the war. In March 1924, for example, John McDougal, the superintendent of Wood Buffalo National Park, received several reports from non-Native trappers of excessive caribou slaughters at the east end of Lake Athabasca near Fond du Lac, Saskatchewan.[25] Four months later, RCMP Cpl. W.H. Bryant reported that four trappers had come to his office at Fort Fitzgerald to complain of "wantonly slaughtered" caribou along the Talston River.[26] Similar reports reached the general public through newspaper articles. In just one example, a story in the *Regina Leader* on 22 July 1926 cited the testimony of the trapper Barney Magnusson that Native hunters near Fort Smith had conducted several wanton caribou slaughters in the two years he had lived in the area.[27] Such complaints against Native hunters prompted urgent calls among federal wildlife officials for more exacting enforcement of the game regulations near the southern border of the Northwest Territories. In response to the allegations of slaughter near Fond du Lac, both McDougal and Maxwell Graham recommended close co-ordination between federal agents and their provincial counterparts.[28]

Although the allegations of mass caribou killing set off alarm bells among federal wildlife officials, at least some observers doubted the authenticity of many of these stories. Four days after the story about Magnusson appeared, the *Winnipeg Free Press* ran an article claiming that northern trappers such as Bearcat Buckley, Old Man Mundy, and Matt Murphy had "laughed" at the idea the caribou around Fort Smith were disappearing. In the case of the alleged Fond du Lac slaughters, the provincial police officer Marcel Chappuis conducted an investigation and found no evidence of a wasteful caribou slaughter, nor had he encountered any excessive killing over the past three years of patrolling the region.[29] Nonetheless, in the summer of 1927, the hunting practices of the Fond du Lac band near Selwyn Lake again became the subject of intense debate after the trappers Fred Riddle and A.G. McCaskill complained of a large and wasteful caribou slaughter near Selwyn, Wholdaia, and Daly Lakes in the Northwest Territories, in which Native hunters had taken only the tongues from the animals. Once again, Chappuis found no evidence of a large caribou massacre. In more general terms, Chappuis reported that the Maurice band at Fond du Lac was "one of the most careful [group of] hunters that are to be found in the Northern Saskatchewan."[30] Further investigation by the Indian agent Gerald Card and the RCMP constable R.H. Clewy revealed that even Riddle's trapping partner, Oscar Johnson, denied that the two men had seen any caribou carcasses killed only for their tongues.[31] In a similar case three years later, the trader Peter Baker reported to Wood Buffalo Park superintendent John McDougal that Native hunters and white trappers had conducted an excessive caribou slaughter east of Fort Smith near Great Slave Lake. When Corporal Burstall of the RCMP was sent to investigate the allegations in May 1930, he found no signs of a wasteful slaughter: non-Native trappers had killed approximately five to six caribou each during the spring migration, while Native hunters had taken fifty to sixty per family, an amount Burstall considered "not excessive."[32] Although some individual Native hunters may have conducted the kind of wasteful slaughter reported, the number of reports that appeared to be built on flimsy evidence or outright falsehood suggests that both the danger of a collapse in the caribou population and the apparent need for more stringent conservation measures were overstated.

What might have prompted these trappers to produce inaccurate reports of caribou massacres? As noted previously, the 1920s were a period of intense competition between Native trappers and a growing population of Euro-Canadian trappers in the Northwest Territories.[33] Crying "foul" over the issue of caribou slaughters may have been an attempt by some non-Natives to undermine the legitimacy of the "special rights" accorded to Native hunters in the Northwest Territories (i.e., no licensing requirements, exclusive access to preserves). At the very least, a generalized contempt for Native hunters is evident in several reports of mass caribou slaughters. In July 1926, the *Winnipeg Free Press* cited the testimony of three trappers, A.C. Spence, Peter Apsit, and T. Hrobjartson, who claimed that Native hunters near The Pas, Manitoba, were killing caribou "for the love of knocking them over," unlike the white trappers, who "do not indulge in the lust for blood."[34] E.J. Gaul, a trader on Baillie Island, echoed these sentiments when he testified to J.F. Moran, a special investigator for the Department of the Interior, that "the natural instinct of the Eskimo is to kill – he will not conserve the game."[35]

It is also likely that some accusations of excessive hunting were the product of the local rumour mill. When Corporal Burstall questioned Peter Baker on his allegations of wasteful slaughters east of Fort Smith, the trader "became very indefinite on the subject and eventually informed me that he had been told this. He could not tell me who had told him."[36] In other cases, caribou that had been the victims of natural accidents, particularly mass drownings at a water crossing, may have been mistaken for carcasses killed and abandoned by Native hunters. Chappuis alluded to this possibility when he reported that hundreds of caribou had died on the thin ice of a lake northeast of Fond du Lac. Because of the frequent occurrence of this type of accident, the provincial police officer warned that it was folly to jump to any quick conclusions about large amounts of dead caribou.[37] Similarly, the discovery of over five hundred drowned caribou along the Hanbury River in the summer of 1929 during an RCMP expedition in search of the missing explorer John Hornby inspired Indian agent Clement Bourget to declare that Native hunters should be absolved of the blame for needless caribou slaughters that had been foisted on them by "trappers and traders of small vision."[38]

Finally, newcomers to the region who had never witnessed the large-scale hunting of a herd animal could misinterpret what they saw. When the trader G.E.G. Craig complained of an excessive slaughter in the Kugaryuak River district in April 1929, the investigating RCMP constable, Richard Wild, paraphrased the following statement by Mr. Purcell at the

East Kugaryuak trading post: "To anyone not familiar with the conditions under which the natives have to live while inland, the amount of caribou they had killed might appear excessive, but when it is taken into consideration that this is their only means of subsistence outside of what supplies they may be able to get from the trading companies on debt, the amount killed was not very large." Based on Wild's reports, Inspector A.N. Eames concluded that "the winter of 1928-29, when the slaughter was said to have taken place, was Craig's first year on the Arctic coast, and in all probability his first experience of caribou and the grounds which they are hunted."[39] Such comments suggest that the widespread criticisms of the Dene and Inuit hunting methods in the 1920s were a product of the cultural prejudices of outsiders who had experienced revulsion at their first sight of a mass slaughter of large mammals. Of course, it is equally possible that the intimacy of police officers, Indian agents, and traders with the Aboriginal communities in which they lived elicited a sympathetic tendency to deny and apologize for local incidents of overhunting. Nonetheless, the body of evidence pointing to a specious origin for many claims of mass caribou slaughter in the 1920s and 1930s is too broad to have been entirely tainted by local bias.[40]

There can be little doubt, however, as to what side of the debate surrounding Aboriginal overkill federal officials adopted as a foundation for the creation of wildlife policy throughout the Northwest Territories in the 1920s. In particular, the allegations of caribou slaughters east of Fond du Lac in the Selwyn Lake region became a rallying point for officials who supported stronger game regulations. In the summer of 1927, both W.H.B. Hoare and the RCMP commissioner, Cortlandt Starnes, responded to the complaints of Riddle and McCaskill with a recommendation to prohibit the killing of caribou in excess of immediate subsistence needs.[41] On 12 January 1928, O.S. Finnie wrote to Hoyes Lloyd, secretary of the Advisory Board on Wildlife Protection, that the reports emanating from the Selwyn Lake region had presented a "most alarming situation."[42] At a meeting held six days later, Finnie bolstered his case somewhat with a photograph the RCMP had obtained from McCaskill depicting several dead caribou east of Fond du Lac. The meeting minutes do not suggest that any attention was afforded to Chappuis' contrary opinions, nor is there any record of the Saskatchewan police officer having been invited to attend the meeting. Furthermore, the photograph itself provides inconclusive evidence of a massive and wasteful caribou slaughter; it shows only a few emaciated caribou that may have died for any number of reasons (see Figure 6.2). The advisory board nevertheless passed a motion in support of a regulation that would prevent the slaughter of caribou in excess of a hunter's personal requirements or those of his or her dependants.[43] Over a year later, on 15 May 1929, a prohibition on the slaughter of caribou, moose, and deer in excess of individual needs, and a ban on killing most female ungulates with young at foot, were incorporated into the game regulations for the Northwest Territories. The revised regulations were also telling, however, for what they omitted. Most important, the "starvation clause" exempting Native hunters from the closed seasons on caribou was removed, and no specific regulation authorized the widespread local trade in caribou meat. As a result, Dene or Inuit groups facing food shortages due to a regional or seasonal scarcity of caribou might not be able to obtain legally an out-of-season or bartered supply.[44]

Native hunters recognized the potentially calamitous implications of the new regulations. In July and August of 1929, Finnie conducted an inspection of the Mackenzie District and reported a "consensus of opinion" that the regulations were too harsh.[45] In July, Bishop Gabriel Breynat wrote to the minister of the interior, Charles Stewart, to inform him that

6.2   A.G. McCaskill's photograph of dead caribou, which he claimed showed a mass slaughter of the animals near Fond du Lac in 1927. LAC C-149547

the new regulations were "causing great disappointment by provoking un-
tolerable new hardships to Natives ... I feel it is my duty to quiet our Natives
and tell them that no human law can prevent them from honestly seeking
life necessities for themselves and families in their own country."[46] As
Breynat's letter suggests, the resentment at the new restrictions on caribou
hunting can be attributed in part to the severe material hardship facing
Dene communities in the Mackenzie Valley during the late 1920s. In the
spring of 1928, a flu epidemic that killed several hundred people proved
disastrous for the local hunting and trapping economy, as many of the de-
ceased were elders with vital knowledge of the bush life.[47] That same year,
a three-year closed season was established on beaver, a mainstay of the
local trapping economy.[48] When copies of the new game regulations were
distributed down the Mackenzie River in the summer of 1929, the added
restrictions on caribou, moose, and muskrat came as a severe blow to
Native communities already under extreme social and economic stress.[49]

Dene hunters opposed the new game regulations not only for contrib-
uting to ongoing material hardship but also as a matter of political principle. In his report on the treaty gatherings held in 1929, Indian Agent
Bourget wrote that Dene communities up and down the Mackenzie Valley had invoked their treaty rights in criticizing the game laws: "The same
motto was repeated to the Department agent viz: that the Government
had promised the Indians that they would hunt and trap forever, as long
as the sun would shine and many more rhetorical flowers, but that in spite
of all that, every year there was new regulations and restrictions, so much
so that they were always anxious to know what would be the next one. At
some posts it was difficult to explain these points to their satisfaction."[50]
Clearly many Dene hunters felt that their right to pursue their usual voca-
tions of hunting, trapping, and fishing in perpetuity had been compromised. Even if the government's conservation policies were sometimes
couched in the benevolent idea of conserving the caribou supply as a
means to maintain the self-reliance of the Native hunter, the crux of the
matter for many northern Aboriginal people remained the issue of who
rightfully controlled access to the caribou herds, not just the maintenance
of adequate numbers to satisfy immediate material needs.

The Northwest Territories Council responded to the protests by recommending the legalization of the local trade in caribou and moose meat
(provided the hunter did not kill more animals than could be sold) so that
Native families who were short of provisions could purchase game from
more fortunate hunters. The subsequent amendments to the new regulations, which received approval from the federal cabinet in November 1929,

also restored to Inuit, Dene, and Métis hunters the privilege of taking game during the closed season if they were in "dire need" of food, provided that no other source of sustenance was available.[51] Although these changes did remove some of the more draconian aspects of the new game regulations, it was also apparent that perceived excessive killing of caribou to satisfy mere hunger rather than actual starvation, even among people who were almost wholly dependent on "bush meat" for food, could still result in criminal sanctions and a possible prison term. The 1929 revisions to the game regulations thus represented an unmistakable advance in what Peter Usher has described as the criminalization of subsistence in the Canadian North.[52] The definitions of "dire need" and of an optimal kill size were now at least nominally the province of federal law enforcement officers and not the people who had staked their survival on the caribou herds for centuries.

The precise impact of the new game regulations on the Native population of the Northwest Territories is difficult to gauge. Provisions against large slaughters and killing caribou out of season seem to have been only sporadically enforced. Up to the end of the Second World War, the federal government's general caribou files contain records of only two charges being laid in the Northwest Territories for killing caribou out of season (both stemming from a single investigation at the community of Rae) and none for slaughters in excess of personal needs.[53] While this does not preclude the possibility of additional arrests, many RCMP officers were reluctant to enforce a law that placed such severe restrictions on the primary food source in the Northwest Territories. Several RCMP reports from the 1930s suggest that Inuit hunters in the Coronation Gulf region were freely taking caribou during the spring and summer months of the closed season, when the animals were massed on their calving grounds near the Bathurst Inlet.[54] When Cpl. L. Basler found the members of a hunting camp near Rae killing caribou outside the closed season in April 1936, he considered it "highly inadvisable" to prosecute, as Chief Susie Abele assured him that the animals were their only means of subsistence.[55] Vague definitions of such concepts as "dire need," and when exactly a caribou slaughter could be described as excessive, added to the inherent difficulty of enforcing the new game regulations over such a wide area. When the game returns for the 1932 hunting season at Fort Rae revealed, for example, that several individual hunters had taken between one hundred and two hundred caribou, Indian Agent Bourget was able to counter accusations of an illegal slaughter with the claim that all the caribou were used to feed large extended families and their dog teams.[56]

In a broad sense, it is likely that Native hunters in the many small bush camps that dotted the northern landscape simply ignored the 1929 game regulations and continued their usual patterns of hunting and trapping as if nothing had changed. There is some indication, however, that government agents at larger settlements were able to establish some measure of control over Native hunters. At the community of Pangnirtung on Baffin Island, the RCMP sergeant O.G. Petty reported in 1930 that he had persuaded many to abandon the "wasteful" practice of slaughtering pregnant females in the spring by reiterating the government's fear that the surrounding country might someday be barren of game.[57] In the late winter of 1933, the new regulations were also strictly enforced at Aklavik, where Native hunters had to request permission from the medical officer of health, J.A. Urquhart, to hunt caribou out of season because of food shortages.[58]

Despite the new restrictions on the scale and season of the caribou hunt, the general policy of Indian Affairs ironically remained the preservation of the self-sufficient hunting and trapping economy as a hedge against expanding relief costs. Thus while reports from government field agents and police officers are replete with accounts of warnings they had proffered against "wanton" caribou hunting, several also refer to the apparent laziness of Native hunters in terms of providing enough food for their families. In June 1928, Cpl. R.A. Williams reported from the Fort Reliance RCMP detachment that he had gone to great pains to impart the government's warnings against excessive caribou slaughters but that many Native hunters in the area killed only four to five caribou at a time even though the herds were abundant south of the Snowdrift River in the winter of 1927-28. Williams was "forced to the conclusion that the local Indians are too lazy to slaughter many caribou ... many camps I have visited had very little caribou meat on hand."[59] In a like manner, Sergeant Petty at Pangnirtung wrote in July 1930 that he had repeatedly discouraged the wasteful killing of caribou but had also "held out no hope of food to the lazy hunter." Petty mused that "to some degree it will seem to the native, that we, who encouraged them to hunt, now to some degree try to prevent their hunting."[60] The government's mixed message on wildlife conservation resulted at least partly from divergent emphases on Native welfare and wildlife conservation within Indian Affairs and the Northwest Territories and Yukon Branch. But the contradictory notion of self-reliance within a framework of state supervision over traditional hunting activities must have appeared to Native hunters as the outgrowth of a singular but perplexing colonial authority.

CARIBOU AND THE MINING FRONTIER

Managing the impact of the hunting and trapping economy in the Canadian North was not the only administrative problem facing federal wildlife officials at the beginning of the 1930s. In 1932, silver and pitchblende were discovered east of Great Bear Lake, and the next year gold deposits were found on the north shore of Great Slave Lake. The ensuing mineral rush dramatically transformed the northern economy: small hydroelectric dams were built, the oil fields at Norman Wells were reopened, supplies were rushed in by air and steamship, and hundreds of non-Native prospectors and labourers poured into the region. How to reconcile the needs of this new industrial economy with the older hunting and trapping life pursued by Native and some non-Native people became one of the primary questions for the northern administration.[61] In particular, meeting the subsistence needs of Native people while placating the demands of miners, prospectors, and restaurant owners for access to the most readily available local source of food – the barren ground caribou – became the subject of a pivotal debate among federal officials.

In November 1932, the Northwest Territories Council responded to the northern mining rush by limiting hunting and trapping licences only to those non-Natives who were residents of the Northwest Territories before 30 June 1932. In effect, no newcomers to the region were permitted to hunt big game or trap fur animals except in cases of extreme need.[62] The regulation appears to have had little effect, however, in the recently established mining community at Cameron Bay. In April 1933, several newspapers reported a large caribou slaughter in the Great Bear Lake region. Although the major source of the story, a miner named Bernard Day, claimed that Native hunters were entirely responsible, a subsequent investigation by RCMP Sgt. E.G. Baker and the district agent, MacKay Meikle, revealed that it was the miners who had illegally killed large numbers of caribou. Sergeant Baker recommended that posters be distributed defining the precise meaning of "dire need" and emphasizing that lawbreakers would be "rigorously prosecuted."[63] The miners at Cameron Bay did receive some sympathetic consideration from some federal officials. J.P. Richards, a senior wildlife official in the Dominion Lands Board, recommended that a special licence be issued allowing miners to take limited quantities of big game.[64] The medical officer of health at Cameron Bay wrote to the minister of the interior that a diet of preserves was insufficient for the miners and that they should be permitted to supply their own food needs until fresh meat could be imported.[65] Conversely, the RCMP super-intendent for the region adamantly opposed the extension of special hunt-ing and trapping rights to non-Native miners. He alleged that the mining community at Cameron Bay had made no effort to import food staples and recommended that the caribou herds be granted protection from new mining communities "in the interests of the native."[66]

The Northwest Territories Council reached a compromise on the issue in November 1933, deciding that non-Natives could obtain hunting and trapping licences after four years' residence in the Northwest Territories.[67] This concession had little immediate impact on the disgruntled mining community, however, as the conviction of the miner Oscar Burstad for killing caribou without a licence that same month renewed demands for hunting and trapping licences for miners. In December, the Northwest Territories Prospectors' Association requested amendments to the game regulations allowing miners and prospectors to kill a limited number of caribou.[68] The Northwest Territories Council nevertheless decided in March 1934 to maintain the status quo: non-Native miners could obtain local fresh meat only from Native hunters (or other holders of a valid hunting licence), preferably at a fair price so that Native hunters would be pro-vided with "an incentive to work."[69]

The tacit support this decision granted to the development of a market hunt for caribou meat is surprising in light of the vehement disdain that most North American wildlife conservationists had held toward this "lower class" practice since the late nineteenth century.[70] Moreover, a strictly enforced small bag limit for non-Native miners might have provided more effective protection of the caribou supply than a market system permitting unrestricted amounts of legally killed caribou to be sold to mining com-munities. Indeed, by the latter half of the 1930s, severe criticism of the commercial trade had emerged: the Hudson's Bay Company's fur trade commissioner complained that almost eight thousand caribou were sold at two mining camps; J.P. Richards also argued that the caribou trade at Yellowknife constituted a "serious drain" on the herds.[71] Roy Gibson, deputy commissioner of the NWT Council and the head of the northern admin-istration, defended the commercial hunt on the grounds that it was in the public interest to afford Native hunters an opportunity to earn cash in-come rather than depend on relief. Although Gibson later had second thoughts about the impact of the commercial slaughter, in 1936 he main-tained that caribou herds hunted near large mining communities were not threatened because they were likely to develop an "intuitive sense" of which areas to avoid during future migrations.[72]

Clearly the northern administration had stepped back somewhat from its fervent pursuit of strict caribou protective regulations in the late 1920s. As with the muskox and the wood bison, it is likely that the administrative changes that had reduced the Northwest Territories and Yukon Branch to a mere bureau within the Dominion Lands Board in 1931 – precipitating the departure of the dedicated wildlife conservationist O.S. Finnie – had dampened general enthusiasm for the development and enforcement of strict conservation measures in the Canadian North. For many northern administrators and field officers in the 1930s, the demands of the non-Native mining community for fresh meat were as important an administrative priority as conserving the caribou. Even the biologist C.H.D. Clarke – one of the first trained scientists to study the caribou and a staunch defender of the "wilderness value" of the species – declared that the commercial activities of Native hunters were "a great aid to development," and the "presence of the caribou herds a great boon to the mining development, which is the white man's portion in this country."[73] Although the distribution of meat to mining communities was not quite on the scale of earlier proposals for a full-scale caribou industry in the Northwest Territories, it shows that the northern administration still believed the commercialization and conservation of wildlife were reconcilable goals. What had once been the white man's burden in the North – the preservation of the world's last great population of herd animals – was now part of the white man's claim stake in this new mining frontier.

CARIBOU, FISH, AND EDUCATION

The focus of wildlife conservation programs in the Northwest Territories shifted perceptibly during the 1930s as federal policy makers moved away from game regulations toward measures designed to influence the hunting practices and material culture of Dene and Inuit communities. The broad program of conservation education aimed at Dene and Inuit hunters during this period included nonregulatory initiatives such as the encouragement of fishing, the development of alternative employment, and the promotion of alternative dog food. In part, this move from regulation toward subtle coercion was a product of administrative pragmatism. Both financial and human resources were extremely scarce throughout the Depression and the war years. The rigorous enforcement of comprehensive game laws that might have seemed possible in the 1920s as new RCMP outposts regularly sprang up in the Northwest Territories now seemed almost a pipe dream as detachments were closed and the number of police officers reduced.[74] Nonetheless, the "education" of Native people in the art of fishing or in "proper" hunting methods also represented the first attempts of the federal government to fundamentally alter the cultures and economies of Native northerners as a means to conserve wildlife. Beginning in the 1930s, Native hunters were not only subjected to the control of formal game regulations but were also introduced to coercive forms of instruction and supervision designed to shape their subsistence cultures in conformity with the conservation agenda of the federal wildlife bureaucracy.

In January 1934, the Department of the Interior issued a questionnaire to field agents and several non-Native trappers in the Northwest Territories asking for opinions on the status of the barren ground caribou. Both groups responded overwhelmingly that too much caribou meat was being "wasted" as dog feed on Native traplines. Dr. J.A. Urquhart professed, for example, that the Dene at Aklavik "do not look ahead to any extent and if they do not fish in September and early October they do not put up enough fish to feed their too numerous dogs with the result that without exception, by Christmas they are feeding cooked oatmeal to their dogs that they should be feeding to their children."[75] Peter McCallum, a trapper and former buffalo ranger at Fort Smith, likewise wrote that "some supervision should be insisted on to prevent too many caribou being killed for dog feed when plenty of fish [are] available in lakes." In summarizing all of this testimony for his superiors, J.P. Richards concluded that Native hunters had made no "serious" attempt to feed their dogs with fish although the majority of rivers and lake in the Northwest Territories were well stocked.[76]

Many Dene and Inuit communities undoubtedly did prefer hunting caribou to fishing, but those who accused Native people of not bothering to fish may have underestimated the importance of this secondary food source in the diets of northern hunters. Dene and Inuit hunters traditionally caught large amounts of fish, particularly when such species as whitefish and lake trout were at their most abundant during the autumn spawning season. Large catches were often frozen or dried, and fish served as an important food source for dogs during the summer and autumn season, when trapping groups were relatively stationary. But the critics of Dene and Inuit subsistence strategies may have overestimated the amount of fish available on a seasonal basis and the practical difficulties involved in eating fish on the trapline. In the winter trapping season, both dogs and humans remained on the move; packing large amounts of preserved fish or stopping frequently to chisel holes and set nets in frozen rivers and lakes where catches were not abundant was likely to be a less effective strategy than killing a moose or caribou opportunistically along the trapline and sharing the spoils between humans and dogs.[77]

Government field staff and senior wildlife officials in Ottawa neverthe-less chose to rely on the anecdotal information provided by non-Native trappers rather than make any serious effort to understand the social and ecological conditions governing Dene and Inuit subsistence practices. In June 1935, a notice was distributed throughout the Northwest Territories warning that "the use of the meat of caribou, moose or deer for dog feed in districts where fish or other kinds of food for dogs are available is not permissible (Figure 6.3)."[78] Two years later, four Native hunters from Fort Chipewyan, Alberta, were fined for killing caribou to feed their dogs while hunting in the Northwest Territories. Even Harold McGill, the director of Indian Affairs and normally a defender of subsistence harvesting, con-cluded that the four Indians were "too lazy to put up fish in the fall," and thus "they deserved no sympathy."[79] In February 1938, the Advisory Board on Wildlife Protection considered limiting each Native hunter in the Northwest Territories to seven dogs after an RCMP report described an Inuit camp of eight families with almost two hundred dogs in the Bathurst Inlet region.[80] Although the proposal never became official policy, infor-mal efforts to limit the amount of caribou used for dog feed remained a key pillar of the caribou conservation program until snowmobiles came into widespread use three decades later.

Federal officials also actively promoted as a conservation measure the idea that fish should replace caribou in the diet of the human population of the Northwest Territories. A major proponent of this policy was Dr. J.A. Urquhart, who continually pressed Native hunters in the Aklavik region to forgo caribou hunting during the September fish runs. In the autumn of 1934, Urquhart became embroiled in a heated dispute with the Indian agent, W.R.M. Truesdell, who had allowed Native hunters to take two caribou each at Arctic Red River during the summer closed season because he believed their summer supply of rabbits and fish had failed. Urquhart vigorously opposed Truesdell's decision, claiming that there were no food shortages at Arctic Red River and that it "was not a hard-ship" to survive on fish for nine to ten weeks.[81] Urquhart's policy of en-couraging fishing over hunting during the summer months in the Aklavik region received tacit support at the most senior levels of the northern administration. For example, Roy Gibson reminded the secretary of Indian Affairs in the spring of 1937 that increased fish production in Native com-munities was an important caribou conservation strategy; if the Natives

PUBLIC ◊ NOTICE

CANADA

IT is unlawful to hunt, kill or molest caribou during the close season.

All persons (including Indians, Eskimos and half-breeds) resident in the Northwest Territories are hereby warned of the consequences of excessive killing of caribou. The use of the meat of caribou, moose or deer for dog feed in districts where fish or other kinds of food for dogs are available is not permissible.

The use of the meat of big game animals as bait for fur bearers is prohibited under Section 31 of the Northwest Game Regulations.

OTTAWA,   T. G. MURPHY,

20th June, 1935   Minister of the Interior

N.W.T. & Y. 152

6.3 Caribou conservation poster, Department of the Interior, 20 June 1935. LAC, RG 85, vol. 1089, file 401-22, pt. 2

did not like fish, Gibson suggested, they could take the trouble to dry meat during the open season. The superintendent of the Mackenzie District similarly wrote that "it is not too much to ask the Indians to put up suffi- cient meat for their needs or to supplement the same with fish or rabbits during the three summer months when the protected species require com- plete protection if they are to survive."[82]

Native hunters resented the attempts of federal officials to supervise their subsistence practices and continued to oppose the imposition of for- mal game regulations throughout the 1930s. In larger towns such as Aklavik, where hunting and trapping were closely supervised, Native hunters took exception to the appeals of local officials to maintain a strict fish-only diet during the closed season on caribou.[83] There were also several formal objections in principle to any game laws that encroached upon the sover- eignty of Native people over their local resources. In November 1934, the Dene band at Fort MacPherson complained to Indian Agent Truesdell that a regulation requiring them to pay for nonresident licences to hunt on their traditional hunting grounds in the Yukon Territory violated the letter of Treaty 11.[84] During a treaty boycott at Fort Resolution in July 1937, the protesting hunters expressed pragmatic concerns that the prohi- bitions on hunting big game had resulted in almost continual hunger on the trapline. The presiding RCMP officer, Sergeant G.T. Makinson, attempted to defend the government's position by pointing to the "star- vation clause" allowing hunting during the closed seasons in cases of dire need. Makinson reported that when he "asked them if they had ever been prosecuted for taken game during the close season, they replied that they had not, but never the less they would like to have the privilege of taking Game for food during the close season."[85] Evidently, the mere idea of an outside authority usurping the traditional right to hunt and trap in the Northwest Territories had provoked the ire of the demonstrators as much as any practical difficulties imposed by the game regulations. More pre- cisely, the recognition of an unrestricted right to hunt and trap on treaty lands was a key political aspiration of the Fort Resolution hunters. Exactly which polity – the federal government or the Dene – had the right to con- trol and manage game was at the root of this conflict, and the "dire need" clause that federal wildlife officials continually promoted as evidence of the liberal nature of the game regulations did not address this fundamen- tal question.

The issue came to a head again in April 1941, when two hunters at Fort Rae, Susie Beaulieu and Edward Zoe, were charged with killing caribou during the spring migration. The RCMP officer who laid the charges,

Const. A.T. Rivett, had found both men skinning a caribou on Marian Lake and claimed that "there is certainly no legitimate reason, or excuse for the killing of caribou at this time of the year. There is none of them in dire need for food, and the widows are issued with a monthly ration from the Indian Department supplies." Chief Jimmy Bruneau saw the issue differently, however, and approached Rivett a few days after the charges were laid to argue that Native hunters had a right to kill caribou during the closed season.[86] At the treaty gathering on 7 July 1941 – where Zoe and Beaulieu were scheduled to go to trial – the Dogrib at Rae refused to take payments until the trials went ahead, claiming once again they had a treaty right to take game at any time during the closed season. After a private meeting with the local chiefs, Indian Agent J.H. Riopel was able to convince the protesters to abandon their boycott.[87] The reward for such acquiescence may have been leniency for the two hunters: although both Zoe and Beaulieu pleaded guilty, Riopel, who presided over the trial, suspended their three-month sentences.[88] Roy Gibson later attributed the controversy at Rae to Riopel's tendency to apply an "overly generous" interpretation of the "dire need" clause, which gave rise to the erroneous idea that Native hunters could kill game at any time of the year.[89] This dismissal of the Rae protests as the product of miscommunication misjudges the extent to which the Zoe and Beaulieu case was a catalyst for the expression of a long-standing political objection among Dene hunters to game regulations that violated what they understood as fundamental treaty rights.

In spite of the calls for a more vigorous prosecution in the Zoe and Beaulieu case, federal officials showed little enthusiasm for broad reforms to the Northwest Territories game regulations during the Second World War. The administrative inertia was at least partly the result of widely divergent opinions among field officers with respect to the regulations governing the sale of meat, the distribution of guns, the use of sled dogs, and the unrestricted bag limit on caribou. After consulting widely with police officers and Indian agents on these issues in the summer of 1938, the RCMP commissioner concluded that "with such a diversity of opinion it is very difficult to arrive at any suitable general regulation."[90] Undoubtedly, the federal government's preoccupation with the war and all its attendant demands on personnel and financial resources curtailed any expansive caribou conservation efforts during this period. Aside from the obvious wartime pressures, however, the advisory board records from 1939 to 1945 suggest that senior wildlife officials considered the sudden crashes in economically important fur-bearer populations to be the most pressing wildlife crisis in the Northwest Territories.[91]

The results of C.H.D. Clarke's study of wildlife conditions in and near the Thelon Game Sanctuary also probably eased the concerns of conservationists about the barren ground caribou. At the annual Dominion-Provincial Wildlife Conference in January 1939, Clarke reported that he had seen a magnificent herd of twenty thousand caribou near the Hanbury River. More important, Clarke estimated a total caribou population of three million animals, using the somewhat questionable method of transposing data on reindeer densities in Alaska to the available grazing range in the Northwest Territories. Although Clarke's estimate paled in comparison to Seton's guess of thirty million caribou, he assured the conference delegates that the earlier estimate was wholly inaccurate and thus could not be used as a baseline indicator of a dramatic crash in the caribou population. Moreover, Clarke used anecdotal reports to suggest that a human kill of 200,000 caribou combined with an annual kill of 400,000 animals by wolves was well within an approximate annual population increment of 750,000 animals. Clarke also invoked the growing concern among ecologists for achieving optimal productivity on wildlife ranges by suggesting that the annual kill might be a useful measure of control on caribou inhabiting the Arctic prairies: "It is clear that were the increase of caribou to go unchecked over the carrying capacity on which our figures are based a disaster would result. Too many caribou is just as bad as too few. Nature's whole set-up seems designed to keep them at or near an average."[92] Although stories of "indiscriminate slaughter" had passed over the desks of northern administrators throughout the 1930s, the best available scientific information at the end of the decade suggested that the overall caribou population was not under any immediate threat from human hunters.

If the crisis mentality surrounding the survival of the caribou herds had eased somewhat, in the early 1940s the northern administration still acted decisively in cases of reported threats to local caribou populations. The apparent decline of the caribou herds on Baffin Island during this period led, in fact, to one of the most intrusive conservation programs yet to be imposed upon Native hunters in the Northwest Territories. The official concern for the Baffin Island herds was spurred by a report issued in June 1943 by the RCMP constable at Lake Harbour, D.P. McLauchlan, that three Inuit families who had spent the previous winter trapping white foxes in the interior of Baffin Island near Nettilling Lake had killed between six hundred and one thousand caribou. The commanding officer for the region, D.J. Martin, deemed this number of caribou "very excessive" and instructed McLauchlan to impress upon the Inuit the need for conservation.[93] By the next winter, high fox prices had attracted fifteen families to the Nettilling Lake district. McLauchlan estimated that these trappers and their dogs would require two to three thousand caribou out of a total Baffin Island herd of fifteen thousand. Roy Gibson, D.L. McKeand (superintendent of the eastern Arctic), and other officials considered several options to curtail the Baffin Island hunt, such as the distribution of reindeer skins from the Mackenzie Delta herds and bison robes from the annual slaughter at Wood Buffalo National Park.[94]

But in the winter and spring of 1945, events increasingly persuaded northern administrators that more dramatic action was necessary to save the Baffin caribou herds. In April, an Inuit deputy police officer, Special Constable Sheutiapik, reported that the hunter Kooloola and an unnamed boy had killed twenty-nine caribou and taken only the choice cuts of meat with no intention of returning for the rest of the animals. Furthermore, the game returns from that winter revealed that two thousand animals had been taken at Nettilling Lake to support seventeen families and their dogs. As a result, McLauchlan proposed sending Kooloola's "bad influence" across the Hudson Strait to Wakeham Bay in northern Quebec, the village from where he had migrated in 1942, and instituting an absolute ban on Inuit hunters wintering inland at Nettilling Lake. The police officer argued that unless the Inuit were forced to spend the winter along the coast near Cape Dorset and Lake Harbour, where there were "plenty of seals for everyone," then the caribou on Baffin Island would become extremely scarce in just a few short years.[95] Although Kooloola eventually received only a stern lecture on "the evil effects of killing excessive caribou" when the Eastern Arctic Patrol passed through the region in July, the removal of Inuit hunters from the Nettilling Lake district was implemented informally when McLauchlan convinced the managers of the Hudson's Bay and Baffin Island Trading Companies not to outfit any hunters to spend the winter in the interior.

By 1947, dissuading Inuit hunters from wintering in the interior of Baffin Island had become official policy. After a group of Inuit hunters complained at the Pangnirtung Christmas celebrations in 1946 that two hunters from the mainland community of Igloolik, Kridluk and Panikpa, had crossed over to Nettilling Lake to trap foxes, the next October Roy Gibson ordered the police to persuade these hunters to move to Clyde River on the north coast of Baffin Island. Gibson justified this policy of coercive relocation as absolutely essential for caribou conservation, arguing that "the main thing is to get these Natives out of the interior and prevent the heavy drain on the caribou. If these methods fail to keep natives from living in the interior on caribou the only recourse will be to declare the area a game sanctuary."[96] No game sanctuary was ever established at Nettilling Lake; presumably Kridluk and Panikpa were persuaded to leave. But the federal government had shown a willingness to compel Native hunters to relocate their seasonal camps and shift their subsistence hunting patterns toward coastal marine mammals as a means of conserving the caribou.

The case of the Baffin Island Inuit provides the starkest indication that federal wildlife conservation programs had moved beyond a basic regulatory approach and instead begun to modify the hunting practices and patterns of the Dene and Inuit. During the 1930s and early 1940s, some northern administrators and federal field agents were willing to observe the game regulations in the breach, primarily to stave off destitution resulting from the collapse of the Dene and Inuit hunting and trapping economy. But the price of such benevolence seems to have been, at least in some locations, the exertion of more direct forms of authority over Dene and Inuit subsistence practices. The exhortations of the police, medical officers, and Indian agents to exploit wildlife resources other than caribou and to move away from areas of high caribou abundance as on Baffin Island suggest that the federal government was beginning to assert tentative control over the material culture of the Dene and the Inuit as a means to conserve caribou. Federal wildlife officials deemed that Dene and Inuit hunters were in need not just of a set of regulations to govern their hunting practices but also of a broad program of conservation education so they could, as the prominent conservationist Harrison Lewis described it, develop "a rational attitude toward the wild life creatures which they utilize, and on which they are largely dependent."[97]

A constructive dialogue between wildlife users and managers was clearly not a feature of the caribou conservation program at this time. Commenting on the enforcement of the summer closed season, Dr. J.A. Urquhart articulated the paternalism that permeated federal wildlife policy during the interwar years: "The Indians cannot be expected to foresee the possible results of an extensive summer hunt, and those who have the best interests of the Indians or Eskimos at heart realize that they must in a large measure do their thinking for them."[98] Such language confirms that wildlife conservation in the Canadian North was part of a broader colonial discourse, one that entailed the imposition of an outside system of wildlife management that proclaimed itself superior to the apparently thoughtless actions of Native hunters. Conservation in the Northwest Territories during this period thus became an ideological crusade rather than a purely pragmatic attempt to reverse the apparent decline of the caribou, an interjection of a supposedly rational approach to wildlife management in a region where, in the view of federal officials, none had ever existed. Yet given the speculative nature of many of the reports detailing mass caribou slaughters in the Northwest Territories and the failure of senior wildlife officials to consider contradictory evidence from their own field agents, the growth of wildlife conservation during this period appears more as a form of institutionalized social control over indigenous people than a reasoned response to a declining caribou population. Although the actual effects of both the game regulations and the conservation education programs were inconsistent across the Northwest Territories, such initiatives as the stricter enforcement of closed seasons, the promotion of fishing, the encouragement of sea mammal hunting, and the coercive relocation of people away from areas of intense hunting activity all laid the groundwork for the much more pervasive caribou conservation programs of the postwar period. Indeed, the policy framework governing caribou conservation in the Northwest Territories took on a sudden and renewed urgency in the 1950s with the advent of the so-called caribou crisis.

7

The Caribou Crisis

S HORTLY AFTER THE EASTER CELEBRATIONS at Fort Resolution in March
1947, Chief Pierre Frise of Rocher River (a small Chipewyan village
on the south shore of Great Slave Lake) returned home to find the
door to his meat shack broken open and one-quarter of his caribou supply
removed. The guilty party in this theft, Frise learned, was none other than
W.H. Day, the forest and game warden for the Fort Resolution region. It
was not the first time, moreover, that Warden Day had deprived Frise of
caribou meat. Only a few days earlier, when the chief arrived at Fort Resolution on 27 March, Warden Day had searched his belongings and found
caribou meat in his carry-all. Because the open season on caribou had ended
almost one month earlier, the warden confiscated the meat and charged
the chief with killing caribou out of season. Determined to ensure that the
charges against Frise would hold up in a court of law, Warden Day travelled sixty kilometres to Rocher River to inspect Frise's meat shed while
the Easter festivities continued at Fort Resolution. If Frise had an ample
supply of meat stored at home, Day reasoned, then the chief would not be
able to claim starvation as his justification for hunting caribou out of season. No search warrant was issued for Frise's shack; Warden Day probably
regarded his unauthorized break and entry into the premises as a minor
indiscretion that was justified in the name of preventing caribou poaching.[1]

Warden Day's aggressive law enforcement tactics provoked an angry
response from Chief Frise. In a letter to the local Indian agent, Frise complained that no notices had been posted to announce that the closed
seasons would be strictly enforced. Frise also questioned the validity of

seasonal restrictions on the caribou hunt, claiming that the closed season "can never be applied to this country as our life depends on meat all year round." He closed with the following demand: "I am hopeful, therefore, that you will be kind enough to take necessary steps to stop the Game Warden from molesting myself and my people for peace's sake."[2]

Frise's petition received some support from the most senior levels of the Indian Affairs bureaucracy. In May 1947, R.A. Hoey, director of the Indian Affairs Branch, informed Deputy Commissioner of the Northwest Territories Roy Gibson that he believed the "starvation clause" in the game regulations allowed Native hunters to take caribou at any time of the year for their own personal use. Hoey wrote that he was "disturbed" by Warden Day's breaking and entering into Frise's shed without a search warrant.[3] While Gibson conceded that Day should have obtained a warrant, and also that some leniency might be exercised for Native hunters who were first offenders against the game laws, he was nevertheless obstinate that the closed seasons must be enforced for the sake of the caribou.[4]

In many respects, this incident exemplified a renewed enthusiasm for caribou conservation among federal administrators as the government turned its attention toward civilian matters following the Second World War. In addition to Gibson's emphasis on the stringent enforcement of the closed seasons, the government introduced several new caribou protective measures in the early postwar period. In July 1947, an order-in-council made it illegal to serve caribou in restaurants, hotels, or any other institution that charged for meals. The same cabinet decree also established a caribou permit system for non-Native residents of the Northwest Territories.[5] The government had enhanced its ability to enforce the game regulations when a warden service was established in 1946 under the auspices of the superintendent of forests and wildlife for the Northwest Territories.[6] A more general growth in the number and variety of federal field agents in the Northwest Territories – welfare officers, teachers, and northern service officers (analogous to Indian agents for the Inuit, but reflecting the policy priorities of the northern administration) – also greatly furthered the ability of the government to supervise and regulate the hunting activities of Aboriginal people within their communities.[7]

Native hunters living near the caribou range responded with no more sympathy to the federal government's renewed conservation agenda than they had in previous decades. In the summer of 1947, several Indian agents from the South Slave region – L.J. Mulvihill from Fort Resolution, J.W. Stewart from Fort Chipewyan, and G.H. Gooderham, the superintendent of the Athabaska Indian agency in Alberta – wrote letters to Hoey outlining local objections to the game regulations. Local Dene hunters were angered that the enforcement of the closed seasons on moose (1 April to 1 September) and caribou (1 March to 1 September), combined with the absolute ban on hunting the wood bison, had deprived them of local fresh meat between the beginning of April and the end of August.[8] Federal officials did show some flexibility on this issue. The open season on male caribou was extended through March, allowing the people of the South Slave region to pursue their ancient tradition of procuring the summer's meat supply during this peak period in the annual northward migration.[9] Such tinkering with the dates of the closed seasons did little, however, to address the broader objection of many Native hunters to *any* enforcement of seasonal hunting restrictions on big game. In his letter to Hoey, Mulvihill reported that the grievances over the closed seasons on big game were rooted in the widespread conviction that the provisions of Treaty 8 included a perpetual guarantee of hunting and trapping rights. Mulvihill went so far as to investigate the veracity of this claim by interviewing two witnesses of the treaty signing at Fort Resolution nearly a half-century earlier, each of whom claimed independently that the government delegation had promised no game laws would ever apply to Native hunters in the treaty area. Mulvihill concluded, "They resent, and my opinion, justly so, the present restrictions on the killing of game for food, which are strictly enforced for the first time this year."[10] Such resentment was not limited to the South Slave region. In December 1947, Warden Parsons reported from the Yellowknife Game Office that the Dogrib chief at Rae, Suzi Abel, was "very disturbed" by the new caribou regulations and remained convinced that, as a matter of principle, there should be no closed season for Native hunters.[11]

Native objections had little impact on a federal wildlife bureaucracy that was determined to apply strict protective regulations to northern caribou hunters. Although spectacular stories of "wanton" caribou slaughters began to fade somewhat from the official and popular discourses on the caribou after the Second World War, a crisis mentality still pervaded the northern administration on the conservation of these animals, particularly after the first aerial surveys of the herds in the late 1940s suggested a much lower population than earlier naturalists and biologists had estimated. More important, the attitude of federal wildlife conservationists toward northern Aboriginal people did not change appreciably during this period. The Native caribou hunt was still regarded as the most severe threat to the caribou population, and the unilateral regulation and control of this hunt by the federal government was still posited as the only way to save the migratory herds of the tundra plains. Like previous caribou conservation policies, proposals to increase managerial control over the hunt did not concentrate solely on the imposition of further game regulations but also on more systemic measures to protect the caribou. The promotion of alternative resources such as fish and marine mammals, the creation of conservation education programs, and the urgent appeals to reduce the amount of caribou fed to sled dogs thus were all pillars of the caribou conservation program in the postwar era.

Official attempts to induce changes in the Dene and Inuit hunting economy became broader and more coercive during this period. As northern development became a mantra for successive governments, preserving the traditional hunting and trapping culture of the northern Native peoples receded from the social policy discourse of northern administrators after the late 1950s. (The Inuit, particularly, were under the sole jurisdiction of an increasingly activist northern administration that was much less sympathetic to the preservation of traditional hunting cultures than their counterparts within the Department of Indian Affairs.)[12] Instead, the northern administration increasingly promoted the advance of a modern industrial economy in the Canadian North, with its potential to provide wage labour for Native workers, as the only realistic means to reduce hunting pressure on the caribou. In the most extreme application of this policy, the federal government relocated Dene and Inuit communities away from the interior caribou herds to areas where they might find employment as industrial labourers. Although caribou conservation was only one of many complex influences on the relocation program, such extreme social control and engineering indicate that the measures designed to mitigate the postwar "caribou crisis" entailed much more than game regulations. By this point, caribou conservation had become one of the most important justifications of government efforts to control the economic and social life of Dene and Inuit communities.

That the Tundra Should Have No Caribou

In the spring of 1948, the Canadian Wildlife Service initiated an ambitious caribou study under the leadership of the mammalogist A.W.F. Banfield. Over the next two years, Banfield and his technical assistants – A.H. Lawrie, A.L. Wilk, John Kelsall, and the soon-to-be famous author Farley Mowat – conducted ground studies and extensive aerial surveys over the tundra and subarctic forests of the Northwest Territories. The relatively new aerial census technique put the investigation at the cutting edge of

postwar wildlife biology, and the result was a remarkably broad study of
almost every aspect of caribou biology from herd movements to rutting
behaviour.[13] Most important for federal wildlife officials, Banfield was able
to provide a population estimate of the mainland caribou herds. In his
final report, which was presented to the Advisory Board on Wildlife Protection in November 1950, Banfield claimed that the caribou herds in the
mainland Northwest Territories and the northern reaches of Alberta, Manitoba, and Saskatchewan comprised only 670,000 animals. Although one
board member, A.E. Porsild, cautioned that this figure should not be compared to the highly speculative earlier estimates of the caribou population,
the notion that the caribou numbered in the thousands rather than millions nevertheless came as something of a shock to federal wildlife officials.[14]
Even more ominous was Banfield's analysis of caribou mortality and repro-
ductive rates. In his comprehensive report, Banfield used the records of
game returns from 1932 to 1950 to estimate an annual human kill of
100,000 caribou in the Northwest Territories: 50,000 by Dene hunters,
30,000 by the Inuit, and 20,000 by non-Native hunters. His estimates of
caribou mortality suggested that wolf predation produced a further annual
loss of 34,000 animals, while disease, accidents, and inclement weather
killed the same number. Banfield projected that the annual mortality rate
from all sources was 178,000 caribou, a number that exceeded the estimated annual calf crop of 145,000 and indicated a 5 percent annual decline in the mainland caribou herds.[15] Although Banfield recognized the
influence of nonanthropogenic ecological factors such as wolf predation
and fire on the winter range, he claimed that the only possible way to stave
off the decline of the barren ground caribou was through control of the
human harvest.[16] His initial submission to the advisory board did contain
recommendations to expand predator control and fire suppression efforts,
but Banfield emphasized the importance of regulating human hunting
through restrictions on the sale of meat and hides, an expansion of the
game warden service, and conservation education programs to prevent
excessive waste on the caribou range.[17]

    Although senior wildlife officials hailed Banfield's study as the first accu-
rate assessment of the caribou population, his results were not universally
accepted as a scientific breakthrough.[18] In a review of the study forwarded
to Harrison Lewis in November 1950, Ian McTaggart-Cowan, a leading
zoologist at the University of British Columbia, questioned Banfield's use
of straight aerial transect lines, a technique that was notoriously inaccurate for a species with such uneven distribution across its range. Indeed, a
glance at the map of Banfield's transect lines reveals an entirely random

network of widely spaced flight paths that were surveyed over an extremely lengthy study period of twenty-four months. McTaggart-Cowan believed that more refinement of this technique was needed: "No reasons are given for assuming accuracy to within 20% and I doubt that the approximation is as close as that. Experiments with deer on limited areas have shown departures from accuracy greatly exceeding this." Based on the speculative nature of the survey results, McTaggart-Cowan disputed Banfield's population estimate and claimed that the total caribou population might still number as many as one million, a figure that suggested no dramatic overall decline if conservative appraisals of the mainland herds in the nineteenth and early twentieth centuries were used as a baseline. The UBC zoologist concluded that population shifts in the caribou population were regional in nature rather than a range-wide phenomenon; therefore regulations that might cause hardship to Native hunters should be imposed only in areas where the local caribou herds were definitely in decline.[19]

Almost four years passed between Banfield's original presentation of his results and the printing of his final report, but there is little indication he incorporated McTaggart-Cowan's criticisms of his work into the manuscript. Although Banfield did suggest that the caribou decline was concentrated regionally in four areas at the northern edge of the migratory routes, he still posited a range-wide annual decline of 32,000 animals. Even with four years to strengthen his arguments in support of this claim, the evidence Banfield marshalled in support of an absolute decline in the barren ground caribou population remained unconvincing at best. To begin with, his calculation for all sources of caribou mortality – a human kill of 100,000, wolf predation of 34,000, and 34,000 additional deaths from disease, weather, and accidents – amounted to an annual mortality of 168,000 animals, not the figure of 178,000 cited in the 1954 report.[20] Whether this was a typographical mistake, a mathematical error, or the omission of an additional cause of caribou mortality, the deaths of 10,000 caribou remain unaccounted for. Moreover, Banfield was aware that other sources of data contradicted his theory of a universal decline in the barren ground caribou. His analysis of the annual departmental caribou questionnaires that had been distributed throughout the Northwest Territories since 1934 revealed, for example, "no clear cut trend in the ratio of the 'increase' [to decrease] reports that would indicate a regular decline."[21] To further complicate the issue, Banfield acknowledged that his research team had not gathered sufficient data to determine the annual loss of caribou to wolf predation and the combined effects of disease, accidents, and weather. The mortality rate of 5 percent he assigned to each of these influences was based on a 1935 study of domesticated reindeer herds in Siberia.[22]

Despite such imprecision, Banfield blamed the impending population decline primarily on Dene and Inuit hunters. He attributed the entire annual caribou deficit to the "improvident and wasteful hunting techniques of the native population" and roundly condemned feeding caribou meat to dogs, careless caching of meat, and the slaughter of caribou beyond the limits of personal need.[23] Unlike many of the earlier reports of wanton Native hunting practices in the Far North, Banfield's report did at least furnish two first-hand accounts of wastage. In August 1948, A.H. Lawrie observed Inuit hunters leaving several whole caribou for later use as dog food on the shores of Nueltin Lake, all of which were lost after rising water froze over the carcasses. Banfield also saw some Inuit hunters fail to utilize several downed caribou and allow an unspecified number of wounded animals to escape during a summer hunt near Contwoyto Lake in 1949.[24] Beyond these two examples, however, Banfield's report did not prove that these practices were widespread and systemic, or that they could account for the annual deficit in the caribou herds. Instead of a quantitative account of the actual impact the allegedly wasteful Dene and Inuit hunting practices might be having on the herds, Banfield defended his allegations of widespread waste with a broad reference to the rumours of caribou slaughters that had been circulating since the late nineteenth century: "Such wastage has been reported by many writers during the last century and the early part of the present century ... From interviews with wardens, traders, missionaries, and trappers in the northern parts of the provinces and the Northwest Territories it is known that excessive wastage is widespread throughout the whole range of the caribou and is indulged in by Indians, Eskimos, and some European Trappers."[25] The possibility that some of these accounts might be the product of local rivalries and the prejudices of outsiders is never discussed in Banfield's report. Wildlife management according to rumour and anecdote thus maintained a residual significance in this apparently modern work of biological science.

The circulation of Banfield's study prompted the creation of a much broader series of game regulations to govern the Dene and Inuit caribou harvest. In December 1951, the NWT Council, which had been granted the exclusive authority to create game regulations under the territorial ordinances after the Northwest Game Act was repealed in 1949, strengthened an existing regulation prohibiting the use of caribou for dog feed when other sources of food were "reasonably available" by banning the practice – widely loathed among federal officials – of feeding caribou to dogs within settled areas.[26] A proposal to restrict the market hunt in the Northwest Territories also gained bureaucratic momentum. This effort was in part a response to long-standing pressure from game administrators in Saskatchewan and Manitoba, who had for many years prohibited white settlers in northern communities from purchasing wild game. The northern administration and Indian Affairs had previously deflected criticism with accusations that the licensing of "outside" sport hunters to kill caribou under provincial regulations did much more to harm the credibility of the caribou conservation program in the eyes of Native hunters.[27] But as Banfield's results began to circulate among federal wildlife officials and northern administrators before the official release of his report, many began to target the local sale of caribou meat as anachronistic in light of the scientific data on the caribou population. The revisions to the game ordinance for 1950 took a small step toward this policy goal, limiting the right to sell caribou meat only to those hunters who held a valid general hunting licence – essentially all Native hunters and the few non-Natives who had held a valid NWT hunting and trapping licence on 3 May 1938. The result was an effective ban on the distribution of caribou meat in trading posts and grocery stores throughout the Northwest Territories.[28]

The new restrictions on the sale of caribou meat provoked at least some opposition from the local population at Fort Resolution. In July 1950, several Native hunters wrote to their member of Parliament, J. Aubrey Simmons, to protest.[29] The superintendent of the Indian agency at Fort Resolution, I.F. Kirkby, suggested in his report on local game conditions that there was widespread opposition because Native hunters could no longer stockpile meat killed during the fall migration by selling it to the local store and buying it back over the course of the winter trapping season. This ad hoc arrangement had allowed them to obtain both badly needed funds in advance of the trapping season and a freezer in which to store meat from the autumn caribou hunt. For Kirkby, the new regulations had all the markings of a policy initiative that paid little heed to local conditions.[30]

Further opposition to this regulation came from within the ranks of the Canadian Wildlife Service. Ward Stevens, a biologist with the CWS who was serving as district administrator in Aklavik, had written to Harrison Lewis in July to argue that the number of caribou killed for the purposes of sale was relatively small, but still necessary in many communities because of the "primitive conditions" that prevailed in the Northwest Territories.[31] The resident CWS biologist at Wood Buffalo National Park, William Fuller, was even blunter, calling the sale issue a "bogey" that was diverting attention from the more serious problem of wastage. Fuller recommended a "buck law" as the most effective means to conserve the caribou population.[32] The issue was finally resolved with a compromise amendment to the game ordinance in 1951 permitting Native hunters alone to sell caribou within twenty miles of a major settlement. An outright ban on trafficking caribou near large, well-supplied communities such as Yellowknife and Fort Smith was finally implemented in July 1952.[33]

Although the controversy over the issue of selling caribou meat did signal some diversity of opinion among CWS biologists, Banfield's allegations of a scarce caribou population hardened attitudes among several federal wildlife officials toward the Aboriginal caribou harvest. Some biologists, such as Stevens and Fuller, continued to espouse the maintenance of the traditional Aboriginal food supply as the fundamental goal of the caribou conservation program – in effect, reconciling the demands of the Native hunting economy with a philosophy that upheld the controlled use of game resources as the highest end of wildlife conservation. But others had concluded from Banfield's study that the relatively liberal game regulations in the Northwest Territories were incompatible with the principles of modern wildlife management. During the advisory board's discussion of the resolution to ban the sale of caribou, the chief of the CWS, Harrison Lewis, invoked the "conclusive" evidence in Banfield's report to argue that when the "learned commission" of 1900 guaranteed perpetual hunting and trapping rights in their treaty promises, they could not have envisioned the kind of wildlife management that would be necessary in the future.[34] The CWS biologist John Kelsall also passionately advocated the idea that caribou conservation measures must supersede even the most basic subsistence requirements of the Dene and Inuit population. Kelsall argued that, though the game regulations could not be enforced efficiently without causing hardship among the Inuit, any effort to cut down the caribou harvest "should be given all consideration possible."[35] The more utilitarian concerns of previous decades – the protection of the Aboriginal food supply and the possible commercial exploitation of the caribou – were no longer at the forefront of caribou conservation strategies in the Northwest Territories. This shift toward a more rigid preservationist philosophy among many CWS biologists strengthened as scientific research suggested further declines in the caribou population throughout the 1950s.

THE FORMATION OF THE CARIBOU CRISIS

In the years immediately following the completion of Banfield's study, scattered reports suggested that the cause of barren ground caribou conservation was not hopeless. A flood of new population data from the Canadian Wildlife Service's continued caribou survey work under the leadership of John Kelsall revealed no clear evidence of a dramatic decline in their population between 1951 and 1953. Although the caribou study was confined for budgetary reasons to the herds migrating between the north side of Great Bear Lake and Great Slave Lake, the so-called Great Bear Lake herd and Radium herd showed a marked increase. Only the Rae herd showed a severe decline, from Banfield's estimate of 210,000 caribou to 138,000 animals in 1951, and a further drop two years later to an estimated 40,000 animals in what Kelsall described as a "widely scattered" caribou herd.[36] Kelsall concluded, however, that the severe decline in the Rae herd could not be attributed to human utilization and disease because the mortality rates from these factors were nowhere near the level where they could cause such a spectacular decimation of the population. In addition, calf counts for these caribou conducted over the winter of 1952-53 had been very high, suggesting an annual herd increment of 29.5 percent. Kelsall therefore reasoned that a major shift in the population had occurred, with over 150,000 caribou migrating to calving grounds east of Bathurst Inlet.[37] Local testimony and Kelsall's own ground and aerial study also suggested that a herd of caribou numbering from 126,000 to 176,000 had inexplicably taken up year-round residence in the Arctic coast region in 1951 and that more than 100,000 animals had remained in the area throughout the winter of 1952-53.[38] As well as pointing to the difficulty of tracking the erratic movements of the caribou, the population data suggested no rapid decline in the Rae herd but a massive outmigration. Indeed, Kelsall's population estimates for the study herds show an increase of almost 70,000 caribou from the time of Banfield's estimates (see Table 7.1).

In spite of figures suggesting an expansion of the caribou population in the best-case scenario, and ambiguity due to erratic herd movements in the worst, Kelsall remained pessimistic about the prospect of conserving the barren ground herds in the Northwest Territories. At a meeting of federal and provincial game officials in June 1953 to discuss the status of the herds, Kelsall dismissed reports from Manitoba and Saskatchewan indicating exceptionally large calf numbers and "heavy" caribou migrations throughout the winter range. And while Kelsall acknowledged the difficulty of estimating the population of the Rae herd due to "variations in distribution," he largely de-emphasized his own herd drift theory by stating that the caribou in this area were "heavily utilized" and "in great danger of being depleted," despite limited data on human utilization of the caribou herds between Great Bear and Great Slave lakes.[39] Perhaps sensing the uncertain nature of the available evidence, the meeting delegates concluded that the existing game regulations in all jurisdictions were adequate for the present.

Kelsall's report did nevertheless inspire a resolution calling for a major federal-provincial co-operative resurvey over the entire range of the barren ground caribou.[40]

In all likelihood, federal wildlife officials expected the new survey to reveal at least some reduction in the caribou population. In the three years since Kelsall had taken control of the caribou study, the public perception of chronic game shortages in the Northwest Territories had become more widespread. Reports of starvation among the inland Inuit of the Keewatin region reached a wide audience through the books and popular articles of such authors as the American biologist Francis Harper and his one-time field assistant Farley Mowat.[41] But perhaps no warning signs could have prepared federal wildlife officials for the catastrophic survey results that appeared in the summer of 1955. According to Kelsall and his co-investigator, Alan Loughrey, the mainland caribou herds had declined to a mere 278,900 animals in the six years since Banfield's estimate of 670,000 animals. The two biologists claimed that their aerial survey was so comprehensive that no significant caribou herds could have been missed in all the mainland range.[42]

The news from further studies only worsened. In 1957, Kelsall was placed in charge of a herd-specific air and ground survey that was undertaken in lieu of a third costly range-wide aerial survey.[43] The new study focused primarily on the large caribou herd that migrated from a winter range in the boreal forests of northern Saskatchewan to spring calving grounds on the tundra in the vicinity of Beverly Lake. Although Kelsall found a dramatic increase in the study herd from 79,354 caribou in 1955 to 142,500 in 1957-58, he assumed that the enlarged population was due entirely to migrations

TABLE 7.1   Caribou population estimates from Great Bear Lake and Great Slave Lake to the Arctic coast, 1948-52

Herd or area	Banfield's survey (1948-49)	Continuing survey (1950-52)
Colville Lake	5,000	–
Great Bear Lake	30,000	34,000
Point MacDonnel	–	11,000
Radium	5,000	10,000
Rae	210,000	138,000
Yellowknife	4,000	–
Adelaide and Sherman Gulfs	500	–
Coastal Caribou	–	126,000
Total	254,500	319,000

SOURCE: John Kelsall, *Continued Barren-Ground Caribou Studies,* Wildlife Management Bulletin, Series 1, No. 12 (Ottawa: Canadian Wildlife Service, 1957), 93.

from the Keewatin caribou herds to the east and the Rae herd to the west. Even more remarkably, Kelsall estimated from a limited survey that the caribou population north of Great Bear Lake numbered only 16,000. Furthermore, he used anecdotal evidence of scarce caribou in northern Manitoba to conclude that the Keewatin herds "certainly numbered less than 40,000," down from 150,000 only two years earlier. Based on all this ambiguous data, Kelsall concluded that the mainland caribou population had declined to a mere 200,000 animals.[44] The CWS biologist placed the responsibility for this apparently grave situation squarely on the shoulders of Native hunters: "The fact that Treaty Indians are not subject to restrictive legislation [in the provinces] has been an obstacle to the maintenance and increase of the caribou population."[45]

Was the caribou population as imperilled by the hunting activities of Native people as Kelsall claimed? Certainly his analysis had an intuitive appeal: too many hunters with guns, too many sled dogs, and too few caribou could only lead to a significant and inevitable crash in the caribou population. But human hunting was only one cause of caribou mortality on the northern range: wolf predation, deep snow, fire on the winter range, and the effect of severe weather on calving could all limit the caribou population. Kelsall's second study did in fact contain a great deal of research on a broad range of ecological factors affecting the caribou herds. His investigation indicated, for example, that forest fires on the caribou's winter range had severely reduced the abundance of their preferred sources of food, such as fruticose lichens. Of course, fire is inherent to the ecology of the taiga forest, but Kelsall claimed that the amount of burning had greatly increased during the mining rush of the 1930s, as prospectors intentionally scorched large areas to clear vegetation from rock surfaces. Thus any large-scale decline in the caribou population might partly be explained by a severe reduction in suitable winter range in the years before the war.[46] A separate study of the relationship between weather and calf survival also suggested a shorter-term limitation on the caribou population: severe wind chill during the calving season might have accounted for extremely low herd increments from 1955 to 1957.[47] Although his own research program pointed to a varied and complex array of ecological influences on the caribou population, Kelsall nevertheless continued to highlight the human hunt as the most significant threat facing the northern herds. The annual caribou kill by hunters in the Northwest Territories had declined to under 15,000 animals, but Kelsall argued in the report of his second study that this rate of human utilization might completely eliminate the caribou population by 1969.[48]

Kelsall's dire predictions of the imminent demise of the mainland herds may have rested on a broadly inaccurate scientific analysis, however. In 1971, the CWS biologist Gerry Parker published a study that questioned the accuracy of Kelsall and Loughrey's population figures, arguing that such factors as the use of wide aerial transects ranging from 0.71 to 1.42 miles, aerial coverage of less than 5 percent of the caribou range, the limited use of aerial photographs, and the failure to adjust population figures for caribou outside the study area or those missed within taiga forests all pointed to an excessively low estimate of the caribou population in 1955. Using the analytical standards of a population survey conducted in 1967, Parker adjusted Kelsall and Loughrey's numbers for the western mainland herds upward from 257,700 to a total of 390,000 caribou.[49] But even with this revision, Kelsall and Loughrey's estimates remain highly questionable. More recent critics have suggested that the potential for error in a range-wide caribou study is difficult to quantify. One group of biologists who conducted a survey of Alaskan caribou in the early 1980s concluded that aerial surveys based on less than 10 percent coverage of the range were "little more than quantitative wild guesses."[50] With such coarse methods and little baseline data to draw on, the studies of Banfield, Kelsall, and Loughrey reveal little about whether the caribou population in the 1950s was stable, had suffered a moderate downturn since the turn of the century, or was in a state of precipitous decline as the CWS biologists claimed.

LIMITING THE CARIBOU HUNT, LIMITING ABORIGINAL RIGHTS

Although Kelsall's caribou surveys included a degree of speculation and conjecture, federal wildlife officials and northern administrators accepted the results with little reservation. Indeed, the assertion that the caribou population had declined from countless millions at the turn of the century to less than one-quarter million at the end of the 1950s provoked the declaration of a "caribou crisis."[51] Immediately after the results of Kelsall's first range-wide survey were released in June 1955, Gordon Robertson, the deputy minister of northern affairs and national resources and commissioner of the Northwest Territories, informed Minister Jean Lesage that the results were "extremely disturbing" and called for abrupt government action to avoid public criticism.[52] At a meeting of federal and provincial wildlife officials held in October 1955 to discuss the situation, delegates generally agreed that Native hunters were "in the right" to kill caribou for their own sustenance and thus supported the decision of the Northwest Territories Council in January 1955 to allow holders of a general hunting licence (Dene, Inuit, and long-time non-Native residents) to kill big game at any time of the year for food purposes.[53] The delegates also concluded, however, that all forms of wastage, including improper caching of meat and the use of caribou for dog feed, should be eliminated through comprehensive conservation education. Where allegations of wasteful slaughters persisted, the delegates proposed stationing a game officer in the area to curb the intensity of the caribou hunt. Fire suppression on the winter range of the caribou was thought to be too expensive, but delegates did recommend expansion of existing predator control programs and the distribution of freezers to aid with the storage of meat killed in the summer months. The most important result of the meeting was the creation of a new federal-provincial Administrative Committee for Caribou Preservation whose purpose was to provide policy recommendations to senior levels of government based on the advice of a separate technical committee composed primarily of CWS scientists and provincial game officers.[54]

The renewed enthusiasm for caribou conservation among the meeting delegates produced several immediate results. Predator control operations begun in the winter of 1952-53 were greatly expanded as strychnine baits were distributed more widely and professional hunters were hired to increase the kill of wolves in the Northwest Territories.[55] The NWT game ordinance was also amended to curtail caribou hunting activities by non-Natives. A regulation allowing special licences for newcomers to the Northwest Territories to take five caribou annually was, for example, rescinded in 1956. That same year, the NWT Council passed a regulation to limit all holders of a general hunting licence who were no longer dependent on "country food" to only one of each big game species per year. Finally, the council effectively banned the sale of caribou to non-Natives in January 1957 by limiting the privilege of buying caribou only to those who held a general hunting licence.[56]

For the most part, these new conservation measures reflected the long-standing policy of preserving the northern food supply primarily for the Dene and Inuit population. Nonetheless, the apparent gravity of the caribou crisis impelled conservationists within government to at least consider more stringent game regulations on Aboriginal subsistence hunters. Some of these were limited in scope, such as the caribou hunting ban that was implemented on Coats and Southampton islands in May 1957 because of reports of a severe decline in the caribou population.[57] Through the late 1950s, however, senior wildlife officials at the federal and particularly the provincial level became increasingly dismissive of the treaty provisions guaranteeing perpetual Aboriginal hunting and trapping rights within the caribou range. Although federal officials had long maintained that the treaties allowed the government to impose game regulations on the Aboriginal hunters of the Northwest Territories, the terms of the Natural Resources Transfer Agreement of 1930 unquestionably prevented the provincial governments from imposing any regulations on the subsistence hunting activities of treaty Indians. This constitutional arrangement meant that any new regulation proposed by the Administrative or Technical Committees for Caribou Conservation would have no effect on Aboriginal hunters on the winter ranges in northern Manitoba, Saskatchewan, and Alberta. At the administrative committee meeting held in October 1957, federal and provincial officials called for a review of treaties and agreements that limited the imposition of conservation measures on the caribou range. This resolution suggested much more than a pragmatic attempt to implement extreme conservation measures such as regional quotas or a five-year closed season on the species. Indeed, the committee adopted a rigidly liberal ideological approach to regulating the caribou harvest, arguing that all hunters should have an equal right to harvest limited resources irrespective of their ethnicity. The final text of the resolution thus rejected any notion of collective Aboriginal rights to a traditional food source that was the material base of Dene and Inuit culture for centuries. It also emphasized the importance of removing the "discriminatory" hunting privileges accorded to treaty Indians.[58]

To justify the abrogation of Aboriginal treaty rights to hunt and trap, federal and provincial wildlife officials argued that state controls over the caribou hunt would benefit Native hunters over the long term. In just one of many examples, Ben Sivertz, the new director of the Northern Administration and Lands Branch, wrote in December 1957 that his sympathies for the "moral obligation" to uphold treaty rights were superseded by the notion "that if the caribou are to be saved we must have adequate legislation applicable to all, regardless of racial origin." It was "in the interest of the Indians to preserve the caribou," and the surrender of their political rights was necessary to save "a resource that is as important, if not more important, to the Indians as any other racial group."[59] Such sentiments represented one of the most thoroughly paternalistic aspects of the federal government's approach to wildlife conservation during this period. According to the conservationist orthodoxy, Native hunters could no longer manage their own affairs; their political rights and freedoms only impeded the more rational guiding hand of state wildlife managers in efforts to save the Dene and Inuit from their own worst excesses.

Almost inevitably, however, the proposal to abrogate Aboriginal treaty rights as part of the caribou conservation program elicited protests from Indian Affairs. In December 1957, Edmund Fulton, the minister responsible for Indian affairs, wrote to the minister of northern affairs, Alvin Hamilton, that the application of strict caribou regulations, particularly if they contained no "starvation clause," would violate the spirit of the treaties both in the provinces and in territories under federal jurisdiction.[60] Hamilton's reply, which was drafted by Sivertz, stated that his department was determined to move ahead with restrictive legislation regardless of Fulton's concerns. The letter claimed that the treaties provided the federal government with the authority to apply game laws that superseded the right to hunt for food. After all, treaty rights to hunt for food would be meaningless if the caribou became extinct.[61]

In accordance with such sentiment, officials within Northern Affairs enacted several broad "non-discriminatory" measures to limit the caribou harvest of Native hunters in the Northwest Territories. In March 1958, the Northwest Territories Council voted to implement one of the administrative committee's key recommendations from the previous year's meeting: the hunting of female caribou east of the Mackenzie River and all caribou under one year old was banned for all in the Northwest Territories, with no "starvation clause" or other formal exemption for Dene or Inuit subsistence hunters. At the same time, feeding caribou meat suitable for human consumption to any domestic animal was banned everywhere in the Northwest Territories, a provision with the potential to cause severe hardship in outlying bush camps where Native hunters depended on sled dogs for transportation. Law enforcement officials were asked to be lenient when infractions did not constitute a repeat offence or a vaguely defined "flagrant violation" of the regulations. The advent of the caribou crisis, however, had led wildlife officials to implement broad restrictions on the caribou harvest regardless of the subsistence requirements of Dene and Inuit hunters.[62]

For all the enthusiasm among federal officials for stricter game regulations in the Northwest Territories, legislative responses to caribou conservation remained limited in scope and effect throughout the provincially controlled portions of the caribou range. Most important, the issue of granting the provinces authority to regulate the Aboriginal harvest was never resolved, despite lengthy negotiations over revisions to the Natural Resources Transfer Agreement. The issue may simply not have been a high priority for the federal cabinet. At a December 1961 meeting of the Administrative Committee for Caribou Preservation, the provincial delegates pushed through a resolution registering their "amazement" that the federal government had taken no action on the necessary legislative amendments that it had proposed three months earlier.[63] When the relevant federal agencies (Indian Affairs, Northern Affairs, and the CWS) again forwarded legislative amendments to cabinet in the spring of 1963, once more no action was taken.[64] At a meeting of the administrative committee held in January 1964, E.L. Paynter, director of fish and game in Saskatchewan, was resigned to the fact that "any program designed to control the killing of caribou must take for granted that nothing can be done with native rights."[65] Of course, the federal government could enact protective legislation in the Northwest Territories, but the continued inability of the provinces to regulate the Aboriginal caribou harvest created a politically awkward situation. Proceeding with some of the more draconian proposals, such as regional quotas or a closure of the caribou season for five years, was bound to spark intense protests and civil disobedience in many Native communities if their counterparts in the provinces were permitted a de facto unregulated caribou hunt.

Federal officials had in fact already received many reports in the late 1950s suggesting that the imposition of strict game regulations in both the provinces and the territories had provoked anger and frustration among the Native population. The Indian Affairs field officer W.G. Turnstead reported in November 1957, for example, that Native hunters at Stony Rapids and Stony Lake, Saskatchewan, had refused to accept hunting permits in response to a legally questionable attempt by provincial game officials to restrict the Native harvest to two caribou per hunter.[66] The unwillingness of the Native population to accept the new quota was so widespread through northern Saskatchewan in the winter of 1957-58 that the regulation proved unenforceable.[67] In a like manner, the chief at Fort Rae, Jimmy Bruneau, responded to the federal cabinet's designation of the caribou as an endangered species by informing Indian Affairs that caribou hunting was a fundamental political right and a part of Dene cultural heritage. According to Bruneau, the Dene hunters at Rae would make every effort to conserve the animals, but they insisted upon the right to kill cows and calves in violation of the game regulations when no other food was available.[68]

At times, even the northern administration's own field officers objected to some of the most severe proposals to change the game regulations. In October 1962, T.H. Butters, the area administrator at Baker Lake, recommended against a proposal from the Technical Committee for Caribou Conservation to strictly prohibit the feeding of any part of the caribou to dogs regardless of whether it was fit for human consumption. Butters claimed that "the land hunter who respects and obeys the law would fore-seeably jeopardize the well-being of his family, lose his teams to starvation, and ultimately be forced into the settlement." A clear majority of field officers who responded to a query on the issue of dog feed supported But-ters' analysis of the proposed regulation.[69]

With both Native hunters and many northern field officers objecting to some of the key policy initiatives of senior wildlife administrators, there was clearly little hope that comprehensive and strict game regulations could be adhered to or enforced in many parts of the Northwest Territories. At an administrative committee meeting held in October 1964, David Munro, the chief of the Canadian Wildlife Service, concluded that legislation to protect the caribou had largely been ineffective because "it evoked little sympathy before the magistrates and the number of enforcement person-nel was small." Munro also claimed that "key administrative agencies ... have seemed unable to accept the fact that [the] human kill has taken any prominent part in the ten- or twenty-fold decrease that has quite obviously occurred."[70] As Munro suggested, too many legal, political, and adminis-trative obstacles stood in the way of far-reaching game regulations to pro-tect the barren ground caribou. Moreover, opponents of stricter game reg-ulations believed many Dene and Inuit communities were so entwined with the seasonal migrations of the caribou that they were not likely to survive a rigidly enforced set of limitations on their slaughter. Almost from the beginning of the caribou crisis, wildlife conservationists thus began to focus less on limiting the caribou hunt through formal regulations and more on a wide-ranging program designed to fundamentally alter the cari-bou culture of northern Aboriginal people.

Controlling Livelihoods, Controlling Lives

By the late 1950s, nonlegislative conservation measures had begun to dominate the federal government's strategy for reversing the apparent decline of the barren ground caribou. This policy shift within the north-ern administration was a response not only to the relative failure of legislative initiatives but also to the willingness of the Department of Indian Affairs to invest a great a deal of money and personnel to support conservation programs that did not threaten the hunting rights of treaty Indians.[71] Several of the Indian Affairs programs – the distribution of high-powered rifles to reduce "crippling loss" among the caribou herds, the sponsorship of predator control hunts, and the construction of underground freezers for the year-round storage of caribou meat – were relatively benign conservation initiatives in terms of their social impacts. But the northern administration (and in some cases Indian Affairs) also promoted several programs that entailed a much more profound upheaval of the human ecology of the Northwest Territories. The distribution of imported foods to Native communities in need, the promotion of fish and marine mammal resources among suitably located communities, and the intensification of conservation education programs were all promoted as the only realistic means to divert human hunting pressure from the remaining caribou herds. The breadth and the reach of such programs suggests that the institutional practice of wildlife conservation had become an integral part of the federal government's postwar programs to control and transform the hunting cultures of northern Aboriginal people.

The colonial discourse behind the caribou conservation program is perhaps most readily revealed in the attempts by the Department of Northern Affairs to "educate" Native hunters on the principles of caribou conservation. Before the onset of the caribou crisis in 1955, conservation education was less a concrete program than an abstract assortment of infrequent poster campaigns and appeals for field officers to do more work with the Natives to prevent wastage or excessive slaughter. After 1955, however, the department produced a broad range of more formal educational material such as filmstrips, booklets, and curriculum supplements for local schools. Much of this material is remarkable for its patronizing tone, as if the intended audience were children rather than adult hunters. A filmstrip commentary claimed, for example, that "in years when there are many animals, food is plentiful and the Eskimos are fat and happy." But because of the impact of wolves and rifles on the caribou, "soon few animals will be left. The herds will become smaller and smaller and the Eskimos will be starving and cold." In subsequent frames, Native hunters were introduced to an RCMP officer who will "tell the Eskimos how they may help save the caribou." His suggestions included digging out wolves' dens, following and killing wounded animals, not killing cows in spring, and "killing only what is needed and not shooting every animal that is to be seen. This is the way young and foolish hunters do much harm because they do not know any better."[72]

In 1956, the department issued a similar publication that can only be described as a children's storybook. Titled *Tuktut*, the Inuktitut word for "caribou," the slim booklet featured simple passages offering advice on caribou conservation with cartoon-like line drawings on the facing pages (see Figure 7.1). Near its beginning, Inuit readers were given a lesson in the government's interpretation of their history: "Your forefathers saw many more caribou than you now see. Had there not been careless killing, this would not be so." Having been informed that any decline in the caribou was solely their own fault, with no mention of itinerant whalers or hide traders at the turn of the century, readers were then instructed in several basic principles of caribou conservation: gather all parts from any animal killed, catch fish to feed dogs, cache meat properly, and kill wolves whenever possible. At one point, the book suggests the time may have come for the Inuit to abandon the caribou hunt due to its inherent inefficiency: "Many of the people live by the sea but they travel by Kamutik [dogsled] far inland to hunt deer. The dogs eat most of the meat from the hunt. When they return they have almost nothing."[73]

Both the form and content of *Tuktut* are imbued with paternalism and condescension toward Inuit culture. The historical analysis manages to mock the hunting culture of the Inuit; the storybook format reinforces the idea that they are childlike in the eyes of the government. Not surprisingly, many Inuit hunters reacted with disdain when northern service officers began to distribute the book throughout the Arctic. On 31 August 1956 an article headlined "Eskimos Deride Ottawa Comics" appeared in the *Edmonton Journal.* The report cites a meeting of the Northwest Territories Council where the elected member from Aklavik, Frank Carmichael, informed his colleagues that *Tuktut* was a "joke among the Eskimos ... He said Eskimos, when given the book, illustrated in comic book fashion, say 'what do you think we are, little children?'"[74] The article provoked Ben Sivertz, at this time chief of the Arctic Division, to solicit opinions on the booklet from all his northern service officers. Although several of these field officers reported no adverse reaction to *Tuktut*, their accounts must be interpreted with caution. For instance, the NSO at Aklavik dismissed Carmichael's comments because one Inuit trapper, Donald Gordon, had found the book interesting.[75] The NSO at Cambridge Bay reported no criticism but also recounted a meeting where resident hunters had complained they could not understand the booklet because it was not printed in the local dialect.[76] Other reports that the booklet was "favourably received" in Frobisher Bay and Churchill may not preclude the possibility that Inuit criticism proceeded behind the backs of the local government field staff.[77] Regardless, at Fort Chimo, Quebec, the NSO regretfully reported that *Tuktut* was received with "cynical amusement."[78] This negative reaction on the part of some Inuit did not inspire a less paternalistic approach to conservation education. When reports of the negative reaction to *Tuktut* reached the volume's illustrator, the northern service officer James Houston, he replied that he was "attempting to imitate the Eskimo style of serious cartoon in

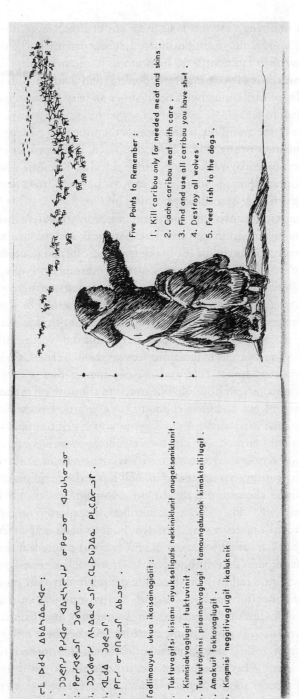

Five Points to Remember:

1. Kill caribou only for needed meat and skins.
2. Cache caribou meat with care.
3. Find and use all caribou you have shot.
4. Destroy all wolves.
5. Feed fish to the dogs.

ᑕᒪ ᐃᕕᐊ ᐃᐸᐃᓴᐃᓐᐊᒋᐊᓕᑦ:

. ᑐᑑᑎᐱ ᑭᓯᐊᓂ ᐊᐃᔪᐠᓴᓕᒍᑎ ᓀᐠᑭᓂᑯᓂ ᐊᓄᐊᐠᓴᓂᐠᓗᓂ .
. ᑭᓂᓯᐊᐠᕙᒍᒋᑦ ᑐᐠᑐᕕᓂᑦ .
l. ᑐᐠᑐᑕᔨᓂᓯ ᐱᓴᐃᓇᐠᕙᒍᒋᑦ - ᑕᒪᐅᓇᒐᑐᐃᓇᐠ ᑭᒪᐠᑕᐃᓕᓗᒋᑦ .
l. ᐊᒪᑯᐃᑦ ᑐᐠᑯᕙᒍᒋᑦ .
. ᑭᖕᒥᓯ ᓀᒋᑎᕙᒍᒋᑦ ᐃᐸᓗᐠᓂᐠ .

ᑕᒪ ᐃᕕᐊ ᐃᐸᐃᓐᐊᐃᕐᖓᑦ :

. ᑐᐱᑎ ᐱᕆᐊᑦ ᐊᐊᐱᑕᓯ ᓱᑉᒥᓐᑦᖓ ᐱᑕᐅᓕᑖᐅᓐᒥ .
. ᓴᐅᔭᕆᓯ ᑐᒃᑖ .
l. ᑐᐠᑕᐠᓴᓂ ᐊᓕᐊᒍᐃᓂ - ᑕᒪᐅᐱᐅᐊᐃ ᑎᒪᐸᐃᐃᓂ .
l. ᐊᕕᑖ ᑐᐠᐊᑐᔭ .
. ᐅᑦᒋ ᖡᓯ ᐊᐱᓯᑦ ᐃᐱᒍᒋ ᐃᐱᓱᓐᐊᓯ ᐃᕕᐊᒍ .

7.1 Page from the conservation booklet *Tuktut*, distributed throughout the Arctic by the Department of Northern Affairs and National Resources in 1956. Northwest Territories Archives N-1992-023, box 33, file 4 this booklet, knowing that this would appeal to those more naïve and charming Eskimo hunters living east of the Mackenzie Delta."[79] Nor did the negative publicity surrounding *Tuktut* prevent the publication of similar material. A second "picture story" booklet titled *Save the Caribou* was printed in 1957, and a comic book titled *A Question of Survival* appeared in 1965 (see Figure 7.2).[80]

In addition to the distribution of educational material, the inauguration of the caribou crisis in 1955 brought about more direct attempts to exercise control over the day-to-day subsistence activities of Dene and Inuit hunters. In order to prevent waste or blatant violations of the game regulations, both the NWT Game Warden Service and the Indian Affairs Branch began to organize supervised caribou hunts beginning in 1955.[81] Field staff from all branches of the northern administration were also directed to teach Native hunters to exploit sources of country food other than caribou. In August 1955, the Northwest Territories Council discussed developing alternative local sources of meat. Proposals ranged from the increased provision of bison meat from Wood Buffalo National Park to a revival of older ideas such as importing herds of domesticated reindeer or yaks. The council members also suggested that nets might be supplied in order to teach Dene and Inuit modern fishing techniques so they could better harvest the resources of large inland lakes and coastal waters.[82] Ben Sivertz was so enthusiastic about this proposal that he called for "an intensive campaign to switch Natives from a 'caribou economy' to a 'fish economy.'"[83]

The notion that expanded fishing projects could reduce human hunting pressure on the caribou also appealed to federal officials who hoped to keep Native hunters from becoming overly reliant on relief. A report forwarded to the Northwest Territories Council in January 1958 on a fishing project at Baker Lake summed up the prevailing sentiment: it was "not considered advisable or desirable to distribute imported foods as such action might tend to destroy all initiative in using fish and other local sources of food."[84] In part, this statement reiterated the long-standing policy of encouraging the Native people of the Northwest Territories to remain self-sufficient hunters rather than wards of the state. It also reflected a more recent debate concerning the relationship of the Inuit to the emerging modern welfare state. After the market for Arctic, or white, foxes, a mainstay of the fur economy north of the treeline, collapsed in the late 1940s, many Inuit came to rely at least partly on new postwar social assistance programs such as the family allowance. Relief outlays to Inuit hunters in the Northwest Territories increased dramatically from $3,978 in 1945 to $68,978 in 1954.[85] A widespread and at times very public debate began to

7.2   Page from the comic book *A Question of Survival*, published by the Canadian Wildlife Service in 1965. Northwest Territories Archives N-1992-023, box 33, file 4

blame the Inuit for their "laziness" and penchant for handouts. Several newspapers in Canada and the United States ran articles and editorials in the early 1950s that were highly critical of the reduced "self-reliance" and "vitality" among the Inuit since the introduction of social welfare to the Far North.[86] The Union Oil Company of California went so far as to place an advertisement in *Newsweek* highlighting the "indolence" of the Inuit as "proof" that the emerging welfare state could only result in "enslavement by security."[87] Although some federal officials dismissed the critics as ideologues bent on discrediting Canada's social welfare programs, others were open to the idea that welfare payments were having detrimental social effects among the Inuit.[88] At a meeting of the federal Committee on Eskimo Affairs held in May 1952, delegates suggested revising welfare policies to discourage the Inuit from giving up life on the land and congregating near larger settlements in the hopes of obtaining social assistance payments.[89] The search for food sources other than caribou can therefore be understood as more than a conservation measure to optimize the production of food resources in the Northwest Territories. It was also part of a program to keep the Inuit off the dole despite the unreliability of an economy based on the Arctic fox and the caribou.

This convergence of northern social policy and the caribou conservation program encouraged the northern administration to pursue local fishing projects with an almost missionary zeal. Perhaps the most urgent attempt to convert a local Inuit group from caribou hunters to fishers occurred at Contwoyto Lake, a large body of water about two hundred kilometres southeast of Coppermine. In March 1957, the RCMP constable T.J. Garvin reported that the Inuit at Contwoyto Lake were living almost exclusively on caribou. Close to three hundred of the animals had apparently been killed there the previous autumn to feed both dogs and humans. Garvin recommended the distribution of fishing nets as the only practical caribou conservation measure.[90] The nets arrived in May but due to an oversight lacked the requisite floats, leads, backing twine, and hanging twine. In August, the game officer F.S. Bailey and a predator control hunter and long-time trapper named Matt Murphy arrived with additional nets for the fishing project. Unfortunately, they brought no boat with them and discovered that the Inuit had only one heavily damaged vessel that was no longer seaworthy. By December, however, the nets could be set under the lake ice, and boats were constructed at the vocational school in Yellowknife for use in the spring of 1959. Nonetheless, the Inuit were able to catch only approximately seventy fish per day, barely sufficient to feed their dogs. The fishing project was not monitored through that summer, and when a flight arrived in August, the Inuit were found to be starving. Although the new fishing equipment had obviously failed to provide a reliable food source, the field officers pressed ahead. Murphy remained in the camp with Game Officer R. Douglas through the autumn of 1959 to assist with the fishing project, but bad weather resulted once again in little more fish being caught than what was needed to keep the dogs alive. Perhaps sensing the precarious nature of the fishing project, the Inuit at Contwoyto Lake killed one thousand caribou in the autumn and early winter of 1959, some apparently for local trade at Coppermine.[91] The next summer, CWS biologists found over five hundred caribou carcasses that had been left on the open tundra with only their hides and tongues removed.[92] On 17 August, Game Officer Douglas reported that Joe Oto-yak, a predator control officer, had suggested that the shaman woman "Old Eda," who "dislikes all government officials," had probably counselled the Inuit to slaughter the caribou.[93]

Why did such large caribou slaughters take place at Contwoyto Lake between the fall of 1959 and the summer of 1960? Inevitably, this question is difficult to answer with archival evidence that omits the voices of the Inuit. Nonetheless, the kill may have constituted a protest against the failure of the fishing project to provide enough food through the previous spring and summer. As the community felt the bite of starvation, Old Eda's general contempt for federal officials may have become more widespread. Perhaps a more likely explanation is that the Contwoyto Lake Inuit actually needed the large numbers of caribou killed in the summer of 1960. When Game Officer Douglas flew to the site to investigate the circumstances surrounding the slaughter in September, several hunters claimed that the hides were absolutely necessary for winter clothing, tents, and sleeping bags. Douglas was, for a game officer, uncommonly sympathetic to these arguments. He reported that approximately six hundred caribou were required to clothe and shelter the thirty-nine Inuit at Contwoyto Lake (twenty hides were required to make a tent for one family). Although some caribou hides had been sold for cash income at Coppermine and Bathurst Inlet, Douglas argued that the white fox population around Contwoyto Lake was so small that caribou hides had become the sole medium of barter for staple goods. Furthermore, the Inuit hunters at Contwoyto Lake lacked enough wooden drying racks to preserve all the meat from a hunt for prime late-summer caribou hides (though much of the "abandoned" meat from the 1960 hunt was actually used to feed the eighty sled dogs in the camp). Finally, Douglas concluded that Contwoyto Lake was "not suitable" for harvesting fish in quantities large enough to divert hunting pressure from the caribou. He recommended instead the construction of ice houses and wire drying racks, the provision of trapping equipment, and the supervision of all hunting activities in the area by a game officer.[94] The following summer, Game Officer J.H. McCauley apparently managed to curb the "excessive slaughter" through the construction of cold storage pits, instruction in the art of drying meat, and the erection of permanent dwellings.[95]

The failure of the fishery at Contwoyto Lake as both a conservation measure and an attempt to diversify the material base of the Inuit economy epitomized much broader problems with the program to convert the Native economy of the Northwest Territories from hunting to fishing. Several other fishing projects experienced similar problems with resource scarcity and a lack of equipment and personnel.[96] In more general terms, however, the idea that the Dene and Inuit could survive on a largely fish diet did not account for the fundamental significance of caribou to their lives. Not only were fish unable to provide the skins to manufacture the clothing and shelter that was absolutely essential for some Native people in the Northwest Territories, they lacked sufficient quantities of nutrients such as iron and protein that were necessary for long-term survival in the Arctic.[97] Dogs also could not maintain their health on a fish diet. The northern service officer at Baker Lake, T.H. Butters, reported in August 1960 that "fish, Ottawa notwithstanding, cannot build dogs strong enough for winter work, of this I am convinced."[98] While the distribution of fishing nets and boats may have improved access to a supplemental food source in many communities, the notion that fish could become the basis of the northern subsistence economy seems, as Butters implied, to have been dreamed up in the offices of civil servants who had little knowledge of local food requirements or environmental conditions.

The idea that northern Natives could live a traditional lifestyle based entirely on local food sources began to fade somewhat in the late 1950s. Several cases of starvation among the Inuit of the Keewatin interior, which gained a high public profile primarily through the popular books of Farley Mowat, strongly indicated that leaving the Inuit to fend for themselves in eastern Arctic tundra regions might have disastrous consequences. In addition, the election of John Diefenbaker's Conservatives in 1957 brought in a government that was committed to a policy of intense industrial development in the Canadian North. As a result, conservation policy in the Northwest Territories shifted further: the provision of wage employment, it was thought, might be the best way to divert Dene and Inuit hunters from their dependence on the caribou. This idea was not entirely new. In 1951, Mowat had advocated a gradual transition from "primitivism to modernism" among the Inuit in his best-selling book *People of the Deer*. Although he later recanted his assimilationist stance in a revised edition of *The Desperate People*, his earlier volume suggested a dramatic expansion of the reindeer industry to provide a secure food supply for the North, the development of the mining industry to employ the Inuit, and finally the enlistment of as many Inuit as possible in the armed forces to provide for continental security.[99] In government circles, the director of the Northern Administration and Lands Branch, F.J.G. Cunningham, proposed an emphasis on wage employment in 1955: "Considering the changes that are even now taking place throughout the Arctic and in our thinking on the future place of Eskimos in the northern economy, it may be that long-term development of native food resources may not be so important now as it was when Eskimos had fewer opportunities of making a living other than by hunting and trapping."[100]

Well into the 1960s, in fact, senior wildlife officials continued to produce comprehensive proposals to modernize the Native economy in the North as a means to conserve caribou. In June 1964, for example, the chief of the Canadian Wildlife Service, David Munro, presented a draft statement on reducing the take of caribou through nonlegislative means to officials from the Education, Welfare, and Industrial divisions of the Northern Administration Branch. The document emphasized work programs for Native hunters, who would perform such tasks as clearing rights-of-way for fire roads or guiding visiting sport hunters and fishers.[101] Munro's draft grew into a larger policy document that was the product of collaboration between the CWS and the Northern Administration Branch; it advocated a radical transformation of the Dene and Inuit economy through vocational education programs, the creation of work programs to develop recreational facilities and roads for a proposed national park near Fort Reliance, and the further development of cottage handicraft industries, all as a means to conserve the caribou population.[102]

Although grand in their design, the proposals to modernize the Inuit economy in the late 1950s and early 1960s never completely displaced programs that were devoted to the development of alternative country food sources. Even Munro's proposals advocated hiring a resource geographer to assess the development of alternative resources for subsistence and cash income. The response of the federal government to the caribou crisis of the 1950s and 1960s was thus dominated by two distinct and contrary policy proposals for "reforming" the Dene and Inuit subsistence economy. On the one hand, the government imposed a kind of "enforced primitivism" based on the development of alternative food sources and the hope that northern Aboriginal people would not become a significant drain on the public welfare purse. On the other, the federal government promoted the idea that some Native hunters might become assimilated to the modern industrial economy. Despite their antithetical relationship, both programs demonstrate how closely caribou conservation initiatives were tied to social and economic policy in the Northwest Territories. This broad expression of state power becomes even more obvious in the relationship between the programs to fundamentally alter the subsistence strategies of northern hunters and those designed to move Dene and Inuit communities away from their traditional hunting grounds to areas "more suitable" for their livelihoods.

MOVING PEOPLE, SAVING CARIBOU

The relocation of Native hunters from areas with a limited game supply to more productive hunting grounds came to be regarded as a cure-all for a range of policy issues in the postwar era. In 1953, several Inuit families were moved from Port Harrison, or Inukjuak, in northern Quebec to the distant High Arctic locations of Craig Harbour (and later Grise Fiord) on Ellesmere Island and Resolute Bay on Cornwallis Island. In the late 1950s, various groups of inland Caribou Inuit were moved from point to point within the Keewatin district and finally from the interior to communities along the west coast of Hudson Bay. Despite repeated claims by the federal government that the moves were carried out in the best interest of willing Inuit participants, the vast majority of scholarly research on this subject has concluded that the relocations were pursued coercively, with participants either unaware of the full implications of relocation or restricted in their choice of where to move.[103] The Inuit representative to the interdepartmental Committee on Eskimo Affairs, Ayaruark, articulated this sentiment at a meeting held on 25 May 1959: "Sometimes Eskimos were over-shadowed by those in authority and this had been evident in cases where they had been moved from one area to another and did not want to go. They had agreed to move only because they were 'over-awed.' It happens sometimes that Eskimos agree to be transferred elsewhere not because they want to but because destitution forces them to accept the offer made to them of transferring elsewhere."[104]

Historians who have researched the relocations have generally pointed to two key policy goals underlying the program: the maintenance of

Canadian sovereignty in the Arctic Archipelago in the case of the Craig Harbour and Resolute Bay relocations, and more broadly, the deterrence of welfare dependency as Native hunters were moved from areas with poor game conditions to locations where they could become self sufficient in their search for country food or wage employment. In addition to these two considerations, however, postwar concerns over the status of the caribou herds in the Northwest Territories also played a part in the development of the relocation policy. Senior officials from the CWS were active participants in the interdepartmental committee that formulated the policy. Relocating Inuit and Dene hunters from the interior regions of the eastern Arctic to coastal areas accorded well with the Canadian Wildlife Service's goal of reducing the human kill of caribou in that region. By the early 1950s, wildlife managers and "people managers" had thus found common cause in their efforts to save both the caribou and the Native hunters of Canada's North.

The sympathetic attitude among federal wildlife officials toward a broad policy of Inuit relocation was readily apparent at the first meeting of what would become the interdepartmental Committee on Eskimo Affairs, held in May 1953. The biologists John Tener and Victor Solman, with their administrative colleague J.P. Richards, all represented the interests of the Canadian Wildlife Service at the meeting. Accordingly, the section of the minutes on conservation and utilization of wildlife emphasized the apparent decline of the caribou over the previous fifty years and invoked the familiar refrain that the solution to this problem lay in "educating the Eskimos themselves to realize the necessity and reasons for sound conservation practices and for making greater use of all the resources of the country, rather than concentrating on those most readily available." The delegates discussed many of the Canadian Wildlife Service's preferred methods of achieving this goal – the distribution of fishing nets, the organization of whale hunts, and restrictions on the number of dogs – but they also suggested a quite novel method of diverting hunting pressure from the caribou. The optimal utilization of country food resources in the Northwest Territories might be achieved, they reasoned, through "the movement of Eskimos from over-populated areas to places where they can be assured of being able to make a better living."[105] A press release issued two days later was equally forthright, declaring that the meeting delegates had concluded the Inuit should be moved to outlying areas because "the concentration of Eskimos at posts and settlements had resulted in the rapid depletion of accessible country produce."[106] One month later, Solman and Tener penned a memo outlining the extreme measures they would support in order to implement a program of relocations from districts with depleted wildlife populations to areas with abundant natural resources: "Eskimo reluctance to move should not preclude moves any more than has been the case in the relocation of prairie farmers under P.F.R.A. [Prairie Farm Rehabilitation Administration] and the expropriation of property and removal of persons for necessary purposes in connection with recent National Defence developments in large areas in Alberta and Saskatchewan."[107]

In spite of such rhetorical support, it is difficult to assess the extent to which the initial relocation of Inuit families from Port Harrison to Ellesmere and Cornwallis islands in July 1953 was influenced by federal conservation policy. At a meeting held to discuss the relocation in August 1953, the main reasons cited for the "experiment" were the federal government's desire to strengthen its sovereign claim over the Arctic Archipelago by having Canadian citizens occupy as much of the region as possible, and also "to see if it is possible for the people to adapt themselves to the conditions of the High North and secure a living from the land."[108] But the broader policy of diverting subsistence hunters from depleted local game populations to other sources of country food provided some context for the latter statement. Writing in November 1960, C.M. Bolger, the administrator of the Arctic, recalled that "part of the history of the scheme was one of a greatly increased population over-burdening a depleted game population. Withdrawal of some hunters from the area not only benefited them but relieved Port Harrison of some of its large human population."[109] Aside from such retrospective comments, however, little evidence ties the Port Harrison relocation specifically to the Canadian Wildlife Service's caribou conservation program. The Ungava caribou resided entirely within Quebec's provincial boundaries, so the CWS was only a minor player in the management of that herd. Furthermore, because the barren ground caribou herds of northern Quebec had been reduced to only a remnant population of a few thousand during the early part of the twentieth century, wildlife officials generally assumed that the law of diminishing returns would prevent the absolute extinction of the species as hunters travelled further from the coast each year to obtain fewer and fewer caribou. It was not until a co-operative federal-provincial study of the Ungava herds was completed in 1956 that biologists became aware that Native hunters were still travelling inland up to three hundred miles in search of scarce caribou.[110] At the time of the High Arctic relocation in 1953, the primary complaint of federal officials was not the vast distances the Port Harrison Inuit travelled in pursuit of declining wildlife herds, but rather their supposed tendency to stay close to the community in order to collect relief payments.[111]

As the perception of an impending caribou crisis strengthened in the mid-1950s, however, the affiliation between relocation programs and conservation policy on the mainland caribou range became more evident. A well-documented case involving the relocation to Churchill of the Sayisi Dene band at Duck Lake, Manitoba, in 1956 reveals a great deal about the contribution of the emerging federal-provincial conservation programs to the relocation policy. The Sayisi Dene band at Duck Lake were major users of caribou and inhabited one of the largest and most reliable caribou crossings in the eastern reaches of the range. Reports that this band routinely conducted large caribou slaughters with many carcasses abandoned had given them a reputation as a "problem" group of hunters. In a 1955 report on the barren ground caribou of Manitoba and the Keewatin District, for instance, the biologist Alan Loughrey identified Duck Lake as one of six settlements in the region where large caribou kills were made annually.[112] At the first federal-provincial meeting to discuss the caribou crisis in October 1955, delegates also identified the Dene bands at Duck Lake and Brochet as the most wasteful caribou hunters on the mainland ranges and recommended that Indian Affairs place an agent in the region to supervise the caribou hunt. Earlier in the meeting, the Manitoba game officer, J.D. Robertson, had shown the participants recent pictures taken by provincial government officials depicting the aftermath of a caribou hunt where over seven hundred animals had been speared at a water crossing and apparently abandoned.[113] One of these pictures, a stark photograph showing several caribou carcasses on the shores of Duck Lake, received wide publicity after it was printed in the *Beaver* the next spring on the front page of an article by A.W.F. Banfield describing the "orgies of killing" that had brought about the caribou crisis.[114] In a similar manner, Robertson's official report on the "carnage" at Duck Lake described "caribou lying scattered over the barrens, some bloated and rotten, others eaten (all but the bones) by ravens. The sight was terrible."[115] The sight of so many dead caribou may have been jarring for Robertson, but the testimony of Sayisi Dene elders and anthropologists suggests that the caribou on the shoreline of Duck Lake had not been abandoned at all but had been left there to freeze, a time-honoured and practical method of preserving food for people and dogs with sub-zero temperatures imminent.[116]

The photographs of the slaughter at Duck Lake nevertheless focused the attention of the federal and provincial governments on what they believed to be the wasteful hunting practices of this particular band. Although

one important impetus for relocation of the Sayisi Dene was the impending closure of the nearby Hudson's Bay Company's trading post, concerns
over the caribou slaughter doubtless played a role.[117] The elder John Solo-
mon has recalled that a meeting held to discuss the move in July 1956
included not only representatives from the federal Indian Affairs Branch
but also officials from Manitoba's Department of Natural Resources, who
had routinely accused the Sayisi Dene of killing excessive numbers of caribou.[118] Furthermore, a memo authored by the supervisor of Indian Affairs
in the region implies some urgency to remove the Sayisi Dene before the
caribou migration in September, or "they will wish to remain for the kill
which might upset all our plans."[119] This memo can be interpreted simply
as a practical recommendation to proceed with the relocation before the
Dene became busily engaged with the caribou hunt, but it may also represent an urgent appeal to prevent a second high-profile slaughter such as
had occurred the previous autumn.

The Sayisi Dene were moved in August 1956 to North River, forty miles
up the Hudson Bay coast from Churchill. After a flood destroyed all the
cabins at North River the following spring, people were slowly moved to
Camp-10, a site on the outskirts of Churchill where alcoholism, violence,
and sexual abuse came to dominate the social fabric of the community.
From the perspective of game officials, however, the relocation was an
unqualified success. At a meeting of the Technical Committee for Caribou
Conservation in November 1959, Robertson noted approvingly that "since
the Duck Lake people had been moved to the coast there had been no
heavy kill at Duck Lake."[120] Similarly, the CWS biologist John Kelsall
blandly noted in his 1968 monograph on the caribou that "a comparable
situation [of large caribou slaughters near trading posts] prevailed at Duck
Lake in northern Manitoba until that post was closed and the resident
Chipewyan Indians moved to Fort Churchill in 1956."[121] The urgency
accorded to the caribou crisis had evidently compelled some game officials
to advocate for the preservation of the remaining herds regardless of the
social cost to the region's Native people.

A similar case at Ennadai Lake in the Keewatin District reveals a comparable story of coercive migration tied to the broader caribou conservation program. By the late 1950s, the northern administration had for many
years classified the small band of just over fifty Inuit at Ennadai Lake as a
"problem" group that was increasingly dependent on handouts from local
government agents. These were, after all, the "Ihalmuit" described in Farley Mowat's *People of the Deer* (1952) and *The Desperate People* (1959), the
symbol of the privation and hunger that had afflicted the Inuit following

the postwar collapse of fox prices and the unreliability of several local caribou migrations. The group first came to the government's attention after
a visiting medical officer from Indian Health Services found in February
1947 that they did not have enough food cached to take them to the
spring, and arranged for food and ammunition to be shipped to the area.
Ongoing reports that the Inuit were congregating near the radio station
operated by the Royal Canadian Corps of Signals at Ennadai Lake in search
of the occasional "handout," combined with the need for semi-annual relief shipments up to 1950, reinforced the image of this Inuit community
as a backward and primitive group in need of a dramatic intervention to
improve their condition. In April 1950, the caribou migration again
missed the Ennadai Lake area and the department recommended relocating this group so they could take part in a commercial fishing venture at
Nueltin Lake. In the summer of 1950, forty-seven Inuit were flown to
Nueltin Lake, only to discover several weeks later that the two traders who
had set up the fishing venture were shutting it down for economic reasons.
A cultural preference for caribou hunting rather than fishing among the
Inuit and poor relations between the Ennadai Lake people and a local group
of Dene had also contributed to the failure of the project. By December
1950 all the Inuit participants in the project had travelled on their own
back to Ennadai Lake.[122]

Caribou were plentiful in the Ennadai Lake region over the next four
years. The abundant food supply eased concerns over the material conditions of the local Inuit, but their apparently wasteful hunting was beginning to cause a great deal of anxiety among northern administrators. In
April 1955, Ben Sivertz wrote to P.A.C. Nichols, manager of the Hudson's
Bay Company's Arctic Division, to request that the company establish a
small post at Ennadai Lake as an incentive to prevent what was thought
to be the extremely wasteful local practice of butchering caribou carcasses
without removing the skins.[123] Nichols responded sceptically, arguing that
such a remote post could not be economically feasible. He nevertheless
offered to trade for the hides at the Padlei post at a low price and distribute them to needy communities throughout the Arctic.[124] The Ennadai
Lake people did not routinely travel to Padlei, however, and Sivertz concluded that the only viable course of action was to move them closer to
the trading post. If persuasion failed to convince the Inuit to move, Sivertz
reasoned that "it can be pointed out to them that we cannot carry on the
present arrangements any longer and that if they persist in staying in this
area, they cannot expect any assistance either from the Department of
Transport station or ourselves."[125]

There was no immediate attempt to move the Inuit from Ennadai Lake in 1955. Nonetheless, the failure of the caribou hunt in the autumn seasons of both 1955 and 1956 and the consequent need to ship relief supplies added weight to the argument that the Ennadai Lake people should be moved to a new location.[126] In June 1956, F.J.G. Cunningham notified Nichols that the northern service officer in the area would soon attempt to convince the Ennadai Lake Inuit of the wisdom of moving east to a site at Henik Lake within forty-five miles of Padlei. Cunningham offered two reasons for the proposed move: the impoverished condition of the Ennadai Lake Inuit due to the failure of the caribou hunt and the "inadequate supervision of the hunting and trading operations of these Natives due largely to the remoteness of the region in relation to the established trading posts and the local administrative offices."[127] Although the extent to which Cunningham's comments reflect the concerns over the issue of abandoned skins and large caribou slaughters is unclear, the Henik Lake relocation was intended to deliver the Inuit to a location where non-Natives might have a better chance of controlling their subsistence hunting practices.

And so the Inuit at Ennadai Lake were moved. In May 1957, fifty-eight Inuit were airlifted to North Henik Lake with tents, ammunition, fish nets, and one month's worth of food supplies. A press release titled "Eskimos Fly to New Hunting Grounds" trumpeted the good fishing, the abundant white fox population, and the plentiful caribou that still migrated through the Henik Lake region.[128] The press release also described the Inuit as volunteers, a highly questionable claim given that the threat of reduced relief distribution was used to compel Inuit co-operation.[129] In any event, the relocation proved to be an unmitigated disaster. The caribou did not come in sufficient numbers to feed the people at this allegedly happy hunting ground during the autumn migration, nor did government officials take sufficient steps to monitor the condition of the Inuit and distribute relief supplies when necessary. Seven people died from the combined effects of starvation and hypothermia at Henik Lake that winter.[130] The deaths received widespread public attention, primarily due to Farley Mowat's gut-wrenching article about Kikkik, who was forced to leave two of her weakened daughters in a snow grave as she fled to Padlei after her husband had been murdered by another starving member of the band.[131]

The incidents at Henik Lake, combined with a second high-profile case of starvation among an Inuit group farther to the north at Garry Lake, prompted a major re-evaluation of federal Inuit policy. According to the new orthodoxy, the frequent failure of the caribou migrations made it impossible to preserve widely dispersed self-sufficient traditional hunting and trapping communities in the remote interior regions of the Northwest Territories. Ignoring the fact that the Henik Lake deaths were a direct result of the department's own intervention in the lives of the Inuit, the northern administration argued that the material culture of the inland "Caribou Eskimos" of the Keewatin District was no longer viable. In April 1958, Alex Stevenson of the Arctic Division wrote, "What has happened to this handful of people, is a forerunner of what is going to happen to all of the Eskimos of this culture. There are many indications of this, but the main one is the decline of the caribou with no visible recovery – the mainstay of a people whose whole life depended for generations on this animal."[132]

For government officials, the solution to this predicament was obvious: more relocations. In May 1958, a memo to cabinet from Alvin Hamilton, the minister of northern affairs and national resources, noted that the incidents at Henik Lake were symptomatic of a broader social collapse and disintegration of the caribou economy in the Keewatin interior. Among the many options considered, Hamilton most clearly supported the creation of a community on the west coast of Hudson Bay designed specifically to "rehabilitate" the interior Keewatin Inuit. He requested $150,000 to establish a settlement where the Caribou Inuit could be trained to develop a diversified economy based on marine resource harvesting, handicraft production, and tourism.[133] The first attempt to establish this planned community, at Whale Cove, failed because of the difficulty of landing supplies in the harbour, but a second community known as the Keewatin Reestablishment Project, or Itavia, was set up just outside Rankin Inlet in the autumn of 1958. In addition to the nearly eighty survivors of the Henik Lake and Garry Lake famines, Inuit families primarily from Baker Lake brought the population of Itavia to 140 by January 1959. Upon arrival, the Inuit were kept employed building housing, caring for a small store, manufacturing handicrafts, and hunting marine mammals.[134] By 1960, however, many of these Inuit families had abandoned the labour training programs and moved to Whale Cove because of their frustration with the pervasive influence of the many white "bosses" at Itavia.[135] In spite of this setback, the northern service officer R.L. Kennedy summed up the prevailing sentiment when he wrote, "The outlook for the interior Eskimos, on the land, appears hopeless to me. I can see no alternative to their grinding poverty except to move the majority of them."[136]

While the Keewatin Reestablishment Project was meant to open new economic vistas for the Inuit, it was also intended as a means to control Inuit modes of subsistence and survival. More precisely, the relocation of the Keewatin Inuit was thought of as a means to bring these inland hunters closer to marine resources and technical training opportunities while keeping them away from the interior caribou herds. Although Hamilton's proposal to cabinet did outline a broad range of benefits arising from an Inuit rehabilitation project on the coast, such as the provision of health and education services, the document also suggests that the relocation of the Inuit might be effective as a caribou conservation measure. If the Keewatin Inuit were concentrated in one coastal community, then "the caribou would be released from the hunting pressure exerted by the Keewatin Eskimos and, with proper conservation measures, might increase and again become the invaluable source of food they were in former years."[137]

Ben Sivertz, director of the Northern Administration and Lands Branch, took this logic one step further with the claim that relocating Native hunters might be the only possible means to effectively introduce restrictive game laws such as a caribou quota. If the inland Inuit continued to live off the land, Sivertz argued, they would need to continue to kill caribou in large numbers. A quota would invite nothing but contempt for the law under such circumstances, and therefore a more all-encompassing transformation of the Inuit subsistence economy was necessary. Sivertz wrote, "The only realistic solution which I can suggest for caribou conservation in Eskimo country is to relieve the pressure of hunting by provision of alternative sources of food and income. The Keewatin re-establishment project is an important beginning in this direction for not only does it provide alternative sources but it makes possible close supervision of all concerned. If this is successful, we will be proposing moderately rapid expansion of this approach throughout the caribou country."[138] These comments are reminiscent of a memo authored by C.M. Bolger, chief of the Arctic Division, three months earlier: "Should quotas be imposed in the Northwest Territories, it is obvious that the suggested quota of five caribou per person for inland Eskimos will not provide such Eskimos with adequate food and clothing for the period of a year. We will therefore have to take steps to supplement the food and clothing for these people unless, of their own volition, they move to the coast where other local resources are available."[139]

Although the primary justification that government officials offered for the relocation program was the improvement of the Inuit economy, Sivertz's and Bolger's comments indicate that reducing the human population in the Keewatin interior accorded well with the priorities of the caribou conservation program. Wildlife conservation in the Northwest Territories demanded not a slight modification of hunting behaviour in order to protect a species believed to be endangered; instead it imposed sweeping and dramatic changes to the way of life of an entire people. Indeed, by the early 1960s, it was hoped that relocating Inuit hunters from their traditional hunting grounds might lead them toward wage employment. At a meeting of the Administrative Committee for Caribou Preservation in February 1965, Bolger highlighted the relocation of several Inuit families to the mining communities of Yellowknife in 1963 and Lynn Lake, Manitoba, in 1964, as well as a recent program to train Inuit to work on the DEW Line: "It is hoped ... such training activities will divert people from caribou hunting."[140]

Ironically, the scientific consensus that had produced the caribou crisis began to dissipate even as the relocations were being promoted as a caribou conservation measure. As early as 1960, extremely large increases in the caribou calf crop were noted, and scattered internal reports began to predict a major population increase by the middle of the decade.[141] In 1966, Robert Ruttan, a former caribou biologist with the CWS, published an article claiming that the mainland caribou had undergone a rapid population surge and now numbered 700,000 animals. He further maintained that a new crisis threatened the herds: a rapidly growing caribou population might outstrip the carrying capacity of its range.[142] Ruttan went so far as to suggest an annual cull of 100,000 animals to prevent mass starvation within the herds. Although senior wildlife officials dismissed Ruttan's assessment of the caribou herds as "dangerous information," a range-wide survey conducted by the CWS biologist Don Thomas in 1967 postulated that the herds had increased significantly to a total of 385,000 animals.[143] The improved population numbers did not immediately assuage the urgent concern over the mainland caribou herds, but the emergence of scientific data suggesting even a moderate increase in the caribou population in many ways marked the end of the so-called caribou crisis.

For over a decade after the inception of the caribou crisis in 1955, the air of urgency surrounding the conservation of this wildlife population had contributed to the imposition of far-reaching changes to the lives of Dene and Inuit hunters in the Northwest Territories. In order to conserve the caribou, federal wildlife officials supported a broad array of coercive programs that seemed to have been designed as much to weaken the political and cultural sovereignty of northern Aboriginal people as to save an endangered species. Throughout the postwar era, the politics of wildlife conservation in the Northwest Territories became increasingly tied to a broad expansion of federal influence over the lives of the Dene and Inuit. During this period the caribou conservation program took on the most visible characteristics of a colonial institution, intent on imposing the cultural norms and economic priorities of the centre as a means to reform the "deficient" hunting cultures of local Aboriginal people living at the periphery. The main tenets of the federal government's response to the caribou crisis – the resettlement schemes intended in part to move Native hunters off the caribou range, the fishing projects that aimed to divert hunting pressure from the caribou, and the employment and training programs that promoted a modernization of the northern economy – all reinforced one basic fact: Native hunters had lost a large measure of control over their lives due to the autocratic imposition of the outside institution of wildlife conservation. Indeed, the caribou conservation program sought to induce fundamental social and cultural changes among the Dene and Inuit, turning subsistence hunters into fishers or industrial labourers and, if necessary, moving them from their traditional hunting grounds so they could fully participate in these new economic "opportunities."

Accordingly, the range of cultural, economic, and ecological choices available to Native hunters in the postwar era was, to a large degree, circumscribed and appropriated by a state authority that placed more faith in scientific expertise and bureaucratic management than in the purely local and supposedly ignorant interests of northern Aboriginal people. The CWS biologist Gerry Parker summed up the prevailing disdain for local Native hunting practices as late as 1972 when he quoted extensively from no less an authority than Warburton Pike to argue that "many people are under the impression that the primitive Indian was a dedicated conservationist," but in reality "nothing could be further from the truth."[144] Such derogatory comments remind the contemporary reader that the practice of wildlife conservation in the Northwest Territories was not a benevolent or visionary attempt to protect the caribou. The expression of state authority over the apparently corrupt local hunting cultures of the Dene and Inuit was a process of coercive change that led many northern Aboriginal communities toward a future that was not of their own making.

Conclusion

I N JUNE 1998, MY WIFE, YOLANDA, AND I were travelling north on the dirt highway leading out of Fort Smith through the endless twilight of a northern summer evening. We had just spent three days hiking in Wood Buffalo National Park, observing sandhill cranes, pelicans, one black bear, and an astonishing variety of boreal songbirds and migratory waterfowl. Nevertheless, we felt a lingering disappointment: the only signs of the park's namesake we had found were scattered tracks and sun-baked dung patties along the Salt River. We soon discovered, however, that we would have had better luck locating bison if we had driven along the road rather than walking the trails. As our car approached the northern boundary of the park, we encountered a herd of well over seventy bison spread out across the highway, no doubt enjoying the abundant grasses at the side of the road and a reprieve from biting insects in this windswept right-of-way. Traffic is rare in this part of the world; we were therefore able to sit on the hood of our car for over three hours observing the herd. For the most part, the bison kept to their grazing, but slowly, almost imperceptibly, a portion of the herd worked their way towards us as they grazed. One of the largest bulls approached so close that we were forced back inside the car. He stared at us for several long minutes through the window; the observers had become the observed. We managed eventually to enact a form of peaceful co-existence with the herd: we would allow them to graze undisturbed just a few feet from us and they would allow us to watch. In time, the herd scattered to the forest as a second car approached with its horn blaring and no intention of slowing down. What was a common annoyance for this local resident had provided an unsurpassed moment of awe and rapture for two outsiders who had never experienced such intimate contact with large wild animals. We were acutely aware that northern Canada remains one of the world's last great reservoirs of wildlife, among the few places with free-roaming herd animals in large numbers. The bison of Wood Buffalo National Park, the caribou of the Arctic interior, and the muskox on the Arctic islands and in the Thelon Game Sanctuary still offer the wilderness enthusiast the same exceptional opportunities for contact with the charismatic megafauna that so enthralled such hunter-naturalists as Warburton Pike, Caspar Whitney, and Ernest Thompson Seton.

Such experiences in the present cannot help but shape our perceptions of the past. The writing of history, as Hayden White has argued, is a process of narrativization that inevitably imposes moral meaning on the chaotic swirl of events that make up our collective experience of earlier times.[1] Although a recent event, the encounter with a once-abundant population of wood bison in one of the world's largest wilderness preserve suggests a certain moral to the history of wildlife conservation in northern Canada. Surely, the mere fact that these animals still exist implies foresight on the part of the government officials who created Wood Buffalo National Park. Through the latter half of the nineteenth century, governments in Canada and the United States did very little to protect the wildlife that was being slaughtered on the Great Plains. In the early decades of the twentieth century, however, Canadian officials adopted a more activist approach to wildlife conservation as they attempted to prevent the destruction of the wood bison, the caribou, and muskox in the Northwest Territories. Meeting a herd of wood bison along a lonely highway could be seen as a monument to their success, a testament to the judicious application of conservation policies in Canada's Northwest Territories.

There is some truth to this narrative. The expansion of a commercial economy in the Northwest Territories in the late nineteenth and early twentieth centuries did pose a real threat to the region's wildlife populations. The influx of trappers, traders, whalers, explorers, and miners from the south led to increased hunting and a commercial trade in the meat and skins of the muskox and the caribou.[2] The participation of Dene and Inuit hunters in this new market hunt for fur and meat extended its reach far inland from the whaling stations of the Arctic coast and the trading posts strung along Great Slave Lake and the Mackenzie Valley. Of course, many ecological factors other than human hunting may account for the decline of a species in a given area, including climate, disease, snow depth, and shifting fire regimes. Nonetheless, the expansion of the robe and meat trade in the latter half of the nineteenth century contributed to the severe reduction of the caribou herds in the lower Mackenzie Valley and the muskox population of the Arctic mainland. In light of such acute wildlife crises, it is tempting to conclude that the northern administration's conservation initiatives were both reasonable and prudent. In particular, measures designed to control the growing commerce in big game, such as the ban on the trade in muskox parts and the restriction of the caribou trade to domestic markets, seem almost to reflect a brave willingness on the part of the federal bureaucracy to challenge the interests of the trading companies and fur auction houses and prevent the commercial overkill that so greatly contributed to the demise of the bison on the Great Plains.

And yet the broad sweep of events surrounding the introduction of federal wildlife conservation programs to northern Canada does not sustain this conclusion. Everywhere within the publications and correspondence of Canada's early conservationists are statements that contradict the "enlightened preservationist" label that has been attached to their endeavours. Those looking for signs of heroic and prototypical environmentalists in the writings of conservation pioneers such as C. Gordon Hewitt, James Harkin, and Maxwell Graham will certainly find rapturous soliloquies attesting to the inherent value of wild creatures, but they will also find praise for the economic importance of Canada's wildlife. The combination of such seemingly contradictory approaches to wildlife conservation was common among those who worked within government natural resource agencies in North America, many of whom were not apt to make fine philosophical distinctions in their arguments for wilderness and wildlife protection.[3] Ultimately, conservationists such as Hewitt, Harkin, and Graham were pragmatic bureaucrats rather than visionaries: they appealed to both the highest ideals of the nature enthusiast and the basest commercial aspirations of the industrialist in an effort to promote their initiatives to as broad an audience as possible.

The abundance of wildlife and unreserved land in the Northwest Territories ensured that commerce was a driving principle behind the early wildlife management programs in this part of Canada. Senior officials such as Maxwell Graham were eager, as we have seen, to place wildlife at the service of specific national interests such as the alleviation of wartime food shortages. On a broader scale, federal wildlife officials were keen to foster linkages between conservation and the advance of a new commercial empire in the Far North. Drawing on the reports of explorers, naturalists, and government agents who extolled a pastoral future for the Canadian North, wildlife officials promoted the establishment of game ranches in the

Northwest Territories, a radical shift in land use patterns they hoped might facilitate further settlement and economic development. One does not have to look very deeply in the historical records to find evidence of this close equation of wildlife conservation with the development of productive agricultural enterprises in the North. Gordon Hewitt's enthusiastic promotion of muskox ranching in his published writings, James Harkin's participation in the muskox and reindeer commission, and Maxwell Graham's support of stocking initiatives within the national parks demonstrate that wildlife policy in the North was based on the rational production orthodoxy of the American progressives.

The enthusiasm among federal wildlife officials for agricultural models of wildlife conservation in the 1920s and 1930s has a close affinity to what James Scott has described as the high modernist faith in the ability of centralized bureaucracies to produce simplified and predictable environments to serve the requirements of industrial production.[4] Officials repeatedly emphasized that the introduction of a simplified agro-economic system to the Canadian North would not only preserve individual species from the vagaries of human and nonhuman predation, but also provide a stable and predictable food supply for the region. As Scott has argued, however, in their rush to improve upon the productive potential of natural systems with narrow management schemes, state bureaucracies often ignore the complexity of local ecosystems and human cultures, an oversight that can bring disastrous consequences.

Indeed, the dogmatic emphasis on production among Canada's early conservationists brought about one of the worst blunders in the history of federal wildlife management: the transfer of thousands of plains bison from southern Alberta to the Wood Buffalo National Park. This project was intended as a comprehensive solution to the dual problem of too many bison on the limited range of Buffalo National Park and too few on the ranges of northern Alberta and the Northwest Territories. But in their zeal to maximize the numbers of bison within Wood Buffalo Park, wildlife managers such as Maxwell Graham neglected to account for the potential ecological impacts of the transfer, most notably the introduction of diseases to the wood bison herds. Ironically, when it was learned two decades later that tuberculosis had spread widely in the northern herds, wildlife scientists identified the central problem of northern bison management as quite the opposite of Graham's: too many bison concentrated on too small a range had allowed for the spread of diseases and raised the possibility of overgrazing on the vast northern bison ranges. For wildlife biologists, the simple solution was to thin the herds by killing large numbers of bison. If the by-products of this slaughter were sold as part of a commercial marketing program, so much the better not only for the herds but also for government coffers. The scheme never eradicated tuberculosis from the bison herds, and the image of government-owned abattoirs conducting large commercial slaughters of wildlife in a national park – even as Native hunters were forbidden to kill the same animals – provides a vivid example of local wildlife resources appropriated by a state management program devoted to the principles of agricultural herd management.

On a broader scale, the earliest articulation of a "productive" wildlife conservation policy regime was linked inseparably to the government's colonial ambitions in the Northwest Territories. The herd animals of the subarctic taiga and the Arctic tundra were to be conserved in part because they provided the only ecologically viable agricultural basis for the expansion of settlement and economic activity. On the advice of explorers and promoters such as Vilhjalmur Stefansson, the federal government envisioned a northward expansion of empire that was novel for its time. Save for the importation of semidomesticated European reindeer herds, agricultural development and settlement in the Canadian North was to be achieved using native wild animals rather than Old World domesticates. This colonization scheme would not have radically altered the faunal composition of the northern tundra, except for the almost inevitable destruction of predatory animals. But the enclosure of northern wildlife on vast ranches would have fundamentally changed the material cultures of the region's Native people, as hunters were coerced into adopting the more sedentary life of ranch hands and herders. Indeed, the proposed conversion of the Arctic landscape from a wildlife commons to an enclosed and domesticated landscape was no less a vision of economic and ecological imperialism than the colonial processes that had transformed much of North America into "neo-European" agricultural landscapes over the previous four centuries.[5] Of course, the North had not been closed to external commercial markets before the advent of agricultural settlement schemes within the federal bureaucracy, having produced furs for global trade since the eighteenth century. Yet the shift among Aboriginal hunters from an almost exclusive focus on subsistence hunting to petty commodity production within a partly commercialized economy had not radically changed the hunting cultures of the North. Other than subtle changes in seasonal movements, the availability of material goods, and trading patterns, the fur trading economy had a great deal of continuity with the "bush life" of the precontact era. The proposed ranching schemes demanded a much broader transformation of economic and social life, however, entailing the marginalization of the hunting and trapping economy, the introduction of capitalism to the region, the transformation of Native hunters into wage labourers, the intensive management of wildlife for the purposes of production, and the further entrenchment of the North as a staple-producing region for southern commodity markets. Although the idea of a pastoral North remained a dream deferred, wildlife enthusiasts within government were more than willing to subordinate their conservation programs to the economic priorities of private capital and the colonial ambitions of an expansionist state.[6]

The federal government's attempts to assert control over northern wildlife populations were also efforts to establish administrative control over Native hunters in the region. By the early twentieth century, the cultural stereotype that cast Native hunters as unruly and improvident killers of wildlife had become firmly entrenched within the conservation discourse. Continued reports of wasteful caribou slaughters and clandestine bison hunts – many of which turned out to be false on investigation – contributed to a general sentiment among federal administrators that Native hunters represented a dire threat to northern wildlife and must therefore be subject to increased regulation and control. The result was dramatic limitations on the ability of Native hunters to access wildlife on their traditional hunting grounds. Beginning with the passage of the Unorganized Territories Game Preservation Act in 1894, the hunting practices of the Dene and the Inuit became increasingly circumscribed by formal game regulations. By the end of the 1920s, Native hunters were subject to closed seasons on valued fur-bearers and waterfowl and were prevented from hunting bison and muskox under any circumstances. Even the caribou hunt – a mainstay of the northern subsistence economy for centuries – was subject to closed seasons that Native hunters were permitted to ignore only if they could prove they were starving. Moreover, Native hunters were excluded both individually and en masse from the traditional hunting and trapping grounds that were enclosed in Wood Buffalo National Park and the Thelon Game Sanctuary. In some locales, particularly the park, the establishment of a game warden service or police detachment provided the federal government with a partial means of direct surveillance and supervisory control over Native hunters. As a result of these changes, many of the most basic aspects of the subsistence cycle that was so fundamental to the lives of the Dene, the Inuit, and the Cree of Wood Buffalo National Park – seasonal movements, fur trapping, and, most important, the gathering of food – were redefined as criminal activities.

The support for these initiatives within government circles was not

monolithic. Throughout the interwar years, the Department of Indian
Affairs consistently opposed game regulations that undermined the ability
of northern Natives to make a living off the land. The department was
motivated in part by concerns over rising relief costs rather than a desire
to defend the viability of traditional Native hunting cultures. But the
sympathetic influence of such senior officials as Duncan Campbell Scott
did stave off more extreme policy proposals from the Northwest Territories
and Yukon Branch and the Advisory Board on Wildlife Protection, such
as the removal of all Native hunters from Wood Buffalo National Park and
the elimination of the starvation clause that prevented the full extension
of closed seasons on caribou to Native hunters. Nonetheless, opposition
within the federal bureaucracy had little effect on the attitudes of senior
wildlife officials and northern administrators such as Maxwell Graham,
O.S. Finnie, and Roy A. Gibson. These men promoted a thoroughly stri-
dent approach to the regulation of Native hunting in the Northwest Territories, including harsh penalties for those convicted of poaching, the
dismissal of the hunting and trapping rights guaranteed in Treaties 8 and
11, and bureaucratic pressure on police and warden services to ensure strict
enforcement of the game laws.

Taken together, these policy initiatives suggest a second moral to this
historical narrative: the institution of wildlife conservation and its attendant legal instruments constituted a deliberate imposition of state power
over independent Aboriginal communities in northern Canada. This argument requires some qualification. As E.P. Thompson has noted, it is far
too easy to simply dismiss the rule of law as a sham – a singular expression
of power on behalf of the ruling classes – without acknowledging its essential role mediating between competing interests within complex societies.[7]
A modern conservationist, for instance, can quite legitimately argue that
in a crisis situation where human hunters knowingly threaten the immediate survival of a species, the intervention of the relevant state authorities
is the most expedient and perhaps the only way to prevent the extinction
of a unique life form. Several points, however, indicate that the intervention of the federal government in the lives of Aboriginal hunters during
the early decades of the twentieth century was more a product of cultural
contempt for Native cultures than a legitimate imposition of state authority to protect endangered species. First, federal wildlife officials based their
case against northern Native hunters as improvident killers of wildlife
more on rumour and conjecture rather than any specific knowledge of
Aboriginal hunting practices. Second, federal officials often based their
conservation policies on the most rudimentary scientific assessments of

the species they were trying to protect, often only the casual observations of naturalists and explorers. For example, the federal government had little evidence other than the questionable reports of the police officer A.M. Jarvis to suggest that Native hunters were killing off the wood bison; several other police reports suggested that moose and caribou rather than bison were the primary quarry for hunters in the South Slave region. Nor was there any solid evidence to suggest that Native hunters were killing muskox in the Thelon-Hanbury region before the creation of the Thelon Game Sanctuary. While the absence of evidence does not mean that no illegal killings took place, the lack of widespread reports of large-scale hunting of bison and muskox suggests that Native hunters were by and large killing more abundant alternatives. Nonetheless, federal officials refused even to consider the idea that existing local systems of wildlife management might have acted as an effective check on the excesses of individual hunters or that a co-operative approach to managing the northern wildlife commons might be a more just and effective approach to achieving their desired conservation objectives. Instead, federal officials were more likely to anticipate Garrett Hardin's call for the imposition of external authority over the commons, positioning themselves as a Leviathan-like presence that would reign supreme over the supposedly improvident traditional hunting cultures of northern indigenous people.[8]

As we have seen, federal wildlife officials hoped to expand their policy framework beyond mere regulation of the hunt and toward direct control over the social lives and material cultures of Dene and Inuit hunters. The earliest manifestation of this policy direction was linked to the broader colonial vision of a pastoral northland. With the introduction of a northern ranching economy, federal wildlife officials hoped that Native people might give up hunting and trapping for the presumably more stable, productive, and docile life of a pastoral herder. But the low biological productivity of the caribou and the muskox and the consequent dampening of enthusiasm for Arctic ranching schemes prevented this particular program of cultural transformation from progressing beyond the few Inuit hunters who became reindeer herders in the Mackenzie Valley.

The attempts of federal conservationists to control the daily subsistence of Native northerners continued through the 1930s, however, and intensified during the postwar period. Recognizing that law enforcement agents could not regulate the hunt over such a vast territory, federal officials in both the northern administration and Indian Affairs found common cause promoting alternative resources as a means to ease hunting pressure on the caribou, and implementing education programs designed to instil a conservationist ethic among the Dene and Inuit. Working through the police, the game warden service, Indian agents, and northern service officers, the federal government distributed nets, boats, and other fishing gear to encourage the consumption of fish and marine mammals instead of caribou. Posters, booklets, filmstrips, and other educational propaganda were distributed throughout the Northwest Territories to promote a more rational approach to wildlife conservation among the Dene and Inuit. Although the government's ability to influence Native hunters was constrained in some locales by the lack of nearby field agents, in other areas the most basic cultural choices available to the Dene and Inuit, such as what food to eat, what tools to use for the hunt, and how to maintain a dog team, all became subject to external authority.

This approach to wildlife conservation took on a particularly coercive hue in the late 1950s and early 1960s as federal officials became convinced that the traditional Dene and Inuit economy was an anachronism given declining wildlife populations and the expansion of industrial resource activities in the region. With increased wage-earning opportunities, Native hunters could become passive workers in a modern capitalist economy rather than subsistence hunters who continually undermined the government's wildlife conservation agenda in the North. This policy received its most overt expression in the relocation of "primitive" Inuit communities from the interior caribou regions of the Keewatin to the Hudson Bay coast, where displaced people received so-called rehabilitation and employment training that would in theory allow them to adopt modern livelihoods as miners, commercial fishers, DEW Line workers, or market-oriented craft producers. Although wildlife conservation was not the only influence on the development of the relocation program, the program appealed to federal wildlife bureaucrats because it removed seemingly reckless hunters from close proximity to the caribou herds. As such, the relocation program represents the most overtly colonial idea to have emerged in six decades of federal wildlife administration in the Northwest Territories. Federal officials decided that the conservation of wildlife in the Northwest Territories required the complete transformation of the cultures that had sustained Dene and Inuit communities for generations. Independent hunters and trappers were to become townsfolk, labourers, or wards of an external authority that sought to control every aspect of their social, cultural, and material lives.

The development of such a broad conservation program can be attributed in part to the expanding role of science in the postwar federal wildlife bureaucracy. The creation of an internal scientific agency in the form of the Canadian Wildlife Service brought enough personnel, funding, and expertise to conduct the first aerial caribou surveys, a census technique that produced estimates of the mainland caribou population in the thousands rather the millions. Although these studies provided only a coarse assessment of the caribou population, they were accepted as accurate markers of a disastrous decline in the mainland caribou population. The CWS biologists tended, moreover, to repeat in their writings the stories of wasteful caribou slaughters that had been circulating in the region for over seven decades, adding an air of scientific legitimacy to the idea that Native hunters were primarily responsible for the decline in caribou numbers. Indeed, the broad participation of CWS biologists in caribou management programs reinforced the notion that the hunting cultures of indigenous people were deficient and in need of expert management and control. Although some of their more radical proposals, such as the campaign to abrogate treaty rights to hunt and trap in the provinces, were never implemented, CWS biologists remained tireless advocates of programs to alter the northern Aboriginal subsistence economy throughout the nearly twenty-five years in which they studied the mainland caribou herds.

In addition to persistent attempts to manage human hunters, the CWS also established direct and intensive forms of managerial control over specific populations of northern wildlife. The increase in predator control operations in response to the postwar caribou crisis, and the intense herding and culling program that was implemented in Wood Buffalo National Park to control disease, suggest that CWS biologists were not averse to slaughtering wildlife if the killing was part of a supposedly rational herd management scheme. The CWS scientists responsible for the culling program did not object even to the blatant commercialization of the bison herds, so long as this pecuniary goal did not completely displace the scientific objective of disease eradication.

Given this willingness to merge wildlife management and marketing programs, it is tempting to adopt the familiar argument that science is an inherently imperialistic form of knowledge dedicated to the control and domination of nature in the service of state commercial interests.[9] But such a generalized analysis overlooks the historical moments when biologists and utilitarian wildlife managers held irreconcilable views. The widespread objections of wildlife biologists in Canada, the United States, and Britain to the Wainwright bison transfer and the heated debates between scientists and managers over the efficacy of predator control operations in the 1920s suggest that the scientific community was not simply a passive servant of state interests. Although the scientific objections to the transfer were grounded in what was perhaps a naïve faith in Frederic Clements' theories of an ideal "balance of nature" free from human influence, biologists before the Second World War were not always compliant advocates of the federal government's intensive wildlife management programs.

By the postwar period, however, the rise of more economic models of ecology (e.g., energy flow, population cycles) and the centralization of wildlife research within the federal bureaucracy had produced a new generation of scientists who were more supportive of the managerial and commercial interests of the state. Although the early Canadian Wildlife Service did not falsify results to serve state objectives, its scientists were more than willing to frame their scientific studies and management programs in terms of the administrative priorities of their bureaucratic masters. Hence a disease control program in Wood Buffalo National Park became intimately tied to the postwar administrative push for economic development in the North. In addition, the tenuous results of the caribou studies were interpreted by both the CWS and the northern administration as a justification for strict wildlife regulations and coercive conservation education programs in the Northwest Territories. The capacity of biologists to assess and manage wildlife over such a vast territory remained limited even in the high-tech age of the aerial survey, but science had become a powerful legitimating force for federal intervention in the lives of humans and wildlife in the more "primitive" regions of the Northwest Territories.

At the intersection of these historical forces – the disdain among conservationists for traditional hunting cultures, the authoritarian approach of the state to wildlife conservation, and the rise of scientific knowledge – lies a wider conclusion regarding the narrative history of wildlife conservation in northern Canada: wildlife conservation in the Northwest Territories was bound to a broad modernization agenda in the region.[10] In pragmatic terms, wildlife conservation was one of the principal reasons that the trappings of modern statecraft – legal codes, bureaucratic management, and a capacity to enforce the law – were imported to northern Canada. The expansion of the state conservation bureaucracy also brought a cadre of scientific "experts" intent on replacing the supposed primitive spontaneity of northern Aboriginal hunting cultures with more modern (i.e., rational) principles of wildlife management. The introduction of legal restrictions on indigenous hunting activities was only one expression of the idea that traditional Aboriginal relationships to nature were somehow lacking. The coercive programs designed to alter the subsistence cycle of Aboriginal people represented perhaps the most profound diffusion of state power over their basic subsistence activities.

In theoretical terms, the attempts of the federal government to control and shape the daily processes of production among northern Native hunters recall Michel Foucault's depiction of the modern state as a pervasive imposition of authority over its citizenry rather than an overtly threatening power. In *Discipline and Punish,* Foucault employs the metaphor of the panopticon – a prison where the guards maintain constant surveillance from a central tower – to argue that discipline in a modern society emerges not from the threat of violence, pain, or death but from the constant observation and supervision of individuals by institutional authorities.[11] Like the denizens of Foucault's panopticon, Native hunters of the Northwest Territories were subject to a state system of wildlife management that emphasized the surveillance and supervision of some of the most intimate aspects of their material lives. Although the vast geography of the Northwest Territories limited the supervisory reach of game wardens, police, and other federal agents, wildlife conservation had nevertheless become a totalizing influence on the lives of many Native hunters in the 1950s and '60s. Indeed, by this time, many Native hunters had lost much of their former independence through coercive policy measures that encouraged them to abandon their traditional lives as caribou hunters and become fishers, whalers, or compliant wage labourers within the modern industrial economy.[12] The federal government had achieved this level of control not through the threat of violence but through more subtle forms of coercion (such as education and relocation) that allowed the state to manage and regulate the most basic aspects of everyday life among the Dene and the Inuit.

Nothing in this analysis is meant to suggest that the Dene and Inuit passively accepted the influence of state conservation programs on their livelihoods. On the contrary, Native hunters in the Northwest Territories – and also the northern Alberta Cree of Wood Buffalo National Park – resisted the federal government's attempts to impose wildlife sanctuaries and game regulations on their traditional hunting grounds through such formal protest methods as treaty boycotts, petitions, and protest letters. Objections to the game laws were a dominant theme in the political discourse of many Native communities by the middle of the twentieth century. In 1950, for example, the anthropologist June Helm reported that, for the people of Jean Marie River, "the restrictions [on hunting] are a source of continual resentment and give rise to such ironic jokes as 'they are going to close mice next.'"[13] The refusal of some hunters to obey the game regulations probably constituted a form of resistance to the federal government's assumption of control over wildlife. Although the motivations of those who broke the game laws are difficult to interpret from an archival record that contains little direct testimony from Aboriginal hunters, the highly politicized nature of the trials in Wood Buffalo Park in the late 1920s and early 1930s and the hostile community reaction to charges laid for "poaching" caribou in the 1940s suggest that breaking the law provided Native hunters with a direct means to register their discontent with federal conservation initiatives. These protests had an instrumental element: many of the participants went to great pains to remind federal officials that the regulation of wildlife harvesting in the Northwest Territories had made an already precarious existence more difficult. But the protests also had a political component, a consistent complaint that the federal government had violated the inherent right of northern Aboriginal people to hunt for food and, in the case of the Dene and the Wood Buffalo Park Cree, breached its obligation to uphold the perpetual hunting and trapping rights guaranteed in Treaties 8 and 11.

Much has changed in the thirty-five years since wildlife management was placed under the control of the Northwest Territories government (and more recently the government of Nunavut). The federal and territorial governments have slowly abandoned the older authoritarian approach to conservation in favour of more co-operative wildlife management. In recent years, the co-management of wildlife populations by scientists and Aboriginal harvesters has become the rule rather than the exception in both federal parks and the vast areas under territorial jurisdiction. Native communities have also been able to take more control over the process of establishing national parks in the Northwest Territories, rejecting protected areas in some cases and establishing others on their own terms through the process of settling land claims.[14] In light of such recent developments, some might question the need to revisit the history of conflict between Native people and conservationists in the Northwest Territories. Surely a thorough examination of the more inclusive contemporary initiatives would constitute a more positive contribution to the causes of conservation and Native cultural survival in the North than would a reiteration of past mistakes.

But can the practice of wildlife conservation in the Northwest Territories be so easily severed from its own past? Paul Nadasdy's recent study of wildlife co-management initiatives in the Yukon suggests that a large measure of the colonialism inherent to previous conservation efforts persists in the contemporary North. According to Nadasdy, an ostensibly co-operative approach to managing bighorn sheep that was implemented in the southwest Yukon in the late 1990s tended to alienate Native hunters from a system that demanded they conform to Euro-Canadian bureaucratic norms and contribute traditional ecological knowledge in a manner consistent with scientific models of understanding wildlife.[15] Shades of the older intensive approaches to wildlife management survive as well. Vehement controversy has developed in the past two decades over proposals to completely eradicate the diseased bison of Wood Buffalo National Park and replace them with a transplanted herd of wood bison.[16] Both the history of conflict between Native hunters and conservationists and the past controversy over intensive wildlife management schemes such as the Wainwright buffalo transfer continue to reverberate through the region.

Indeed, if we were to return to the road leading out of Wood Buffalo National Park with a more thorough knowledge of the history of wildlife conservation in the region, an encounter with a herd of bison might raise more questions than answers. How many of the bison we encountered that night were infected with tuberculosis or brucellosis? How many of their ancestors were killed in the disease control and meat production programs in the park? Is the continued ban on bison hunting in the park a lingering source of discontent for Native hunters in the region? Any presumption of historical success for the federal government's wildlife conservation programs must, in the end, be measured against the answers to such questions. The free-roaming herds of northern bison, caribou, and muskox may have survived to the present day, but so too has the memory of wildlife conservation as a projection of federal government power over both humans and nature in the Northwest Territories.

Appendix

TABLE A.1 Federal administrative units with primary control over wildlife in the Northwest Territories, 1894-1966

Year	Branch or bureau	Department
1894	North-West Mounted Police*	Interior
1911	Forestry Branch	Interior
1917	Parks Branch	Interior
1922	Northwest Territories and Yukon Branch	Interior
1931	Dominion Lands Board	Interior
1934	Lands, Northwest Territories and Yukon Branch	Interior
1936	Lands, Parks and Forests Branch	Mines and Resources
1947	Lands and Development Services Branch	Mines and Resources
1950	Development Services Branch	Resources and Development
1951	Northern Administration and Lands Branch	Resources and Development
1952	Northern Administration and Lands Branch	Northern Affairs and National Resources
1959	Northern Administration Branch	Northern Affairs and National Resources
1966	Northern Administration Branch	Indian and Northern Affairs

* The mounted police were responsible only for enforcing wildlife laws. There was no branch or bureau specifically devoted to the administration of wildlife in the Northwest Territories during this early period.

Major Events in the History of Conservation in the Northwest Territories

1894 Unorganized Territories Game Preservation Act becomes the first conservation legislation with clauses specific to wildlife in the Canadian North. It offers full protection to the wood bison and a closed season on muskox applicable only to non-Native hunters.

1897 North-West Mounted Police begin patrols in the wood bison ranges of the South Slave region.

1898 François Byskie is convicted of bison poaching in Fort Smith. He is the first Aboriginal hunter to be charged under the Game Preservation Act north of the sixtieth parallel.

1899 Treaty 8 delegation visits the Northwest Territories to secure land cessions from Native groups.

1911 Department of the Interior's Forestry Branch is granted authority over the administration of wildlife in the Northwest Territories. A game warden service is established at Fort Smith.

1916 The federal government establishes the interdepartmental Advisory Board on Wildlife Protection.

1917 Northwest Game Act establishes closed seasons on a variety of game, including caribou, and a ban on killing muskox throughout the year (with exceptions for Native hunters who are starving). Responsibility for wildlife in the Northwest Territories transferred to the Parks Branch.

1919 National Conference on Conservation of Game, Fur-Bearing Animals and other Wild Life is held in February. A royal commission is established to investigate the potential of reindeer and muskox industries in the Northwest Territories.

1921 First federal government administrative office in the Northwest Territories opens. The NWT commissioner, W.W. Cory, appoints six members to the Northwest Territories Council. Treaty 11 is signed with Native groups in the Mackenzie River region. The federal government also creates the Northwest Territories and Yukon Branch, the first administrative unit devoted to the Northwest Territories.

1922 Wood Buffalo National Park established. The administration of wildlife policy and Wood Buffalo National Park becomes the responsibility of the Northwest Territories and Yukon Branch.

1923 The Peel River, Yellowknife, and Slave River Game Preserves are created for the exclusive use of Native hunters.

1924 Ban on muskox hunting in the Northwest Territories applied to Native hunters, who had previously been exempt if they were starving.

1925 The transfer of plains bison from Buffalo National Park at Wainwright to Wood Buffalo National Park begins and continues until 1928.

1926 The boundary of Wood Buffalo National Park is extended south of the Peace River to create the "park annex." The Arctic Islands Game Preserve is established.

1927 The Thelon Game Sanctuary is created.

1928 First slaughter of bison in Wood Buffalo National Park for relief purposes.

1929 An amendment to the game regulations makes it illegal for any person to enter the Thelon Game Sanctuary without a permit. The game regulations are also amended to remove the "starvation clause" allowing Native hunters to kill caribou during the closed season when in dire need of food. The new regulations also prevent the slaughter of game in excess of personal need and the killing of most female big game species with young at foot. Due to vigorous protests, the starvation clause is reinstated in November.

1931 As a result of the transfer of responsibility over natural resources from the federal government to the western provinces in 1930, the Department of the Interior is reorganized and the Northwest Territories and Yukon Branch is abolished. The administration of NWT wildlife falls to the Dominion Lands Board.

1934 Name of Dominion Lands Board changed to Lands, Northwest Territories and Yukon Branch.

1936 C.H.D. Clarke begins his biological survey of the Thelon Game Sanctuary. The functions of the Department of the Interior are merged into the Department of Mines and Resources along with the departments of Mines, Indian Affairs, and Immigration and Colonization. The Northwest Territories is administered under the auspices of the Bureau of Northwest Territories and Yukon Affairs within the Lands, Parks and Forests Branch. The branch's director, Roy A. Gibson, becomes the effective administrative chief of the Northwest Territories.

1945 A superintendent of forests and wildlife is appointed for the Northwest Territories.

1946 A game warden service is established with posts at Fort Norman, Aklavik, Yellowknife, and Fort Simpson.

1947 The Dominion Wildlife Service is created. The administration of the Northwest Territories is assigned to the Northwest Territories and Yukon Service within the Lands and Development Services Branch. Roy Gibson maintains his position as director of this branch and remains the effective administrative chief of the North-west Territories. The federal government organizes the first major study of the barren ground caribou herds (A.W.F. Banfield is hired to lead the study in January 1948). A ban on serving caribou in restaurants, hotels, or other institutions that charge for meals is implemented, sparking a lengthy battle with Catholic missionaries who run schools and hospitals.

1949 The authority to create game regulations is shifted from the federal cabinet to the Northwest Territories Council. The council remains an appointed body until 1951, when three of eight members are to be elected.

1950 Reorganization results in the dissolution of the Department of Mines and Resources and the creation of the Department of Resources and Development. The administration of the Northwest Territories is placed under the Northern Administration Service within the Development Services Branch (Roy Gibson remains director of the latter). The right to sell caribou meat is limited to those who held a general hunting licence before 3 May 1938. The continuing study of the caribou herds comes under the leadership of John Kelsall. The survey work is confined to the Rae herd that inhabits a large region between Great Slave and Great Bear lakes, but Kelsall estimates at the end of his study that the mainland caribou population has dropped to 278,900 animals.

1951 The Northern Administration Service becomes the Northern Administration and Lands Branch. Feeding caribou to dogs in settled areas is banned.

1953 Inuit families from Port Harrison, Quebec, are relocated to Ellesmere and Cornwallis islands. The Department of Resources and Development is renamed the Department of Northern Affairs and National Resources. The first commercial slaughter of bison in Wood Buffalo National Park takes place.

1955 Native hunters who hold a general hunting licence are permitted to hunt game other than bison and muskox at any time of the year so long as it is for subsistence purposes. Administrative and technical committees for caribou preservation are established to co-ordinate scientific research and conservation programs across political boundaries.

1956 The boundary of the Thelon Game Sanctuary is altered to accommodate mining interests. A.W.F. Banfield's article declaring a "caribou crisis" appears in the *Beaver*. The Sayisi Dene band at Duck Lake, Manitoba, is relocated to Churchill.

1957 A study of the Saskatchewan caribou herd begins under the leader-
      ship of John Kelsall. At the end of the study Kelsall estimates that
      only 200,000 caribou remain on the Arctic mainland ranges. Cari-
      bou can only be sold among holders of a general hunting licence.
      Caribou hunting is banned on Coats and Southampton islands. The
      Ennadai Lake Inuit are relocated to Henik Lake and starvation ensues
      in the winter of 1957-58.

1958 A ban is implemented on hunting female caribou east of the Mac-
      kenzie River and animals under one year of age everywhere in the
      Northwest Territories. Feeding caribou to dogs is banned every-
      where in the Northwest Territories. The survivors of the Henik Lake
      disaster are relocated to the Keewatin Reestablishment Project on
      the west coast of Hudson Bay.

1959 The Northern Administration and Lands Branch is renamed the
      Northern Administration Branch.

1964 Transfer of Wood Buffalo National Park to the National Parks
      Branch begins.

1965 The transfer of authority over Wood Buffalo National Park from the
      Northern Administration Branch to the National and Historic Parks
      Branch is set in motion, to be completed four years later.

1966 Department of Northern Affairs and National Resources is replaced
      with the Department of Indian and Northern Affairs. The biologist
      Robert Ruttan claims that the mainland caribou herds have recov-
      ered to 700,000 animals.

1967 Devolution of control over local government and services from the
      federal to the territorial government begins. This devolution of
      authority takes place over the next three years and gradually includes
      the administration of wildlife (except in national parks and federal
      game sanctuaries). Final commercial slaughter of bison in Wood
      Buffalo National Park. The CWS biologist Don Thomas conducts a
      major resurvey of the barren ground caribou population and esti-
      mates that 385,000 animals inhabit the mainland ranges.

Notes

This volume is primarily a study of archival documents. Newspaper articles cited throughout the notes are too numerous to list in the bibliography of primary sources. The vast majority of these articles came from clippings within the government records consulted at Library and Archives Canada and the Northwest Territories Archives. In some cases, original articles were consulted when clippings were in poor condition.

Foreword: The Enigmatic North

1 Derek Hayes, *Historical Atlas of the Arctic* (Vancouver, BC: Douglas and McIntyre; Seattle, WA: University of Washington Press, 2003).
2 Warburton Pike, "Authors Preface to the Original Edition [1891]," *The Barren Ground of Northern Canada* (New York: E.P. Dutton, 1917), v-ix.
3 Eric Wilson, *A Spiritual History of Ice: Romanticism, Science, and the Imagination* (New York: Palgrave Macmillan, 2003).
4 See among others, Carl C. Berger, "The True North Strong and Free," in *Nationalism in Canada,* ed. Peter Russell (Toronto: McGraw-Hill, 1966), 3-26; R.G. Haliburton, "The Men of the North and Their Place in History" microform CIHM 27014 (Ottawa: 1869); David Heinimann, "'Latitude Rising': Historical Continuity in Canadian Nordicity," *Journal of Canadian Studies* 28, 3 (1993): 134-39. Sherrill E. Grace, *Canada and the Idea of North* (Montreal and Kingston: McGill-Queen's University Press, 2001) derives her title in part from Canadian pianist and composer Glenn Gould's "Idea of North" suite in his Solitude trilogy. Her cultural/literary analysis taps into a broad stream of literary celebration and cultural scrutiny with northern emphases, to which the contributions of Margaret Atwood and John Moss are particularly worth note. See Margaret Atwood, *Survival: A Thematic Guide to Canadian Literature* (Toronto: Anansi, 1972); Margaret Atwood, *Strange Things: The Malevolent North in Canadian Literature* (Oxford: Clarendon Press, 1995); and John Moss, *Enduring*

Dreams: An Exploration of Arctic Landscape (Don Mills, ON: Anansi, 1994). Matthew Evenden points to the role of the North in Canadian historical scholarship in his "The Northern Vision of Harold Innis," *Journal of Canadian Studies* 34, 3 (Autumn 1999): 162-86.

5 W.L. Morton, ed., *The Shield of Achilles: Aspects of Canada in the Victorian Age/Le bouclier d'Achille: regards sur le Canada de l'ere victorienne* (Toronto: McClelland and Stewart, 1968); Janice Cavell, "The Second Frontier: The North in English-Canadian Historical Writing," *Canadian Historical Review* 83, 3 (2003): 364-84; J.L. Granatstein, "A Fit of Absence of Mind: Canada's National Interest in the North to 1968," in *The Arctic in Question*, ed. E.J. Dosnan (Toronto: Oxford University Press 1976), 13-33. See also Shelagh Grant, "Northern Nationalists: Visions of 'A New North,' 1940-1950," in *For Purposes of Dominion: Essays in Honour of Morris Zaslow*, ed. Kenneth S. Coates and William R. Morrison (North York: Captus Press 1989), 47-70.

6 George M. Dawson, "On Some of the Larger Unexplored Regions of Canada," microform CIHM 06094 (Ottawa: 1890); Pike, *Barren Ground*, 1. I am indebted to Matt Dyce, a doctoral student in Geography at UBC. His fine MA thesis, "A Souvenir from the North: Images, Narratives, and Power in the Athabaska-Mackenzie River Basin, 1882-1914" (Carleton University, 2006), set me thinking about some of the issues discussed in these pages, and guided me to some of the most pertinent literature, especially the piece by Agnes Laut (see below). I am indebted as well to Jono Peyton, also in the UBC doctoral program in Geography, who commented helpfully on a draft version of these reflections.

7 Caspar Whitney, *On Snow Shoes to the Barren Grounds: Twenty-Eight Hundred Miles after Musk-Oxen and Wood-Bison* (New York: Harper and Brothers, 1896), 2, 1.

8 Elihu Stewart, *Down the Mackenzie and up the Yukon in 1906* (Toronto: Bell and Cockburn, 1913), 23.

9 Agnes Laut, "The Twentieth Century Is Canada's: The Romantic Story of a People Just Discovering Their Own Country," *World's Work* 15 (1907): 8499-8517; Ernest J. Chambers, ed., *Canada's Fertile Northland: A Glimpse of the Enormous Resources of Part of the Unexplored Regions of the Dominion* (Ottawa: Government Printing Bureau, 1907).

10 Laut, "The Twentieth Century"; William C. Wonders, ed., *Canada's Changing North* (Toronto: McClelland and Stewart, 1971).

11 Richard Harrington, *The Face of the Arctic: A Cameraman's Story in Words and Pictures of Five Journeys into the Far North* (New York: Henry Schuman, 1952), 8; *National Geographic* (October 1949): 7, cited in Matthew Farish, "Frontier Engineering: From the Globe to the Body in the Cold War Arctic," *The Canadian Geographer* 50, 2 (June 2006): 177-96.

12 Hamilton quoted in Graeme Wynn, *Canada and Arctic North America: An Environmental History* (Santa Barbara, CA; ABC-Clio, 2007); extract from *Imperial Oil Review* 49, 5 (1965): 13, in Wonders, ed., *Canada's Changing North*, 212-13.

13 Thomas Berger, *Northern Frontier, Northern Homeland: The Report of the Mackenzie Valley Pipeline Inquiry*, 2 vols. (Ottawa: Ministry of Supply and Services Canada, 1977).

14 Shelagh D. Grant *Sovereignty or Security?: Government Policy in the Canadian North, 1936-1950* (Vancouver: UBC Press, 1988); Shelagh D. Grant, "Sovereignty, Stewardship and Security in the Evolution of Canadian Northern Policy, 1940-1950" (MA thesis, Trent University, 1982); Morris Zaslow, *The Opening of the Canadian North, 1870-1914* (Toronto: McClelland and Stewart, 1971); Morris Zaslow, *The Northward*

Expansion of Canada 1914-1967 (Toronto: McClelland and Stewart, 1988); Janet Foster, *Working for Wildlife: The Beginning of Preservation in Canada* (Toronto: University of Toronto Press, 1978); Alexander J. Burnett, *A Passion for Wildlife: The History of the Canadian Wildlife Service* (Vancouver: UBC Press, 2003); George Colpitts, *Game in the Garden: A Human History of Wildlife in Western Canada to 1940* (Vancouver: UBC Press, 2002); Tina Loo, *States of Nature: Conserving Canada's Wildlife in the Twentieth Century* (Vancouver: UBC Press, 2006).

15 For examples, see E.P. Thompson, *Whigs and Hunters: The Origin of the Black Act* (London: Allen Lane, 1975); Ramachandra Guha, *The Unquiet Woods: Ecological Change and Peasant Resistance in the Himalayas* (Berkeley: University of California Press, 2000); K. Sivaramakrishnan, *Modern Forests: Statemaking and Environmental Change in Colonial Eastern India* (Stanford, CA: Stanford University Press, 1999); Jane Carruthers, *The Kruger National Park: A Social and Political History* (Pietermaritzburg: University of Natal Press, 1995); Karl Jacoby, *Crimes against Nature: Squatters, Poachers, Thieves, and the Hidden History of American Conservation* (Berkeley: University of California Press, 2001); Louis S. Warren, *The Hunter's Game: Poachers and Conservationists in Twentieth-Century America* (New Haven, CT: Yale University Press, 1997); Mark D. Spence, *Dispossessing the Wilderness: Indian Removal and the Making of the National Parks* (New York: Oxford University Press, 1999); Bruce W. Hodgins and Jonathan Bordo, "Wilderness, Aboriginal Presence and the Land Claim," in *Co-Existence? Studies in Ontario-First Nations Relations,* ed. Bruce W. Hodgins, Shawn Heard, and John S. Milloy (Peterborough, ON: Frost Centre, 1992), 67-80; Theodore (Ted) Binnema and Melanie Niemi, "'Let the Line Be Drawn Now': Wilderness, Conservation and the Exclusion of Aboriginal People from Banff National Park in Canada," *Environmental History* 11 (October 2006): 724-50.

16 Kenneth S. Coates and William R. Morrison, *The Alaska Highway in World War II: The US Army of Occupation in Canada's Northwest* (Norman, OK: University of Oklahoma Press, 1992), 85; Loo, *States of Nature,* 93-111. For a summary and extension of the work by Elton and his associates as well as a useful bibliography, see Charles H. Smith, "Spatial Trends in Canadian Snowshoe Hare, *Lepus americanus,* Population Cycles," *Canadian Field-Naturalist* 97, 2 (1983): 151-60.

17 For a summary, see Loo, *States of Nature,* passim; Aldo Leopold, *Game Management* (New York, London: C. Scribner's Sons, 1933).

18 Quoted in Barry Potyondi, *Dual Allegiance: The History of Wood Buffalo National Park, 1929-1965* (Ottawa: Parks Canada, 1981), 173, and cited in Loo, *States of Nature,* 143.

INTRODUCTION: WILDLIFE AND CANADIAN HISTORY

1 O.S. Finnie, "A Letter from the Government to the Indian People," 1 April 1924, RG 85, vol. 768, file 5208, Library and Archives Canada (LAC).

2 There has been considerable debate as to whether the wood bison is a distinct subspecies of the plains bison. Yet even those critics who balk at assigning distinct species status to the wood bison agree that the animal's physical characteristics (e.g., darker and thicker fur) suggest that it is a unique ecotype. Thus, for the period before 1925, I employ the term "wood bison" for the buffalo herds of northern Alberta and the Northwest Territories. I use the more generic "northern bison" for the herds of Wood

Buffalo National Park in the period after 1925, when the release of several thousand plains bison south of Fort Smith ensured that the wood bison were no longer the majority of the park's bison population and could no longer be considered a pure strain of a distinct subspecies. For an overview of the competing poles of the taxonomy debate, see Valerius Geist, "Phantom Subspecies: The Wood Bison *Bison bison 'athabascae'* Rhoads 1897 Is Not a Valid Taxon, but an Ecotype," *Arctic* 44, 4 (December 1991): 283-300; and C.G. Van Zyll de Jong, *A Systematic Study of Recent Bison, with Particular Consideration of the Wood Bison* (Bison bison athabascae *Rhoads 1898*), Publication in Natural Sciences no. 6 (Ottawa: National Museums of Canada, 1989).

3 Although this study focuses on the Northwest Territories, the first three chapters also discuss the impact of wildlife policy on the Cree of northern Alberta. Many were affected by federal game laws because they lived within or in close proximity to Wood Buffalo National Park. I have therefore included the Cree in more general discussions of wildlife policy in Wood Buffalo National Park throughout the manuscript, unless the subject is clearly political conflict and policy developments in the Northwest Territories.

4 Gibson to J.R.E. Bouchard, District Administrator, Aklavik, 24 November 1949, RG 85, vol. 1088, file 406-13, pt. 5, LAC.

5 Harry Hopkins, *The Long Affray: The Poaching Wars, 1760-1914* (London: Secker and Warburg, 1985).

6 See John Mackenzie, *The Empire of Hunting: Hunting, Conservation, and British Imperialism* (New York: Manchester University Press, 1981); William K. Storey, "Big Cats and Imperialism: Lion and Tiger Hunting in Kenya and Northern India, 1898-1930," *Journal of World History* 2, 2 (1991): 135-73; William Beinhart, "Empire, Hunting and Ecological Change in Southern and Central Africa," *Past and Present* 128 (1990): 162-86.

7 Karl Jacoby, *Crimes against Nature: Squatters, Poachers, Thieves and the Hidden History of American Conservation* (Berkeley: University of California Press, 2001); Mark David Spence, *Dispossessing the Wilderness: Indian Removal and the Making of the National Parks* (Oxford: Oxford University Press, 1999); Philip Burnham, *Indian Country, God's Country: Native Americans and the National Parks* (Washington, DC: Island Press, 2000); Robert H. Keller and Michael F. Turek, *American Indians and National Parks* (Tucson: University of Arizona Press, 1998); Louis Warren, *The Hunter's Game: Poachers and Conservationists in Twentieth Century America* (New Haven, CT: Yale University Press, 1997).

8 See Janet Foster, *Working for Wildlife: The Beginnings of Preservation in Canada*, 2nd ed. (Toronto: University of Toronto Press, 1998); J. Alexander Burnett, *A Passion for Wildlife: The History of the Canadian Wildlife Service* (Vancouver: UBC Press, 2003); and Michel F. Girard, *L'écologisme retrouvé: Essor et decline de la Commission de la conservation du Canada* (Ottawa: University of Ottawa Press, 1994).

9 Loo's study was released very late in the production of the present volume, but it is a brilliant examination of the race, class, and gender dimensions of the popular back-to-nature and conservation movement in Canada. See Tina Loo, *States of Nature: Conserving Canada's Wildlife in the Twentieth Century* (Vancouver: UBC Press, 2006). See also Dan Gottesman, "Native Hunting and the Migratory Birds Convention Act: Historical, Political and Ideological Perspectives," *Journal of Canadian Studies* 13, 3 (Fall 1983): 67-89. Regional studies that are critical of the early conservation movement include Bill Parenteau, "Care, Control and Supervision: Native People in the

Canadian Atlantic Salmon Fishery, 1867-1900," *Canadian Historical Review* 79, 1 (March 1998): 1-35; Bill Parenteau, "A 'Very Determined Opposition to the Law': Conservation, Angling Leases, and Social Conflict in the Canadian Atlantic Salmon Fishery, 1867-1914," *Environmental History* 9, 3 (July 2004): 436-63; Nancy B. Bouchier and Ken Cruickshank, "'Sportsmen and Pothunters': Environment, Conservation and Class in the Fishery of Hamilton Harbour, 1858-1914," *Sport History Review* 28 (1997): 1-18; and Tina Loo, "Making a Modern Wilderness: Conserving Wildlife in Twentieth-Century Canada," *Canadian Historical Review* 82, 1 (March 2001): 92-121. Alan MacEachern's recent book on the national parks in Atlantic Canada traces a history of conflict between local people and the Parks Branch over the expropriation of land. MacEachern, *Natural Selections: National Parks in Atlantic Canada, 1935-1970* (Montreal and Kingston: McGill-Queen's University Press, 2001). Finally, George Colpitts' recent work on wildlife in western Canada and Robert McCandless' volume on the Yukon discuss a broad range of human cultural and social relationships to wildlife, but both devote at least some space to the conflict between wildlife conservationists and local people within their respective regions. McCandless, *Yukon Wildlife: A Social History* (Edmonton: University of Alberta Press, 1985); Colpitts, *Game in the Garden: A Human History of Wildlife in Western Canada to 1940* (Vancouver: UBC Press, 2002).

10 For a discussion of Muir, Leopold, and other "wilderness prophets," see Roderick Nash, *Wilderness and the American Mind*, 3rd ed. (New Haven, CT: Yale University Press, 1982); and Max Oelschlaeger, *The Idea of Wilderness from Prehistory to the Age of Ecology* (New Haven, CT: Yale University Press, 1991). For works that tend to emphasize the contributions of sport hunters to the development of wildlife conservation, see James Trefethen, *An American Crusade for Wildlife* (New York: Boone and Crocket Club, 1975); and John F. Reiger, *American Sportsmen and the Origins of Conservation*, 3rd ed. (Corvallis: Oregon State University Press, 2001). For an account of the progressive conservation movement, see Samuel Hays, *Conservation and the Gospel of Efficiency: The Progressive Conservation Movement, 1890-1920* (New York: Atheneum, 1959).

11 Foster, *Working for Wildlife*, 222, 13-14.

12 Girard, *L'écologisme retrouvé*. Girard's study of the Commission of Conservation is wide ranging, and only chapter 5 is devoted to wildlife issues.

13 Burnett, *A Passion for Wildlife*.

14 Maxwell Graham, *Canada's Wild Buffalo: Observation in the Wood Buffalo Park* (Ottawa: Department of the Interior, 1923), 11.

15 See John Gunion Rutherford, James Stanley McLean, and James Bernard Harkin, *Report of the Royal Commission to Investigate the Possibilities of the Reindeer and Musk-Ox Industries in the Arctic and Sub-Arctic Regions of Canada* (Ottawa: King's Printer, 1922).

16 See C. Gordon Hewitt, *The Conservation of the Wild Life of Canada* (New York: Charles Scribner's Sons, 1921), 136-42.

17 For works that identify a distinct preservationist stream of thought among North American nature advocates, see Foster, *Working for Wildlife;* Nash, *Wilderness and the American Mind;* and Oelschlaeger, *Idea of Wilderness.* In contrast, George Altmeyer has claimed that the wider early conservation movement in Canada served both a "doctrine of unselfishness" and a "doctrine of utilization." Altmeyer, "Three Ideas of Nature in Canada, 1893-1914," in *Consuming Canada: Readings in Environmental History,*

ed. Pam Gaffield and Chad Gaffield (Toronto: Copp Clark, 1995), 105. For an excellent summary and analysis of this debate over the relative emphasis on preservationist sentiment and the "doctrine of usefulness" in Canadian national parks policy, see MacEachern, *Natural Selections*, 34-46. For recent works from the United States that question the preservationist versus conservationist distinction, see Richard West Sellars, *Preserving Nature in the National Parks: A History* (New Haven, CT: Yale University Press, 1997); and Alfred Runte, *National Parks: The American Experience,* 3rd ed. (Lincoln: University of Nebraska Press, 1997), 138-54. Peder Anker has recently argued that British and South African ecologists integrated both preservationist and managerial approaches to conservation in the first half of the twentieth century. Anker, *Imperial Ecology: Environmental Order in the British Empire, 1895-1945* (Cambridge: Harvard University Press, 2001), 197.

18 Doug Weiner, *Models of Nature: Ecology, Conservation and Cultural Revolution in Soviet Russia* (Pittsburgh: University of Pittsburgh Press, 2000).

19 This contradictory stance was typical of the wider cultural and aesthetic antimodernist movement that emerged in Europe and North America between 1880 and 1920. T.J. Jackson Lears' classic study of antimodernism, *No Place of Grace,* rarely touches on the rise of the wilderness and "back to nature" movements in the early twentieth century, but his account of the search for authentic experience among the North American upper classes who believed that modern civilization had created an overly artificial lifestyle is broadly applicable to the contradictory blend of managerial and romantic ideals promoted by early conservationists. According to Lears, Americans who embraced antimodern symbolism readily accommodated their backward-looking sentiments to modern precepts such as efficiency, productivity, and commercialism. The antimodern ideal was, in a sense, repackaged as both a commodity and a therapeutic experience that would contribute to greater efficiency and managerial acumen among the bourgeoisie. Lears, *No Place of Grace: Antimodernism and the Transformation of American Culture, 1880-1920* (New York: Pantheon, 1981). For a discussion of antimodernism in Canada, see the essays by Ian MacKay, Lynda Jessup, Gerta Moray, and Ruth B. Phillips in Lynda Jessup, ed., *Antimodernism and Artistic Experience: Policing the Boundaries of Modernity* (Toronto: University of Toronto Press, 2001).

20 See Ernest Thompson Seton, *Two Little Savages; Being the Adventures of Two Boys Who Lived as Indians and What They Learned* (New York: Grosset and Dunlap, 1911); Ernest Thompson Seton, *The Gospel of the Redman: An Indian Bible* (London: Psychic Press, 1970); Arthur Heming, *Spirit Lake* (New York: Macmillan, 1907); Grey Owl, *The Men of the Last Frontier* (London: Country Life, 1934). For discussions of the dominant society's images of North American Native people in the late nineteenth and early twentieth centuries, see S. Elizabeth Bird, *Dressing in Feathers: The Construction of the Indian in American Popular Culture* (Boulder, CO: Westview, 1996); Joe Sawchuck, ed., *Images of the Indian: Portrayals of Native People,* Readings in Aboriginal Studies vol. 4 (Brandon, MB: Bearpaw Publishing, 1995); and Daniel Francis, *The Imaginary Indian: The Image of the Indian in Canadian Culture* (Vancouver: Arsenal, 1993).

21 For the distinction between settler colonies and exploitation colonies where a minority European administration ruled over a majority indigenous population, see Jürgen Osterhammel, *Colonialism: A Theoretical Overview* (Princeton: Markus Wiener Publishers, 1999). For a general discussion of colonialism, see D.K. Fieldhouse, *Colonialism*

1870-1945: An Introduction (London: Weidenfeld and Nicolson, 1981). For the colonization of western Canada, see Sarah Carter, *Aboriginal People and Colonizers of Western Canada to 1900* (Toronto: University of Toronto Press, 1998); Doug Owram, *The Promise of Eden: The Canadian Expansionist Movement and the Idea of West, 1856-1900* (Toronto: University of Toronto Press, 1999); and R. Cole Harris, *The Resettlement of British Columbia: Essays on Colonialism and Geographic Change* (Vancouver: UBC Press, 1997). For a work that interprets western expansion in the United States through the lens of colonialism, see Jeffrey Ostler, *The Plains Sioux and U.S. Colonialism from Lewis and Clark to Wounded Knee* (Cambridge: Cambridge University Press, 2004).

22 See Morris Zaslow, *The Opening of the Canadian North, 1870-1914* (Toronto: McClelland and Stewart, 1971).

23 Although James Scott's work on the efforts of the modern state to effectively colonize the ecological and social spaces inhabited by rural peasants with homogenous and overly simple management schemes is a major influence and inspiration for the present volume, examples such as this suggest that Scott's analysis may not place enough emphasis on contradictory and variable attitudes among state actors towards the denizens of hinterland regions. See Scott, *Seeing Like a State: How Certain Schemes to Improve the Human Condition Have Failed* (New Haven, CT: Yale University Press, 1998). For an overview of colonialism that emphasizes variability among state and colonial actors, see Nicholas Thomas, *Colonialism's Culture: Anthropology, Travel and Government* (Princeton: Princeton University Press, 1994).

24 The idea of a colonial culture is useful here because it encompasses the multifaceted expressions of colonialism that fall outside a formal definition of the phenomenon as the rule of one country over a foreign people. If the Aboriginal people were not technically a foreign people, their cultures were (and to a certain extent remain) alien to Canada's mainstream European settler cultures. The expansion of the federal government's influence in the Northwest Territories in the early twentieth century thus involved many elements of a paternalistic colonial government (e.g., the imposition of an unelected government, an absence of local consultation, a movement toward cultural assimilation). For further elaboration on the multifaceted expression of a colonial culture among the Western nations, see Thomas, *Colonialism's Culture*, 16-17.

25 Some readers might wonder whether Wood Buffalo National Park, the subject of the first three chapters of this study, can properly be considered part of the Northwest Territories. Although a large portion of this park lies within Alberta, both bison and the Cree and Chipewyan hunters in the region were subject to the control and supervision of the federal conservation bureaucracy from very early in the twentieth century. The southern section of Wood Buffalo National Park may therefore be considered effectively an extension of the federal government's authority over wildlife and people in the Northwest Territories.

26 For a more detailed overview of the Dene subgroups, see June Helm, ed., *Subarctic*, vol. 6 of *Handbook of North American Indians* (Washington: Smithsonian Institution, 1981), 271-360. Lengthy ethnographic descriptions of each Inuit group can be found in David Damas, ed., *Arctic*, vol. 5 of *Handbook of North American Indians* (Washington: Smithsonian Institution, 1984), 391-507 (the Inuvialuit of the Mackenzie Delta are described on pp. 347-58).

27 See Maria Devine, "The First Northern Métis: An Overview of the Historical Context for the Emergence of the Earliest Métis in Canada's North," in *Picking Up the*

Threads: Métis History in the Mackenzie Basin, ed. Métis Heritage Association of the Northwest Territories (Winnipeg: Métis Heritage Association of the Northwest Territories, 1998), 5-28; Jennifer L. Bellman and Christopher C. Hanks, "Northern Métis and the Fur Trade," in *Picking up the Threads,* 29-68; and David M. Smith, *Moose-Deer Island House People: A History of the Native People of Fort Resolution,* National Museum of Man Mercury Series, Canadian Ethnology Service Paper no. 81 (Ottawa: National Museums of Canada, 1982), 68-71.

28 For a description of the animals that formed the basis of the Dene economy, see Beryl C. Gillespie, "Major Fauna in the Traditional Economy," in Helm, *Subarctic,* 15-18. For the animals central to the Inuit economy, see Milton M.R. Freeman, "Arctic Ecosystems," in Damas, *Arctic,* 36-48.

29 For a detailed anthropological description of the seasonal subsistence round of a Dene "bush community" in the middle of the twentieth century, see June Helm, *The People of Denendeh: Ethnohistory of the Indians of Canada's Northwest Territories* (Montreal and Kingston: McGill-Queen's University Press, 2000), 21-90.

30 See ibid., 63-71; June Helm and David Damas, "The Contact-Traditional All Native Community in the Canadian North," *Anthropologica* 5 (1963): 9-21; Takashi Irimoto, *Chipewyan Ecology: Group Structure and Caribou Hunting System* (Osaka: National Museum of Ethnology, 1981); Hugh Brody, *Living Arctic: Hunters of the Canadian North* (Vancouver: Douglas and McIntyre, 1987); Henry S. Sharp, "The Caribou-Eater Chipewyan: Bilaterality, Strategies of Caribou Hunting and the Fur Trade," *Arctic Anthropology* 14, 2 (1977): 35-40; James G.E. Smith, "Local Band Organization of the Caribou-Eater Chipewyan," *Arctic Anthropology* 13, 1 (1976): 12-24; James G.E. Smith, "Economic Uncertainty in an 'Original Affluent Society': Caribou and Caribou-Eater Chipewyan Adaptive Strategies," *Arctic Anthropology* 15, 1 (1978): 68-88; and George Wenzel, *Clyde Inuit Adaptation and Ecology: The Organization of Subsistence,* National Museum of Man Mercury Series, Canadian Ethnology Service Paper no. 77 (Ottawa: National Museums of Canada, 1981).

31 George Blondin, *Yamoria the Lawmaker: Stories of the Dene* (Edmonton: NeWest, 1997); Penny Petrone, ed., *Northern Voices: Inuit Writings in English* (Toronto: University of Toronto Press, 1992).

32 See Gail Beaulieu, ed., *That's the Way We Lived: An Oral History of the Fort Resolution Elders* (Yellowknife: Government of the Northwest Territories, 1987). Full transcripts of the interviews in this collection can be found in the Fort Resolution Community Education Council Fonds, acc. N-1993-016, Northwest Territories Archives. See also Sharone Maldaver, ed., *As Long as I Remember: Elders of the Fort Smith, Northwest Territories Region Talk about Bush Life and Changes They Have Seen* (Fort Smith: Cascade Graphics, 1993); Alan Fehr, Nicole Davis, and Scott Black, eds., *Nàhn' Kak Geenjit Gwich'n Ginjik (Gwich'in Words about the Land)* (Inuvik: Gwich'in Renewable Resource Board, 1997); and Hattie Mannik and David Webster, eds., *Oral Histories: Baker Lake, Northwest Territories* (Ottawa: National Historic Parks and Sites Directorate, Environment Canada, 1993). I chose not to conduct my own oral history study involving those elders in the Northwest Territories who have memories of the conflicts described in this book for several reasons. First, when I worked in the Northwest Territories as an adult educator, the Chipewyan people in my home community of Fort Resolution constantly joked and complained about how they had been treated as objects of study in the past by anthropologists, consultants, and various other researchers.

As a non-Native outsider living in that village, almost six months passed before I felt people were trusting enough to speak openly with me about even the most mundane topics, much less the issues surrounding game conservation in the region. I thus have serious doubts as to whether a community-by-community set of "drop-in" interviews covering several towns and villages in all the regions of the Northwest Territories would have yielded useful results. Due to the restrictions imposed by distance, time, and resources, oral history projects in the Canadian North are probably best done over a long period within a single community (collaboratively with local researchers or exclusively as a local endeavour) rather than as a broad regional study. Second, the available archival sources contain more than enough material to fill one volume; I hope that additional future NWT oral history collections will devote at least some space to the issues raised in this book.

33 Shepard Krech III, *The Ecological Indian: Myth and History* (New York: W.W. Norton, 1999).
34 Ibid., 208.
35 John A. Livingston, *The Fallacy of Wildlife Conservation* (Toronto: McClelland and Stewart, 1981).

CHAPTER 1: MAKING SPACE FOR WOOD BISON

1 Routledge, Patrol Report, Fort Saskatchewan to Fort Simpson, in "Report of the Royal Northwest Mounted Police," *Sessional Papers of the Dominion of Canada*, no. 15 (1899): 88, 95-96.
2 Dan Gottesman, "Native Hunting and the Migratory Birds Convention Act: Historical, Political and Ideological Perspectives," *Journal of Canadian Studies* 13, 3 (Fall 1983): 67-89.
3 For a discussion, see Marilyn Dubasak, *Wilderness Preservation: A Cross-Cultural Comparison of Canada and the United States* (New York: Garland Publishing, 1990), 23-25.
4 Janet Foster, *Working for Wildlife: The Beginnings of Preservation in Canada*, 2nd ed. (Toronto: University of Toronto Press, 1998), 30, 84.
5 Alan MacEachern, *Natural Selections: National Parks in Atlantic Canada, 1935-1970* (Montreal and Kingston: McGill-Queen's University Press, 2001), provides an excellent account of the impact on local people of land expropriation for the creation of Cape Breton Highlands, Prince Edward Island, Fundy, and Terra Nova national parks.
6 The hunters affected by the creation of the park included those living in (and near) such communities as Hay River, Fort Resolution, Fort Smith, and Fort Fitzgerald. After the park boundary was extended south of the Peace River in 1926, the Cree hunters of Fort Chipewyan, Fort MacKay, and Little Red River also came under the regulatory authority of the park administration. Although in general Chipewyan hunters were concentrated at the north end of the park and Cree hunters closer to the south, the ethnic composition of the local population is complicated and difficult to delineate in a simple manner. All the communities near the park also contained Métis trappers and traders, as well as a significant non-Native population after the First World War. For an overview and discussion, see Patricia A. McCormack, "Chipewyans Turn Cree: Governmental and Structural Factors in Ethnic Processes," in *For*

the *Purposes of Dominions: Essays in Honour of Morris Zaslow*, ed. Kenneth S. Coates and William R. Morrison (Toronto: Captus Press, 1989), 125-38.

7 Wood Buffalo National Park was created by order-in-council P.C. 2498, 18 December 1922. The extension of the boundary south of the Peace River to its present-day configuration was accomplished by order-in-council P.C. 1444, 24 September 1926. The provisions allowing hunting and trapping in the park are in each piece of legislation. Copies in RG 13, vol. 2128, file 156807, Library and Archives Canada (LAC).

8 For an overview of the physical characteristics of the wood bison, see L.N. Carbyn, S.M. Oosenbrug, and D.W. Anions, *Wolves, Bison and the Dynamics Related to the Peace-Athabasca Delta in Canada's Wood Buffalo National Park,* Circumpolar Research Series no. 4 (Edmonton: Canadian Circumpolar Institute, University of Alberta, 1993), 40-41.

9 John Schultz, "Report of the Select Committee of the Senate Appointed to Inquire into the Resources of the Great Mackenzie Basin," Appendix 1, *Senate Journals* (1888), 310.

10 William Ogilvie, "Report on the Peace River and Tributaries," *Sessional Papers of the Dominion of Canada,* no. 13 (1893).

11 L.W. Herchmer to Comptroller, Royal Northwest Mounted Police, 3 October 1893, RG 18, series A-1, vol. 489, file 381-15, pt. 2, LAC.

12 Warburton Pike, *The Barren Ground of Northern Canada* (New York: Macmillan, 1892), 145; Caspar Whitney, *On Snow-Shoes to the Barren Grounds: Twenty-Eight Hundred Miles after Musk-Oxen and Wood-Bison* (New York: Harper and Brothers, 1896), 116-17. For an overview of wood bison population estimates from this period, see J. Dewey Soper, "History, Range and Home Life of the Northern Bison," *Ecological Monographs* 2, 4 (October 1941): 360-63.

13 Samuel Hearne, *A Journey from Prince of Wales's Fort in Hudson's Bay to the Northern Ocean, 1769, 1770, 1771, 1772,* ed. Richard Glover (Toronto: Macmillan, 1958), 161; and Alexander Mackenzie, *Voyages from Montreal on the River St. Laurence through the Continent of North America to the Frozen and Pacific Oceans in the Years 1789 and 1793,* ed. John W. Garvin (Toronto: Radisson Society of Canada, 1927), 267. For a discussion of the inaccuracy of the bison population estimates near the turn of the century, see Theresa A. Ferguson, "The 'Jarvis Proof': Management of Bison, Management of Bison Hunters and the Development of a Literary Tradition," *Proceedings of the Fort Chipewyan/Fort Vermilion Bicentennial Conference,* 23-24 September 1988, ed. P.A. McCormack and R.G. Ironside, Occasional paper 28 (Edmonton: Boreal Institute for Northern Studies), 9-10. The biologist William Fuller argues that estimates of the bison population before the age of the aerial survey were merely "intelligent guesses." Fuller, *The Biology and Management of the Bison of Wood Buffalo National Park,* Wildlife Management Bulletin Series 1, no. 16 (Ottawa: Canadian Wildlife Service, 1962), 8.

14 L.W. Herchmer to Comptroller, Royal Northwest Mounted Police, 3 October 1893, RG 18, series A-1, vol. 489, file 381-15, pt. 2, LAC.

15 L.W. Herchmer to Comptroller, Royal Northwest Mounted Police, 8 March 1894, ibid.

16 An Act for the Preservation of Game in the Unorganized Portions of the North-west Territories of Canada, 57-58 Victoria, *Statutes of Canada,* 7th Parliament, 4th Session (1894), c. 31, 221-26.

17 See J.A. Allen, "Northern Range of the Bison," *American Naturalist* 2 (1887): 624;

Ogilvie, "Report on the Peace River," 39; and Whitney, *On Snow-Shoes*, 116. Recent scientific research has suggested that snow depths of only fifty to sixty centimetres can contribute to bison calf mortality and that accumulations of sixty-five to seventy-five centimetres can cause adults to become stressed as uncovering food and moving become laborious. For a summary of this work, see Carbyn, Oosenbrug, and Anions, *Wolves, Bison and Dynamics*, 67-79.

18 For an overview of factors that may lead to declines in the wood bison population, see Carbyn, Oosenbrug, and Anions, *Wolves, Bison and Dynamics*, 92-233.

19 For a full discussion of Aboriginal fire use and the impact of burning on the northern bison, see Henry T. Lewis, "Maskuta: The Ecology of Indian Fires in Northern Alberta," *Western Canadian Journal of Anthropology* 7, 1 (1977): 15-52; and Henry T. Lewis, *A Time for Burning: Traditional Indian Uses of Fire in Western Canadian Boreal Forest*, Occasional Publication no. 17 (Edmonton: Boreal Institute for Northern Studies, 1982).

20 One stream of contemporary research on the more recent decline of the bison population in Wood Buffalo National Park has argued that multiple factors ranging from habitat alteration to disease to wolf predation have all contributed to the downward trend. See Ludwig N. Carbyn, Nicholas J. Lunn, and Kevin Timoney, "Trends in the Distribution and Abundance of Bison in Wood Buffalo National Park" *Wildlife Society Bulletin*, 26, 3 (Fall 1998), 463-70; M.J. Peterson, "Wildlife Parasitism, Science, and Management Policy," *Journal of Wildlife Management* 55, 4 (1991), 782-89.

21 A.M. Jarvis, Northern Patrol, Appendix L, "Report of the Northwest Mounted Police," *Sessional Papers of the Dominion of Canada*, no. 15 (1898): 162; 170-72.

22 *Parliamentary Debates*, vol. 38, 7th Parliament, 4th Session (1 June 1894), 3538.

23 See René Fumoleau, *As Long as This Land Shall Last: A History of Treaty 8 and Treaty 11, 1870-1939* (Toronto: McClelland and Stewart, 1975). The text of Treaty 8 is on pp. 70-73.

24 Ibid. See in particular the edited transcripts of interviews with Susie Abel, Angus Beaulieu, Johnny Beaulieu, John Jean Marie Beaulieu, Pierre Drygeese, Johnny Tassie, Pierre Frisé, Frank Norn, Henry Drygeese, and Pierre Michel on pp. 89-99.

25 An Act to Amend the Unorganized Territories Game Preservation Act, 1894, 62-63 Victoria, *Statutes of Canada*, 8th Parliament, 4th Session (1899), c. 20, 151; An Act Further to Amend the Unorganized Territories Game Preservation Act, 1894, 2 Edward VII, *Statutes of Canada*, 9th Parliament, 2nd Session (1902), c.12, 81.

26 See RG 18, vol. 489, file 381-15, pt. 2, LAC. A patrol report from this file, submitted on 21 February 1900 by Corporal Trotter to his commanding officer in Fort Saskatchewan, stated that Native hunters had killed four or five buffalo near Peace Point. According to Trotter, the hunters claimed ignorance of the legislation extending the ban from 1899 to 1902 as their "only excuse." A report from the 30 July 1901 *Edmonton Bulletin* describing the seizure of fourteen wood bison from Native hunters who were similarly not notified of the extension is in the same file.

27 For a discussion of wolf predation on bison calves as the key factor limiting the herd size, see Corporal Field to C.O. NWMP, 5 March 1902, and Fred White, Comptroller, RNWMP, to Acting Deputy Minister, Department of the Interior, 5 March 1904, RG 18, vol. 489, file 381-15, pt. 2, LAC. For a discussion of using poison or a bounty to reduce the wolf population, see "Excerpt, Fort Chipewyan Police Diary," October 1904, and Field to Commissioner, RNWMP, 10 June 1907, ibid.

28 Report of Inspector A.M. Jarvis, C.M.G., on Wood Buffalo in the Mackenzie District, Appendix N, "Report of the Royal Northwest Mounted Police," *Sessional Papers of the Dominion of Canada*, no. 28 (1907): 123-24.

29 Jarvis to Commissioner, RNWMP, 22 September 1908, RG 18, vol. 489, file 381-15, pt. 2, LAC.

30 Report of Inspector Jarvis, C.M.G., on Wood Buffalo in the Mackenzie District, Appendix N, "Report of the Royal Northwest Mounted Police," *Sessional Papers of the Dominion of Canada*, no. 28 (1907): 125-26.

31 See "Wild Buffalo in the Far North in Danger of Extinction," *Ottawa Free Press*, 16 August 1907, and an untitled report in the *Edmonton Bulletin*, 2 December 1907; clippings in RG 18, vol. 489, file 381-15, pt. 2, LAC.

32 Ernest Thompson Seton, *The Arctic Prairies* (New York: Harper and Row, 1911), 39, 318-20.

33 Ibid., 20, 174. Preble's assessment of the situation was more measured than Seton's and Jarvis'. He acknowledged that precise information on the population of the bison herds was difficult to obtain. He stated that wolves might be a factor limiting the growth of the bison populations, but also briefly noted Jarvis' assertion that illegal killing of the bison was the key factor causing the decline in the herds. Edward A. Preble, *A Biological Investigation of the Athabaska-Mackenzie Region Prepared under the Direction of Dr. C. Hart Merriam* (Washington, DC: Government Printing Office, 1908), 149.

34 Fred White to Frank Oliver, 18 November 1907, and White to Major Perry, 22 November 1907, RG 18, vol. 489, file 381-15, pt. 2, LAC.

35 Sergeant Field to Commissioner, RNWMP, 10 February 1908, RG 18, vol. 489, file 381-15, pt. 2, LAC.

36 Frank Pedley to Frank Oliver, 10 February 1908, ibid.

37 J. Hursell, Justice of the Peace, to Routledge, 16 March 1908, ibid.

38 E. Rowfag, E. Nagle and Trading Co., to Supt. Routledge, 23 July 1908, ibid.

39 The archival record contains other letters to Routledge and other RNWMP officials that are highly critical of Jarvis and Seton. See A. Bower Perry to Routledge, 25 January 1908, and Max G. Hamilton to Routledge, 16 March 1908, ibid. Routledge's report is dated 13 April 1908, ibid.

40 Extract of a Report from Inspector Field, 1 November 1911, ibid.

41 Campbell to Mulloy, 30 March 1911, RG 85, vol. 665, file 3911, pt. 1, LAC.

42 Bell to Campbell, 9 July 1912, ibid.

43 E.H. Finlayson to Campbell, 9 March 1914, RG 85, vol. 664, file 1390, pt. 1, LAC.

44 For a discussion of Mulloy's resignation, see Robert Campbell to W.W. Cory, 11 February 1913, RG 85, vol. 665, file 3911, pt. 1, LAC. Campbell was informed of the transfer of authority over northern wildlife in a memo from Cory dated 5 March 1917, RG 85, vol. 665, file 3911, pt. 2, LAC.

45 See Andrew Isenberg, *The Destruction of the Bison: An Environmental History, 1750-1920* (Cambridge: Cambridge University Press, 2000), 180-81.

46 The proposals for the buffalo enclosure are contained in a series of reports and correspondence among Bell, Mulloy, McCallum, and Campbell. See Bell to Campbell, 16 January 1912, Mulloy to Campbell, 9 July 1913, Bell to Campbell, 8 December 1913, and Bell to Campbell, 28 February 1914, RG 85, vol. 665, file 3912, pt. 1, LAC.

47 For Graham's role in the creation of Nemiskam Antelope Preserve, see Foster, *Working*

for Wildlife, 96-104. For his instrumental role suggesting the idea of uniform cross-border migratory bird regulations, see Kurkpatrick Dorsey, *The Dawn of Conservation Diplomacy: U.S.-Canadian Wildlife Protection Treaties in the Progressive Era* (Seattle: University of Washington Press, 1998), 188-89.

48 Graham to Harkin, 30 June 1912, RG 85, vol. 665, file 3911, pt. 1, LAC.

49 Graham to Harkin, 7 December 1912, ibid.

50 Ibid.

51 See Foster, *Working for Wildlife,* 13-14.

52 Graham to Harkin, 10 December 1912, RG 85, vol. 664, file 3910, pt. 1, LAC.

53 Graham briefly attended the Ontario Agricultural College and was a farmer for six years before he joined the civil service in 1906. Foster, *Working for Wildlife,* 97.

54 Graham to Harkin, 3 January 1913, RG 85, vol. 665, file 3911, pt. 1, LAC. It appears there was general support within the Parks Branch for the idea of an enclosed northern buffalo park at least until 1915. A senior official within the branch, F.H.H. Williamson, stated that the Parks Branch was looking for a suitable area to locate an enclosed wood bison herd. Williamson, "Game Preservation in Dominion Parks," *Proceedings of the Committee on Fisheries, Game and Fur-Bearing Animals, Commission of Conservation, November 1-2, 1915* (Toronto: Methodist Book and Publishing House, 1916), 132-33.

55 Graham to Harkin, 16 October 1912, ibid.

56 Aldo Leopold, *Game Management* (New York: Charles Scribner's Sons, 1933), 3.

57 Graham's idea of managing bison as domestic ranch animals was not unique. Even in the immediate aftermath of the broader collapse of the North American bison population, utilitarian values influenced leading bison conservationists. For example, George Bird Grinnell recommended in 1892 that the US Department of Agriculture should buy all the remaining domestic bison in the country to set up an experimental breeding station and attempt the cross-breeding of bison and cattle. Grinnell, "The Last of the Buffalo," *Scribner's Magazine* 12, 3 (September 1892); reprinted New York: Arno, 1970, 274-77.

58 Graham to Harkin, 7 December 1912, RG 85, vol. 665, file 3911, pt. 1, LAC.

59 Ibid.

60 For example, the hunter-naturalist H.V. Radford wrote to Franklin W. Hooper, president of the American Bison Society, to argue emphatically that Native hunters were not killing the wood bison, that they were pleased the wood bison were being protected by law, and that expropriation of their hunting grounds for a preserve would be resented in a manner that might do more harm than good to the cause of bison preservation. Radford to Hooper, 20 June 1911, RG 85, vol. 665, file 3911, pt. 2, LAC. For other reports that Native hunters were not killing wood bison, see Francis Harper, Geological Survey of Canada, *Annual Report,* 1914, ibid.; Henry J. Bury, "Report on Buffalo Protection," 25 October 1915, RG 85, file 3912, pt. 1, LAC; George Mulloy's patrol report to Robert Campbell, 9 July 1913, ibid.; and Charles Camsell, "The Wood Buffalo Range of Northern Alberta," 21 November 1916, RG 85, vol. 1390, file 406-13, pt. 1, LAC.

61 Harkin to W.W. Cory, 18 April 1916, RG 85, vol. 1390, file 406-13, pt. 1, LAC. See also Maxwell Graham, "Statement as to the Causes That Led Up to the Creation of the Wood Buffalo Park," 4 June 1924, ibid., which indicates that Graham drafted this letter for Harkin.

62 Minister of Interior to Governor General in Council, 3 July 1916, RG 85, vol. 664, file 1310, pt. 1, LAC.

63 For a summary of correspondence surrounding this issue, see Maxwell Graham, "Statement as to the Causes That Led Up to the Creation of the Wood Buffalo Park," 4 June 1924, RG 85, vol. 1390, file 406-13, pt. 1, LAC. Williamson's comments to Harkin are contained in a letter dated 8 August 1916, RG 85, vol. 665, file 3911, pt. 2, LAC. The possibility that wartime budget restrictions killed the park proposal is suggested in a letter from the ornithologist Percy Taverner to Harkin, 31 January 1916, RG 85, vol. 664, file 3910, pt. 1, LAC.

64 W.W. Cory, Deputy Minister of the Interior, to Robert Campbell, 5 March 1917, RG 85, vol. 665, file 3911, pt. 2, LAC.

65 A growing body of literature from the field of environmental history suggests that the state is not a one-dimensional entity that automatically militates against local patterns of resource use. See Mahesh Rangarajan, "Environmental Histories of South Asia: A Review Essay," *Environment and History* 2 (1996): 129-43; Richard Grove, *Green Imperialism: Colonial Expansion, Tropical Island Edens and the Origins of Environmentalism, 1600-1860* (Cambridge: Cambridge University Press, 1995); Satpal Sangwan, "From Gentlemen Amateurs to Professionals: Reassessing the Natural Science Tradition in Colonial India, 1780-1840," in *Nature and the Orient: The Environmental History of South and Southeast Asia,* ed. Richard H. Grove, Vinita Damodaran, and Satpal Sangwan (Delhi: Oxford University Press, 1995), 209-36; and K. Siviramakrishnan, "The Politics of Fire and Forest Regeneration in Colonial Bengal," *Environment and History* 2 (1996): 145-94.

66 For a discussion, see Mark Dickerson, *Whose North? Political Change, Political Development, and Self-Government in the Northwest Territories* (Vancouver: UBC Press, 1992), 28-60. See also Morris Zaslow, *The Northward Expansion of Canada, 1914-1967* (Toronto: McClelland and Stewart, 1988), 188. For a discussion of the policy as applied in the Yukon Territory, see Ken S. Coates, *Best Left as Indians: Native-White Relations in the Yukon Territory, 1840-1973* (Montreal and Kingston: McGill-Queen's University Press, 1993).

67 Arthur Meighen, "Address of Welcome," in *National Conference on Conservation of Game, Fur-Bearing Animals and Other Wild Life, 18-19 February 1919,* ed. Commission of Conservation of Canada (Ottawa: King's Printer, 1919), 5.

68 Duncan Campbell Scott, "The Relation of Indians to Wild Life Conservation," in Commission of Conservation, *National Conference,* 21.

69 James Harkin, "Wild Life Sanctuaries," in Commission of Conservation, *National Conference,* 49.

70 F. Bradshaw, "Comment," in Commission of Conservation, *National Conference,* 27.

71 John McLean to Harkin, 23 July 1914, RG 85, vol. 664, file 3910, pt. 2, LAC.

72 For a report on the meeting, see Harkin to W.W. Cory, 18 April 1916, RG 85, vol. 664, file 3910, pt. 1, LAC.

73 For Graham's first proposal to create Caribou Mountains National Park, see Minister of Interior to Governor General, 30 June 1914, RG 85, vol. 664, file 3910, pt. 1, LAC. For a summary of McLean's and Conroy's influence on the failure of the proposed order-in-council, see Maxwell Graham, "Statement as to the Causes That Led Up to the Creation of the Wood Buffalo Park," 4 June 1924, RG 85, vol. 1390, file 406-13, pt. 1, LAC.

74 Minutes, Advisory Board on Wildlife Protection, 18 June 1920, RG 10, vol. 4085, file 496,658-1A, LAC.

75 F.H. Kitto, "Report on the Natural Resources of the Mackenzie District and Their Economic Development," Natural Resources Intelligence Branch, Department of the Interior, 1920, RG 10, vol. 4092, file 549,036, LAC.

76 Harkin to Cory, 29 February 1921, RG 85, vol. 1390, file 406-13, pt. 1, LAC.

77 F.V. Siebert to F.C.C. Lynch, Superintendent, Natural Resources Intelligence Branch, 22 July 1922, ibid.

78 Maxwell Graham, *Canada's Wild Buffalo: Observation in the Wood Buffalo Park* (Ottawa: Department of the Interior, 1923), 11.

79 H.J. Bury to Deputy Minister, Indian Affairs, 13 April 1916, RG 85, vol. 664, file 3910, pt. 1, LAC. How much of this support for the park was filtered through Bury's own perception of his negotiations with the chiefs is open to question. Despite his position within Indian Affairs, Bury was a strong supporter of the national park proposal. See also H.J. Bury, "Report on the Game and Fisheries of Northern Alberta and the Northwest Territories," 6 November 1915, RG 85, vol. 664, file 3910, pt. 2, LAC.

80 Kitto's discussion with Chief Squirrel is summarized in a series of untitled notes dated 26 June 1920 on his survey of the buffalo range, RG 10, vol. 4085, file 496,658-1A, LAC. The non-Native population in the area that now comprises the Northwest Territories and Nunavut increased from 137 people in 1901 to 519 in 1911. Morris Zaslow, *The Opening of the Canadian North, 1870-1914* (Toronto: McClelland and Stewart, 1971), 238.

81 Minutes, Advisory Board on Wildlife Protection, 18 June 1920, RG 10, vol. 4085, file 496,658-1A, LAC.

82 Fumoleau, *As Long as This Land,* 255.

83 "Buffalo Range Would Deprive Alberta of 100 Square Miles of Territory Say Northmen," *Edmonton Bulletin,* 18 October 1922, 5.

84 Ibid.

85 McLean to Harkin, 22 July 1920, RG 10, vol. 4085, file 496,658-1A, LAC.

86 Minutes, Advisory Board on Wildlife Protection, 12 April 1921, RG 85, vol. 1390, file 406-13, pt. 1, LAC.

87 Graham to O.S. Finnie, 31 October 1922, ibid.

88 Graham, *Canada's Wild Buffalo,* 10.

CHAPTER 2: CONTROL ON THE RANGE

1 F.H. Kitto, "The Survival of the American Bison in Canada," *Geographical Journal* 63 (May 1924): 431.

2 McDougal to O.S. Finnie, Director, Northwest Territories and Yukon Branch, 2 March 1926, RG 85, vol. 1213, file 400-2-3, pt. 1, Library and Archives Canada (LAC).

3 O.S. Finnie, "Statement as to the Need for Eliminating Indians as Well as Other Hunters and Trappers from the Wood Buffalo Park," 25 January 1926, RG 85, vol. 1213, file 400-2-3, pt. 1, LAC.

4 For a summary of the treaty negotiations, see René Fumoleau, *As Long as This Land Shall Last: A History of Treaty 8 and Treaty 11, 1870-1939* (Toronto: McClelland and Stewart, 1975), 150-224.

5 Mark Dickerson, *Whose North? Political Change, Political Development, and Self-Government in the Northwest Territories* (Vancouver: UBC Press, 1992), 31-32; Shelagh Grant, *Sovereignty or Security? Government Policy in the Canadian North, 1936-1950* (Vancouver: UBC Press, 1988), 18-19.

6 Finnie created the preserves after lobbying from the superintendent of Wood Buffalo Park, John McDougal, and the Catholic bishop Gabriel Breynat. Kerry Abel, *Drum Songs: Glimpses of Dene History* (Montreal and Kingston: McGill-Queen's University Press, 1993), 188-95. For the petitions of Native hunters regarding game preserves, see Fumoleau, *As Long as This Land,* 248-50. A fourth game preserve encompassing the Arctic Archipelago was created in 1926 by order-in-council P.C. 1146, 19 July 1926; copy in RG 13, vol. 924, file 6101, part A, LAC.

7 See O.S. Finnie, "Statement as to the Need for Eliminating Indians as Well as Other Hunters and Trappers from the Wood Buffalo Park," 25 January 1926, RG 85, vol. 1213, file 400-2-3, pt. 1, LAC. See also Finnie to Graham, 13 January 1926, RG 85, vol. 1213, file 400-2-3, vol. 1, LAC.

8 For Finnie's requests to remove treaty Indians from the park, see Finnie to W.W. Cory, Deputy Minister of the Interior, 30 November 1925, and Finnie to R.A. Gibson, Assistant Deputy Minister of the Interior, 9 December 1925, RG 85, vol. 1213, file 400-2-3, pt. 1, LAC.

9 Scott to Stewart, 29 December 1925, RG 85, vol. 1213, file 400-2-3, pt. 1, LAC.

10 Graham to Finnie, 21 November 1922, RG 85, vol. 1390, file 406-13, pt. 1, LAC.

11 Ibid. For an account of the poaching incident, see Maxwell Graham, *Canada's Wild Buffalo: Observation in the Wood Buffalo Park* (Ottawa, Department of the Interior, 1923), 11.

12 The notice is quoted in a letter from Graham to Finnie, 23 July 1925, RG 85, vol. 1390, file 406-13, pt. 1, LAC.

13 Finnie to the Olson brothers, 20 June 1923, ibid.

14 An article in the *Edmonton Bulletin* stated that "a number" of white trappers who had claimed squatters' rights had been ordered out of the park. "Trappers Warned Off the Northern Buffalo Range," *Edmonton Bulletin,* 9 July 1923, 2.

15 H.E. Brownlea for park superintendent to Finnie, 9 July 1923, RG 85, vol. 1390, file 406-13, pt. 1, LAC.

16 McDougal submitted a report on the meeting to Finnie on 1 August 1924. RG 85, vol. 1213, file 400-2-3, pt. 1, LAC.

17 Cornwall to Finnie, 14 April 1924, RG 85, vol. 1390, file 406-13, pt. 1, LAC.

18 See Morris Zaslow, *The Northward Expansion of Canada, 1914-1967* (Toronto: McClelland and Stewart, 1988), 131-34.

19 "Trappers Warned Off the Northern Buffalo Range," *Edmonton Bulletin,* 9 July 1923, 2.

20 Information on the Conibear family was gleaned from a newspaper obituary for Kenneth Conibear. Tom Hawthorn, "Kipling of the North," *Globe and Mail,* 6 November 2002, R9.

21 Population data from the years 1921 to 1931 suggests that 30 to 40 percent of the newcomers to the Northwest Territories were European immigrants. Peter Usher, "Societies and Economies in the North," in *The Historical Atlas of Canada,* vol. 3, ed. Donald Kerr and Deryck W. Holdsworth (Toronto: University of Toronto Press, 1990), plate 58. Although no specific data are available on returned soldiers, in 1920 F.H. Kitto reported a concern about two veterans who were trying to scratch out a

living on a homestead near Peace Point. See Kitto's notes on his survey of the Mackenzie District, 26 June 1920, RG 10, vol. 4085, file 496,658-1A, LAC.

22 Graham, *Canada's Wild Buffalo*, 11.

23 Finnie to McDougal, 23 July 1925, RG 85, vol. 1213, file 400-2-3, pt. 1, LAC.

24 Finnie to McDougal, 27 August 1924, RG 85, vol. 1213, file 400-2-3, pt. 1, LAC.

25 See Graham to Finnie, 23 July 1925, RG 85, vol. 1213, file 400-2-3, pt. 1, LAC.

26 Petition to H.E. Hume, 3 September 1932, RG 85, vol. 1213, file 400-2-3, pt. 2, LAC. Hume's response was forwarded to McDougal, 6 October 1932, ibid.

27 Finnie, "Notes on an Official Visit to Wood Buffalo Park, Aug.-Sept. 1925," RG 85, vol. 1391, file 406-13, pt. 2, LAC.

28 Finnie to Gibson, 9 December 1925, RG 85, file 400-2-3, pt. 1, LAC.

29 William Rowan, report on expedition to Wood Buffalo National Park submitted to O.S. Finnie, 17 December 1925, RG 85, vol. 763, file 5021, LAC.

30 McDougal to Finnie, 2 March 1926, RG 85, vol. 1213, file 400-2-3, pt. 1, LAC.

31 Finnie to McDougal, 24 December 1925, ibid.

32 Maxwell Graham to T.R.L. MacInnes, 6 October 1925, RG 85, vol. 1391, file 406-13, pt. 2, LAC.

33 See Finnie to Scott, 9 December 1925, RG 85, vol. 1213, file 400-2-3, pt. 1, LAC.

34 Scott to Charles Stewart, 29 December 1925, ibid.

35 Although I found no list of the warden staff dated prior to 1931, records covering the year 1925 include reports, correspondence, or references to wardens Klukas, Arden, Murphy, Dempsey, D'Aoust, McDermott, Bennett, Milne, Browning, and Wyatt. RG 85, vol. 1213, file 400-2-3, pt. 1, and RG 85, vol. 1391, file 406-13, pts. 1A, 2, LAC. By 1931, there were thirteen game wardens patrolling the enlarged Wood Buffalo National Park area. RG 85, vol. 152, file 420-2, pt. 2, LAC.

36 Kitto reported in 1920 that only six RCMP detachments with a staff of two officers and a dozen noncommissioned officers in total constituted the whole police force for the Mackenzie Valley region. F.H. Kitto, "Report on the Natural Resources of the Mackenzie District and their Economic Development," Natural Resources Intelligence Branch, Department of the Interior, 1920, RG 10, vol. 4092, file 549,036, LAC.

37 McDougal to Finnie, 2 March 1926, RG 85, vol. 1213, file 400-2-3, pt. 1, LAC.

38 O.S. Finnie, "Statement as to the Need for Eliminating Indians as Well as Other Hunters and Trappers from the Wood Buffalo Park," 25 January 1926, RG 85, vol. 1213, file 400-2-3, pt. 1, LAC.

39 Warden G.D. Murphy to Superintendent McDougal, 3 February 1925, RG 85, vol. 1213, file 400-2-3, pt. 1, LAC.

40 Extract from Warden Arden's diary, 9 March 1926, RG 85, vol. 1391, file 406-13, pt. 2-A, LAC.

41 Finnie to Scott, 30 April 1926, RG 85, vol. 1213, file 400-2-3, pt. 1, LAC; Scott to Finnie, 17 May 1926, ibid.

42 See C. Gordon Hewitt, "The Coming Back of the Bison," *Natural History* 19, 6 (1919): 553-65.

43 For the problems associated with the bison irruption at Buffalo National Park, see RG 84, vol. 111, file BU232, LAC. For the controversy over the film, see "Kill Buffalo as Movie Men Make Pictures," *Ottawa Journal,* 27 October 1923, and "To Kill Buffalo in a Humane Way," *Ottawa Citizen,* 17 October 1923.

44 Cory to Harkin, 26 May 1923, RG 85, vol. 1390, file 406-13, pt. 1, LAC.

45 Graham to Finnie, 28 May 1923, ibid.

46 A summary of the meeting is contained in a document titled "Memorandum for Fyle," 5 June 1923, ibid.

47 See Graham's discussion of tuberculosis with Finnie in response to a letter from Dean Rutherford, Faculty of Agriculture, University of Saskatchewan, 9 April 1925, RG 85, vol. 1391, file 406-13, pt. 1-A, LAC. For the decision to dispense with tuberculosis testing, see A.G. Smith to Harkin, 16 April 1924, RG 85, vol. 1390, file 406-13, pt. 1, LAC.

48 Maxwell Graham, "Finding Range for Canada's Buffalo," *Canadian Field-Naturalist* 38 (December 1924): 189.

49 Francis Harper, letter to the editor, *Canadian Field-Naturalist* 39 (February 1925): 45; W.E. Saunders, letter to the editor, *Canadian Field-Naturalist* 39 (May 1925): 118. For a further protest letter, see A. Brazier Howell, American Bison Society, to Harkin, 13 April 1925, RG 85, vol. 1391, file 406-13, pt. 1-A, LAC. A resolution opposing the transfer was passed by the Society of Mammalogists at its April 1925 meeting.

50 Rowan was no stranger to controversy. Since 1920 he had feuded with University of Alberta president Henry Tory, who pressured Rowan to conduct much of his path-breaking work on migratory birds at home and in his spare time because it did not accord with the program of applied and economically useful scientific research that Tory hoped to build at the university. Marianne Gosztonyi Ainley, "Rowan vs. Tory: Conflicting Views of Scientific Research in Canada," *Scientia Canadensis* 12, 1 (Spring-Summer 1988): 3-21.

51 The letters of Bensley, Cameron, and Frazer were sent to Rowan on 3 April 1925 and forwarded to Stewart on 23 April 1925. RG 85, vol. 1391, file 406-13, pt. 1-A, LAC.

52 For a summary, see Thomas Dunlap, *Saving America's Wildlife: Ecology and the American Mind, 1850-1990* (Princeton, NJ: Princeton University Press, 1988), 48-61. The historian Richard West Sellars has argued that the conflict between "no nonsense" wildlife managers from the older naturalist school and the growing number of university-trained biologists dominated the political history of wildlife management in US national parks well into the 1960s. Sellars, *Preserving Nature in the National Parks: A History* (New Haven, CT: Yale University Press, 1997), 91-148, 204-66.

53 Maxwell Graham, "Statement Concerning the Transfer of Buffalo from the Park at Wainwright, Alberta, to the Southern Range of the Wood-Buffalo in Northern Alberta, Prepared from Memoranda Supplied by the Parks and Northwest Territories Branches," 25 June 1925, RG 85, vol. 1391, file 406-13, pt. 2, LAC.

54 Graham, *Canada's Wild Buffalo*, 12.

55 Graham, "Finding Range for Canada's Buffalo," 189.

56 Janet Foster, *Working for Wildlife: The Beginnings of Preservation in Canada*, 2nd ed. (Toronto: University of Toronto Press, 1998), 221.

57 C. Gordon Hewitt, *The Conservation of the Wild Life of Canada* (New York: Charles Scribner's Sons, 1921), 136-42. Many of these "cattalo" or "beefalo" were later raised in a special enclosure at Buffalo National Park in Wainwright.

58 For an account of the episode involving Lloyd and Lewis, see J. Alexander Burnett, "A Passion for Wildlife: A History of the Canadian Wildlife Service, 1947-1997," *Canadian Field-Naturalist* 13, 1 (January-March 1999): 12.

59 A Canadian Zoologist, "The Passing of the Wood Bison," *Canadian Forum* (July 1925): 301-5.

60 For detailed statements on the numbers of Wainwright bison shipped each year (including data on sex ratios and cost), see RG 85, vol. 768, file 5164, pts. 1-3, LAC.

61 For favourable press reports, see "Alberta Buffalo Sent Far North, Like New Home," *Calgary Herald*, 1 February 1926; "Buffalo Now Secure," *Ottawa Citizen*, 20 March 1926; Earl Gaye, "Plains Buffalo Take Kindly to New Home Around Fort Smith," *Edmonton Journal*, 28 July 1928; John F. Ariza, "A Vanishing American Comes Back," *Baltimore Sun*, 17 August 1930. In January 1926, the deputy minister of the interior, W.W. Cory, wrote to Finnie from Washington to report that he had managed to persuade Hornaday and Seymour of the sound reasoning behind the transfer program. Garretson also wrote to Finnie later that year to say he was pleased that the Wainwright bison were "doing nicely." Cory to Finnie, 28 January 1926, and Garretson to Finnie, 24 March 1926, RG 85, vol. 1391, file 406-13, pt. 2, LAC. Although criticism was somewhat muted in the wake of the transfer, it did not dissipate entirely. Dr. James Ritchie denounced the project in the prestigious journal *Nature*. Ritchie, "The American Bison: A Questionable Experiment," *Nature* 117 (20 February 1926): 275. And in 1932, the Harvard scientist Thomas Barbour described the transfer as "one of the most tragic examples of bureaucratic stupidity in all history." Barbour, review of *Wild Beasts To-day*, by Harold Shepstone, *Science* 76, 1978 (25 November 1932): 491.
62 For reports on the Wainwright bison in their new habitat, see Warden Report Extracts, July 1926, RG 85, vol. 1391, file 406-13, pt. 2, LAC.
63 Finnie to J.A. McDougal, 7 May 1925, RG 85, vol. 1391, file 406-13, pt. 1A, LAC.
64 Warden Dempsey, Patrol Report, 7 January 1925, RG 85, vol. 1391, file 406-13, pt. 2, LAC.
65 Joussard to Department of Indian Affairs, 18 March 1926, RG 85, vol. 1391, file 406-13, pt. 2A, LAC.
66 Woodman's report was contained in a letter to D. Christie, 30 November 1925. Finnie forwarded a copy of the letter to Deputy Minister W.W. Cory with a recommendation to expand the park on 23 December 1925. RG 85, vol. 1391, file 406-13, pt. 2, LAC.
67 John A. McDougal, "Report of Expedition to Baril Lake with Wardens Dempsey, Watt and McDermott," 3 February 1926, RG 85, vol. 1391, file 406-13, pt. 2A, LAC.
68 The conversation is described in a letter from Finnie to Graham, 15 March 1926, ibid.
69 McDougal to Finnie, 25 March 1926, ibid.
70 The petition, dated 16 April 1926, was signed by Police Magistrate John Wylie, Colin Fraser (whom McDougal had cited as a supporter of the proposal), James Fraser, H. Mecredi, A.G. Mecredi, and Bishop Joussard. RG 85, vol. 1213, file 400-2-3, pt. 1, LAC.
71 Finnie to R.A. Gibson, Assistant Deputy Minster, Department of Interior, 16 June 1926, RG 85, vol. 1391, file 406-13, vol. 2A, LAC.
72 Order-in-council P.C. 1444, 18 September 1926. A copy was found in RG 85, vol. 1391, file 406-13, vol. 2-A, LAC. For a discussion of the broad powers accorded to the park superintendent to deny entry to non-permit-holders, see Finnie to McDougal, 28 September 1926, RG 85, vol. 1391, file 406-13, vol. 2A, LAC.
73 K.R. Daly to Finnie, 11 September 1926, ibid.
74 Barry Potyandi, "Dual Allegiance: The History of Wood Buffalo National Park, 1929-65," manuscript, 1981, 5-6, Wood Buffalo National Park Library, Fort Smith, NWT.
75 Both the Burke and Ada investigations are described in the report of Murphy to McDougal, 5 April 1928, RG 85, vol. 1391, file 406-13, pt. 3, LAC. The trapper in question is probably Ada Bouchie (also called Adam Boucher).
76 See Patricia A. McCormack, "Chipewyans turn Cree: Governmental and Structural Factors in Ethnic Processes," in *For the Purposes of Dominions: Essays in Honour of*

Morris Zaslow, ed. Kenneth S. Coates and William R. Morrison (Toronto: Captus Press, 1989), 125-138.

77 For summaries of warden activities, see Reports on the Duties of the Game Wardens, January 1932, and also the individual patrol reports in RG 85, vol. 152, file 420-2, pt. 2, LAC. For details on the creation of trails and cabins in Wood Buffalo National Park, see H.E. Hume, Chairman, Dominion Lands Board, to J.A. McDougal, 3 May 1932, ibid.

78 McDougal to Finnie, 13 June 1931, RG 85, vol. 1213, file 400-2-3, pt. 1A, LAC.

79 Whiteknife replied that he did not care if his permit was cancelled. As the wardens had been instructed not to use force to gain access to boats, the matter was left there. Warden Dempsey to McDougal, 5 June 1931, ibid.

80 Extract from Warden McDermott's diary, 5 June 1926, RG 85, vol. 1391, file 406-13, pt. 2A, LAC.

81 McDougal to Finnie, 7 June 1926, RG 85, vol. 769, file 5222, pt. 1, LAC.

82 Theophile was deemed an accessory because he shot at the bison and consumed the meat. Each man had the option of paying a fine – $500 for the heavier sentence and $200 for the lighter sentence – but both chose jail terms, presumably because payment was beyond their means. McDougal to Finnie, 3 July 1926, ibid.

83 All cases of bison poaching are amply documented in RG 85, vol. 769, file 5222, pt. 1, LAC. For the Watsuga case, see Warden Mike Dempsey to McDougal, 21 May 1934, ibid. The details of the other unsolved case are contained in Const. L.H. Crozier, RCMP, "Unlawful Killing of Buffalo in Wood Buffalo," 28 December 1935, RG 85, vol. 769, file 5222, pt. 1, LAC.

84 Records from the licence year ending 30 June 1932 indicate that of 295 permits issued to hunt and trap in the park, 189 were for south of the Peace River. See J.P. Richards to H.E. Hume, 20 July 1933, RG 85, vol. 1391, file 406-13, vol. 3, LAC.

85 For a summary, see Zaslow, *Northward Expansion*, 130-40. See also Peter Usher, "The Growth and Decay of the Trading and Trapping Frontiers in the Western Canadian Arctic," *Canadian Geographer* 19, 4 (1975): 308-20.

86 For the record of the arrests, the charges, and the reaction of the hunters, see Wakwan's Statement Made at Cabin #6, 22 March 1930, RG 85, vol. 769, file 5222, pt. 1, LAC. See also Dempsey's report to McDougal, 24 March 1930, ibid.

87 Dempsey to McDougal, 5 June 1930, ibid.

88 McDougal to Finnie, 3 July 1926, ibid.

89 Dempsey to McDougal, 23 July 1930, RG 85, vol. 152, file 420-2, pt. 2, LAC.

90 Gladu to McDougal, 10 June 1932, RG 85, vol. 769, file 5222, pt. 1, LAC.

91 Gladu to McDougal, 8 April 1934, ibid. Gladu was reinstated on compassionate grounds at a Northwest Territories Council meeting on 17 October 1934. See R.A. Gibson, Asst. Deputy Minister of the Interior, to Maj.-Gen. J.H. MacBrien, Commissioner, RCMP, 1 November 1934, ibid.

92 Joseph Wagwah [Wakwan], to the District Agent, Department of the Interior, Fort Smith, NWT, 16 July 1937, RG 85, vol. 769, file 5222, pt. 2, LAC. Wakwan was not reinstated until November 1949, almost two decades after his original offence. R.A. Gibson, Deputy Commissioner, NWT, to J.W. Burton, District Administrator, Fort Smith, 17 November 1949, RG 85, vol. 769, file 5222, pt. 2, LAC.

93 Ireland to Mike Dempsey, 5 June 1931, RG 85, vol. 1213, file 400-2-3, vol. 1-A, LAC.

94 Const. L.H. Crozier, Report, "Unlawful Killing of Buffalo in Wood Buffalo," 28 December 1935, RG 85, vol. 769, file 5222, pt. 1, LAC.

95 Order-in-council P.C. 2589, 14 December 1933; copy in RG 85, vol. 1213, file 400-2-3, pt. 2A, LAC.

96 Dr. J.E. Amyot, Indian Agent, Report on Treaty Trip and Payment to the Indians of the Great Slave Lake Agency for 1935, 31 July 1935, ibid.

97 Dempsey to Acting District Agent P.E. Trudel, 17 March 1936, RG 85, vol. 153, file 420-2, pt. 3, LAC.

98 Chief Seypekaham to MacKay Meikle, 13 July 1938, RG 85, vol. 1213, file 400-2-3, pt. 2-A, LAC.

99 Gibson to D.G. Hogan, 16 August 1935, RG 85, vol. 1213, file 400-2-3, pt. 2-A, LAC.

100 See, for example, the rejection letters sent to Francis Bourassa (28 July 1936), Father Picard on behalf of Joe Cortrae and Julien Cris (19 August 1936), Narcisse Shott (19 August 1936), Isadore Voyageur (19 November 1936), and George Dachuk (1 December 1936), RG 85, vol. 845, file 7744, pt. 1, LAC.

101 See "List of Persons Ineligible for Licenses or Permits to Hunt and Trap in the Wood Buffalo Park," RG 85, vol. 845, file 7744, pt. 2, LAC.

102 Dempsey to Meikle, 20 February 1937, RG 85, vol. 845, file 7744, pt. 2, LAC.

103 Tuckaroo's permit application form is not dated, but the district agent, A.L. Cumming, rejected the appeal on 19 November 1936. RG 85, vol. 845, file 7744, pt. 1, LAC.

104 Benoit to P.W. Head, Indian Agent, 9 July 1940, RG 85, vol. 845, file 7744, pt. 2, LAC. Benoit's application was in a letter from J.A. Urquhart, Acting Superintendent of Wood Buffalo National Park, to Head, 25 July 1940, ibid.

105 A.L. Cumming to R.A. Gibson, 16 December 1937, RG 85, vol. 845, file 7744, pt. 1, LAC.

106 St. Cyr to Urquhart, 28 December 1939, RG 85, vol. 845, file 7744, pt. 2, LAC.

107 The background to the Boucher case is contained in a report from Dempsey to Meikle, 20 February 1937, RG 85, vol. 845, file 7744, pt. 1, LAC. The "gambling" comment is in a rejection of Boucher's first application for a permit, which was sent to Indian Agent Henry Lewis on 3 April 1935, ibid.

108 Mrs. Adam Boucher to Fort Smith, 27 February 1936, ibid.

109 Boucher to "Wood Buffalo Head," 8 January 1937, ibid.

110 An RCMP report on the conclusion of Boucher's case, dated 15 August 1939, is filed in RG 85, vol. 904, file 10345, LAC.

111 Warden Dempsey reported that "in view of Adam Boucher having stated in his letter to Ottawa that he will enter the park to trap without a permit if his application is refused the staff will be advised to keep a close check on his movements to prevent him hunting and trapping without a permit." Dempsey to Superintendent Meikle, 10 February 1937, RG 85, vol. 845, file 7744, pt. 1, LAC.

112 Karl Jacoby, *Crimes against Nature: Squatters, Poachers, Thieves and the Hidden History of American Conservation* (Berkeley: University of California Press, 2001); Ramachandra Guha, *The Unquiet Woods: Ecological Change and Peasant Resistance in the Himalaya*, expanded ed. (Berkeley: University of California Press, 2000). For Guha's theoretical discussion of peasant protest movements, see pp. 185-96.

113 For an estimate of twelve thousand animals, based on various warden reports, see McDougal to Finnie, 23 February 1931, RG 85, vol. 1391, file 406-13, LAC.

114 For McDougal's proposal, see his letter to Finnie, 31 May 1927, RG 85, vol. 1391, file 406-13, pt. 2-A, LAC. Finnie's proposals are contained in an undated letter to H.H. Rowatt, RG 85, vol. 768, file 5164, vol. 3, LAC. Since Finnie refers to his regret at being obliged to leave the department, it is reasonable to assume that it was written in 1931, when the Northwest Territories and Yukon Branch was dissolved.

115 Soper's report is contained in a memo to Finnie, 3 November 1931, RG 85, vol. 1200, file 400-15-1, LAC. Soper's undated instructions are located in the same file.
116 H.H. Rowatt to H.E. Hume, 8 February 1932, RG 85, vol. 768, file 5164, pt. 3, LAC.
117 For details of warden duties in Wood Buffalo National Park, see records of the patrol reports in RG 85, vol. 152, file 420-2, LAC.
118 Extract from Sgt. G.T. Makinson's report, Fort Resolution, NWT, 3 July 1937, RG 85, vol. 1213, file 400-2-3, pt. 2A, LAC.
119 Thomas H. Birch, "The Incarceration of Wildness: Wilderness Areas as Prisons," in *The Great New Wilderness Debate*, ed. J. Baird Callicott and Michael P. Nelson (Athens: University of Georgia Press, 1998), 443-70.

CHAPTER 3: PASTORAL DREAMS

1 J.A. Urquhart, "Notice to All Indians: Protect the Muskrats and Beaver," 15 April 1940, RG 10, vol. 8409, file 191/20-14-1, pt. 1, Library and Archives Canada (LAC).
2 Clarke to Hoyes Lloyd, 29 January 1940, RG 85, vol. 1392, file 406-13, pt. 3A, LAC; J. Dewey Soper, "History, Range and Home Life of the Northern Bison," *Ecological Monographs* 2, 4 (October 1941): 394.
3 For a discussion of the general decline in fur-bearers in the early 1940s, see "Recommendations of Committee Appointed to Enquire into Certain Fur Conservation Problems in Wood Buffalo Park," 16 July 1945, RG 84, vol. 1214, file 400-2-3, pt. 3, LAC. On moose, see "Statement Showing the Number of Moose Taken in Wood Buffalo Park during the Period 1931-32 to 1944-45 Inclusive," RG 85, vol. 1214, file 400-2-3, pt. 3A, LAC.
4 For a summary of Elton's work and an overview of the economic emphasis of the "new" ecology in the 1930s, see Donald Worster, *Nature's Economy: A History of Ecological Ideas,* 2nd ed. (Cambridge: Cambridge University Press, 1994), 291-314. For an overview of Elton's early ecological ideas, see his *Animal Ecology* (London: William Clowes and Sons, 1947), first printed in 1927.
5 In September 1938 the federal bureaucrats on the Northwest Territories Council acknowledged the importance of Elton's work on northern wildlife and suggested that the National Research Council fund the research. Minutes of the 82nd Session of the Northwest Territories Council, 20 September 1938, RG 85, vol. 3241, file 600,352, pt. 6, LAC. A summary of Elton's research in northern Canada and the reaction of Canadian wildlife officials can be found in Minutes, Advisory Board on Wildlife Protection, 7 September 1938, RG 22, vol. 4, file 14, LAC. The results of this research were published in Elton's comprehensive study of wildlife cycles, *Voles, Mice and Lemmings: Problems in Population Dynamics* (Oxford: Clarendon, 1942).
6 J.L. Grew, "Preliminary Report of a Reconnaissance Survey of Muskrat and Water Conditions in the Athabasca Delta," December 1938, RG 85, vol. 1392, file 406-13-1, pt. 1, LAC.
7 For a summary of the fur enhancement projects, including their apparent impact on the muskrat populations, see R.A. Gibson to K.M. Cameron, Chief Engineer, Department of Public Works, 29 March 1946, RG 85, vol. 1393, file 406-13-1, pt. 2, LAC. For Meikle's comments, see his letter to Gibson, 28 June 1943, ibid.
8 The report is attached to a memo from J.P. Richards to A.L. Cumming, 2 April 1940, ibid.

9   The change in the muskrat season is discussed in J.D. Melling, Indian Agent, "Diary of Treaty Trip – Athabaska Agency, 1942," 4 July 1942, RG 10, vol. 8409, file 191/20-14-1, pt. 1, LAC.

10 Soper to R.A. Gibson, Deputy Minister, Department of Mines and Resources, 30 May 1945, RG 85, vol. 1214, file 400-2-3, pt. 3, LAC. For the full report on Soper's second survey of the park's wildlife in 1945, including his recommendation for a closed season on beaver, see Soper, "Report on Wildlife Investigations in Wood Buffalo Park and Vicinity, Alberta and Northwest Territories, Canada," report, National Parks Bureau, Department of Mines and Resources, 1945, Wood Buffalo National Park Library.

11 J.D. Melling, Indian Agent, "Diary of Treaty Trip – Athabaska Agency, 1942," 4 July 1942, RG 10, vol. 8409, file 191/20-14-1, pt. 1, LAC. A ban on trapping marten was implemented for the whole of the Northwest Territories in July 1943. R.A. Gibson to J.A. Urquhart, Acting Superintendent, Wood Buffalo National Park, 19 August 1943, RG 85, vol. 1214, file 400-2-3, pt. 3, LAC.

12 J.D. Melling, Indian Agent, "Diary of Treaty Trip – Athabaska Agency, 1942," 4 July 1942, RG 10, vol. 8409, file 191/20-14-1, pt. 1, LAC.

13 For a summary of Riopel's report, see Gibson to Meikle, 19 September 1944, RG 85, vol. 1097, file 472-3, pt. 2A, LAC.

14 The committee did nevertheless recommend a ban on beaver hunting, a group trapping system specific to Wood Buffalo Park, and a program to stock the park with beaver from other parts of the country. See J.D Soper, J.L. Grew, M. Meikle, and M. Dempsey, "Recommendations of Committee Appointed to Enquire into Certain Fur Conservation Problems in Wood Buffalo Park," 16 July 1945, RG 85, vol. 1214, file 400-2-3, pt. 3, LAC.

15 Extract from the Minutes of the 162nd Session of the Northwest Territories Council, 5 September 1945, RG 85, vol. 1214, file 400-2-3, pt. 3A, LAC. The controversy over group trapping areas was not unique to Wood Buffalo National Park. In 1950, a group system was imposed in the Mackenzie Delta region near Aklavik with strong opposition from local trappers. For an overview, see Peter Clancy, "State Policy and the Native Trapper: Post-War Policy toward Fur in the Northwest Territories," in *Aboriginal Resource Use in Canada: Historical and Legal Aspects*, ed. Kerry Abel and Jean Friesen (Winnipeg: University of Manitoba Press, 1991), 191-218.

16 Chief John Cowie to A.H. Gibson, 5 February 1946, RG 85, vol. 1214, file 400-2-3, pt. 3A, LAC.

17 Between 1938 and 1951, twenty-eight convictions were recorded for violations of the game regulations other than killing bison. Six of these convictions were for setting snares (all between 1942 and 1944). Records of the convictions are in RG 10, vol. 8409, file 191/20-14-1, pt. 1-2; RG 85, vol. 888, files 9356 and 9358; RG 85, vol. 995, file 15878; RG 85, vol. 959, file 13523; RG 85, vol. 940, file 12599; RG 85, vol. 153, file 420-2, pt. 3; RG 85, vol. 1191, file 400-2-3, all LAC. This list is highly likely to be only partial, due to the scattered nature of police and warden records from the South Slave region.

18 Horace Halcrow to T.A. Crerar, 26 October 1940, RG 85, vol. 1214, file 400-2-3, pt. 3, LAC. There were six convictions in the park for breaking into muskrat houses between 1942 and 1948.

19 Reports of widespread anthropogenic burning in the park are contained in a letter from R.A. Gibson, Director, Lands, Parks and Forests Branch, to H.W. McGill, Director, Indian Affairs Branch, 31 October 1940, RG 10, vol. 8409, file 191/20-14-1,

pt. 1, LAC. See also P.W. Head, Indian Agent, Fort Chipewyan, to Secretary, Indian Affairs Branch, 24 November 1940, ibid. There are many reports of "lots" of fires in the warden reports covering the period from 1938 to 1953. See RG 85, vol. 153, file 420-2, pt. 3, and vol. 310, file 420 2/199 1, LAC. For a discussion of the traditional burning in the Alberta boreal forest as a conscious, deliberate, and adaptive environmental management strategy, see Henry T. Lewis, *A Time for Burning: Traditional Indian Uses of Fire in Western Canadian Boreal Forest,* Occasional Publication no. 17 (Edmonton: Boreal Institute for Northern Studies, 1982), 30-46.

20 Gibson to Eugene Oldham, Superintendent, Wood Buffalo National Park, 22 November 1947, RG 85, vol. 1214, file 400-2-3, pt. 3A, LAC.

21 For a discussion of the number of wardens and the weak pattern of law enforcement in Wood Buffalo National Park during the 1930s, see Barry Potyandi, "Dual Allegiance: The History of Wood Buffalo National Park, 1929-65," manuscript, 1981, 33-38, Wood Buffalo National Park Library, Fort Smith, NWT. For a record of the number of wardens in Wood Buffalo Park, see the warden reports in RG 85, vol. 153, file 420-2, pt. 3, LAC.

22 For a discussion of the many families that fell into dire poverty in Wood Buffalo National Park after 1939, see Extract from the Minutes of the 120th Session of the Northwest Territories Council, 7 January 1941, RG 85, vol. 1214, file 400-2-3, pt. 3, LAC.

23 Minutes, Advisory Board on Wildlife Protection, 22 January 1946, RG 22, vol. 14, file 4, LAC.

24 Excerpt from Letter from Fifth Meridian Post, n.d., RG 85, vol. 1214, file 400-2-3, pt. 3A, LAC. The letter was forwarded to R.A. Gibson, Deputy Commissioner, NWT, in a letter from Mr. Chesshire, General Manager, Fur Trade Department, Hudson's Bay Company, on 15 April 1946.

25 John Cowie to A.H. Gibson, Acting Agent and Superintendent, Wood Buffalo National Park, 5 February 1946, ibid.

26 See Dr. J. Melling, "Report of Meeting with Chief and Councillors of Indians Living in 'B' and 'C' Areas of the Wood Buffalo Park," 3 February 1943, RG 10, vol. 8409, file 191/20-14-1, pt. 1, LAC.

27 For the legal ruling, see T.L. Cory, Legal Advisor, to A.L. Cumming, 4 May 1943, RG 85, vol. 1214, file 400-2-3, pt. 3, LAC.

28 For a summary of the problems faced by hunters expelled from the park, see Dr. J. Melling, Indian Agent, to Secretary, Indian Affairs Branch, 8 October 1942, RG 10, vol. 8409, file 191/20-14-1, pt. 1, LAC. Federal officials attempted to alleviate the situation by issuing permits to destitute exiles from the park to hunt and trap in the Northwest Territories. See R.A. Gibson, Deputy Commissioner, NWT, to Dr. H.W. McGill, Director, Indian Affairs Branch, 7 November 1942, ibid.

29 Cowie to C. Pant Schmidt, 18 May 1944, ibid.

30 Meikle to Gibson, 27 June 1945, RG 85, vol. 1214, file 400-2-3, pt. 3, LAC. For the record of Meikle's concern about bison protection and evicted hunters returning to the park, see J.W. Stewart, Indian Agent, to C. Pant Schmidt, Inspector of Indian Agencies, 1 August 1944, RG 10, vol. 8409, file 191/20-14-1, pt. 1, LAC.

31 See Extracts from E.G. Oldham's Report, 1947-48, RG 85, vol. 1214, file 400-2-3, pt. 3A, LAC; and William Fuller, "Status of Wildlife in Wood Buffalo Park," 27 April 1951, RG 85, vol. 1254, file 406-13, vol. 4A, LAC.

32 For the new muskrat regulations, see "Regulations Respecting the Preservation of

Game in Wood Buffalo National Park," authorized by order-in-council P.C. 5588, 3
November 1949; copy in RG 85, vol. 1214, file 400-2-3, pt. 3A, LAC. For the lifting of
the beaver ban north of the Peace River, see order-in-council P.C. 341, 23 January 1952;
copy in RG 85, vol. 1214, file 400-2-3, pt. 5, LAC. For the lifting of the ban south of
the Peace River, see order-in-council P.C. 4157, 1 October 1952, ibid.

33 See B.I. Love, "Survey of Animals and Surroundings, Wood Buffalo Park, NWT, Aug.
4-27, 1944," RG 85, vol. 1392, file 406-13, pt. 3A, LAC.

34 For a summary of patrol duties during this period, see the warden reports in RG 85,
vol. 153, file 420-2, pt. 3, LAC.

35 For a report of Soper's "shock" at the condition of Wood Buffalo Park, see Harrison
Lewis to A.L. Cumming, 10 December 1945, RG 85, vol. 1392, file 406-13, pt. 4, LAC.
See also H.L. Holman, District Forest Officer, to R.A. Gibson, 17 August 1949, ibid.

36 For a summary of Oldham's comments (which were not written down), see J.P.
Richards to A.L. Cumming, 11 March 1947, RG 85, vol. 1392, file 406-13, pt. 4, LAC.

37 For a record of the decline in moose, see "Statement Showing the Number of Moose
Taken in Wood Buffalo Park during the Period 1931-32 to 1944-45 Inclusive," RG 85,
vol. 1214, file 400-2-3, pt. 3A, LAC. Records of caribou scarcity in the region surrounding the park are found in an extract from MacKay Meikle's letter to R.A. Gibson, 29 September 1944, RG 85, vol. 1097, file 472-3, pt. 2A, LAC; and J.P. Richards
to A.L. Cumming, 2 October 1945, ibid. The caribou migration did arrive in the
southern part of the park in February 1947 for the first time in many years, according
to the report of Warden F. McCall, RG 85, vol. 318, file 420-2/199-1, LAC.

38 Meikle's comments are typed on a memo from J.P. Richards to A.L. Cumming, 12
February 1947, RG 85, vol. 1214, file 400-2-3, pt. 3A, LAC.

39 Records of the yearly slaughter are in RG 85, vol. 1097, file 472-3, pts. 2, 2A, LAC.

40 Extracts from E.G. Oldham's Report, 1947-48, ibid.

41 C.H.D. Clarke to A.L. Cumming, 2 February 1944, RG 85, vol. 1097, file 472-3, pt.
2A, LAC.

42 See Worster, *Nature's Economy*, 291-316. The American historians Thomas Dunlap and
Richard West Sellars have argued that wildlife scientists in the United States often
opposed intensive wildlife management schemes well into the 1960s. Sellars, *Preserving Nature in the National Parks: A History* (New Haven, CT: Yale University Press,
1997): 91-148, 204-66; Dunlap, "Ecology, Nature and Canadian National Park Policy:
Wolves, Elk and Bison as a Case Study," in *To See Ourselves/To Save Ourselves: Ecology
and Culture in Canada*, ed. Rowland Lorimer and Michael M'Gonigle, Proceedings
of the Annual Conference of the Association for Canadian Studies, University of Victoria, 31 May to 1 June 1990 (Montreal: Association for Canadian Studies, 1991), 139-
67; and Dunlap, "Wildlife, Science, and the National Parks, 1920-1940," *Pacific Historical Review* 59, 2 (May 1990): 187-202. In contrast, Alan MacEachern's recent work
on the national parks in the Atlantic provinces suggests there was a growing alliance
between bureaucratic managers and wildlife scientists in Canada in the interwar years
and during the postwar period. MacEachern, *Natural Selections: National Parks in
Atlantic Canada, 1935-1970* (Montreal and Kingston: McGill-Queen's University Press,
2001), 190-203. For a specific and convincing reply to Dunlap's assertion that wildlife
scientists led the Canadian Parks Branch to abandon predator control policies, see
Alan MacEachern, "Rationality and Rationalization in Canadian National Parks
Predator Policy," in *Consuming Canada: Readings in Environmental History*, ed. Pam
Gaffield and Chad Gaffield (Toronto: Copp Clark, 1995), 197-212.

43 For the growth of the Canadian Wildlife Service through the 1950s, and the agency's attentiveness to practical management questions, see J. Alexander Burnett, "A Passion for Wildlife: A History of the Canadian Wildlife Service, 1947-1997," *Canadian Field-Naturalist* 13, 1 (January-March 1999): 31-34.

44 Minutes, Tenth Dominion-Provincial Conference on Wildlife, 22-24 February 1945, RG 22, vol. 4, file 13, LAC.

45 "Summary of Buffalo Reduction by Park, 1951-1966," RG 84, vol. 2239, WB 299, pt. 2, LAC.

46 Patricia McCormack, "The Political Economy of Bison Management in Wood Buffalo National Park," *Arctic* 45, 4 (December 1992): 371-73. For various accounts of the broader northern resource development program, see Kenneth J. Rea, *The Political Economy of the Canadian North: An Interpretation of the Course of Development in the Northwest Territories of Canada to the Early 1960s* (Toronto: University of Toronto Press, 1968); Edgar J. Dosman, *The National Interest: the Politics of Northern Development, 1968-75* (Toronto: McClelland and Stewart, 1975); and Peter Clancy, "Working on the Railway: A Case Study in Capital-State Relations," *Canadian Public Administration* 30, 3 (Fall 1987): 452-71.

47 For records of timber berths in Wood Buffalo National Park, see RG 84, vol. 2237, file 206-503m, pts. 2-4, LAC. For records of the Lake Claire fishery and proposals to reduce the park boundary to open areas for resource development, see RG 85, acc. 1997-98/076, box 73, file 406-13, pts. 5-9, LAC.

48 B.I. Love, "Survey of Animals and Surroundings, Wood Buffalo Park, NWT, Aug. 4-27, 1944," RG 85, vol. 1392, file 406-13, pt. 3A, LAC.

49 W.E. Stevens, "Bison Slaughter in Wood Buffalo Park, January, 1950," RG 85, vol. 1254, file 406-13, pt. 4A, LAC.

50 See William Fuller, "Buffalo Report – Wood Buffalo Park," n.d., RG 85, vol. 157, file 472-3, pt. 3, LAC; and "Second Aerial Census of Northern Bison, 20-31 January 1951," RG 85, vol. 1254, file 406-13, pt. 4A, LAC.

51 Harrison Lewis to R.A. Gibson, 25 September 1950, RG 85, vol. 1097, file 472-3, pt. 2A, LAC; J.P. Kelsall to H.F. Lewis, 19 September 1950, ibid.

52 Extract from Warden Taylor's November Report, Little Buffalo River, 1948, RG 85, vol. 1097, file 472-3, pt. 2A, LAC.

53 Harrison Lewis to William Fuller, 17 November 1951, RG 85, vol. 157, file 472-3, pt. 3, LAC.

54 Chief Warden Essex to W.G. Brown, 18 January 1951, ibid.

55 F.E. Graesser, "Report – Investigations of Buffalo, Wood Buffalo Park," 29 December 1950, RG 85, vol. 157, file 472-3, pt. 3, LAC.

56 See B.I. Love to G.E.B. Sinclair, Director, Northern Administrations and Lands Branch, 31 March 1952, RG 85, vol. 158, file 472-3, pt. 6A, LAC.

57 See Appendix A, "Outline of Future Operating Procedures in Connection with the Slaughtering of Buffalo in Wood Buffalo National Park," C.W. Jackson to the Deputy Minister, Department of Agriculture, 22 August 1951, RG 85, vol. 157, file 472-3, pt. 3, LAC.

58 J.W. Burton, Acting Chief, Conservation and Management Services, to J.G. Wright, Acting Chief, Northern Administration Division, 6 July 1951, ibid.

59 W.E. Stevens, "Bison Report – September 1954," Wood Buffalo National Park Library, Fort Smith, NWT.

60 Minutes, Advisory Board on Wildlife Protection, 31 January 1951, RG 22, vol. 16, file

69, LAC. For R.A. Gibson and Lewis's support of the expanded slaughter as a caribou conservation initiative, see Lewis to Gibson, 25 September 1950, RG 85, vol. 1097, file 472-3, pt. 2A, LAC, and Gibson to W.G. Brown, District Administrator, 30 September 1950, ibid.

61 F.J.G. Cunningham, "Alternative Sources of Meat for the People of the North," Memorandum for the Commissioner of the Northwest Territories, 25 November 1955, RG 85, vol. 1255, file 472-1, pt. 1, LAC.

62 Fraser to Jackson, 4 August 1954, RG 85, vol. 1255, file 472-1, pt. 1, LAC.

63 Cunningham to H.T. Anderson, Manager, P. Burns and Co., 14 December 1954, RG 85, vol. 1255, file 472-1, pt. 1, LAC.

64 Extract of article by Father Brown from the November 1955 issue of the *Aklavik Journal*, published at the RC Mission, Aklavik, RG 85, vol. 1255, file 472-1, pt. 1, LAC. A resident of Fort Smith, Roger Brunt, also noted the injustice associated with higher local prices for buffalo meat when compared with the choice cuts flown out of Fort Smith for the southern market. Writing in 1976, Brunt recalled that local people were not allowed to buy the export meat, while "gut bags" containing scraps of kidney and guts were sold to Native people for two dollars. One presumes the gut bags were used for dog feed, but Brunt does not specify. Brunt, "The Decline and Fall of the Last Free Roaming Buffalo Herds in the World Taking Place in Wood Buffalo National Park and the Grand Detour, Hook Lake Area of the Northwest Territories, Canada," manuscript, 15 April 1976, Wood Buffalo National Park Library, Fort Smith, NWT.

65 Fraser to Cunningham, 19 November 1954, RG 85, vol. 1255, file 472-1, pt. 1, LAC.

66 Stevens to Cunningham, 22 September 1956, RG 84, vol. 2237, file WB232, pt. 4, LAC.

67 For a report from the superintendent of Wood Buffalo National Park on plans for the first test and slaughter program, see B.E. Olson, "Buffalo Management 1957-58 – Testing and Slaughtering Program," 29 July 1957, ibid.

68 For a report on the specialty food program, see Robertson to J.A. McDonald, Assistant Secretary to the Treasury Board, 7 May 1962, RG 85, acc. 1997-98/0878, box 80, file 472-3, pt. 19, LAC.

69 For a report on the buffalo marketing program, see E.A. Côté, Deputy Minister, Northern Affairs and National Resources, to Minister Arthur Laing, 30 October 1964, RG 85, acc. 1997-98/076, box 79, file 471-4, pt. 5, LAC. For an example of a press release connected to the marketing program, see "Sweetgrass Buffalo – New Delicacy from the North," 16 January 1962, RG 84, vol. 2237, file WB232, pt. 4. LAC. For records of the Royal York event, see V. Vokes to Robert Ardblaster, Divisional Sales Manager, Joseph E. Seagram and Sons, Ltd., 9 March 1962, RG 85, acc. 1997-98/076, box 80, file 472-3, pt. 19, LAC.

70 For the instructions to ship the meat, see a telex from the Regional Director, Northern Administration Branch, to Olson, 29 March 1967, RG 84, vol. 2239, file WB299, pt. 2, LAC.

71 N.S. Novakowski, "Estimates of the Bison Population in Wood Buffalo Park and the Northwest Territories Based on Transect and Total Counts," February 1961, RG 84, vol. 2237, file WB232, pt. 4, LAC.

72 For a record of Novakowski's "dressing down," see J.R.B. Coleman to B.G. Sivertz, 4 April 1961, ibid. For a report on the slaughter, see B.E. Olson, "Wood Buffalo National Park: Buffalo Round-up, Testing and Slaughter Program, 1961," RG 84, vol. 2239, file WB299, pt. 2, LAC.

73 B.E. Olson to C.L. Merrill, 28 October 1962, ibid.

74 These events are summarized in "Report on the Anthrax Outbreak among the Buffalo Herds," Northwest Territories Council Sessional Paper 5, 1963 (First Session), RG 109, vol. 37, file WLWB 200, pt 1, LAC.

75 The decision to depopulate the Grand Detour herds was taken at a meeting of the Anthrax Committee on 17 July 1964. RG 84, vol. 587, file WB210-1, pt. 1, LAC. The data on the meat salvage operation come from two separate memos from R.A. Hodgkinson, Acting Administrator of the Mackenzie, to Director, 1 December 1964, RG 109, vol. 37, file WLWB 200, LAC; and 12 March 1965, RG 85, acc. 1997-98/076, box 80, file 472-3, pt. 22, LAC. For a report on the inoculation program from January to June 1965, see N.S. Novakowski, memo to Chief, Canadian Wildlife Service, 4 June 1965, RG 109, vol. 37, file WLWB 200, pt. 1, LAC.

76 William Fuller, *The Biology and Management of the Bison of Wood Buffalo National Park*, Wildlife Management Bulletin Series 1, no. 16 (Ottawa: Queen's Printer, 1962), 45.

77 N.S. Novakowski and L.P.E. Choquette, "Proposed Five-Year Management Plan for Bison in Wood Buffalo National Park," RG 84, vol. 2237, file WB210-1, pt. 2, LAC.

78 For a discussion of the decision not to proceed with the disease eradication program, see McCormack, "Political Economy of Bison Management," 373.

79 In a 1965 overview, Ward Stevens wrote that the predator control program "was designed to protect bison from wolves so that they could be converted to Sweet Grass T-bones. That was in the era when the Canadian Wildlife Service was slaughtering wolves to protect caribou, so no one had clean hands in the matter and no one cried halt." The predator control program actually contravened Parks Branch policy. Stevens, "Wolf Control in Wood Buffalo National Park," 3 May 1965, RG 84, vol. 2238, WB266, pt. 1, LAC. Parks Director J.R.B. Coleman ordered predator control discontinued in the park on 4 June 1965, partly because he thought the wolves would aid in the herd thinning effort that was so central to the anthrax control program. Coleman to Regional Director, Western Region, 4 June 1965, ibid.

80 Because of the anthrax outbreaks that hit the area throughout the 1960s, bison hunting outside the park was closed from 1962 to 1968. See Jack Van Camp, "Predation on Bison," in *Bison Ecology in Relation to Agricultural Development in the Slave River Lowlands, NWT*, ed. H.W. Reynolds and A.W.L. Hawley, Canadian Wildlife Service Occasional Paper no. 63 (Ottawa: Minister of Supply and Services, 1987), 25-33. Federal officials consistently asserted that it was unwise to allow human hunting of buffalo in the park because of disease. See, for example, F.J.G. Cunningham to Dr. K.F. Wells, Veterinary Director General, 4 March 1957, RG 84, vol. 2237, WB232, pt. 4, LAC.

81 Sivertz to R.G. Robertson, Deputy Minister, 15 January 1958, RG 85, acc. 1997-98/076, box 73, file 406-13, pt. 6, LAC.

82 B.E. Olson to Warden Lorne Lapp, Fifth Meridian, Wood Buffalo Park, 17 February 1961, RG 84, vol. 2237, file WB232, pt. 4, LAC. Seven years earlier, in May 1954, a meeting of the Little Red River Cree band passed a resolution calling on the superintendent of Wood Buffalo National Park to hold an organized hunt near Fifth Meridian trading post so that families could take one buffalo each. See R.I. Eklund, Fur Supervisor, to Director, Indian Affairs Branch, 27 July 1954, RG 10, vol. 8409, file 191/20-14-1, pt. 2, LAC.

83 See C.L. Merrill, Administrator of the Mackenzie, to B.G. Sivertz, Director, Northern Administration Branch, 22 February 1961, RG 84, vol. 2237, file WB232, pt. 4, LAC.

84 Dan Frandsen, Robert Redhead, Bill Dolan, Ron Davies, and Jeff Dixon, "Park Conservation Plan: Wood Buffalo National Park," report, Wood Buffalo National Park, March 1988, section 10.
85 Brief of the Deninoo Association of Fort Resolution to the Northwest Territories Council, January 1969, RG 85, acc. 1997-98/076, box 74, file 406-13, pt. 8, LAC.
86 Brief of the Thebacha Association to the Northwest Territories Council, January 1969, ibid.
87 Loughrey to J.H. Gordon, Acting Deputy Minister, 26 February 1969, RG 85, acc. 1997-98/076, box 73, file 406-14, pt. 8, LAC. Loughrey did recommend that a pilot project involving Native management of one hundred bison might be a reasonable alternative to the Thebacha proposal.
88 The anthropologist Michael Asch has argued that Dene notions of land title are intimately tied to a sense of ownership over local wildlife. In the Dene worldview, "wild" animals are regarded in a manner much more akin to European notions of domesticates than to the modern idea of wildlife as a public resource. Asch, "Wildlife: Defining the Animals the Dene Hunt and the Settlement of Aboriginal Land Claims," *Canadian Public Policy* 15, 2 (1989): 205-19.
89 See Park Superintendent Olson's report to D.B. Coombs, Regional Director, 28 September 1967, RG 84, vol. 2239, WB299, pt. 2, LAC.
90 The transition to a "hands-off" management philosophy was quite gradual. Massive round-ups, corralling, and vaccination took place throughout the 1970s in an effort to control anthrax. For an overview, see McCormack, "Political Economy of Bison Management," 373.
91 See B.E. Olson to D.B. Coombs, Regional Director, 11 October 1967, RG 84, vol. 2227, file WB 3-1, pt. 1, LAC.
92 Hugo Fischer, Legal Advisor, to Alex J. Reeve, Acting Director, National and Historic Parks Branch, 20 November 1968, ibid.
93 See E.P Thompson, *Whigs and Hunters: The Origins of the Black Act* (London: Pantheon Books, 1975).
94 For a brief overview of the evolution of policy toward Native hunting rights in Canada's national parks, see Juri Peepre and Philip Dearden, "The Role of Aboriginal Peoples," in *Parks and Protected Areas in Canada: Planning and Management,* 2nd ed., ed. Philip Dearden and Rick Rollins (Toronto: Oxford University Press, 2002), 323-32.
95 Canada National Parks Act, 2000, *Statutes of Canada,* c. 32, Second session, 36th Parliament. For an overview and discussion, see Ken M. East, "Joint Management of Canada's Northern Parks," in *Resident People and National Parks: Social Dilemmas and Strategies in International Conservation,* ed. Patrick C. West and Steven R. Brechin (Tucson: University of Arizona Press, 1991), 333-45.
96 For Justice Delores Hansen's ruling, see *Mikisew Cree First Nation v. Canada (Minister of Canadian Heritage),* 2001 FCT 1426. http://decisions.fct-cf.gc.ca. For the 2005 ruling, see *Mikisew Cree First Nation v. Canada (Minister of Canadian Heritage),* 3 S.C.R. 388; 2005 SCC 69.
97 Department of Indian and Northern Affairs, "Salt River First Nation, Canada, and the Government of the Northwest Territories Initial Final Treaty Land Entitlement," news release 2-01261, 23 November 2001, http://www.ainc-inac.gc.ca/nr/prs. See also Department of Indian and Northern Affairs, "Smith's Landing Becomes Newest First Nation in Alberta," news release 2-00129, 6 May 2000.

98 Canada National Parks Act, 2000, s. 37(3). See also Peepre and Dearden, "Role of Aboriginal Peoples," 336.
99 Wood Buffalo National Park Game Regulations, N 14.01-SOR/78-830, http://laws.justice. gc.ca/N 14.01/SOR-78-830/text.html, ss, 24(1), 29(1), 30(1). The Wildlife Advisory Board may set out conditions governing the power of the park superintendent to issue and revoke licences (subject to the approval of the federal cabinet), but the final say on individual permit allocations remains with the park authorities. See Canada National Parks Act, 2000, s. 37(3).

CHAPTER 4: THE POLAR OX

1 C. Gordon Hewitt, *The Conservation of the Wild Life of Canada* (New York: Charles Scribner's Sons, 1921), 89-101.
2 Ibid., 316.
3 Ibid., 318.
4 J.A. Allen, *Otogentic and Other Variations in Muskoxen, with a Systematic Review of the Muskox Group, Recent and Extinct,* Memoirs of the American Museum of Natural History, vol. 1, part 4, (New York: American Museum of Natural History, 1913). For further discussion, see Edward A. Preble, *A Biological Investigation of the Athabaska-Mackenzie Region Prepared under the Direction of Dr. C. Hart Merriam* (Washington, DC: Government Printing Office, 1908), 150-55.
5 Ernest Thompson Seton, *The Lives of Game Animals,* vol. 3, pt. 2 (Garden City, NJ: Doubleday, 1929), 618-20.
6 W.H.B. Hoare, *Conserving Canada's Musk-Oxen, Being an Account of an Investigation of Thelon Game Sanctuary, 1928-29, with a Brief History of the Area and an Outline of Known Facts Regarding the Musk-ox* (Ottawa: King's Printer, 1930), 41-48.
7 R.M Anderson, "Notes on the Musk-Ox and the Caribou," Appendix B in Hoare, *Conserving Canada's Musk-Oxen,* 49-53.
8 Extremely detailed data on the Hudson's Bay Company's muskox skin trade are in a letter from Maxwell Graham to James Harkin, 23 June 1914, RG 85, vol. 664, file 3910, pt. 2, Library and Archives Canada (LAC). For a slightly different data set, see John Tener, *Muskoxen in Canada: A Biological and Taxonomic Review,* Canadian Wildlife Service Monograph 2 (Ottawa: Queen's Printer, 1965), 114-15. In a more general reference, the anthropologist Paul F. Wilkinson has estimated that at least sixteen thousand muskox were killed for robes between 1860 and 1916, a figure that accords reasonably well with Graham's data. Wilkinson, "The History of Musk-ox Domestication," *Polar Record* 17, 106 (1974): 14.
9 For an overview of the popularity of northern Canada among British sport hunters after the completion of the railway, see R.G. Moyles and Doug Owram, *Imperial Dreams and Colonial Realities: British Views of Canada 1880-1914* (Toronto: University of Toronto Press, 1988), 61-86. For eyewitness accounts of muskox trophy hunts, see Frank Russell, *Explorations in the Far North: Being the Report of an Expedition under the Auspices of the University of Iowa during the Years 1892, '93, and '94* (Iowa City: University of Iowa Press, 1898), 108-24; J.W. Tyrrell, *Across the Sub-Arctic of Canada, a Journey of 3,200 Miles by Canoe and Snowshoe through the Barren Lands* (London: T. Fisher Unwin, 1898), 108-9; Caspar Whitney, *On Snow-Shoes to the Barren Grounds:*

Twenty-Eight Hundred Miles after Musk-Oxen and Wood-Bison (New York: Harper and Brothers, 1896), 216-23; Henry Toke Munn, *Prairie Trails and Arctic By-Ways* (London: Hurst and Blackett, 1932), 70-71; David T. Hanbury, *Sport and Travel in the Northland of Canada* (London: Edward Arnold, 1904), 39, 225, 234; and Warburton Pike, *The Barren Ground of Northern Canada* (New York: Macmillan, 1892), 5, 103-5, 168-69.

10 See William Barr, *Back from the Brink: The Road to Muskox Conservation in the Northwest Territories,* Komatik series no. 3 (Calgary: The Arctic Institute of North America, 1991), cited in Lyle Dick, *Muskox Land: Ellesmere Island in the Age of Contact* (Calgary: University of Calgary Press, 2001), 410-13.

11 At a meeting of the Advisory Board on Wildlife Protection on 30 October 1924, Lauge Koch, a geologist and cartographer with the Danish government, informed those present that MacMillan killed three to four hundred muskox on Ellesmere Island each year from 1913 to 1918, a figure that suggests a much higher rate of killing by Arctic explorers than the numbers cited in Barr's report. See Minutes, Advisory Board on Wildlife Protection, 30 October 1924, RG 10, vol. 4085, file 496,658-1B, LAC.

12 D.R. Urquhart, *Life History and Current Status of the Muskoxen in the NWT* (Yellowknife: Department of Renewable Resources, NWT, 1982), 3-9; Peter C. Lent, *Muskoxen and Their Hunters: A History* (Norman: University of Oklahoma Press, 1999), 36-45.

13 Ernest Thompson Seton, *The Arctic Prairies* (New York: Harper and Row, 1911), 235.

14 Russell, *Explorations in the Far North,* 117, 124; J.W. Tyrrell, "Report on the Country North and East of Great Slave Lake," 1901, RG 85, vol. 1087, file 401-22, pt. 1, LAC; Hanbury, *Sport and Travel,* 27.

15 Stefansson's career is summarized in Richard Diubaldo, *Stefansson and the Canadian Arctic* (Montreal and Kingston: McGill-Queen's University Press, 1978).

16 Stefansson to Borden, 8 January 1914, MG 36 H, Borden Papers, vol. 785, 101514-101520, LAC.

17 Stefansson to Sifton, 8 February 1914, RG 85, vol. 665, file 3914, pt. 1, LAC.

18 Graham to James Harkin, 26 March 1914, RG 85, vol. 664, file 3910, pt. 2, LAC.

19 Graham to James Harkin, 23 June 1914, ibid.

20 Henry J. Bury, "Report on the Game and Fisheries of Northern Alberta and the Northwest Territories," 6 November 1915, RG 85, vol. 664, file 3910, pt. 2, LAC.

21 Allen, *Otogentic and Other Variations,* 206.

22 An Act Respecting Game in the Northwest Territories of Canada, *Statutes of Canada,* 7-8 George V, vol. 1, c. 36, s. 1, 337-43. The events leading up to the passage of the Northwest Game Act are summarized in Hewitt, *Conservation of Wild Life,* 258-60, and C. Gordon Hewitt, *Conservation of Wild Life in Canada in 1917: A Review,* reprinted from the Ninth Annual Report of the Commission of Conservation (Ottawa, 1918).

23 For Scott's philosophy toward subsistence hunters in the North, see his paper "Relation of Indians to Wild Life Conservation," in *National Conference on Conservation of Game, Fur-Bearing Animals and Other Wild Life, 18-19 February 1919,* ed. Commission of Conservation of Canada (Ottawa: King's Printer, 1919), 19-21.

24 N. Jérémie, *Twenty Years of York Factory, 1694-1714: Jérémie's Account of Hudson Bay and Strait* (Ottawa: Thurnburn and Abbot, 1926), quoted in Paul F. Wilkinson, "The Domestication of the Muskoxen," *Polar Record* 15, 98 (1971): 683.

25 For a summary of the proposals to domesticate the muskox in the late eighteenth and nineteenth centuries, including the quotation from Pennant, see Wilkinson, "History of Musk-Ox Domestication," 14-16. Pennant is probably best remembered as one of

Gilbert White's correspondents in the classic work *A Natural History of Selborne* (1788; New York: Penguin, 1977).

26 See Graham's report to Harkin on the muskox, 23 June 1914, RG 85, vol. 664, file 3910, pt. 2, LAC.

27 Vilhjalmur Stefansson, *The Northward Course of Empire* (New York: Harcourt Brace and Company, 1922), 140-41.

28 Vilhjalmur Stefansson, "Possible New Domestic Animals for Cold Countries," memo to Sir Richard McBride, 9 February 1917; copy forwarded by Hewitt to Harkin, 28 November 1918, RG 85, vol. 1203, file 401-3, pt. 1, LAC. Stefansson's ideas on the "liveable north" are summarized in his books *The Friendly Arctic: The Story of Five Years in the Polar Region* (New York: Macmillan, 1922) and, particularly, *Northward Course of Empire*.

29 These events are summarized in Diubaldo, *Stefansson and the Canadian Arctic,* 137-42; and Stefansson, *Northward Course of Empire,* 137-67. Roosevelt's letter to Stefansson is printed in full on pp. 163-64 of the latter volume.

30 For Stefansson's entreaties to Harkin to change the name of the muskox, see his letters dated 15 October 1920 and 13 November 1920 in the J.B. Harkin Papers, MG 30, E-169, vol. 2, LAC. For an overview, see William A. Waiser, "Canada Ox, Ovibos, Woolox ... Anything But Musk-ox," in *For the Purposes of Dominions: Essays in Honour of Morris Zaslow,* ed. Kenneth S. Coates and William R. Morrison (Toronto: Captus Press, 1989), 189-99.

31 Minutes, Advisory Board on Wildlife Protection, 28 February 1916, RG 10, vol. 4084, file 496,658, LAC.

32 Waiser, "Canada Ox, Ovibos, Woolox," 192.

33 For a summary of these events, see Diubaldo, *Stefansson and the Canadian Arctic,* 142-45.

34 Harkin's participation in the royal commission is not surprising. He had taken a personal interest in the idea of introducing reindeer to parts of northern Canada at least since 1913, asserting that the initiative would "offer a simple solution to the matter of a permanent food supply for the native population." Harkin to W.W. Cory, 10 June 1913, RG 17, vol. 1188, docket 228571, LAC. See also M. Graham to Harkin, 5 June 1913, ibid. For a summary of the circumstances surrounding Stefansson's lease, including the failed attempt to release over six hundred Norwegian reindeer on Baffin Island in November 1921, see Diubaldo, *Stefansson and the Canadian Arctic,* 147-60.

35 For example, the whaling captain George Comer testified that the meat was inferior to beef, but Frank Hennessy, a former member of Captain Bernier's Arctic expedition, attested to the superior qualities of the meat compared with beef. Transcripts of the testimony of all witnesses are bound in a separate unpublished volume, RG 33-105, vol. 1, LAC.

36 John Gunion Rutherford, James Stanley McLean, and James Bernard Harkin, *Report of the Royal Commission to Investigate the Possibilities of the Reindeer and Musk-ox Industries in the Arctic and Sub-Arctic Regions of Canada* (Ottawa: King's Printer, 1922), 16. Hornaday's comments are in Appendix L, 52-54.

37 Ibid., 14-15, 36.

38 A proposal to remove muskox from Ellesmere and domesticate them in the protected environment of Anticosti Island had emerged in response to the royal commission, but O.S. Finnie, director of the Northwest Territories and Yukon Branch, explained to the deputy minister in August 1924 that no muskox had been captured because the

few ships that passed through the region were rarely able to stay long enough to search for the animals. Finnie to W.W. Cory, 25 August 1924, RG 85, vol. 1203, file 401-3, pt. 1, LAC.

39 Comer to Stefansson, 19 July 1919, RG 10, vol. 1203, file 401-3, pt. 1, LAC.

40 Cory to A.A. McLean, Comptroller, Royal Northwest Mounted Police, 18 July 1919, and McLean to Cory, 24 July 1919, ibid.

41 The letter is summarized in a report on the status of Canadian sovereignty in the Arctic islands prepared for a technical advisory committee established to investigate the issue. "Memo Re: Northern Islands, Prepared for Information, Technical Advisory Board Meeting, November 10th, 1920," n.d., MG 30, E-169, vol. 2, LAC.

42 Rasmussen to the Administration of the Colonies of Greenland, 8 March 1920, RG 85, vol. 1203, file 401-3, pt. 1, LAC.

43 Danish Minister to Earl Curzon of Keddleton, 12 April 1920, ibid.

44 Stefansson to Harkin, 15 May 1920, ibid.

45 Harkin to Cory, 16 June 1929, ibid.

46 "Memo Re: Northern Islands. Prepared for Information, Technical Advisory Board Meeting, November 10th, 1920," n.d., MG 30, E-169, vol. 2, LAC.

47 For an account of the establishment of these posts, see William R. Morrison, *Showing the Flag: The Mounted Police and Canadian Sovereignty in the North, 1894-1825* (Vancouver: UBC Press, 1985). The Danish government acquiesced in 1921 to a program of muskox conservation on Ellesmere. Most important, Denmark agreed to prohibit any trading of muskox skins through Rasmussen's Greenland post. See Harkin to Cory, 29 June 1921, RG 85, vol. 1203, file 401-3, pt. 1, LAC.

48 Rutherford, McLean, and Harkin, *Report of the Royal Commission*, 14-15. My reading of the royal commission transcripts concludes, however, that very few witnesses were critical of Inuit hunting practices. See RG 33-105, vol. 1, LAC.

49 See Graham to Finnie, 16 November 1923, RG 85, vol. 1203, file 401-3, pt. 1, LAC; and Finnie to Hoyes Lloyd, 20 November 1923, ibid.

50 Order-in-council P.C. 555, 8 April 1924; copy in RG 85, vol. 1203, file 401-3, pt. 1, LAC. The advisory board resolution calling for complete protection of the muskox is quoted in full.

51 See "Canada Takes Steps to Protect Musk Ox," *Christian Science Monitor*, 28 September 1924; "Cow Buffalo and Musk-Ox," *Ottawa Citizen*, 28 August 1924; "Canada Protects Musk-Ox from Total Extinction," *Brandon Sun*, 11 August 1924; "Conservation of Canada's Musk-Ox," *Wetawiskin Times*, 7 August 1924; clippings in RG 85, vol. 1203, file 401-3, pt. 1, LAC.

52 Hoare to Finnie, 10 August 1926, RG 85, vol. 1383, file 401-3, pt. 2, LAC.

53 Caulkin to Officer Commanding, "G" Division, Edmonton, 14 August 1925, ibid.

54 Finnie to Cory, 5 November 1925, and Anderson to Finnie, 17 November 1925, ibid.

55 Harkin to Cory, 12 November 1925, ibid. Harkin hoped that a "superstition" might be found within the Inuit hunting camps that would brand offenders against the game laws as deviants and outcasts.

56 Minutes, Advisory Board on Wildlife Protection, 19 November and 2 December 1925, RG 13, vol. 924, file 6101, pt. B, LAC.

57 Finnie to Starnes, 16 December 1926, RG 85, vol. 1203, file 401-3, pt. 1, LAC. In keeping with the new policy, two Inuit hunters, Khow-joack and Pookeenak Hayes, were not charged with poaching after killing two muskox near Back River because the men

had not been informed of the new regulation. O.G. Petty, Chesterfield Inlet Detachment, to Officer Commanding, RCMP Headquarters, 1 June 1926, RG 85, vol. 1383, file 401-3, pt. 2, LAC.

58 See No author, *Canoeists' Reflections on Arctic Cairn Notes* (Toronto: Betelgeuse Books, 1997).

59 M.T. Kelly, "The Land before Time," *Saturday Night* 104, 7 (July 1989), 74; David Pelly, *Thelon: River Sanctuary* (Hyde Park, ON: Canadian Recreational Canoeing Association, 1996).

60 J.W. Tyrrell, "Report on the Country North and East of Great Slave Lake," 1901, RG 85, vol. 1087, file 401-22, pt. 1, LAC.

61 For Hornby's recommendation, see Minutes, Advisory Board on Wildlife Protection, 19 November 1925, RG 13, vol. 924, file 6101, pt. B, LAC.

62 Minutes, Advisory Board on Wildlife Protection, 28 May 1926, RG 13, vol. 924, file 6101, pt. B, LAC.

63 The article, entitled "Sanctuary for Musk-Ox," was reprinted in "The Fifth Column," *Ottawa Morning Citizen*, 12 August 1927; clipping in RG 85, vol. 1383, file 401-3, pt. 2, LAC.

64 Finnie to Lloyd, 15 June 1926, RG 13, vol. 924, file 6101, pt. A, LAC.

65 "Trappers Are Resentful of New Rulings," *Edmonton Journal*, 27 July 1927; clipping in RG 85, vol. 1383, file 401-3, pt. 2, LAC. Other clippings from the same file include "Trappers Here to Fight New Regulations," *Edmonton Bulletin*, 25 July 1927, and "Trappers Will Fight Edict of Government," *Edmonton Journal*, 12 August 1927.

66 "Trappers Here to Fight New Regulations," *Edmonton Bulletin*, 25 July 1927.

67 Minutes of the 13th Session of the Northwest Territories Council, 3 February 1932, RG 10, vol. 3238, file 300,352, pt. 2, LAC.

68 Minutes, Advisory Board on Wildlife Protection, 29 February 1932, RG 10, vol. 4085, file 496,658-1, pt. 4, LAC.

69 Hoare's instructions are summarized in the introduction to his diary of his journey to the Thelon, MG 30 B138, LAC.

70 Hoare, *Conserving Canada's Muskoxen*, 12. See also Hoare's diary, 5 May 1928, MG 30 B138, LAC.

71 Hoare, *Conserving Canada's Muskoxen*, 12.

72 See Hoare's diary, 26 July 1929, MG 30, B138, LAC.

73 Hoare, *Conserving Canada's Muskoxen*, 48.

74 See Hoare's diary, 9 August 1929, MG 30, B138, LAC.

75 See Pelly, *Thelon*, 70-72.

76 Minutes of the 80th Session of the Northwest Territories Council, 19 April 1938, RG 10, vol. 3241, file 600,352, pt. 6, LAC.

77 For a discussion of the rationale for the amendment, see Finnie to R.A. Gibson, Acting Deputy Minister of the Interior, 13 November 1929, RG 85 vol. 1383, file 401-3, pt. 2, LAC. The regulation was amended by order-in-council P.C. 2265, *Canada Gazette* 63, 23 (20 November 1929): 2079-80.

78 "Extract from F.M. Steel's report November 1935 – Snyder Expedition, Mackenzie District, File 7883," n.d., RG 85, vol. 1383, file 401-3, pt. 2, LAC.

79 "Extract from the Report on the Harry Snyder 1935 Barren Lands Expedition, Northwest Territories," 31 January 1936, ibid.

80 Ramachandra Guha, *The Unquiet Woods: Ecological Change and Peasant Resistance in*

the Himalaya, expanded ed. (Berkeley: University of California Press, 2000), 55-58. In a similar case, indigenous hunters living near Kenya's Amboseli National Park intentionally poached wildlife in the late 1960s as a form of protest against restrictive hunting regulations in the game preserve portion of the park. David Western, "Ecosystem Conservation and Rural Development: The Case of Amboseli," in *Natural Connections: Perspectives in Community-Based Conservation,* ed. David Western and R. Michael Wright (Washington, DC: Island Press, 1994), 15-52.

81 "Extract from the Report on the Harry Snyder 1935 Barren Lands Expedition," RG 85, vol. 1383, file 401-3, pt. 2, LAC.

82 See Acting Lance Corporal W.J.G. Smith, RCMP, Fort Reliance, to Officer Commanding, Fort Smith, 17 April 1937, RG 85, vol. 1249, file 401-3, pt. 4, LAC.

83 Clarke to R.A. Gibson, Deputy Commissioner, NWT, 16 June 1938, ibid. See also C.H.D. Clarke, *A Biological Investigation of the Thelon Game Sanctuary,* National Museum of Canada Bulletin no. 96, Biological Series no. 25 (Ottawa: Department of Mines and Resources, Mines and Geology Branch, 1940), 9-11.

84 Hoare to R.M. Anderson, 14 July 1936, RG 85, vol. 1383, file 401-3, pt. 2, LAC.

85 Report of Const. W.J.G. Stewart, Fort Reliance, to Officer Commanding, Fort Smith, 18 September 1936, RG 85, vol. 1249, file 401-3, pt. 4, LAC.

86 Clarke, *Biological Investigation,* 76. For Hoare's estimate, see *Conserving Canada's Musk-Oxen,* 48.

87 Camsell to Wood, 6 July 1937, RG 22, vol. 866, file 40-6-5, LAC.

88 Minutes of the 80th Session of the Northwest Territories Council, 19 April 1938, RG 10, vol. 3241, file 600,352, pt. 6, LAC.

89 Minutes of the 84th Session of the Northwest Territories Council, 19 October 1938, Ibid.

90 Based on the testimony of local trappers and officials, the Northwest Territories Council concluded that no muskox poaching had occurred in the sanctuary through the winter of 1937-38. Ibid. But three hunters were arrested for killing muskox in the sanctuary in 1939. Lent, *Muskoxen and Their Hunters,* 163.

91 Tener, *Muskoxen in Canada,* 102.

92 In 1955 Const. G.E. Heapy reported that the Hudson's Bay Company post manager at Cambridge Bay had stated that the Inuit did not "go out of their way" to kill muskox but would hunt them if in dire need of food. Heapy to Commanding Officer "G" Division, 14 April 1955, RG 109, vol. 23, file WLT 200, pt. 3, LAC. One large slaughter of seventy muskox took place at Nose Lake in the winter of 1955-56 because of acute hunger among the local Inuit. See A.J. Boxer, Northern Service Officer, to Chief of the Arctic Division, 19 December 1955, ibid. Reports of smaller-scale and very infrequent poaching incidents in cases of acute hunger through the 1950s and 1960s are in RG 85, vol. 1249, file 401-3, pts. 4 and 4a, LAC; and RG 109, vol. 23-4, file WLT 200, pts. 3-4 and 6-8, LAC. Even the police were forced to kill muskox when hunger threatened. In August 1960, an RCMP constable on patrol with an Inuit special constable and four Inuit hunters killed two muskox on Devon Island to avoid starvation. See W.G. Fraser, Officer Commanding "G" Division, RCMP, to W.W. Mair, Chief, CWS, 2 August 1960, RG 109, vol. 24, file WLT 200, pt. 6, LAC. In none of these cases were charges laid. Charges were laid and fines of $50 levied against several hunters in August 1962 after they killed muskox when caribou were readily

available in the region surrounding the Spence Bay RCMP detachment. See Const. J.W. Pringle, RCMP, "Angotitayak – N.W.T. Game Ordinance" and "Kadloo et al. – N.W.T. Game Ordinance," 14 August 1962, RG 109, vol. 24, file WLT 200, pt. 7, LAC. Charges were also laid after a muskox was killed because it had entered a hunting camp near Baker Lake and was believed to be dangerous. The hunter Koonungnak was fined $200. Area Administrator, Baker Lake to Regional Administrator, Churchill, 16 September 1963, ibid.

93 See F.J.G. Cunningham to Commissioner, RCMP, 9 February 1956, RG 85, acc. 1997-98/076, box 73, file 406-7, pt. 3, LAC. A copy of the ordinance amending the boundaries, dated 23 January 1956, is in the same file.

94 Stefansson set off a dispute between the United Kingdom and the Soviet Union when he convinced his company, the Hudson Bay Reindeer Company, to send a party to Wrangel Island in 1921 to claim British sovereignty. The matter was not resolved until 1926, and the British were more angered than impassioned by Stefansson's brash move. The explorer subsequently lost his privileged position with Canadian officials. See Diubaldo, *Stefansson and the Canadian Arctic,* 161-87.

95 Minutes, Advisory Board on Wildlife Protection, 15 January 1951, RG 85, vol. 1249, file 401-3, pt. 4, LAC. The federal government continued to fund the domestication experiment after the capture of the calves. A contract dated 28 June 1960 between Teal and the Crown provided $2,500 for research reports related to the domestication experiments in Vermont after the project had run into financial difficulty. See Minister of Northern Affairs and National Resources to Teal, RG 109, vol. 24, file WLT 200, pt. 6, LAC.

96 For a report on the calf capture in 1954, see Teal to W.W. Mair, Chief, CWS, 3 September 1954, RG 109, vol. 23, file WLT 200, pt. 2, LAC. For the 1955 capture, see W.A. Fuller, "Report on the Teal Expedition," RG 109, vol. 23, file WLT 200, pt. 3, LAC.

97 John J. Teal, Jr., "Golden Fleece of the Arctic," *Atlantic Monthly* 201, 3 (March 1958): 81.

98 See John J. Teal, Domesticating the Wild and Wooly Musk Ox," *National Geographic* 137, 6 (June 1970), 862-79. In the mid- to late 1960s Teal established unsuccessful projects in Fort Chimo, Quebec, and Bardu, Norway, and a third project at Fairbanks, Alaska, that had moderate success after the muskox were moved several times. They finally settled in the Matanuska River Valley north of Anchorage in 1986. See Lent, *Muskoxen and Their Hunters,* 238. A second farmer, Al Oeming, received a permit (with the blessing of the Canadian Wildlife Service) to take six muskox calves from the Thelon Game Sanctuary in March 1958 for his game farm in Alberta. See Oeming to John Tener, 12 March 1959, RG 109, vol. 24, file WLT 200, pt. 6, LAC. Oeming obtained a second permit in 1964 and captured six more calves from the Thelon River area that August. See W.E. Stevens, Regional Superintendent, CWS, to David Munro, Chief, CWS, 2 September 1964, RG 109, vol. 24, file WLT 200, pt. 8, LAC. In 1957 the Department of Northern Affairs and National Resources rejected the idea of establishing a muskox farm in the North due to the projected cost and a presumed lack of interest on the part of the Inuit. The policy statement suggested that muskox ranches might be established after further research on the species. R.G. Robertson, "Departmental Policy Statement on the Muskoxen," 4 February 1959, ibid.

99 See Alfred Crosby, *Ecological Imperialism: The Biological Expansion of Europe, 900-1900* (Cambridge: Cambridge University Press, 1986).

CHAPTER 5: LA FOULE! LA FOULE!

1 See Suzanne Zeller, *Inventing Canada: Early Victorian Science and the Idea of a Trans-continental Nation*, (Toronto: University of Toronto Press, 1987).

2 See, for example, John Schultz, "Report of the Select Committee of the Senate Appointed to Inquire into the Resources of the Great Mackenzie Basin," Appendix 1, *Senate Journals*, 1888; and Ernest J. Chambers, ed., *Canada's Fertile Northland: A Glimpse of the Enormous Resources of Part of the Unexplored Regions of the Dominion* (Ottawa: Government Printing Bureau, 1907).

3 Carl Berger, *Science, God and Nature in Victorian Canada* (Toronto: University of Toronto Press, 1982), 3.

4 For a classic historical account of the relationship of romanticism and imperialism to the nineteenth-century hunting cult, see John Mackenzie, *The Empire of Nature: Hunting, Conservation, and British Imperialism* (Manchester: Manchester University Press, 1988), 26-28. See also Theodore Roosevelt, *African Game Trails: An Account of the African Wanderings of an American Hunter-Naturalist* (New York: Scribner's, 1926); and Frederick Selous, *A Hunter's Wanderings in Africa* (London: R. Bentley, 1890).

5 For a discussion of the historical manifestation of the Victorian hunting cult in western Canada, see Tina Loo, "Of Moose and Men: Hunting for Masculinities in British Columbia, 1880-1939," *Western Historical Quarterly* 32 (Autumn 2001): 296-319; Tina Loo, "Making a Modern Wilderness: Conserving Wildlife in Twentieth-Century Canada," *Canadian Historical Review* 82, 1 (March 2001): 92-121; and Greg Gillespie, "'I Was Well Pleased with Our Sport among the Buffalo': Big-Game Hunters, Travel Writing and Cultural Imperialism in the British North American West, 1847-72," *Canadian Historical Review* 83, 4 (December 2002): 555-84.

6 This idea was applied broadly to the entire northwest of Canada after 1870. For a discussion, see George Colpitts, *Game in the Garden: A Human History of Wildlife in Western Canada to 1940* (Vancouver: UBC Press, 2002).

7 Loo, "Of Moose and Men."

8 For an overview of the growth and extent of hunters' influence on the wildlife conservation movement in the United States, see John F. Reiger, *American Sportsmen and the Origins of Conservation*, 3rd ed. (Corvallis: Oregon State University Press, 2001).

9 See James Tober, *Who Owns the Wildlife? The Political Economy of Conservation in Nineteenth-Century America* (Westport, CT: Greenwood Press, 1981), 48-49.

10 C. Gordon Hewitt, *The Conservation of the Wild Life of Canada* (New York: Charles Scribner's Sons, 1921), 1-2, 11-12.

11 Warburton Pike, *The Barren Ground of Northern Canada* (New York: Macmillan, 1892), 274.

12 Ibid., 82, 83-84.

13 J.W. Tyrrell, *Across the Sub-Arctic of Canada, a Journey of 3,200 Miles by Canoe and Snowshoe through the Barren Lands* (London, T. Fisher Unwin, 1898), 85.

14 Joseph Burr Tyrrell, "An Expedition through the Barren Lands of Northern Canada," *Geographical Journal* 4, 5 (1894): 442.

15 Frank Russell, *Explorations in the Far North: Being the Report of an Expedition under the Auspices of the University of Iowa during the Years 1892, '93, and '94* (Iowa City: University of Iowa Press, 1898), 88.

16 David T. Hanbury, *Sport and Travel in the Northland of Canada* (London: Edward Arnold, 1904), 44.

17 Ernest Thompson Seton, *The Arctic Prairies* (New York: Harper and Row, 1911), 220, 259.
18 Henry Toke Munn, *Prairie Trails and Arctic By-Ways* (London: Hurst and Blackett, 1932), 58. Seton claimed in *The Arctic Prairies* that Munn had seen the caribou at Artillery Lake in July 1892, but Munn's travelogue indicates the incident took place in the summer of 1894.
19 Ernest Thompson Seton, *The Lives of Game Animals*, vol. 3, pt. 2 (Garden City, NJ: Doubleday, 1929), 135, 117.
20 The following six large groups of caribou migrate through at least part of the present-day Northwest Territories and Nunavut: the Kaminuriak herd of the Keewatin District west of Hudson Bay, the Northeastern Mainland herd of the northern Keewatin and Melville Sound regions, the Beverly herd of northern Saskatchewan and the central Arctic plains, the Bathurst herd that winters north of Yellowknife and summers on the central Arctic coast, the Bluenose herd that ranges from the Mackenzie River to the western Arctic coast, and the Porcupine herd of the northeastern Yukon that migrates into a small corner of the Northwest Territories near Aklavik and Fort McPherson. For a summary of caribou biology and migratory habits, see Doug Urquhart, "Biology," in *People and Caribou in the Northwest Territories,* ed. Ed Hall (Yellowknife: Department of Renewable Resources, NWT, 1989).
21 Rutherford's comments are contained in transcripts of the royal commission's hearings, Appendix 1, Evidence before the Commission, 12 May 1920, RG 33-105, vol. 1, Library and Archives Canada (LAC).
22 Seton, *Arctic Prairies,* 220.
23 Ibid., xi (his emphasis).
24 For a discussion of this romanticism, see Shelagh Grant, *Sovereignty or Security? Government Policy in the Canadian North, 1936-1950* (Vancouver: UBC Press, 1988), 19-20.
25 G.H. Blanchet, "An Exploration into the Northern Plains North and East of Great Slave Lake, Including the Source of the Coppermine River," *Canadian Field-Naturalist* 39 (February 1925): 31; and vol. 39 (January 1925): 15.
26 John Hornby, "Barren Land Caribou (*Rangifer arcticus*)," n.d., RG 85, vol. 1087, file 401-22, pt. 1, LAC. He revised and reprinted these notes in "Wild Life in the Thelon River Area, Northwest Territories, Canada," *Canadian Field-Naturalist* 48, 7 (October 1934): 105-111.
27 Pike, *Barren Ground of Northern Canada,* 48.
28 Russell, *Explorations in the Far North,* 227.
29 Hanbury, *Sport and Travel,* 43, 149.
30 Caspar Whitney, *On Snow-Shoes to the Barren Grounds: Twenty-Eight Hundred Miles after Musk-Oxen and Wood-Bison* (New York: Harper and Brothers, 1896), 212-14.
31 Pike, *Barren Ground of Northern Canada,* 48; Whitney, *On Snow-Shoes,* 241.
32 For an overview of the complex relationships between sport hunters and their guides, see Loo, "Of Moose and Men," 312-18. For a case study of Native guides in the Atlantic salmon fishery, see Bill Parenteau, "'Care, Control and Supervision': Native People in the Canadian Atlantic Salmon Fishery, 1867-1900," *Canadian Historical Review* 79, 1 (March 1998): 1-35.
33 Pike, *Barren Ground of Northern Canada,* 192.
34 Whitney, *On Snow-Shoes,* 242.
35 For archaeological and anthropological studies of Native hunting strategies in northern Canada, see David A. Morrison, *Caribou Hunters in the Western Arctic: Zooarchaeology of the Rita-Claire and Bison Skull Sites.* Mercury Series, Archaeological Survey of

Canada Paper 157 (Hull: Canadian Museum of Civilization, 1997); Bryan C. Gordon, *Of Men and Herds in Barrenland Prehistory,* Mercury Series, Archeological Survey Paper 28 (Ottawa: National Museum of Man, 1975); Bryan C. Gordon, "Prehistoric Chipewyan Harvesting at a Barrenland Caribou Water Crossing," *Western Canadian Journal of Anthropology* 7, 1 (1977): 69-83; Margaret W. Morris, "Great Bear Lake Indians: A Historical Demography and Human Ecology," pt. 1, *Musk-Ox* 11 (1972): 3-27; Henry S. Sharp, "The Caribou-Eater Chipewyan: Bilaterality, Strategies of Caribou Hunting and the Fur Trade," *Arctic Anthropology* 14, 2 (1977): 35-40; and James G.E. Smith, "Economic Uncertainty in an 'Original Affluent Society': Caribou and Caribou Eater Chipewyan Adaptive Strategies," *Arctic Anthropology* 15, 1 (1978): 68-88.

36 For a discussion of the importance of fat to balance the high protein content of the northern hunter's diet, see Hugh Brody, *Living Arctic: Hunters of the Canadian North* (Vancouver: Douglas and McIntyre, 1987), 59-67.

37 Roderick MacFarlane, "Notes on Mammals Collected and Observed in the Northern Mackenzie River District, Northwest Territories of Canada, with Remarks on Explorers and Explorations of the Far North," *Proceedings of the United States National Museum,* vol. 27 (Washington, DC: Government Printing Office, 1905), 680.

38 Pike, *Barren Ground of Northern Canada,* 48.

39 Shepard Krech III, "Throwing Bad Medicine: Sorcery, Disease and the Fur Trade among the Kutchin and other Northern Athapaskans," in *Indians, Animals and the Fur Trade: A Critique of Keepers of the Game,* ed. Shepard Krech III (Athens: University of Georgia Press, 1981), 75-108.

40 Peter Usher has suggested that as many as six hundred American whalers on Herschel Island needed to be fed from local caribou supplies in the late nineteenth century. Usher, "The Canadian Western Arctic: A Century of Change," *Anthropologica,* n.s., 13, 1-2 (1971): 169-83.

41 Gordon, "Prehistoric Chipewyan Harvesting," 78; Robin Ridington, "Knowledge, Power and the Individual in Subarctic Hunting Societies," *American Anthropologist* 90, 1 (1988): 107.

42 June Helm, *The People of Denendeh: Ethnohistory of the Indians of Canada's Northwest Territories* (Montreal and Kingston: McGill-Queen's University Press, 2000), 64-65.

43 See Sharp, "Caribou-Eater Chipewyan." See also Brody, *Living Arctic;* and George Wenzel, *Clyde Inuit Adaptation and Ecology: The Organization of Subsistence,* National Museum of Man Mercury Series, Canadian Ethnology Service Paper no. 77 (Ottawa: National Museums of Canada, 1981).

44 Michael A.D. Ferguson, Robert P. Williamson, and François Messier, "Inuit Knowledge of Long Term Changes in a Population of Arctic Tundra Caribou," *Arctic* 51, 3 (1998): 202-19; Michael A.D. Ferguson and François Messier, "Collection and Analysis of Traditional Ecological Knowledge about a Population of Arctic Tundra Caribou," *Arctic* 50, 1 (1997): 17-28; Anne Gunn, G. Arlooktoo, and D. Kaomayak, "The Contribution of Ecological Knowledge of Inuit to Wildlife Management in the Northwest Territories," in *Traditional Knowledge and Renewable Resource Management,* ed. M.M.R. Freeman and L.N. Carbyn, Occasional Publication no. 23 (Edmonton: Boreal Institute for Northern Studies, 1988), 22-30; Harvey Feit, "Self Management and State Management: Forms of Knowing and Managing Northern Wildlife," in Freeman and Carbyn, *Traditional Knowledge,* 72-91; Peter Usher, "Indigenous Management

Systems and the Conservation of Wildlife in the Canadian North," *Alternatives* 14 (1987): 3-9.

45 In just one example, the government agent at Fort Smith, A.J. Bell, cited eyewitness reports of Chipewyan hunters at Fond du Lac having killed thousands of caribou with spears and removed only their tongues. Bell's report is quoted extensively in a letter from R.H. Campbell to W.W. Cory, 8 January 1912, RG 85, vol. 664, file 3910, pt. 1, LAC.

46 Stefansson to Borden, 8 January 1914, MG 36 H, Borden Papers, vol. 785, 101514-101520, LAC.

47 Stefansson to Sifton, 8 February 1914, RG 85, vol. 665, file 3914, pt. 1, LAC. Stefansson's attitude to these slaughters was contradictory over the course of his career. He claimed in his popular book, *The Friendly Arctic*, that large caribou slaughters were actually a conservation measure employed by the Inuit to avoid the wastage of meat. With a large slaughter, Stefansson reasoned, an Inuit hunting party could camp by the game for several days and consume all the meat, whereas transporting the meat from a scattered kill presented more of a logistical problem. Stefansson, *The Friendly Arctic: The Story of Five Years in the Polar Region* (New York: Macmillan, 1922), 283.

48 Hewitt's memorandum is reproduced in a letter from C. Sifton to W.W. Cory, 8 August 1914, RG 85, vol. 665, file 3914, pt. 1, LAC.

49 Graham to Harkin, 2 September 1914, RG 85, vol. 665, file 3914, pt. 1, LAC.

50 Henry J. Bury, "Report on the Game and Fisheries of Northern Alberta and the Northwest Territories," 6 November 1915, RG 85, vol. 664, file 3910, pt. 2, LAC.

51 See Graham to Harkin, 7 December 1915, RG 85, vol. 664, file 3910, 2, LAC.

52 For an overview of Hewitt's address to the Commission of Conservation, see Janet Foster, *Working for Wildlife: The Beginnings of Preservation in Canada*, 2nd ed. (Toronto: University of Toronto Press, 1998), 174-75.

53 For a summary of the events leading up to the passage of the Northwest Game Act, see Hewitt, *Conservation of Wild Life*, 258-60; C. Gordon Hewitt, *Conservation of Wild Life in Canada in 1917: A Review*, reprinted from the Ninth Annual Report of the Commission of Conservation (Ottawa, 1918), 8-9; and Foster, *Working for Wildlife*, 172-78.

54 An amendment to the Northwest Game Act in 1920 finally allowed cabinet to set closed seasons by order-in-council. See J.B. Harkin, "Report of the Commissioner of Dominion Parks," *Sessional Papers of the Dominion of Canada*, no. 25 (1921): 13.

55 An Act Respecting Game in the Northwest Territories of Canada, *Statutes of Canada*, 7-8 George V, vol. 1, c. 36, s. 1, 337-43.

56 Perry's comments are taken from "Commissioner's Report, Royal Northwest Mounted Police," *Sessional Papers of the Dominion of Canada*, no. 28 (1919): 20. For Harkin's comments, see "Report of the Commissioner of Dominion Parks," *Sessional Papers of the Dominion of Canada*, no. 25 (1920): 7.

57 F.H. Kitto, "Report on the Natural Resources of the Mackenzie District and Their Economic Development, Made in the Summer of 1920," Department of the Interior, Natural Resources Intelligence Branch, RG 10, vol. 4092, file 549036, LAC, 18.

58 René Fumoleau, *As Long as This Land Shall Last: A History of Treaty 8 and Treaty 11, 1870-1939* (Toronto: McClelland and Stewart, 1975), 125-30.

59 Hewitt, *Conservation of Wild Life*, 1.

60 For an overview, see Samuel Hays, *Conservation and the Gospel of Efficiency: The Progressive Conservation Movement, 1890-1920* (New York: Atheneum, 1959).

61 Hewitt, *Conservation of Wild Life*, 66. Janet Foster claims that Hewitt objected to the commercialization of the caribou, based on comments he made before the Commission of Conservation in 1918 regarding the desirability of using domesticated reindeer rather than wild caribou as a meat supply for northern Canada. Although Hewitt did promote the introduction of reindeer to the Canadian North, the quotation cited here, as well as others cited later on in this chapter, suggests that he was not opposed to a commercial caribou slaughter in the Northwest Territories. See Foster, *Working for Wildlife*, 163.

62 Graham to Harkin, 2 September 1914, RG 85, vol. 665, file 3914, pt. 1, LAC.

63 For example, see two long letters from Graham to Harkin, 2 September 1914 and 27 October 1917, RG 85, vol. 665, file 3914, pt. 1, LAC. See also Hewitt, *Conservation of Wild Life*, 56-71.

64 Seton, *Lives of Game Animals*, vol. 3, pt. 2, 117.

65 Henry J. Bury, "Report on the Game and Fisheries of Northern Alberta and the Northwest Territories," 6 November 1915, RG 85, vol. 664, file 3910, pt. 2, 18, LAC.

66 See Kurkpatrick Dorsey, *The Dawn of Conservation Diplomacy: US-Canadian Wildlife Protection Treaties in the Progressive Era* (Seattle: University of Washington Press, 1998), 221-31.

67 Edmund Russell, *War and Nature: Fighting Humans and Insects with Chemicals from World War I to Silent Spring* (Cambridge: Cambridge University Press, 2001).

68 F.H.H. Williamson to W.W. Cory, 28 October 1917, RG 85, vol. 665, file 3914, pt. 1, LAC.

69 Graham to Harkin, 27 October 1917, ibid.

70 Graham's final recommendations are contained in a letter to Harkin, 24 April 1918, ibid. In addition to caribou, Harkin suggested that seal, whale, and even ptarmigan netted by Native hunters might help to alleviate the food shortage. Harkin to R.M. Anderson, 26 February 1918, ibid.

71 The reasons for abandoning the proposed slaughter are outlined in "Caribou Can't Offset Shortage in Meat," *Conservation* 7, 5 (May 1918): 18. See also J.B. Harkin, "Report of the Commissioner of Dominion Parks," *Sessional Papers of the Dominion of Canada*, no. 25 (1918): 13.

72 See W.H.P. Jarvis to Harkin, 2 October 1918, RG 85, vol. 1087, file 401-22, pt. 1, LAC. Jarvis, it seems, never got over the official rejection of his idea. During the Second World War, he wrote several letters to the editor of the *Globe and Mail* urging the shipment of wild caribou to England and suggesting that reported crashes of Royal Air Force planes over Berlin due to frozen controls could have been prevented had a northern air flight training centre been established. W.H.P. Jarvis, letters to the editor, *Globe and Mail*, 18 November 1940 and 18 October 1941; clippings in RG 85, vol. 1088, file 401-22, pt. 3, LAC.

73 Harkin to Jarvis, 23 November 1918, RG 85. vol. 1087, file 401-22, pt. 1, LAC.

74 John Gunion Rutherford, James Stanley McLean, and James Bernard Harkin, *Report of the Royal Commission to Investigate the Possibilities of the Reindeer and Musk-ox Industries in the Arctic and Sub-Arctic Regions of Canada* (Ottawa: King's Printer, 1922), 31, 36-38.

75 Blanchet, "Exploration into the Northern Plains," 55.

76 Capt. J.C. Critchell-Bullock, "An Expedition to Sub-Arctic Canada," *Canadian Field-Naturalist* 45 (February 1931): 33.

77 Capt. J.C. Critchell-Bullock, "An Expedition to Sub-Arctic Canada," *Canadian Field-Naturalist* 44 (March 1930): 55.

Chapter 6: To Save the Wild Caribou

1 The description of the Northwest Territories and Yukon Branch as a "shackled admin-istration" comes from chapters 3 and 4 of Diamond Jenness, *Canada*, vol. 2 of *Eskimo Administration*, Arctic Institute of North America Technical Report no. 14, May (Montreal: Arctic Institute of North America, 1964). Mark Dickerson has argued that the federal government's role in the Northwest Territories from 1921 to 1950 was more activist, a series of deliberate and dynamic policy initiatives in the fields of education, health, welfare, and education. Dickerson, *Whose North? Political Change, Political Development, and Self-Government in the Northwest Territories* (Vancouver: UBC Press, 1992), 28-60.

2 See the minutes contained in RG 10, vol. 4085, file 658-1; RG 22, vol. 4, file 14; RG 22, vol. 16, file 69, all Library and Archives Canada (LAC).

3 For an overview, see Dickerson, *Whose North?* 29-30. The other three members of the expanded NWT Council (in addition to Cory, Finnie, and Gibson) were J.W. Green-way, commissioner of Dominion lands, Charles Camsell, deputy minister of mines, and Lt.-Col. Cortlandt Starnes, assistant commissioner, RCMP.

4 Finnie's instructions to Hoare, in a letter dated 14 May 1924, appear at the beginning of the lay missionary's final report. W.H.B. Hoare, *Report of Investigations Affecting Eskimo and Wild Life, District of Mackenzie, 1924-1925-1926* (Department of the Inte-rior, Northwest Territories and Yukon Branch). The report consists of two parts, dated 1 August 1925 and 17 January 1927.

5 Ibid., 1 August 1925, 12-13; 17 January 1927, 37.

6 Ibid., 1 August 1925, 12.

7 Ibid., 13.

8 Ibid., 17 January 1927, 40-43.

9 Ibid., 1 August 1925, 11. In the late 1930s, the biologist C.H.D Clarke described the presumption of a former massive migration of the interior caribou herds to the Arc-tic islands as one of the significant fallacies of the early theories on caribou migration. Clarke, *A Biological Investigation of the Thelon Game Sanctuary*, National Museum of Canada Bulletin no. 96, Biological Series no. 25 (Ottawa: Department of Mines and Resources, Mines and Geology Branch, 1940), 95-98. Although there may have been some interchange between the Peary caribou of the Arctic islands and the barren ground caribou, little is known of the extent to which Peary caribou migrated south to the Arctic mainland or the barren ground caribou to the Arctic islands. See Frank Miller, "Caribou," in *Wild Mammals of North America: Biology, Management, and Economics*, ed. J.A. Chapman and G.A. Feldhamer (Baltimore: Johns Hopkins Uni-versity Press, 1982), 923-24.

10 Hoare, *Report of Investigations*, 17 January 1927, 39-40.

11 Ibid., 39.

12 Reference to Barnes' report was made in Minutes, Advisory Board on Wildlife Pro-tection, 2 November 1926, RG 13, vol. 924, file 6101, pt. A, LAC. See also the reports of Const. Gibson, 10 February 1924, Inspector Stuart T. Wood, 30 April 1924, Const.

D.F. Robinson, 1 June 1926, Cpl. O.G. Petty, 1 June 1926, RG 10, vol. 4085, file 496,658-1B, LAC.

13 Minutes, Advisory Board on Wildlife Protection, 30 March 1925, RG 10, vol. 4085, file 496,658-1B, LAC.

14 Minutes, Advisory Board on Wildlife Protection, 19 November 1925, RG 13, vol. 924, file 6101, pt. B, LAC.

15 Minutes, Advisory Board on Wildlife Protection, 20 February 1926, RG 10, vol. 4085, file 496,658-1B, LAC.

16 See Minutes, Advisory Board on Wildlife Protection, 29 and 30 April, 1 and 5 May 1925, ibid. A report from the RCMP inspector Stuart T. Wood on his time with Rasmussen on Herschel Island stated that the Danish explorer thought the Inuit held life very cheaply. Rasmussen's assessment came only one month after two Inuit were hanged at Herschel Island for the murder of RCMP Corporal Doak. An attempt was also made on Rasmussen's life at the Hudson's Bay Company post on the Kent Peninsula. See Wood, "Re: Knud Rasmussen – Explorer," 30 April 1924, ibid. For details on the high-profile murder cases involving Inuit people, see William Morrison, *Showing the Flag: The Mounted Police and Canadian Sovereignty in the North, 1894-1925* (Vancouver: UBC Press, 1985), 158-61. See also "Commissioner's Report, Royal Canadian Mounted Police," *Sessional Papers of the Dominion of Canada* 21 (1923): 35-43.

17 See Minutes, Advisory Board on Wildlife Protection, 29 April and 1 May 1925, RG 10, vol. 4085, file 496,658-1B, LAC.

18 For an overview of Rasmussen's attitude to the Inuit, see his popular travelogue, *Across Arctic America: Narrative of the Fifth Thule Expedition* (New York: Greenwood Press, 1927).

19 Minutes, Advisory Board on Wildlife Protection, 30 March 1925, RG 10, vol. 4085, file 496,658-1B, LAC.

20 Minutes, Advisory Board on Wildlife Protection, 11 March 1926, RG 13, vol. 924, file 6101, pt. B, LAC.

21 Order-in-council P.C. 1146, 19 July 1926; copy extracted from the *Canada Gazette* of 21 July 1926, ibid.

22 Minutes, Advisory Board on Wildlife Protection, 15 January and 1 May 1925, RG 10, vol. 4085, file 496,658-1B, LAC. For the discussion of the draft memo to the NWT Council, see minutes of 20 July 1926, RG 13, vol. 924, file 6101, pt. B, LAC.

23 Order-in-council P.C. 2265, *Canada Gazette* 60, 9 (28 August 1926): 595.

24 See A.E. Porsild, *Reindeer Grazing in Northwest Canada: Report of an Investigation of Pastoral Possibilities in the Area from the Alaska-Yukon Boundary to Coppermine River* (Ottawa: King's Printer, 1929). For a summary of the reindeer project up to the late 1970s, see Erhard Treude, "Forty Years of Reindeer Herding in the Mackenzie Delta, NWT," *Polarforschung* 45, 2 (1975), 129-48.

25 McDougal to Finnie, 24 March 1924, RG 85, vol. 1087, file 401-22, pt. 1, LAC.

26 Bryant to Officer Commanding, Mackenzie Sub-District, RCMP, 15 July 1924, ibid.

27 "Urges Action Be Taken to Stay Slaughter of Cariboo," *Regina Leader*, 22 July 1926; clipping in RG 85, vol. 1087, file 401-22, pt. 1, LAC.

28 See McDougal to Finnie, 24 March 1924, and Graham to Finnie, 29 April 1924, ibid.

29 Chappuis' investigation is referred to in a letter from Graham to Finnie, 29 October 1924, ibid.

30 Riddle's original complaint is contained in a letter to Finnie on 20 June 1927, ibid.

See also "Report of A.G. McCaskill, Trapper, Hinde Lake," June 1927, ibid. For the results of the provincial police investigation, see M. Chappuis to Gerald Card, 2 July 1927, ibid.

31 See Const. R.I.I. Clewy, "Report re Complaint – Alleged Unlawful Slaughter of Caribou, Selwyn Lake District, Fond du Lac, Saskatchewan," 22 July 1927, ibid.

32 Corporal Burstall, Report from Fort Smith Detachment to Officer Commanding, Great Slave Lake Sub-District, 10 May 1930, ibid.

33 René Fumoleau, *As Long as This Land Shall Last: A History of Treaty 8 and Treaty 11, 1870-1939* (Toronto: McClelland and Stewart, 1975), 239-41.

34 "Northern Trappers Attest Magnusson's Statement of Wanton Cariboo Slaughter," *Winnipeg Free Press,* 31 July 1926; clipping in RG 85, vol. 1087, file 401-22, pt. 1, LAC.

35 "Evidence of E.J Gaul, Baillie Island – Re: Caribou – J.F. Moran Report, 1928," RG 85, vol. 798, file 6556, LAC.

36 Corporal Burstall, Report from Fort Smith Detachment to Officer Commanding, Great Slave Lake Sub-District, 10 May 1930, RG 85, vol. 1087, file 401-22, pt. 1, LAC.

37 M. Chappuis to Gerald Card, 2 July 1927, ibid.

38 C. Bourget, "Report of the Treaty Trip of the Great Slave Lake Agency," 9 September 1929, ibid.

39 Const. Richard Wild to Officer Commanding, Western Arctic Sub-district, 5 September 1929, ibid.; Inspector A.M. Eames, "Reported Slaughter of Caribou – East Kugaryuak District," 6 May 1930, ibid.

40 In addition to the reports already mentioned from the 1920s, the archival record contains many questionable reports of caribou slaughters made by non-Natives during the 1930s. When the trapper W.F. Cooke reported in March 1935, for example, that caribou carcasses were being left to rot near Rocher River, the RCMP constable at Fort Smith reported that Cooke admitted he heard the story from Alexan King, who was "well known for careless handling of the truth." Const. W.T. James, RCMP, Ft. Smith Detachment, Report, 4 May 1935, ibid. Also in March 1935, H.A. Swanson, a trader at Cameron Bay, complained of caribou meat being left to rot in the district. Cpl. J.H. Davies of the RCMP claimed, however, that he had found no evidence of meat being wasted. See H.A. Swanson to Turner, 2 March 1935, RG 85, vol. 1089, file 401-22, pt. 2, LAC. See also Cpl. J.H. Davies, RCMP, to Officer Commanding, Fort Smith, 15 November 1935, ibid. In January 1938, the pilot W.J. Windrum claimed that the caribou herds had declined in northern Saskatchewan and adjacent areas in the Northwest Territories because Native hunters were slaughtering the herds indiscriminately and using the meat as bait on the trapline. Two months later, the inspector commanding of the subdivision at Prince Albert, Saskatchewan, reported that his officers had investigated and found no evidence of an indiscriminate slaughter in the region. See "Ruthless Slaughter," *Saskatoon Star-Phoenix,* 8 January 1938; clipping in RG 85, vol. 1089, file 401-22, pt. 2, LAC. See also F.W. Schultz, Inspector Commanding, Prince Albert Sub-Division, to Officer Commanding, "F" Division, Saskatchewan, 16 February 1938, ibid. In February 1939 one of the RCMP constables at Eskimo Point was highly critical of a claim made by the trapper George Lush that "Indians kill caribou as long as their ammunition will last." Const. Wilkinson questioned many of the local Inuit hunters, who said they had not seen any Indians in the region for quite some time. The police officer concluded that "these trappers are trying to make as much trouble for the Indians as possible, in order to keep them out of

the district, as Lush stated once, they are a nuisance and should be prevented from coming into the Territories [from Manitoba]." See Const. E.E. Wilkinson, RCMP, Eskimo Point, to Officer Commanding, Eastern Arctic Sub-Division, 18 February 1939, RG 85, vol. 1088, file 401-22, pt. 3, LAC.

41 Hoare to Finnie, 23 July 1927, RG 85, vol. 1087, file 401-22, pt. 1, LAC; Starnes to Finnie, 20 September 1927, ibid.

42 Finnie to Lloyd, 12 January 1928, ibid.

43 Minutes, Advisory Board on Wildlife Protection, 18 January 1928, RG 13, vol. 924, file 6101, pt. A, LAC.

44 The new regulations were drafted and approved at a special meeting of the Advisory Board on Wildlife protection held 29 April 1929. For the revisions to the NWT game regulations, see order-in-council P.C. 807, *Canada Gazette* 67, 47 (15 May 1929): 2079.

45 "Extract from Report of O.S. Finnie, on his Inspection of Mackenzie District, July and August 1929," RG 10, vol. 3237, file 600,352, pt. 1, LAC.

46 Breynat also wrote to Finnie and Duncan Campbell Scott on 3 July 1929. All three telegrams are quoted in Fumoleau, *As Long as This Land,* 283.

47 See George Blondin, *Yamoria the Lawmaker: Stories of the Dene* (Edmonton: NeWest, 1997), 38-39; and June Helm, *The People of Denendeh: Ethnohistory of the Indians of Canada's Northwest Territories* (Montreal and Kingston: McGill-Queen's University Press, 2000), 140-43.

48 Native trappers were allowed to take limited amounts of beaver as a relief measure on an ad hoc basis. See Minutes, Advisory Board on Wildlife Protection, 10 March 1927, RG 13, vol. 924, file 6101, pt. A, LAC.

49 Kerry Abel, *Drum Songs: Glimpses of Dene History* (Montreal and Kingston: McGill-Queen's University Press, 1993), 199.

50 C. Bourget, "Report of the Treaty Trip of the Great Slave Lake Agency," 9 September 1929, RG 85, vol. 1087, file 401-22, pt. 1, LAC.

51 Order-in-council P.C. 2265, *Canada Gazette* 63, 23 (7 December 1929): 2079. The Northwest Territories Council voted to authorize the sale of meat from caribou and moose during open season and to permit the killing of game out of season by those in "dire need" of food at the meeting held 29 October 1929. See Minutes of the 10th Session of the NWT Council, RG 10, vol. 3237, file 600,352, pt. 1, LAC. The local trade in caribou meat and skins had been conducted at least since the first trading posts were established in the middle of the nineteenth century and primarily served areas where caribou had been in short supply. See Philip Godsell, *Arctic Trader: The Account of Twenty Years with the Hudson's Bay Company* (New York: G. Putnam's Sons, 1932), 275-76.

52 Peter Usher, "Contemporary Aboriginal Land, Resource, and Environmental Regimes: Origins, Problems, and Prospects," report prepared for the Land Resource and Environment Regimes Project, February 1996, in *For Seven Generations: An Information Legacy of the Royal Commission on Aboriginal Peoples,* ed. Royal Commission on Aboriginal Peoples, CD-ROM (Ottawa: Libraxus, 1997).

53 Const. Rivett, RCMP, to Officer Commanding, Ft. Smith Sub-Division, 15 August 1941, RG 85, vol. 1088, file 401-22, pt. 3, LAC. Four Native hunters were also prosecuted and fined for killing caribou out of season to feed their dogs at Fort Chipewyan, Alberta, in April 1937. See H.W. McGill, Director of Indian Affairs, to Deputy Minister, 22 April 1937, RG 85, vol. 1089, file 401-22, pt. 2, LAC.

54 See Const. S.E. Alexander, St. Roch Detachment, RCMP, to Officer Commanding, Aklavik, 27 April 1937, ibid. See also Acting Lance Corporal G. Abraham, Copper- mine Detachment, RCMP, to Officer Commanding, Aklavik, 6 May 1938, ibid.

55 Cpl. L. Basler, RCMP, Rae Detachment, to Officer Commanding, Rae Detachment, 28 April 1936, ibid.

56 For the game returns at Fort Rae for 1932, see H.E. Hume to Major MacBrien, Com- missioner, RCMP, 4 May 1933, RG 85, vol. 1087, file 401-22, pt. 1, LAC. Bourget's response is contained in a letter to Hume dated 8 November 1933, ibid.

57 Sgt. O.G. Petty to Officer Commanding, RCMP, Ottawa, "Re: Sec. 31 – Game Reg- ulations – Excessive Slaughter of Game By Natives," 30 June 1930, ibid.

58 Dr. J.A. Urquhart to H.E. Hume, 28 February 1933, ibid.

59 Cpl. R.A. Williams, RCMP, Reliance Detachment, to C. Trundle, Officer Com- manding, Great Slave Lake Sub-district, 1 June 1928, ibid.

60 Sgt. O.G. Petty, RCMP, Pangnirtung, to Officer Commanding, Headquarters, Ottawa, 31 July 1930, ibid.

61 See Morris Zaslow, *The Northward Expansion of Canada, 1914-1967* (Toronto: McClelland and Stewart, 1988), 174-202.

62 For a summary, see J.P. Richards to H.E. Hume, Chair, Dominion Lands Board, 7 October 1933, RG 85, vol. 1087, file 401-22, pt. 1, LAC.

63 Sgt. E.G. Baker, RCMP, "Slaughter of Cariboo – Great Bear Lake," 11 August 1933, ibid.

64 Richards to H.E. Hume, 26 September 1933, ibid.

65 T.O. Byrnes to T.G. Murphy, 26 August 1933, ibid.

66 Report of Supt. T.H. Irvine, Officer Commanding, "G" Division, to J.H. MacBrien, RCMP Commissioner, 24 October 1933, ibid.

67 See H.H. Rowatt to H.J.H. MacBrien, 28 November 1933, ibid.

68 See H.H. Rowatt to H.J.H. MacBrien, 27 December 1933, ibid.

69 Extract of Minutes of the 51st Session of the Northwest Territories Council, 15 March 1934, ibid.

70 For a discussion, see James Tober, *Who Owns the Wildlife? The Political Economy of Conservation in Nineteenth-Century America* (Westport, CT: Greenwood Press, 1981), 52-58.

71 Ralph Parsons to R.A. Gibson, Director, Lands, Parks and Forests Branch, 16 June 1936, RG 85, vol. 1089, file 401-22, pt. 2, LAC; J.P. Richards to A.L. Cumming, 30 November 1938, ibid.

72 Gibson to Ralph Parsons, 22 June 1936, ibid.

73 Clarke, *Biological Investigation*, 112.

74 From 1930 to 1938, the size of the RCMP force in the Northwest Territories declined from ninety-eight to eighty personnel. In the Mackenzie Valley alone, three detach- ments were closed and the personnel reduced from fifty-two to thirty-one people. For a summary, see Zaslow, *Northward Expansion*, 192-93.

75 Urquhart to J. Lorne Turner, Chair, Dominion Lands Board, 31 January 1934, RG 85, vol. 1087, file 401-22, pt. 1, LAC.

76 See Richards to H.H. Rowatt, Deputy Minister, 11 April 1934, ibid.

77 See Margaret W. Morris, "Great Bear Lake Indians: A Historical Demography and Human Ecology," pt. 1, *Musk-Ox* 11 (1972): 12-13; Henry S. Sharp, "The Caribou- Eater Chipewyan: Bilaterality, Strategies of Caribou Hunting and the Fur Trade,"

Arctic Anthropology 14, 2 (1977): 35-40; and James G.E. Smith, "Economic Uncertainty in an 'Original Affluent Society': Caribou and Caribou Eater Chipewyan Adaptive Strategies," *Arctic Anthropology* 15, 1 (1978): 71-72. Although comprehensive statistical information is lacking, Inspector Christianson with Indian Affairs reported in August 1936 that virtually all dog food at Fort Norman, Fort Good Hope, Aklavik, and Simpson was fish, while fish comprised 50 percent of dog feed at Fort Resolution, 10 percent at Fort Reliance, and 25 percent at Fort Rae and Yellowknife. "Extract of Report of Inspector Christenson, Dept. of Indian Affairs," 18 August 1936, RG 85, vol. 1089, file 401-22, pt. 2, LAC.

78 "Public Notice," 20 June 1935, ibid.

79 H.W. McGill, Director, Indian Affairs, to R.A. Gibson, 22 April 1937, RG 85, vol. 1089, file 401-22, pt. 2, LAC.

80 Minutes, Advisory Board on Wildlife Protection, 7 February 1938, RG 22, vol. 4, file 14, LAC; Const. S.E. Alexander to Officer Commanding, Western Arctic Sub-Division, 27 April 1937, RG 85, vol. 1089, file 401-22, pt. 2, LAC.

81 Urquhart to J. Lorne Turner, 14 July 1934, ibid.

82 Gibson to T.R.L. MacInnes, 2 April 1937, ibid; A.L. Cumming to Gibson, 22 June 1937, ibid.

83 Supt. Irvine, RCMP, to T.R.L. MacInnes, 4 February 1937, ibid.

84 W.M. Truesdell to J. Lorne Turner, Chair, Dominion Lands Board, 16 November 1934, ibid.

85 Extract from Sgt. G.T. Makinson's "Report Re: Treaty Indians, Fort Resolution, Refusal to Accept Treaty Payment," 3 July 1937, ibid.

86 Const. A.T. Rivett, RCMP, Rae Detachment, Report, 29 April 1941, RG 85, vol. 932, file 12231, LAC.

87 Const. A.T. Rivett, RCMP, Rae Detachment, to Officer Commanding, Fort Smith, 15 August 1941, RG 85, vol. 1089, file 401-22, pt. 2, LAC.

88 See Const. A.T. Rivett, RCMP, Rae Detachment, "Report on Conclusion of Case," 4 August 1941, RG 85, vol. 932, file 12231, LAC.

89 Gibson to H.W. McGill, Director, Indian Affairs, 6 October 1941, RG 85, vol. 932, file 12232, LAC.

90 See Memorandum Re: Taking of Caribou for Food Purposes, Summary of Correspondence, 27 December 1939, RG 85, vol. 1088, pt. 3, LAC.

91 See RG 22, vol. 4, file 14, LAC.

92 C.H.D. Clarke, Address on Caribou Given at the Provincial-Dominion Wildlife Conference 16 January 1939, RG 22, vol. 4, file 13, LAC. Clarke's results were published in 1940 in his monograph, *A Biological Investigation of the Thelon Game Sanctuary.* For the influence of such concepts as "cropping" game populations to fit the carrying capacity of their range on wildlife management practices in the Canadian national parks during this period, see Alan MacEachern, *Natural Selections: National Parks in Atlantic Canada, 1935-1970* (Montreal and Kingston: McGill-Queen's University Press, 2001), 190-203.

93 Const. D.P. McLauchlan, RCMP, Lake Harbour Detachment, to Officer Commanding, "G" Division, 30 June 1943, RG 85, vol. 1088, file 401-22, pt. 3, LAC; Insp. D.J. Martin to Commissioner, RCMP, 21 October 1943, ibid. The biologist T.H. Manning also suggested in a scientific paper that wasteful hunting was occurring on Baffin Island. Manning, "Notes on the Mammals of South and Central West Baffin Island," *Journal of Mammalogy* 12, 11 (1943): 47-59.

94 Const. D.P. McLauchlan, RCMP, Lake Harbour Detachment, to Officer Commanding, "G" Division, 1 June 1944, RG 85, vol. 1088, file 401-22, pt. 3, LAC. For comments on the distribution of buffalo and reindeer, see D.L. McKeand to Gibson, 16
October 1944, ibid., and Gibson to Commissioner, RCMP, 3 November 1944, ibid.

95 Const. D.P. McLauchlan, RCMP, Lake Harbour Detachment, to Officer Commanding, "G" Division, 14 and 15 April 1945, ibid.

96 Gibson to Commissioner, RCMP, 1 October 1947, ibid.

97 Minutes, Advisory Board on Wildlife Protection, 28 November 1940, RG 22, vol. 4,
file 14, LAC.

98 Urquhart to J. Lorne Turner, 31 October 1934, RG 85, vol. 1089, file 401-22, pt. 2,
LAC.

Chapter 7: The Caribou Crisis

1 For a detailed report, see Eugene Oldham, Superintendent of Forests and Wildlife,
Bureau of the Northwest Territories and Yukon Affairs, to R.A. Gibson, 29 May 1947,
RG 85, vol. 1088, file 401-22, pt. 3, Library and Archives Canada (LAC).

2 Frise to W.P. Earle, 11 April 1947, ibid.

3 Hoey to Gibson, 30 May 1947, ibid.

4 Gibson to E. Oldham, 18 June 1947, ibid. Chief Frise's case was concluded when he
pleaded guilty to the charges and was given a severe warning. See Const. G.R. Brown,
RCMP, Fort Resolution, to Officer Commanding, Fort Smith, 12 April 1948, RG 85,
vol. 1088, file 401-22, pt. 4, LAC.

5 Order-in-council P.C. 2567, 3 July 1947; copy in RG 85, vol. 1088, file 401-22, pt. 3,
LAC.

6 Game warden offices were established at Fort Resolution, Aklavik, Fort Norman, Fort
Simpson, and Yellowknife. See "Extracts Regarding Caribou Populations from the
1947 Reports of Forest and Wildlife Wardens in Mackenzie District," n.d., RG 85, vol.
1088, file 401-22, pt. 3, LAC.

7 For an overview of changes to the northern administration, see Mark Dickerson,
*Whose North? Political Change, Political Development, and Self-Government in the
Northwest Territories* (Vancouver: UBC Press, 1992), 61-87.

8 The letters are summarized in a report from J.P. Richards to MacKay Meikle, Chief
of the Mackenzie Division, 25 September 1947, RG 85, vol. 1088, file 401-22, pt. 3, LAC.

9 See Minutes, Advisory Board on Wildlife Protection, 17 November 1947, RG 22, vol.
4, file 14, LAC.

10 Mulvihill to Hoey, 17 July 1947; quoted in Kerry Abel, *Drum Songs: Glimpses of Dene
History* (Montreal and Kingston: McGill-Queen's University Press, 1993), 217.

11 "Extracts Regarding Caribou Populations from the 1947 Reports of Forest and Wildlife Wardens in Mackenzie District," n.d., RG 85, vol. 1088, file 401-22, pt. 3, LAC.

12 Authority over "Eskimo Affairs" rested with the northern administration rather than
Indian Affairs because, until a Supreme Court decision in 1935, the Inuit were not
included in the definition of "Indian" under the British North America Act and thus
were never included in the terms of the Indian Act. For an overview, see Frank Tester
and Peter Kulchyski, *Tammarniit (Mistakes): Inuit Relocation in the Eastern Arctic,
1939-63* (Vancouver: UBC Press, 1994), 13-42.

13 See A.W.F. Banfield, *Preliminary Investigation of the Barren-Ground Caribou*, Wildlife Management Bulletin Series 1, no. 10 (Ottawa: Canadian Wildlife Service, 1954), pt. 1, 2-7. For an early summary of the study, see A.W.F. Banfield, *The Barren-Ground Caribou* (Ottawa: Department of Resources and Development, 1951), 13-14.

14 Minutes, Advisory Board on Wildlife Protection, 6 November 1950, RG 22, vol. 16, file 69, LAC.

15 Banfield, *Preliminary Investigation*, pt. 2, 70. Banfield's estimate of an annual human kill of 100,000 animals was based on the average annual kill at the trading posts, with an increase of 15 percent on the assumption that hunters were under-reporting their kill (see p. 68).

16 Ibid., pt. 2, 71.

17 His recommendations are printed in full in Minutes, Advisory Board on Wildlife Protection, 6 November 1950, RG 22, vol. 16, file 69, LAC.

18 The advisory board accepted Banfield's results as the "most reliable estimate of the caribou population to date." Ibid.

19 McTaggart-Cowan to Lewis, 2 November 1950, ibid.

20 Banfield, *Preliminary Investigation*, pt. 2, 70.

21 Ibid., pt. 1, 37. For the results of these questionnaires for the years 1948-49, see RG 85, vol. 1089, file 401-22-4, pt. 16, LAC.

22 Banfield, *Preliminary Investigation*, pt. 1, 44, 51.

23 Ibid., pt. 2, 70.

24 Ibid., pt. 2, 55-56, 59.

25 Ibid., pt. 2, 60.

26 In order to confine the use of caribou for dog meat to the trapline, the ordinance also banned feeding caribou to dogs within four miles of any settlement in the Mackenzie District. See "Extract from the Votes, Proceedings and Debates of the NWT Council Meeting in Yellowknife, December 1951," RG 85, vol. 1089, file 401-22, pt. 6, LAC. A recent controversy has erupted over the allegations of Inuit elders that RCMP officers slaughtered large numbers of their dogs in the 1950s and 1960s as part of a campaign to assert control over their livelihoods. The RCMP claimed before the Standing Committee on Aboriginal Affairs that the killings were carried out as part of a program to control disease among dog teams and reduce the dangers presented by strays in the community. See Greg Younger-Lewis, "Police Explanation Sheds Little Light on Dog Slaughter," *Nunatsiaq News*, 11 March 2005, http://www.nunatsiaq. com. Given the distaste for large dog teams among federal wildlife officials, it is tempting to conclude that the dog killings were connected to the caribou conservation program. I found no references, however, to the deliberate killing of dogs as a conservation measure in the voluminous archival files on caribou conservation.

27 See Minutes, Dominion-Provincial Wildlife Conference, 3 June 1949, RG 22, vol. 16, file 68, LAC.

28 For details on the proposed regulation, see "Proposed Revisions of NWT Game Ordinance for 1950," 3 August 1950, RG 85, vol. 1088, file 401-22, pt. 4, LAC. Gibson confirmed that the ban on the sale of caribou meat had been passed, in a letter to Aubrey Simmons, 9 September 1950, ibid.

29 The letter was sent to Simmons on 25 July 1950 and signed by Chief Alexie Jean Marie Beaulieu, Pierre Phressie, and Samuel Simmons. Roy Gibson referred to the petition in a letter to Aubrey Simmons, 9 September 1950, ibid.

30 I.F. Kirkby, "Fort Resolution Indian Agency: Report on Fur and Game Conditions in this Area," n.d., ibid.
31 Stevens to Lewis, 6 July 1950, ibid.
32 W.A. Fuller, "Comments Concerning the Northwest Game Ordinance," 3 August 1950, ibid.
33 See "Caribou Protective Legislation," n.d., RG 85, acc. 1997-98/076, file 401-22, pt. 22, LAC. For a summary, see Peter Clancy, *Native Hunters and the State: The "Caribou Crisis" in the Northwest Territories,* Studies in National and International Development Occasional Paper no. 87-101 (Kingston: Queen's University, 1987), 11.
34 Minutes, Advisory Board on Wildlife Protection, 17 March 1950, RG 22, vol. 16, file 69, LAC.
35 Kelsall to H. Lewis, 7 November 1950, RG 85, vol. 1088, file 401-22, pt. 4, LAC.
36 John P. Kelsall, *Continued Barren-Ground Caribou Studies,* Wildlife Management Bulletin Series 1, no. 12 (Ottawa: Canadian Wildlife Service, 1957), 6-25.
37 John P. Kelsall, "Barren-Ground Caribou Movements in the Canadian Arctic," *North American Wildlife Conference Proceedings* 19 (1954): 551-61.
38 Kelsall, *Continued Barren-Ground Caribou Studies,* 17-22. In retrospect, it is not surprising that Kelsall had difficulty tracking the movements of and overlap among the migratory caribou herds. His five study herds were made up of what are now understood to be the discrete Bathurst and Bluenose caribou herds.
39 Minutes of Meeting, "Barren-Ground Caribou," 18 June 1953, RG 22, vol. 270, file 40-6-3, pt. 2, LAC. In the final printed report on his studies, for example, Kelsall used game returns from 1946 to 1950, which showed a variable harvest of from 2,500 to just over 8,000 animals in the region, to produce a "theoretical annual kill" of 8,105.6 caribou. Kelsall, *Continued Barren-Ground Caribou Studies,* 27-28.
40 Minutes of Meeting, "Barren-Ground Caribou," 18 June 1953, RG 22, vol. 270, file 40-6-3, pt. 2, LAC.
41 See Farley Mowat, *People of the Deer* (Toronto: McClelland and Stewart, 1951); Francis Harper, "In Caribou Land: Exploration in One of the Least-Known Sections of Canada, Where Timber Meets the Tundra," *Natural History* 58, 5 (May 1949): 224-31, 239-49; and Francis Harper, *The Barren Ground Caribou of Keewatin* (Lawrence: University Press of Kansas, 1955).
42 John Kelsall and A.G. Loughrey, "Barren Ground Caribou Re-survey 1955," n.d., RG 22, vol. 865, file 40-6-3, pt. 3, LAC. See also "Appreciation of the Mainland Caribou Situation – Eastern Mackenzie and Keewatin Districts," 15 August 1955, RG 22, vol. 270, file 40-6-3, pt. 2, LAC.
43 See Minutes, Administrative Committee for Caribou Preservation, 4 June 1956, RG 22, vol. 865, file 40-6-3, pt. 3, LAC.
44 John P. Kelsall, *Co-operative Studies of Barren-Ground Caribou, 1957-58,* Wildlife Management Bulletin Series 1, no. 15 (Ottawa: Canadian Wildlife Service, 1960), 24-26.
45 Ibid., 93.
46 See ibid., 102-9. See also John P. Kelsall, "Forest Fire on the Caribou Winter Ranges," n.d., RG 85, vol. 1250, file 401-22, pt. 14. For further elaboration on the impact of forest fires on the caribou winter ranges, see George Wilby Scotter, *Effects of Forest Fires on the Winter Range of Barren-Ground Caribou in Northern Saskatchewan,* Wildlife Management Bulletin Series 1, no. 18 (Ottawa: Canadian Wildlife Service, 1964). For a historical overview, see Anthony G. Gulig, "'Determined to Burn off the Entire

Country': Prospectors, Caribou, and the Denesuliné in Northern Saskatchewan, 1900-1940," *American Indian Quarterly* 26, 3 (Summer 2002): 335-59.

47 Kelsall, *Co-operative Studies of Barren-Ground Caribou,* 51-62.

48 Ibid., 92.

49 Gerry R. Parker, *Trends in the Population of Barren-Ground Caribou of Mainland Canada over the Last Two Decades: A Re-Evaluation of the Evidence,* Canadian Wildlife Service Occasional Paper 10 (Ottawa: Queen's Printer, 1972), 5.

50 R.D. Cameron, K.R. Whitten, W.T. Smith, and D.J. Reed, "Sampling Errors Associated with Aerial Transect Surveys of Caribou," in *Proceedings of the Second North American Caribou Workshop,* ed. Thomas C. Meredith and Arthur M. Martell, McGill Subarctic Research Paper no. 40 (Montreal: Centre for Northern Studies and Research, McGill University, 1985), 282. Possible sources of error during aerial surveys include variable observer biases due to fatigue, boredom, poor light, snow glare, air speed, inaccurate definition of the transect width, and difficulties counting individuals within large caribou herds. For an overview, see Douglas C. Heard, "Caribou Census Methods Used in the Northwest Territories," in Meredith and Martell, *Proceedings,* 229-38.

51 For a popular treatment of the caribou crisis, see A.W.F. Banfield, "The Caribou Crisis," *Beaver,* Outfit 286 (Spring 1956): 3-6. Similar popular articles and monographs were issued by government bureaucrats and scientists throughout the caribou crisis. See, for example, John Tener, "The Present Status of the Barren-Ground Caribou," *Canadian Geographical Journal,* 60, 3 (1960): 98-105; John P. Kelsall, "Barren-Ground Caribou and Their Management," *Canadian Audubon Magazine* (November-December 1963): 2-7; and Fraser Symington, *Tuktu: The Caribou of the Northern Mainland* (Ottawa: Queen's Printer, 1965).

52 Robertson to Lesage, Minister of Northern Affairs and National Resources, 6 July 1955, RG 22, vol. 270, file 40-6-3, pt. 2, LAC.

53 This liberalization of the game regulations was the result of political pressure from Indian Affairs and a growing frustration with the impossibility of enforcing the game regulations in remote areas. See Ben Sivertz, Acting Director, Northern Administration and Lands Branch, to R.G. Robertson, Commissioner, NWT, 23 August 1955, ibid.

54 Minutes, Federal-Provincial Meeting on Barren-Ground Caribou, 13 October 1955, ibid.

55 For the initial proposal to expand the predator control program, see "Brief Presented to Northwest Territories Council, 1 September 1955," Alexander Stevenson Fonds, N-1992-023, box 33, file 1, Northwest Territories Archives (NWTA). For an overview of predator control efforts in the Northwest Territories in the 1950s and 1960s, see NWT Council, Sessional Paper no. 8, Second Session, 1964, 20 October 1964, RG 85, acc. 1997-98/076, file 401-22, pt. 22, LAC.

56 The changes to the Game Ordinance for 1956 are summarized in a letter from F.J.G. Cunningham, Director, Northern Administration and Lands Branch, to Commissioner, RCMP, 12 February 1957, RG 85, vol. 1250, file 401-22. pt. 14, LAC. The general hunting licence was generally restricted to Dene, Inuit, and Métis hunters "living the life of a native," but non-Natives who had lived in the Northwest Territories since 1938 were also permitted to hold one.

57 A copy of the order to close the season, dated 6 May 1957, is in the Alexander Stevenson Fonds, N-1992-023, box 33, file 1, NWTA.

58 Minutes, Administrative Committee for Caribou Preservation, 3-4 October 1957, RG 22, vol. 865, file 40-6-3, pt. 4, LAC.

59 Sivertz to E.A. Cote, Asst. Deputy Minister of Northern Affairs and National Resources, 23 December 1957, ibid.

60 E.D. Fulton, Minister of Citizenship and Immigration, to Hamilton, 5 December 1957, ibid.

61 Hamilton to Fulton, 24 December 1957, RG 85, vol. 1495, file 401-22, pt. 17, LAC.

62 The March 1957 amendments to the game ordinance were enclosed in a letter from R.G. Robertson to A. Hamilton, Minister of Northern Affairs and National Resources, 3 March 1957, RG 85, acc. 1997-98, box 68, file 401-22-5. pt. 3, LAC.

63 Minutes, Administrative Committee for Caribou Preservation, 1 December 1961, RG 85, acc. 1997-98/076, box 68, file 401-22-5-1, pt. 1, LAC.

64 See a report from H.R. Conn presented to the Administrative Committee for Caribou Preservation, 17 April 1963, ibid.

65 Minutes, Administrative Committee for Caribou Preservation, 27 January 1964, ibid.

66 See W.G. Turnstead, Diary for the Month of November 1957, RG 22, vol. 865, file 40-6-3, pt. 4, LAC.

67 Paynter's attempt to enforce a quota of two caribou per hunter "regardless of racial origin" constituted a clear violation of the Natural Resources Transfer Agreement. For a summary of Paynter's policies, see "Caribou Management Policy for 1957-58, Saskatchewan," RG 85, vol. 865, file 40-6-3, pt. 4, LAC. In Manitoba, a year-round closed season on caribou was established in 1957, but the regulation did not apply to treaty Indians. See Minutes, Technical Committee for Caribou Conservation, 13-15 November 1958, RG 85, acc. 1997-98/076, box 68, file 401-22-5, pt. 3, LAC.

68 For a summary of Bruneau's comments, see W.G. Brown to H.M. Jones, 25 May 1961, RG 85, acc. 1997-98/076, box 67, file 401-22, pt. 20, LAC.

69 T.H. Butters to Regional Administrator, 28 October 1961, RG 85, acc. 1997-98/076, box 67, file 401-22, pt. 20, LAC. The field staff to the proposed ban can be found in a memo from C.L. Merrill, Administrator of the Mackenzie Region, to W.G. Brown, ibid.

70 Minutes, Administrative Committee for Caribou Preservation, 20 June 1964, RG 85, acc. 1997-98/076, box 67, file 401-22, pt. 22, LAC.

71 For a summary of the contributions of Indian Affairs to the caribou conservation program and the department's rationale for participating, see E.D. Fulton, Minister of Citizenship and Immigration, to A. Hamilton, Minister of Northern Affairs and National Resources, n.d., RG 22, vol. 865, file 40-6-3, pt. 4, LAC.

72 "Filmstrip Commentary on Conservation of the Caribou," n.d. [circulated in 1955], RG 85, vol. 1250, file 401-22, pt. 11, LAC. This filmstrip was based on the conservation sections of *The Book of Wisdom for Eskimo,* a government publication intended to improve the lives of the Inuit through information on subjects ranging from wildlife to personal hygiene.

73 A copy of *Tuktut* is in the Alexander Stevenson Fonds, N-1992-023, box 33, file 4, NWTA. The only publishing data is that the booklet was produced by the Department of Northern Affairs and National Resources.

74 "Eskimos Deride Ottawa Comics," *Edmonton Journal,* 31 August 1956; clipping in RG 85, vol. 1250, file 401-22, pt. 13, LAC.

75 A.J. Boxer to Chief, Arctic Division, 19 September 1956, ibid.

76 Jameson Bond to Sivertz, 31 October 1956, RG 85, vol. 1250, file 401-22, pt. 14, LAC.
77 See Doug Wilkinson, northern service officer, to Ben Sivertz, 25 September 1956, RG 85, vol. 1250, file 401-22, pt. 13, LAC; W.G. Kerr, NSO, to Sivertz, 21 September 1956, ibid.
78 J.G. Walton to Sivertz, 20 September 1956, RG 85, vol. 1250, file 401-22, pt. 13, LAC.
79 Houston to Sivertz, 31 October 1956, RG 85, vol. 1250, file 401-22, pt. 14, LAC. Houston was well known for having set up several successful Inuit handicraft co-operatives in the eastern Arctic.
80 *Save the Caribou* was created and printed by the Education Division of the Northern Administration and Lands Branch in 1957; copy in RG 85, vol. 1250, file 401-22, pt. 14, LAC. The Canadian Wildlife Service printed *A Question of Survival* in 1965; copy in Alexander Stevenson Fonds, N-1992-023, box 33, file 4, NWTA.
81 A description of the supervised hunting program is contained in a memo from W.E. Stevens, superintendent of game, to all NWT game wardens, 3 January 1956, RG 85, vol. 1250, file 401-22, pt. 12, LAC.
82 See F.J.G. Cunningham, Director, Northern Administration and Lands Branch, "Alternative Sources of Meat for the People of the North," memorandum for the commissioner of the NWT, 25 November 1955, RG 85, vol. 1255, file 472-1, pt. 1, LAC.
83 Sivertz to R.G. Robertson, Deputy Minister, 8 August 1956, RG 85, vol. 1250, file 401-22, pt. 13, LAC.
84 Council of the Northwest Territories, Report on the Conservation of Caribou, 2 January 1958, Alexander Stevenson Fonds, N-1992-023, box 33, file 3, NWTA.
85 See "Relief Issued to the Eskimos," n.d., RG 22, vol. 254, file 40-8-1, pt. 3, LAC.
86 See, for example, "Eskimos Hunting Less Since Pensions Granted," *Globe and Mail*, 17 May 1952; and "The Government and the Eskimos," *Calgary Herald*, 5 June 1952; clippings in RG 22, vol. 254, file 40-8-1, pt. 3, LAC.
87 See "What Price Kanaukyaksait?" advertisement, *Newsweek*; clipping stamped 27 January 1953, in RG 22, vol. 254, file 40-8-1, pt. 3, LAC.
88 For a rebuke of the criticisms levelled at the government's welfare policies, see George Davidson, Deputy Minister of Welfare, to Harry Young, Commissioner of the Northwest Territories, 21 January 1953, ibid.
89 See "Summary of the Proceedings at a Meeting on Eskimo Affairs Held May 19 and 20, 1952, in the Board Room of the Confederation Building, Ottawa," ibid. For an extensive summary of the development of Inuit welfare policy, see Tester and Kulchyski, *Tammarniit (Mistakes)*, 43-101.
90 Const. T.J. Garvin, RCMP, "Report Re: Caribou Conservation – Coppermine Area," 23 April 1958, RG 85, acc. 1997-98/076, box 67, file 401-22, pt. 18, LAC.
91 See J.E. Bryant, Superintendent of Game, "Report on Contwoyto Lake Fishing Project," 29 December 1959, RG 85, acc. 1997-98/076, box 67, file 401-22, pt. 19, LAC.
92 E.H. McEwen to Chief, Canadian Wildlife Service, 6 August 1960, RG 85, acc. 1997-98/076, box 67, file 401-22, pt. 20, LAC.
93 Douglas to J.E. Bryant, 17 August 1960, ibid.
94 R. Douglas, "Utilization of the Caribou by the Eskimos of Contwoyto Lake," n.d., RG 85, vol. 1944, file A-401-22, pt. 1, LAC.
95 See E. Kuyt, "Thelon River – 1961, Caribou Movements, Segregation Data," n.d., RG 85, acc. 1997-98/076, Box 67, file 401-22, pt. 21.
96 In October 1957, for example, the game officer F.S. Bailey reported that the people of

Snowdrift failed to catch many fish as part of a program sponsored by Indian Affairs. Bailey to W.E. Stevens, Superintendent of Game, 19 October 1957, RG 85, vol. 1495, file 401-22, pt. 17, LAC. In the summer of 1957, RCMP Sergeant Abraham at Eskimo Point organized and supervised a relatively successful beluga whale fishery, but the hunt was abandoned the next year due to a lack of supervisory personnel. See "Meat Substitutes for Caribou," NWT Sessional Paper no. 17, 1959, RG 85, vol. 1944, file A-401-22, LAC.

97 For a discussion, see Tester and Kulchyski, *Tammarniit (Mistakes)*, 256.

98 Butters to R.L. Kennedy, Regional Administrator, 25 August 1960, RG 85, vol. 1944, file A-401-22, LAC.

99 Mowat, *People of the Deer*, 332-38. Mowat's rejection of assimilation can be found in *The Desperate People*, rev. ed. (Toronto: McClelland-Bantam, 1975), 210-13.

100 F.J.G. Cunningham to Deputy Minister, 8 June 1955, RG 22, vol. 270, file 40-6-3, pt. 2, LAC.

101 Munro's original proposal was titled "Draft Statement on the Barren-Ground Caribou." It was presented at a meeting held 28 May 1964 of officials from the CWS and the Northern Administration and Lands Branch. See G. Abramson, Projects Section, Industrial Division, memo for file, 1 June 1964, RG 85, acc. 1997-98/076, box 68, file 401-22-5, pt. 5, LAC.

102 "Barren-Ground Caribou and Northern Development – A Proposal," Appendix A, Northwest Territories Council, Sessional Paper no. 8, Second Session, 1964, Alexander Stevenson Fonds, N-1992-023, box 33, file 3, NWTA. The success of these work programs was decidedly mixed. Although Inuit art from the eastern Arctic has sold throughout the globe, a nickel mine that opened at Rankin Inlet in 1957 and provided ample jobs for the Inuit in that region closed after only five years of operation. At a meeting of the administrative committee in February 1965, C.M. Bolger, the assistant director of the Northern Administration Branch, worried that Inuit vocational trainees might find only limited employment opportunities outside of a few positions that had been created along the DEW Line radar system. See Minutes, Administrative Committee for Caribou Preservation, 25 February 1965, RG 85, acc. 1997-98/076, box 68, file 401-22-5-1, pt. 2, LAC.

103 A study commissioned by the Department of Indian Affairs and Northern Development in 1990 exonerated the government of any wrongdoing in relation to the Inuit relocations. Hickling Corporation, "Assessment of the Factual Basis of Certain Allegations Made before the Standing Committee on Aboriginal Affairs Concerning the Relocation of Inukjuak Inuit Families in the 1950s," report submitted to Department of Indian and Northern Affairs, 1990. Responses to the Hickling report have overwhelmingly argued that the relocation program was coercive and a violation of international and domestic human rights laws. See Shelagh Grant, "A Case of Compounded Error: The Inuit Resettlement Project, 1953, and the Government Response, 1990," *Northern Perspectives* 19, 1 (1991): 3-29; Alan R. Marcus, "Out in the Cold: Canada's Experimental Inuit Relocation to Grise Fiord and Resolute Bay," *Polar Record* 27, 163 (1991): 285-95; Alan R. Marcus, *Relocating Eden: The Image and Politics of Inuit Exile in the Canadian Arctic* (Hanover, NH: University Press of New England, 1995); Russel Lawrence Bash, "High Arctic Relocations: International Norms and Standards," research report, in *For Seven Generations: an Information Legacy of the RCAP*, ed. Royal Commission on Aboriginal Peoples, CD-ROM (Ottawa: Libraxus, 1997); Tester and Kulchyski, *Tammarniit (Mistakes)*.

104 Minutes, Tenth Meeting of the Committee on Eskimo Affairs, 25 May 1959, RG 109, vol. 35, file WLT 300-2, pt. 1, LAC.
105 "Meeting on Eskimo Affairs Held in the Board Room of the Confederation Building on the 19th and 20th of May, 1952," RG 22, vol. 254, file 40-8-1, pt. 3, LAC.
106 Press Release, Editorial and Information Division, Department of Resources and Development, 22 May 1952, RG 22, vol. 254, file 40-8-1, pt. 2, LAC.
107 Solman and Tener to J.A. Smart, 4 June 1952, RG 22, vol. 254, file 40-8-1, pt. 3, LAC.
108 "Minutes of a Meeting Held at 10:00 AM August 10, 1953, in Room 304, Langevin Block, to Discuss the Transfer of Certain Eskimo Families from Northern Quebec to Cornwallis and Ellesmere Island," RG 22, vol. 254, file 40-8-1, pt. 4, LAC.
109 Bolger to Director, Northern Administration Branch, 15 November 1960, RG 85, vol. 1392, file 1012-13, pt. 5, LAC. Over two decades after the original relocations, Alex Stevenson, an employee with Arctic Services at the time of the High Arctic relocations, used almost the same terms to describe the purpose of the program. Stevenson to Gunther Abraham, Chief, Social Development Division, Indian and Northern Affairs, 30 November 1977, Alexander Stevenson Fonds, N-1992-023, box 24, file 14, NWTA.
110 See A.W.F. Banfield and J.S. Tener, "A Preliminary Study of the Ungava Caribou," n.d., RG 85, vol. 1495, file 401-22, pt. 15, LAC.
111 See F.J.G. Cunningham, Director, Northern Administration and Lands Branch, 10 March 1953, RG 22, vol. 254, file 40-8-1, pt. 4, LAC.
112 See A.G Loughrey, "Recommendations from Manitoba and Keewatin Barren-Ground Caribou Re-Survey, 1955," n.d., RG 85, vol. 1250, file 401-22, pt. 13, LAC.
113 Minutes, Federal-Provincial Meeting on Barren Ground Caribou, 13 October 1955, RG 22, vol. 270, file 40-6-3, pt. 2, LAC.
114 Banfield, "Caribou Crisis," 3.
115 J.D. Robertson, "Caribou Slaughter – Duck Lake" (Manitoba Game Branch Officer's Report, 1955); quoted in John P. Kelsall, *The Migratory Barren-Ground Caribou of Northern Canada*, Canadian Wildlife Service Monograph 3 (Ottawa: Queen's Printer, 1968), 219.
116 See Virginia Petch, "The Relocation of the Sayisi Dene of Tadoule Lake," research report, Royal Commission on Aboriginal Peoples, *For Seven Generations*. A documentary film on the relocation of the Sayisi Dene features an interview with the hunter Charlie Learjaw, who claimed that the caribou were left above the shoreline of Duck Lake as food for dogs and people. Alan Code and Mary Code, directors, *Nu Ho Ne Yeh – Our Story*, VHS video (Whitehorse: Treeline Productions, 1995).
117 See Petch, "Relocation of the Sayisi Dene."
118 See Ila Bussidor and Üstün Bilgen-Reinhart, *Night Spirits: The Story of the Relocation of the Sayisi Dene* (Winnipeg: University of Manitoba Press, 1997), 45.
119 R.D. Ragan, departmental memo, 27 July 1956, quoted ibid., 44-45.
120 Minutes, Technical Committee on Caribou Preservation, 13 November 1959, RG 85, acc. 1997-98/076, box 68, file 401-22-5, pt. 4, LAC.
121 Kelsall, *Migratory Barren-Ground Caribou*, 227.
122 The events surrounding the Nueltin Lake relocation were reconstructed from an undated report forwarded by Gordon Sinclair to the deputy commissioner of the Northwest Territories on 7 April 1952, "Eskimos Living in the Nueltin Lake-Kazan River Areas of the District of Keewatin, NWT," RG 22, vol. 254, file 40-8-1, pt. 2, LAC. For a retrospective report, see Sivertz to Deputy Minister, "Background of

Henik Lake Eskimos," 9 March 1959, Alexander Stevenson Fonds, N-1992-023, box 24, file 6, NWTA.

123 Sivertz to Nichols, 28 April 1955, RG 85, vol. 1250, file 401-22, pt. 9, LAC.

124 Nichols to Sivertz, 6 May 1955, ibid. The price was kept low so as not to provide an incentive for killing caribou for the hides alone.

125 Sivertz to W.G. Kerr, Northern Service Officer, 17 May 1955, ibid.

126 R.A.J. Phillips to Director, Northern Administration and Lands Branch, 20 October 1958, Alexander Stevenson Fonds, N-1992-023, box 24, file 6, NWTA.

127 Cunningham to Nichols, 25 June 1956, ibid.

128 "Eskimos Fly to New Hunting Grounds," press release, Department of Northern Affairs and National Resources, 24 May 1957, ibid.

129 See Tester and Kulchyski, *Tammarniit (Mistakes)*, 220.

130 The events at Henik Lake in the winter of 1957-58 are summarized in a report from R.A.J. Phillips to Sivertz, "Starvation among the Eskimos in the Winter of 1957-58," 29 October 1958, Alexander Stevenson Fonds, N-1992-023, box 24, file 6, NWTA. For a more critical assessment of the failure of government agents to properly monitor the situation at Henik Lake, see Tester and Kulchyski, *Tammarniit (Mistakes)*, 233-37.

131 See Farley Mowat, "The Two Ordeals of Kikkik," *Maclean's*, 31 January 1959, 12-15, 42-26. A revised version of this article appears as the thirteenth chapter of Mowat's *The Desperate People*.

132 Alex Stevenson to R.A.J. Phillips, 16 April 1958, Alexander Stevenson Fonds, N-1992-023, box 24, file 6, NWTA.

133 Hamilton, memo to Cabinet, 9 May 1958, ibid.

134 See "Keewatin Reestablishment Project," 14 July 1959, ibid.

135 For an overview, see F.G. Vallee, *Kabloona and the Eskimo in the Central Keewatin* (Ottawa: Canadian Research Centre for Anthropology, St. Paul University, 1967), 54-56.

136 R.L. Kennedy, northern service officer, to Chief, Arctic Division, 22 December 1958, RG 85, vol. 1382, file 1012-13, pt. 5, LAC.

137 Hamilton, memo to Cabinet, 9 May 1958, Alexander Stevenson Fonds, N-1992-023, box 24, file 6, NWTA.

138 Sivertz to J.R.B. Coleman, 11 December 1958, RG 85, acc. 1997-98/076, box 67, file 401-22, pt. 18, LAC.

139 Bolger, memo for file, 11 September 1958, ibid.

140 Minutes, Administrative Committee for Caribou Preservation, Edmonton, 25 February 1965, RG 85, acc. 1997-98/076, box 68, file 401-22-5-1, pt. 2, LAC.

141 See "The Current Barren-Ground Caribou Situation," NWT Sessional Paper no. 8, Second Session, 23 June 1960, RG 85, vol. 1944, file A-401-22, pt. 1, LAC. The first report of increased caribou numbers came from a survey of the Keewatin herds conducted by R.A. Ruttan and a Mr. Look, assistant superintendent of game at Churchill. "Report on the Keewatin Herds," 28 July 1965, RG 85, acc. 1997-98/076, box 68, file 401-22, pt. 23, LAC.

142 R.A. Ruttan, "New Crisis for the Barren-Ground Caribou," *Country Guide* 85, 11 (November 1966): 24-25.

143 Minutes, Administrative Committee for Caribou Preservation, 15 July 1966, RG 85, acc. 1997-98/076, box 68, file 401-22-5-1, pt. 2, LAC; Donald C. Thomas, *Population Estimates of Barren-Ground Caribou, March to May, 1967*, Canadian Wildlife Service Report Series no. 9 (Ottawa: Queen's Printer, 1969), 42.

144 Gerry R. Parker, *Biology of the Kaminuriak Population of Barren-Ground Caribou, Part 1*, Canadian Wildlife Service Report Series no. 20 (Ottawa: Information Canada, 1972), 74.

CONCLUSION

1 Hayden White, *The Content of the Form: Narrative Discourse and Historical Representation* (Baltimore: Johns Hopkins University Press, 1987). For the application of White's ideas to environmental history, see William Cronon, "A Place for Stories: Nature, History and Narrative," *Journal of American History* 78 (March 1992): 1347-77.

2 Peter Usher, "The Canadian Western Arctic: A Century of Change," *Anthropologica*, n.s., 13, 1-2 (1971), 169-83.

3 See Richard West Sellars, *Preserving Nature in the National Parks: A History* (New Haven, CT: Yale University Press, 1997). See also chapter 2 of Alan MacEachern, *Natural Selections: National Parks in Atlantic Canada, 1935-1970* (Montreal and Kingston: McGill-Queen's University Press, 2001), 25-46.

4 James C. Scott, *Seeing Like a State: How Certain Schemes to Improve the Human Condition Have Failed* (New Haven, CT: Yale University Press, 1998).

5 See Alfred Crosby, *Ecological Imperialism: The Biological Expansion of Europe, 900-1900* (Cambridge: Cambridge University Press, 1986).

6 For an overview of this phenomenon in other resource sectors, see Kenneth J. Rea, *The Political Economy of the Canadian North: An Interpretation of the Course of Development in the Northwest Territories of Canada to the Early 1960s* (Toronto: University of Toronto Press, 1968). For an examination of the intimate association between the state and resource industries at the provincial level, see H.V. Nelles, *The Politics of Development: Forests, Mines and Hydro-Electric Development in Ontario, 1849-1941* (Toronto: University of Toronto Press, 1974).

7 E.P. Thompson, *Whigs and Hunters: the Origins of the Black Act* (London: Pantheon Books, 1975), 258-69.

8 Garrett Hardin, "The Tragedy of the Commons," *Science* 162 (1968): 1243-48.

9 For general critiques of the "mastery" of nature by science, see Vandana Shiva, *Monocultures of the Mind: Perspectives on Biodiversity and Biotechnology* (London: Zed, 1993); and Donna Haraway, *Simians, Cyborgs and Women: The Reinvention of Nature* (New York: Routledge, 1991).

10 The modernization of traditional hunting cultures through the imposition of wildlife conservation measures was repeated in other parts of the globe. See, for example, Roderick P. Neumann, "The Postwar Conservation Boom in British Colonial Africa," *Environmental History* 7, 1 (January 2002): 22-47.

11 Michel Foucault, *Discipline and Punish: The Birth of the Prison* (New York: Vintage, 1979).

12 This interpretation was derived in part from Frank James Tester and Peter Kulchyski, *Tammarniit (Mistakes): Inuit Relocation in the Eastern Arctic, 1939-63* (Vancouver: UBC Press, 1994).

13 June Helm, *The People of Denendeh: Ethnohistory of the Indians of Canada's Northwest Territories* (Montreal and Kingston: McGill-Queen's University Press, 2000), 35.

14 Throughout the 1970s, the Dene community of Lutsel'ke was able to maintain a

united front during community consultations and prevent the creation of a national park in their traditional territory on the east arm of Great Slave Lake. See Kerry Abel, *Drum Songs: Glimpses of Dene History* (Montreal and Kingston: McGill-Queen's University Press, 1993), 254. For more on the creation of national parks through the land claims process, see Juri Peepre and Philip Dearden, "The Role of Aboriginal Peoples," in *Parks and Protected Areas in Canada: Planning and Management,* 2nd ed., Philip Dearden and Rick Rollins (Toronto: Oxford University Press, 2002), 323-32.

15 Paul Nadasdy, *Hunters and Bureaucrats: Power, Knowledge and Aboriginal-State Relations in the Southwest Yukon* (Vancouver: UBC Press, 2003).

16 See Environmental Assessment Panel, *Northern Diseased Bison* (Ottawa: Minister of Supply and Services, 1990). For a survey of Aboriginal perspectives on the slaughter proposal, see Theresa A. Ferguson and Clayton Burke, "Aboriginal Communities and the Northern Buffalo Controversy," in *Buffalo,* ed. John Foster, Dick Harrison, and I.S. MacLaren (Edmonton: University of Alberta Press, 1992). For scientific studies critical of the slaughter proposal, see L.N. Carbyn, S.M. Oosenbrug, and D.W. Anions, *Wolves, Bison and the Dynamics Related to the Peace-Athabasca Delta in Canada's Wood Buffalo National Park,* Circumpolar Research Series no. 4 (Edmonton: Canadian Circumpolar Institute, University of Alberta, 1993); and Ludwig N. Carbyn, Nicholas J. Lunn, and Kevin Timoney, "Trends in the Distribution and Abundance of Bison in Wood Buffalo National Park," *Wildlife Society Bulletin* 26, 3 (Fall 1998): 463-70.

Bibliography

ARCHIVAL SOURCES

Library and Archives Canada, Ottawa

RG 10, Department of Indian Affairs
RG 13, Department of Justice
RG 17, Department of Agriculture
RG 18, Royal Canadian Mounted Police
RG 22, Department of Indian and Northern Affairs
RG 33-105, Royal Commission on Reindeer and Musk-ox Industries
RG 84, Canadian Parks Service
RG 85, Northern Affairs Program
RG 109, Canadian Wildlife Service
MG 36 H, Borden Papers
MG 30 B-138, William Henry Beere Hoare Diaries
MG 30 E-169, J.B. Harkin Papers

Northwest Territories Archives, Prince of Wales Northern Heritage Centre, Yellowknife

Accession N-1992-023, Alexander Stevenson Fonds
Accession N-1993-016, Fort Resolution Community Education Council Fonds

Wood Buffalo National Park Library, Fort Smith

Brunt, Roger. "The Decline and Fall of the Last Free Roaming Buffalo Herds in the World Taking Place in Wood Buffalo National Park and the Grand Detour, Hook Lake Area of the Northwest Territories, Canada," Manuscript, 15 April 1976.
Potyandi, Barry. "Dual Allegiance: The History of Wood Buffalo National Park, 1929-65." Manuscript, 1981.
Soper, J. Dewey. "Report on Wildlife Investigations in Wood Buffalo Park and Vicinity,

Alberta and Northwest Territories, Canada." National Parks Bureau, Department of Mines and Resources, 1945.

OTHER SOURCES

Abel, Kerry. *Drum Songs: Glimpses of Dene History.* Montreal and Kingston: McGill-Queen's University Press, 1993.

Ainley, Marianne Gosztonyi. "Rowan vs. Tory: Conflicting Views of Scientific Research in Canada." *Scientia Canadensis* 12, 1 (Spring-Summer 1988): 3-21.

Allen, J.A. "Northern Range of the Bison." *American Naturalist* 2 (1887): 624.

–. *Otogentic and Other Variations in Muskoxen, with a Systematic Review of the Muskox Group, Recent and Extinct.* Memoirs of the American Museum of Natural History, vol. 1, part 4. New York: American Museum of Natural History, 1913.

Altmeyer, George. "Three Ideas of Nature in Canada, 1893-1914." In *Consuming Canada: Readings in Canadian Environmental History,* ed. Chad Gaffield and Pam Gaffield, 96-118. Toronto: Copp Clark, 1995.

Anderson, George. "Enemies of the Caribou." *Beaver,* Outfit 268, 1 (June 1937): 30-32.

Anker, Peder. *Imperial Ecology: Environmental Order in the British Empire, 1895-1945.* Cambridge: Harvard University Press, 2001.

Asch, Michael. *Home and Native Land: Aboriginal Rights and the Canadian Constitution.* Toronto: Methuen, 1984.

–. "Wildlife: Defining the Animals the Dene Hunt and the Settlement of Aboriginal Rights Claims." *Canadian Public Policy* 15, 2 (1989): 205-19.

Banfield, A.W.F. *The Barren-Ground Caribou.* Ottawa: Department of Resources and Development, 1951.

–. "The Caribou Crisis." *Beaver,* Outfit 286 (Spring 1956): 3-6.

–. *Preliminary Investigation of the Barren-Ground Caribou.* Wildlife Management Bulletin Series 1, no. 10. Ottawa: Canadian Wildlife Service, 1954.

Banfield, A.W.F., and N.S. Novakowski. *The Survival of the Wood Bison (Bison bison athabascae Rhoads) in the Northwest Territories.* Natural History Paper 8. Ottawa: National Museum of Canada, 1960.

Barbour, Thomas. Review of *Wild Beasts Today,* by Harold Shepstone. *Science* 76, 1978 (25 November 1932).

Bash, Russel Lawrence. "High Arctic Relocations: International Norms and Standards." Research report. In Royal Commission on Aboriginal Peoples, *For Seven Generations: An Information Legacy of the Royal Commission on Aboriginal Peoples.* CD-ROM. Ottawa: Libraxus, 1997.

Beaulieu, Gail, ed. *That's the Way We Lived: An Oral History of the Fort Resolution Elders.* Yellowknife: Government of the Northwest Territories, 1987.

Beinhart, William. "Empire, Hunting and Ecological Change in Southern and Central Africa." *Past and Present* 128 (1990): 162-86.

Bellman, Jennifer L., and Christopher C. Hanks. "Northern Métis and the Fur Trade." In *Picking up the Threads: Métis History in the Mackenzie Basin,* 29-68, ed. Métis Heritage Association of the Northwest Territories. Winnipeg: Métis Heritage Association of the Northwest Territories, 1998.

Berger, Carl. *Science, God and Nature in Victorian Canada.* Toronto: University of Toronto Press, 1982.

Birch, Thomas H. "The Incarceration of Wildness: Wilderness Areas as Prisons." In

The Great New Wilderness Debate, ed. J. Baird Callicott and Michael P. Nelson, 443-70. Athens: University of Georgia Press, 1998.

Bird, S. Elizabeth, ed. *Dressing in Feathers: The Construction of the Indian in American Popular Culture*. Boulder, CO: Westview, 1996.

Blanchet, G.H. "An Exploration into the Northern Plains North and East of Great Slave Lake, Including the Source of the Coppermine River." Serialized in *Canadian Field-Naturalist* 38 (December 1924): 183-87; 39 (January 1925): 12-17; 39 (February 1925): 30-35; 39 (March 1925): 52-55.

Blondin, George. *Yamoria the Lawmaker: Stories of the Dene*. Edmonton: NeWest, 1997.

Bouchier, Nancy B., and Ken Cruickshank. "'Sportsmen and Pothunters': Environment, Conservation and Class in the Fishery of Hamilton Harbour, 1858-1914." *Sport History Review* 28 (1997): 1-18.

Bradshaw, F. "Comment." In *National Conference on Conservation of Game, Fur-Bearing Animals and Other Wild Life, 18-19 February 1919*, ed. Commission of Conservation of Canada, 19-21. Ottawa: King's Printer, 1919.

Breummer, F. "The Caribou Hunt." *North* 15, 3 (1968): 2-9.

Bristow, Joseph. *Empire Boys: Adventures in a Man's World*. London: Harper Collins, 1991.

Brody, Hugh. *Living Arctic: Hunters of the Canadian North*. Vancouver: Douglas and McIntyre, 1987.

Burch, E.S. "Muskox and Man in the Central Canadian Subarctic, 1689-1974." *Arctic* 30, 3 (1977): 135-54.

Burnett, J. Alexander. *A Passion for Wildlife: The History of the Canadian Wildlife Service*. Vancouver: UBC Press, 2003. Originally published as "A Passion for Wildlife: A History of the Canadian Wildlife Service, 1947-1997," *Canadian Field-Naturalist* 13, 1 (January-March 1999): 1-183.

Burnham, Philip. *Indian Country, God's Country: Native Americans and the National Parks*. Washington, DC: Island Press, 2000.

Bussidor, Ila, and Üstün Bilgen-Reinhart. *Night Spirits: The Story of the Relocation of the Sayisi Dene*. Winnipeg: University of Manitoba Press, 1997.

Cameron, R.D., K.R. Whitten, W.T. Smith, and D.J. Reed. "Sampling Errors Associated with Aerial Transect Surveys of Caribou." In *Proceedings of the Second North American Caribou Workshop*, ed. Thomas C. Meredith and Arthur M. Martell, 273-83. McGill Subarctic Research Paper no. 40. Montreal: Centre for Northern Studies and Research, McGill University, 1985.

Canadian Zoologist. "The Passing of the Wood Bison." *Canadian Forum* (July 1925): 301-5.

Carbyn, Ludwig N., Nicholas J. Lunn, and Kevin Timoney. "Trends in the Distribution and Abundance of Bison in Wood Buffalo National Park." *Wildlife Society Bulletin* 26, 3 (Fall 1998): 463-70.

Carbyn, Ludwig N., S.M. Oosenbrug, and D.W. Anions. *Wolves, Bison and the Dynamics Related to the Peace-Athabasca Delta in Canada's Wood Buffalo National Park*. Circumpolar Research Series no. 4. Edmonton: Canadian Circumpolar Institute, University of Alberta, 1993.

Carter, Sarah. *Aboriginal People and Colonizers of Western Canada to 1900*. Toronto: University of Toronto Press, 1998.

Chambers, Ernest J., ed. *Canada's Fertile Northland: A Glimpse of the Enormous Resources of Part of the Unexplored Regions of the Dominion.* Ottawa: Government Printing Bureau, 1907.

Clancy, Peter. *Native Hunters and the State: The "Caribou Crisis" in the Northwest Territories.* Studies in National and International Development Occasional Paper no. 87-101. Kingston: Queen's University, 1987.

–. "State Policy and the Native Trapper: Post War Policy toward Fur in the NWT." In *Aboriginal Resource Use in Canada: Historical and Legal Aspects,* ed. Kerry Abel and Jean Friesen, 191-218. Winnipeg: University of Manitoba Press, 1991.

–. "Working on the Railway: A Case Study in Capital-State Relations." *Canadian Public Administration* 30, 3 (Fall 1987): 452-71.

Clarke, C.H.D. *A Biological Investigation of the Thelon Game Sanctuary.* National Museum of Canada Bulletin no. 96, Biological Series no. 25. Ottawa: Department of Mines and Resources, Mines and Geology Branch, 1940.

–. "Report on Development of the Reindeer Industry – Mackenzie District." NWT Lands, Parks and Forests Branch, Department of Mines and Forests, Ottawa, 1942.

Coates, Kenneth S. *Best Left as Indians: Native-White Relations in the Yukon Territory, 1840-1973.* Montreal and Kingston: McGill-Queen's University Press, 1993.

Coates, Kenneth S., and William R. Morrison, eds. *For the Purposes of Dominions: Essays in Honour of Morris Zaslow.* Toronto: Captus Press, 1989.

Code, Alan, and Mary Code, directors. *Nu Ho Ne Yeh – Our Story.* VHS video. Whitehorse: Treeline Productions, 1995.

Colpitts, George. *Game in the Garden: A Human History of Wildlife in Western Canada to 1940.* Vancouver: UBC Press, 2002.

Commission of Conservation of Canada. *National Conference on Conservation of Game, Fur-Bearing Animals and Other Wild Life, 18-19 February 1919.* Ottawa: King's Printer, 1919.

Critchell-Bullock, Capt. J.C. "An Expedition to Sub-Arctic Canada." Serialized in *Canadian Field-Naturalist* 44 (March 1930): 53-59; 44 (April 1930): 81-87; 44 (May 1930): 111-17; 44 (September 1930): 141-45; 44 (October 1930): 156-63; 44 (November 1930): 187-97; 44 (December 1930): 207-13; 45 (January 1931): 11-19; 45 (February 1931): 31-35.

Cronon, William. "A Place for Stories: Nature, History and Narrative." *Journal of American History* 78 (March 1992): 1347-77.

–. "The Trouble With Wilderness; or, Getting Back to the Wrong Nature." In *Uncommon Ground: Re-thinking the Human Place in Nature,* ed. William Cronon, 69-90. New York: W.W. Norton, 1986.

Crosby, Alfred. *Ecological Imperialism: the Biological Expansion of Europe, 900-1900.* Cambridge: Cambridge University Press, 1986.

Damas, David, ed. *Arctic.* Vol. 5 of *Handbook of North American Indians.* Washington, DC: Smithsonian Institution, 1984.

Deprez, Paul. *The Pine Point Mine and the Development of the Area South of Great Slave Lake.* Winnipeg: Centre for Settlement Studies, University of Manitoba, 1973.

Devine, Maria. "The First Northern Métis: An Overview of the Historical Context for the Emergence of the Earliest Métis in Canada's North." In *Picking up the Threads: Métis History in the Mackenzie Basin,* ed. Métis Heritage Association of the Northwest Territories, 5-28. Winnipeg: Métis Heritage Association of the Northwest Territories, 1998.

Dick, Lyle. *Muskox Land: Ellesmere Island in the Age of Contact.* Calgary: University of Calgary Press, 2001.

Dickerson, Mark. *Whose North? Political Change, Political Development, and Self-Government in the Northwest Territories.* Vancouver: UBC Press, 1992.

Diubaldo, Richard. *Stefansson and the Canadian Arctic.* Montreal and Kingston: McGill-Queen's University Press, 1978.

Dorsey, Kurkpatrick. *The Dawn of Conservation Diplomacy: US-Canadian Wildlife Protection Treaties in the Progressive Era.* Seattle: University of Washington Press, 1998.

Dosman, Edgar J. *The National Interest: the Politics of Northern Development, 1968-75.* Toronto: McClelland and Stewart, 1975.

Dubasak, Marilyn. *Wilderness Preservation: A Cross-Cultural Comparison of Canada and the United States.* New York: Garland Publishing, 1990.

Dunlap, Thomas. "Ecology, Nature and Canadian National Park Policy: Wolves, Elk and Bison as a Case Study." In *To See Ourselves/To Save Ourselves: Ecology and Culture in Canada,* ed. Rowland Lorimer and Michael M'Gonigle, 139-67. Proceedings of the Annual Conference of the Association for Canadian Studies, University of Victoria, 31 May to 1 June 1990. Montreal: Association for Canadian Studies, 1991.

–. *Saving America's Wildlife: Ecology and the American Mind, 1850-1990.* Princeton, NJ: Princeton University Press, 1988.

–. "Wildlife, Science, and the National Parks, 1920-1940." *Pacific Historical Review* 59, 2 (May 1990): 187-202.

East, Ken M. "Joint Management of Canada's Northern Parks." In *Resident People and National Parks: Social Dilemmas and Strategies in International Conservation,* ed. Patrick C. West and Steven R. Brechin, 333-45. Tucson: University of Arizona Press, 1991.

Elton, Charles. *Animal Ecology.* London: William Clowes and Sons, 1947.

–. *Voles, Mice and Lemmings: Problems in Population Dynamics.* Oxford: Clarendon, 1942.

Environmental Assessment Panel. *Northern Diseased Bison.* Ottawa: Minister of Supply and Services, 1990.

Fehr, Alan, Nicole Davis, and Scott Black, eds. *Nàhn' Kak Geenjit Gwich'n Ginjik (Gwich'in Words about the Land).* Inuvik: Gwich'in Renewable Resource Board, 1997.

Feit, Harvey. "Self Management and State Management: Forms of Knowing and Managing Northern Wildlife." In *Traditional Knowledge and Renewable Resource Management,* ed. M.M.R. Freeman and L.N. Carbyn, 72-91. Occasional Publication no. 23. Edmonton: Boreal Institute for Northern Studies, 1988.

Ferguson, Michael A.D., and François Messier. "Collection and Analysis of Traditional Ecological Knowledge about a Population of Arctic Tundra Caribou." *Arctic* 50, 1 (1997): 17-28.

Ferguson, Michael A.D., Robert P. Williamson, and François Messier. "Inuit Knowledge of Long Term Changes in a Population of Arctic Tundra Caribou." *Arctic* 51, 3 (1998): 202-19.

Ferguson, Theresa A. "The 'Jarvis Proof': Management of Bison, Management of Bison Hunters and the Development of a Literary Tradition." *Proceedings of the Fort Chipewyan/Fort Vermilion Bicentennial Conference,* 23-24 September 1988, ed. P.A. McCormack and R.G. Ironside, 299-304. Occasional paper 28. Edmonton: Boreal Institute for Northern Studies.

Ferguson, Theresa A., and Clayton Burke. "Aboriginal Communities and the Northern Buffalo Controversy." In *Buffalo,* ed. John Foster, Dick Harrison, and I.S. MacLaren, 189-206. Edmonton: University of Alberta Press, 1992.

Ferguson, Theresa A., and Frank LaViolette. "A Note on Historical Mortality in a Northern Bison Population." *Arctic* 45 (March 1992): 47-50.

Fieldhouse, D.K. *Colonialism 1870-1945: An Introduction.* London: Weidenfeld and Nicolson, 1981.

Foster, Janet. *Working for Wildlife: The Beginnings of Preservation in Canada.* 2nd ed. Toronto: University of Toronto Press, 1998.

Foucault, Michel. *Discipline and Punish: The Birth of the Prison.* New York: Vintage, 1979.

Francis, Daniel. *The Imaginary Indian: The Image of the Indian in Canadian Culture.* Vancouver: Arsenal, 1993.

Frandsen, Dan, Robert Redhead, Bill Dolan, Ron Davies, and Jeff Dixon. "Park Conservation Plan: Wood Buffalo National Park." Report. Wood Buffalo National Park, March 1988.

Freeman, M.M.R. "Assessing Movement in an Arctic Caribou Population." *Journal of Environmental Management* 3 (1975): 251-57.

–, ed. *Proceedings: First International Symposium on Renewable Resources and the Economy of the North.* Ottawa: Association of Canadian Universities for Northern Studies and the Man and the Biosphere Program, 1981.

Freeman, M.M.R., and L.N. Carbyn, eds. *Traditional Knowledge and Renewable Resource Management.* Occasional Publication no. 23. Edmonton: Boreal Institute for Northern Studies, 1988.

Fuller, William A. *The Biology and Management of the Bison of Wood Buffalo National Park.* Wildlife Management Bulletin Series 1, no. 16. Ottawa: Canadian Wildlife Service, 1962.

Fumoleau, René. *As Long as This Land Shall Last: A History of Treaty 8 and Treaty 11, 1870-1939.* Toronto: McClelland and Stewart, 1975.

Geist, Valerius. "Phantom Subspecies: The Wood Bison *Bison bison 'athabascae'* Rhoads 1897 Is Not a Valid Taxon, But an Ecotype." *Arctic* 44, 4 (December 1991): 283-300.

Gillespie, Greg. "'I Was Well Pleased with Our Sport among the Buffalo': Big-Game Hunters, Travel Writing and Cultural Imperialism in the British North American West, 1847-72." *Canadian Historical Review* 83, 4 (December 2002): 555-84.

Girard, Michel F. *L'écologisme retrouvé: Essor et decline de la Commission de la conservation du Canada.* Ottawa: University of Ottawa Press, 1994.

Godsell, Philip H. *Arctic Trader: The Account of Twenty Years with the Hudson's Bay Company.* New York: G.P. Putnam's Sons, 1932.

Gordon, Bryan C. *Of Men and Herds in Barrenland Prehistory.* National Museum of Man, Mercury Series, Archeological Survey Paper 28. Ottawa, 1976.

–. "Prehistoric Chipewyan Harvesting at a Barrenland Caribou Water Crossing." *Western Canadian Journal of Anthropology* 7, 1 (1977): 69-83.

Gottesman, Dan. "Native Hunting and the Migratory Birds Convention Act: Historical, Political and Ideological Perspectives." *Journal of Canadian Studies* 13, 3 (Fall 1983): 67-89.

Graham, Maxwell. *Canada's Wild Buffalo: Observation in the Wood Buffalo Park.* Appendix by F.V. Seibert. Ottawa: Department of the Interior, 1923.

–. "Finding Range for Canada's Buffalo." *Canadian Field-Naturalist* 38 (December 1924): 189.

Grant, Shelagh. "A Case of Compounded Error: The Inuit Resettlement Project, 1953, and the Government Response, 1990." *Northern Perspectives* 19, 1 (1991): 3-29.

–. *Sovereignty or Security? Government Policy in the Canadian North, 1936-1950.* Vancouver: UBC Press, 1988.

Grey Owl. *The Men of the Last Frontier.* London: Country Life, 1934.

Grinnell, George Bird. "The Last of the Buffalo." *Scribner's Magazine* 12, 3 (September 1892). Reprinted New York: Arno, 1970.

Grove, Richard. *Ecology, Climate and Empire: Colonialism and Global Environmental History.* Cambridge: White Horse Press, 1997.

–. *Green Imperialism: Colonial Expansion, Tropical Island Edens and the Origins of Environmentalism, 1600-1860.* Cambridge: Cambridge University Press, 1995.

Grumbine, R. Edward. "Reflections on 'What Is Ecosystem Management?'" *Conservation Biology* 11, 1 (February 1997): 41-47.

Guha, Ramachandra. *The Unquiet Woods: Ecological Change and Peasant Resistance in the Himalaya.* Expanded ed. Berkeley: University of California Press, 2000.

Gulig, Anthony G. "'Determined to Burn off the Entire Country': Prospectors, Caribou, and the Denesuliné in Northern Saskatchewan, 1900-1940." *American Indian Quarterly* 26, 3 (Summer 2002): 335-59.

Gunn, Anne, G. Arlooktoo, and D. Kaomayak. "The Contribution of Ecological Knowledge of Inuit to Wildlife Management in the Northwest Territories." In *Traditional Knowledge and Renewable Resource Management*, ed. M.M.R. Freeman and L.N. Carbyn, 22-30. Occasional Publication no. 23. Edmonton: Boreal Institute for Northern Studies, 1988.

Gunn, Anne, Chris Shank, and Bruce McLean. "The History, Status and Management of Muskoxen on Banks Island." *Arctic* 44, 3 (September 1991): 188-95.

Hamilton, John David. *Arctic Revolutions: Social Change in the Northwest Territories: 1935-1994.* Toronto: Dundurn, 1994.

Hanbury, David T. *Sport and Travel in the Northland of Canada.* London: Edward Arnold, 1904.

Haraway, Donna. *Simians, Cyborgs and Women: The Reinvention of Nature.* New York: Routledge, 1991.

Hardin, Garrett. "The Tragedy of the Commons." *Science* 162 (1968): 1243-48.

Harkin, James. "Wild Life Sanctuaries." In *National Conference on Conservation of Game, Fur-Bearing Animals and Other Wild Life, 18-19 February 1919*, ed. Commission of Conservation of Canada, 46-50. Ottawa: King's Printer, 1919.

Harper, Francis. *The Barren Ground Caribou of Keewatin.* Lawrence: University Press of Kansas, 1955.

–. "In Caribou Land: Exploration in One of the Least-known Sections of Canada, Where Timber Meets the Tundra." *Natural History* 58, 5 (May 1949): 224-31, 239-40.

–. Letter to the editor. *Canadian Field-Naturalist* 39 (February 1925): 45.

Harris, R. Cole. *The Resettlement of British Columbia: Essays on Colonialism and Geographic Change.* Vancouver: UBC Press, 1997.

Hays, Samuel. *Conservation and the Gospel of Efficiency: The Progressive Conservation Movement, 1890-1920.* New York: Atheneum, 1959.

Hearne, Samuel. *A Journey from Prince of Wales's Fort in Hudson's Bay to the Northern Ocean, 1769, 1770, 1771, 1772*, ed. Richard Glover. Toronto: MacMillan, 1958.

Helm, June, ed. *The People of Denendeh: Ethnohistory of the Indians of Canada's Northwest Territories.* Montreal and Kingston: McGill-Queen's University Press, 2000.

–. *Subarctic.* Vol. 6 of *Handbook of North American Indians.* Washington, DC: Smithsonian Institution, 1981.

Helm, J., and David Damas. "The Contact-Traditional All Native Community in the Canadian North." *Anthropologica* 5 (1963): 9-21.

Heming, Arthur, *Spirit Lake.* New York: MacMillan, 1907.

Hewitt, C. Gordon. "The Coming Back of the Bison." *Natural History* 19, 6 (1919): 553-65.

–. *Conservation of Wild Life in Canada in 1917: A Review.* Reprinted from the Ninth Annual Report of the Commission of Conservation (Ottawa, King's Printer, 1918).

–. *The Conservation of the Wild Life of Canada.* New York: Charles Scribner's Sons, 1921.

Hickling Corporation. "Assessment of the Factual Basis of Certain Allegations Made before the Standing Committee on Aboriginal Affairs Concerning the Relocation of Inukjuak Inuit Families in the 1950s." Report submitted to the Department of Indian and Northern Affairs, 1990.

Hoare, W.H.B. *Conserving Canada's Musk-Oxen, Being an Account of an Investigation of Thelon Game Sanctuary, 1928-29, with a Brief History of the Area and an Outline of Known Facts Regarding the Musk-Ox.* Ottawa: King's Printer, 1930.

–. *Report of Investigations Affecting Eskimo and Wild Life, District of Mackenzie, 1924-1925-1926.* Department of the Interior, Northwest Territories and Yukon Branch. Part 1, 1 August 1925 and Part 2, 17 January 1927.

Hopkins, Harry. *The Long Affray: The Poaching Wars, 1760-1914.* London: Secker and Warburg, 1985.

Hornby, John. "Wild Life in the Thelon River Area, Northwest Territories, Canada." *Canadian Field-Naturalist* 48, 7 (October 1934): 105-11.

Irimoto, Takashi. *Chipewyan Ecology: Group Structure and Caribou Hunting System.* Osaka: National Museum of Ethnology, 1981.

Isenberg, Andrew C. *The Destruction of the Bison, An Environmental History, 1750-1920.* Cambridge: Cambridge University Press, 2000.

Jacoby, Karl. *Crimes against Nature: Squatters, Poachers, Thieves and the Hidden History of American Conservation.* Berkeley: University of California Press, 2001.

Jenness, Diamond. *Canada.* Vol. 2 of *Eskimo Administration.* Arctic Institute of North America Technical Report no. 14, May. Montreal: Arctic Institute of North America, 1964.

Jérémie, N. *Twenty Years of York Factory, 1694-1714: Jérémie's Account of Hudson Bay and Strait.* Ottawa: Thurnburn and Abbot, 1926. Quoted in Paul F. Wilkinson, "The Domestication of the Muskoxen," *Polar Record* 15, 98 (1971): 683.

Jessup, Lynda, ed. *Antimodernism and Artistic Experience: Policing the Boundaries of Modernity.* Toronto: University of Toronto Press, 2001.

Keller, Robert H., and Michael F. Turek. *American Indians and National Parks.* Tucson: University of Arizona Press, 1998.

Kelly, M.T. "The Land before Time." *Saturday Night* 104, 7 (July 1989): 68-75.

Kelsall, John P. "Barren-Ground Caribou and Their Management." *Canadian Audubon Magazine* (November-December 1963): 2-7.

–. "Barren-Ground Caribou Movements in the Canadian Arctic." *Transactions of the North American Wildlife Conference* 19 (1954): 551-60.

–. *Continued Barren-Ground Caribou Studies.* Wildlife Management Bulletin Series 1, no. 12. Ottawa: Canadian Wildlife Service, 1957.

–. *Co-operative Studies of Barren-Ground Caribou, 1957-58.* Wildlife Management Bulletin Series 1, no. 15. Ottawa: Canadian Wildlife Service, 1960.

–. *The Migratory Barren-Ground Caribou of Northern Canada.* Canadian Wildlife Service Monograph 3. Ottawa: Queen's Printer, 1968.

Kitto, F.H. "The Survival of the American Bison in Canada." *Geographical Journal* 63 (1930): 431-37.

Klein, D.R. "Fire, Lichens and Caribou." *Journal of Range Management* 35, 3 (1982): 390-95.

Krech, Shepard III. *The Ecological Indian: Myth and History.* New York: W.W. Norton, 1999.

–. "Throwing Bad Medicine: Sorcery, Disease and the Fur Trade among the Kutchin and other Northern Athapaskans." In *Indians, Animals and the Fur Trade: A Critique of Keepers of the Game,* ed. Shepard Krech III, 75-108. Athens: University of Georgia Press, 1981.

Lears, T.J. Jackson. *No Place of Grace: Antimodernism and the Transformation of American Culture, 1880-1920.* New York: Pantheon, 1981.

Lent, Peter C. *Muskoxen and Their Hunters: A History.* Norman: University of Oklahoma Press, 1999.

Leopold, Aldo. *Game Management.* New York: Charles Scribner's and Sons, 1933.

Lewis, Henry T. "Maskuta: The Ecology of Indian Fires in Northern Alberta." *Western Canadian Journal of Anthropology* 7, 1 (1977): 15-52.

–. *A Time for Burning: Traditional Indian Uses of Fire in Western Canadian Boreal Forest.* Occasional Publication no. 17. Edmonton: Boreal Institute for Northern Studies, 1982.

Livingston, John A. *The Fallacy of Wildlife Conservation.* Toronto: McClelland and Stewart, 1981.

Loo, Tina. "Making a Modern Wilderness: Conserving Wildlife in Twentieth-Century Canada." *Canadian Historical Review* 82, 1 (March 2001): 92-121.

–. "Of Moose and Men: Hunting for Masculinities in British Columbia, 1880-1939." *Western Historical Quarterly* 32 (Autumn 2001): 296-319.

MacEachern, Alan. *Natural Selections: National Parks in Atlantic Canada, 1935-1970.* Montreal and Kingston: McGill-Queen's University Press, 2001.

–. "Rationality and Rationalization in Canadian National Parks Predator Policy." In *Consuming Canada: Readings in Environmental History,* ed. Pam Gaffield and Chad Gaffield, 197-212. Toronto: Copp Clark, 1995.

MacFarlane, Roderick. "Notes on Mammals Collected and Observed in the Northern Mackenzie River District, Northwest Territories of Canada, with Remarks on Explorers and Explorations of the Far North." *Proceedings of the United States National Museum,* vol. 27. Washington, DC: Government Printing Office, 1905.

Mackenzie, Alexander. *Voyages from Montreal on the River St. Laurence through the Continent of North America to the Frozen and Pacific Oceans in the Years 1789 and 1793,* ed. John W. Garvin. Toronto: Radisson Society of Canada, 1927.

Mackenzie, John. *The Empire of Hunting: Hunting, Conservation, and British Imperialism.* Manchester: Manchester University Press, 1981.

Maldaver, Sharone, ed. *As Long as I Remember: Elders of the Fort Smith, Northwest*

Territories Region Talk about Bush Life and Changes They Have Seen. Fort Smith: Cascade Graphics, 1993.

Mannik, Hattie, and David Webster, eds. *Oral Histories: Baker Lake, Northwest Territories.* Ottawa: National Historic Parks and Sites Directorate, Environment Canada, 1993.

Manning, T.H. "Notes on the Mammals of South and Central West Baffin Island." *Journal of Mammalogy* 12, 11 (1943): 47-59.

–. "Remarks on the Physiography, Eskimos and Mammals of Southampton Island, NWT." *Canadian Geographical Journal* 24, 1 (1942): 17-33.

Marcus, Alan R. "Out in the Cold: Canada's Experimental Inuit Relocation to Grise Fiord and Resolute Bay." *Polar Record* 27, 163 (1991): 285-96.

–. *Relocating Eden: The Image and Politics of Inuit Exile in the Canadian Arctic.* Hanover, NH: University Press of New England, 1995.

Martin, Calvin. *Keepers of the Game: Indian-Animal Relationships and the Fur Trade.* Berkeley: University of California Press, 1978.

McCandless, Robert. *Yukon Wildlife: A Social History.* Edmonton: University of Alberta Press, 1985.

McCormack, Patricia A. "Chipewyans Turn Cree: Governmental and Structural Factors in Ethnic Processes." In *For the Purposes of Dominions: Essays in Honour of Morris Zaslow,* ed. Kenneth S. Coates and William R. Morrison, 125-38. Toronto: Captus Press, 1989.

–. "The Political Economy of Bison Management in Wood Buffalo National Park." *Arctic* 45, 4 (December 1992): 367-80.

Meighen, Arthur. "Address of Welcome." In *National Conference on Conservation of Game, Fur-Bearing Animals and Other Wild Life, 18-19 February 1919,* ed. Commission of Conservation of Canada, 5. Ottawa: King's Printer, 1919.

Miller, Frank. "Caribou." In *Wild Mammals of North America: Biology, Management, and Economics,* ed. J.A. Chapman and G.A. Feldhamer, 923-59. Baltimore: Johns Hopkins University Press, 1982.

Morris, Margaret W. "Great Bear Lake Indians: A Historical Demography and Human Ecology," pt. 1. *Musk-Ox* 11 (1972): 3-27.

Morrison, David A. *Caribou Hunters in the Western Arctic: Zooarchaeology of the Rita-Claire and Bison Skull Sites.* Mercury Series, Archaeological Survey of Canada Paper 157. Hull: Canadian Museum of Civilization, 1997.

Morrison, William R. *Showing the Flag: The Mounted Police and Canadian Sovereignty in the North, 1894-1925.* Vancouver: UBC Press, 1985.

Moss, John. *Enduring Dreams: An Exploration of Arctic Landscape.* Toronto: Anansi, 1994.

Mowat, Farley. *The Desperate People,* rev. ed. Toronto: McClelland-Bantam, 1975.

–. *People of the Deer.* Toronto: McClelland and Stewart, 1952.

Moyles, R.G., and Doug Owram. *Imperial Dreams and Colonial Realities: British Views of Canada 1880-1914.* Toronto: University of Toronto Press, 1988.

Munn, Henry Toke. *Prairie Trails and Arctic By-Ways.* London: Hurst and Blackett, 1932.

Nadasdy, Paul. *Hunters and Bureaucrats: Power, Knowledge and Aboriginal-State Relations in the Southwest Yukon.* Vancouver: UBC Press, 2003.

Nash, Roderick. *Wilderness and the American Mind.* 3rd ed. New Haven, CT: Yale University Press, 1982.

Nelles, H.V. *The Politics of Development: Forests, Mines and Hydro-Electric Development in Ontario, 1849-1941.* Toronto: University of Toronto Press, 1974.

Neumann, Roderick P. "The Postwar Conservation Boom in British Colonial Africa." *Environmental History* 7, 1 (January 2002): 22-47.

No author. *Canoeists' Reflections on Arctic Cairn Notes.* Toronto: Betelgeuse Press, 1997.

Oelschlaeger, Max. *The Idea of Wilderness: From Prehistory to the Age of Ecology.* New Haven, CT: Yale University Press, 1991.

Osterhammel, Jürgen. *Colonialism: A Theoretical Overview.* Princeton: Markus Wiener Publishers, 1999.

Ostler, Jeffrey. *The Plains Sioux and U.S. Colonialism from Lewis and Clark to Wounded Knee.* Cambridge: Cambridge University Press, 2004.

Owram, Doug. *The Promise of Eden: The Canadian Expansionist Movement and the Idea of West, 1856-1900.* Toronto: University of Toronto Press, 1999.

Parenteau, Bill. "'Care, Control and Supervision': Native People in the Canadian Atlantic Salmon Fishery, 1867-1900." *Canadian Historical Review* 79, 1 (March 1998): 1-35.

–. "A 'Very Determined Opposition to the Law': Conservation, Angling Leases, and Social Conflict in the Canadian Atlantic Salmon Fishery, 1867-1914." *Environmental History* 9, 3 (July 2004): 436-63.

Parker, Gerry R. *Biology of the Kaminuriak Population of Barren-Ground Caribou, Part 1.* Canadian Wildlife Service Report Series no. 20. Ottawa: Information Canada, 1972.

–. *Distribution of Barren-Ground Caribou Harvest in Northcentral Canada.* Canadian Wildlife Service Occasional Paper 15. Ottawa: Queen's Printer, 1972.

–. *Trends in the Population of Barren-Ground Caribou of Mainland Canada over the Last Two Decades: A Re-evaluation of the Evidence.* Canadian Wildlife Service Occasional Paper 10. Ottawa: Queen's Printer, 1972.

Peepre, Juri, and Philip Dearden. "The Role of Aboriginal Peoples." In *Parks and Protected Areas in Canada: Planning and Management,* 2nd ed., ed. Philip Dearden and Rick Rollins, 323-32. Toronto: Oxford University Press, 2002.

Pelly, David. *Thelon: River Sanctuary.* Hyde Park, ON: Canadian Recreational Canoeing Association, 1996.

Petch, Virginia. "The Relocation of the Sayisi Dene of Tadoule Lake." Research report. In Royal Commission on Aboriginal Peoples, *For Seven Generations: An Information Legacy of the Royal Commission on Aboriginal Peoples.* CD-ROM. Ottawa: Libraxus, 1997.

Peterson, M.J. "Wildlife Parasitism, Science, and Management Policy." *Journal of Wildlife Management* 55, 4 (1991): 782-89.

Petrone, Penny, ed. *Northern Voices: Inuit Writings in English.* Toronto: University of Toronto Press, 1992.

Pike, Warburton. *The Barren Ground of Northern Canada.* New York: Macmillan, 1892.

Porsild, A.E. "Reindeer and Caribou Grazing in Northern Canada." *Transactions of the North American Wildlife Conference* 7 (1942): 381-91.

–. *Reindeer Grazing in Northwest Canada: Report of an Investigation of Pastoral Possibilities in the Area from the Alaska-Yukon Boundary to Coppermine River.* Ottawa: King's Printer, 1929.

Preble, Edward A. *A Biological Investigation of the Athabaska-Mackenzie Region Prepared under the Direction of Dr. C. Hart Merriam.* Washington, DC: Government Printing Office, 1908.

Pruitt, W.O. "Snow as a Factor in the Winter Ecology of the Barren Ground Caribou." *Arctic* 12, 3 (1959): 159-79.

Rangarajan, Mahesh. "Environmental Histories of South Asia: A Review Essay." *Environment and History* 2 (1996): 129-43.

Rasmussen, Knud. *Across Arctic America: Narrative of the Fifth Thule Expedition.* New
York: Greenwood Press, 1927.

Raup, H.M. *Botanical Investigations in Wood Buffalo National Park.* National Museums of Canada Bulletin no. 74, Biological Series no. 20. Ottawa: National Museums of Canada, 1935.

Rea, Kenneth J. *The Political Economy of the Canadian North: An Interpretation of the
Course of Development in the Northwest Territories of Canada to the Early 1960s.*
Toronto: University of Toronto Press, 1968.

Reiger, John F. *American Sportsmen and the Origins of Conservation.* 3rd ed. Corvallis:
Oregon State University Press, 2001.

Ridington, Robin. "Knowledge, Power and the Individual in Subarctic Hunting Societies." *American Anthropologist* 90, 1 (1988): 48-110.

Ritchie, James. "The American Bison: a Questionable Experiment." Supplement to
Nature 117 (20 February 1926): 275.

-. "*Bison bison athabascae*, Rhoads." *Nature* 119, 2985 (15 January 1927): 95-96.

Roe, Frank G. *The North American Buffalo: A Critical Study of the Species in Its Wild
State.* 2nd ed. Toronto: University of Toronto Press, 1970.

Roosevelt, Theodore. *African Game Trails: An Account of the African Wanderings of an
American Hunter-Naturalist.* New York: Scribner's, 1926.

Rowan, William. "Canada's Buffalo." *Country Life* 66 (1929): 358-60.

Royal Commission on Aboriginal Peoples. *For Seven Generations: An Information Legacy
of the Royal Commission on Aboriginal Peoples.* CD-ROM. Ottawa: Libraxus, 1997.

Runte, Alfred. *National Parks: The American Experience.* 3rd ed. Lincoln: University
of Nebraska Press, 1997.

Russell, Edmund. *War and Nature: Fighting Humans and Insects with Chemicals from
World War I to Silent Spring.* Cambridge: Cambridge University Press, 2001.

Russell, Frank. *Explorations in the Far North: Being the Report of an Expedition under
the Auspices of the University of Iowa during the Years 1892, '93, and '94.* Iowa City:
University of Iowa Press, 1898.

Rutherford, John Gunion, James Stanley McLean, and James Bernard Harkin. *Report
of the Royal Commission to Investigate the Possibilities of the Reindeer and Musk-Ox
Industries in the Arctic and Sub-Arctic Regions of Canada.* Ottawa: King's Printer, 1922.

Ruttan, R.A. "New Crisis for the Barren-Ground Caribou." *Country Guide* 85, 11
(November 1966): 24-25.

Sabin, Paul. "Voices from the Hydrocarbon Frontier: Canada's Mackenzie Valley
Pipeline (1974-1977)." *Environmental History Review* 19, 1 (1995): 17-48.

Sangwan, Satpal. "From Gentlemen Amateurs to Professionals: Reassessing the Nat-
ural Science Tradition in Colonial India, 1780-1840." In *Nature and the Orient: The
Environmental History of South and Southeast Asia,* ed. Richard Grove, Vinita
Damodaran, and Satpal Sangwan, 212-36. Delhi: Oxford University Press, 1995.

Saunders, W.E. Letter to the editor. *Canadian Field-Naturalist* 39 (May 1925): 118.

Sawchuck, Joe, ed. *Images of the Indian: Portrayals of Native People.* Readings in Aboriginal Studies, vol. 4. Brandon, MB: Bearpaw Publishing, 1995.

Schultz, John. "Report of the Select Committee of the Senate Appointed to Inquire into the Resources of the Great Mackenzie Basin." Appendix 1, *Senate Journals*, 1888.

Scott, Duncan Campbell. "The Relation of Indians to Wild Life Conservation." In *National Conference on Conservation of Game, Fur-Bearing Animals and Other Wild Life*, ed. Commission of Conservation of Canada, 19-21. Ottawa: King's Printer, 1919.

Scott, James C. *Seeing Like a State: How Certain Schemes to Improve the Human Condition Have Failed*. New Haven, CT: Yale University Press, 1998.

Scotter, George Wilby. *Effects of Forest Fires on the Winter Range of Barren-Ground Caribou in Northern Saskatchewan*. Wildlife Management Bulletin Series 1, no. 18. Ottawa: Canadian Wildlife Service, 1964.

Seibert, F.V. "Some Notes on Canada's So-Called Wood Buffalo." *Canadian Field-Naturalist* 39 (1925): 204-6.

Sellars, Richard West. *Preserving Nature in the National Parks: A History*. New Haven, CT: Yale University Press, 1997.

Selous, Frederick. *A Hunter's Wanderings in Africa*. London: R. Bentley, 1890.

Seton, Ernest Thompson. *The Arctic Prairies*. New York: Harper and Row, 1911.

–. *The Gospel of the Redman: An Indian Bible*. London: Psychic Press, 1970.

–. *The Lives of Game Animals*, vol. 3, pt. 2. Garden City, NJ: Doubleday, 1929.

–. *Two Little Savages; Being the Adventures of Two Boys Who Lived as Indians and What They Learned*. New York: Dover Publications, 1903.

Sharp, Henry S. "The Caribou-Eater Chipewyan: Bilaterality, Strategies of Caribou Hunting and the Fur Trade." *Arctic Anthropology* 14, 2 (1977): 35-40.

–. "The Chipewyan Hunting Unit." *American Ethnologist* 4, 2 (1978): 377-93.

Shiva, Vandana. *Monocultures of the Mind: Perspectives on Biodiversity and Biotechnology*. London: Zed, 1993.

Sivaramakrishnan, K. "The Politics of Fire and Forest Regeneration in Colonial Bengal." *Environment and History* 2 (1996): 145-94.

Smith, David M. *Moose-Deer Island House People: A History of the Native People of Fort Resolution*. National Museum of Man Mercury Series, Canadian Ethnology Service Paper no. 81. Ottawa: National Museums of Canada, 1982.

Smith, James G.E. "Economic Uncertainty in an 'Original Affluent Society': Caribou and Caribou-Eater Chipewyan Adaptive Strategies." *Arctic Anthropology* 15 (1978): 68-88.

–. "Local Band Organization of the Caribou-Eater Chipewyan." *Arctic Anthropology* 13, 1 (1976): 12-24.

Soper, J. Dewey. "History, Range and Home Life of the Northern Bison." *Ecological Monographs* 2, 4 (October 1941): 348-412.

–. "Wood Buffalo Park: Notes on the Physical Geography of the Park and Its Vicinity." *Geographical Review* 29 (1939): 383-99.

Spence, Mark David. *Dispossessing the Wilderness: Indian Removal and the Making of the National Parks*. Oxford: Oxford University Press, 1999.

Stefansson, Vilhjalmur. *The Friendly Arctic: The Story of Five Years in the Polar Region*. New York: Macmillan, 1922.

–. *My Life with the Eskimo*. New York: Macmillan, 1913.

–. *The Northward Course of Empire*. New York: Harcourt Brace, 1922.

Storey, William K. "Big Cats and Imperialism: Lion and Tiger Hunting in Kenya and Northern India, 1898-1930." *Journal of World History* 2, 2 (1991): 135-73.

Symington, Fraser. *Tuktu: The Caribou of the Northern Mainland.* Ottawa: Queen's Printer, 1965.

Teal, John J. Jr. "Domesticating the Wild and Wooly Musk Ox." *National Geographic* (June 1970): 863-79.

–. "Golden Fleece of the Arctic." *Atlantic Monthly* 201, 3 (March 1958): 76-81.

Tener, John S. *Muskoxen in Canada: A Biological and Taxonomic Review.* Canadian Wildlife Service Monograph 2. Ottawa: Queen's Printer, 1965.

–. "The Present Status of the Barren-Ground Caribou." *Canadian Geographical Journal* 60, 3 (1960): 98-105.

Thomas, Donald C. *Population Estimates of Barren-Ground Caribou, March to May, 1967.* Canadian Wildlife Service Report Series no. 9. Ottawa: Queen's Printer, 1969.

Tester, Frank, and Peter Kulchyski. *Tammarniit (Mistakes): Inuit Relocation in the Eastern Arctic, 1939-63.* Vancouver: UBC Press, 1994.

Thomas, Nicholas. *Colonialism's Culture: Anthropology, Travel and Government.* Princeton: Princeton University Press, 1994.

Thompson, E.P. *Whigs and Hunters: The Origins of the Black Act.* London: Pantheon Books, 1975.

Tober, James. *Who Owns the Wildlife? The Political Economy of Conservation in Nineteenth-Century America.* Westport, CT: Greenwood Press, 1981.

Trefethen, James. *An American Crusade for Wildlife.* New York: Boone and Crocket Club, 1975.

Treude, Erhard. "Forty Years of Reindeer Herding in the Mackenzie Delta, NWT." *Polarforschung* 45, 2 (1975): 129-48.

Tyrrell, Joseph Burr. "An Expedition through the Barren Lands of Northern Canada." *Geographical Journal* 4, 5 (1894): 437-50.

Tyrrell, J.W. *Across the Sub-Arctic of Canada, a Journey of 3,200 Miles by Canoe and Snowshoe through the Barren Lands.* London: T. Fisher Unwin, 1898.

Urquhart, Doug. "Biology." In *People and Caribou in the Northwest Territories,* ed. Ed Hall, 60-69. Yellowknife: Department of Renewable Resources, NWT, 1989.

–. *Life History and Current Status of the Muskoxen in the NWT.* Yellowknife: Department of Renewable Resources, NWT, 1982.

Usher, Peter. "The Canadian Western Arctic: A Century of Change." *Anthropologica* 13, 1-2 (1971): 169-83.

–. "Contemporary Aboriginal Land, Resource, and Environmental Regimes: Origins, Problems, and Prospects." Report prepared for the Land Resource and Environment Regimes Project, February 1996. In Royal Commission on Aboriginal Peoples, *For Seven Generations: An Information Legacy of the Royal Commission on Aboriginal Peoples.* CD-ROM. Ottawa: Libraxus, 1997.

–. "The Growth and Decay of the Trading and Trapping Frontiers in the Western Canadian Arctic." *Canadian Geographer* 19, 4 (1975): 308-20.

–. "Indigenous Management Systems and the Conservation of Wildlife in the Canadian North." *Alternatives* 14 (1987): 3-9.

–. *Property, the Basis of Inuit Hunting Rights, A New Approach.* Ottawa: Inuit Committee on National Issues, 1986.

–. "Property Rights: The Basis of Wildlife Management." In *National and Regional Interests in the North: Third National Workshop on People, Resources and the Environment North of 60, 1-3 June 1983*, 389-90. Ottawa: Canadian Arctic Resources Committee, 1984.

–. "Societies and Economies in the North." In *The Historical Atlas of Canada*, vol. 3, ed. Donald Kerr and Deryck W. Holdsworth, plate 58. Toronto: University of Toronto Press, 1990.

Vallee, F.G. *Kabloona and the Eskimo in the Central Keewatin*. Ottawa: Canadian Research Centre for Anthropology, St. Paul's University, 1967.

Van Camp, Jack. "Predation on Bison." In *Bison Ecology in Relation to Agricultural Development in the Slave River Lowlands, NWT*, ed. H.W. Reynolds and A.W.L. Hawley, 25-33. Canadian Wildlife Service Occasional Paper no. 63. Ottawa: Minister of Supply and Services, 1987.

Van Zyll de Jong, C.G. *A Systematic Study of Recent Bison, with Particular Consideration of the Wood Bison* (Bison bison athabascae *Rhoads 1898*). Publication in Natural Sciences no. 6. Ottawa: National Museums of Canada, 1989.

Waiser, William A. "Canada Ox, Ovibos, Woolox ... Anything but Musk-ox." In *For the Purposes of Dominions: Essays in Honour of Morris Zaslow*, ed. Kenneth S. Coates and William R. Morrison, 189-99. Toronto: Captus Press, 1989.

Warren, Louis. *The Hunter's Game: Poachers and Conservationists in Twentieth Century America*. New Haven, CT: Yale University Press, 1997.

Weaver, Sally. *Making Canadian Indian Policy: The Hidden Agenda, 1968-70*. Toronto: University of Toronto Press, 1981.

Weiner, Doug. *Models of Nature: Ecology, Conservation and Cultural Revolution in Soviet Russia*. Pittsburgh: University of Pittsburgh Press, 2000.

Wenzel, George. *Animal Rights, Human Rights: Ecology, Economy and Ideology in the Canadian North*. Toronto: University of Toronto Press, 1991.

–. *Clyde Inuit Adaptation and Ecology: The Organization of Subsistence*. National Museum of Man Mercury Series, Canadian Ethnology Service Paper no. 77. Ottawa: National Museums of Canada, 1981.

West, Douglas A. "Re-Searching the North in Canada: An Introduction to the Canadian Northern Discourse." *Journal of Canadian Studies* 26, 2 (Summer 1991): 108-119.

Western, David. "Ecosystem Conservation and Rural Development: The Case of Amboseli." In *Natural Connections: Perspectives in Community-Based Conservation*, ed. David Western and R. Michael Wright, 15-52. Washington, DC: Island Press, 1994.

White, Gibert. *A Natural History of Selborne*. 1788. Reprint, New York: Penguin, 1977.

White, Hayden. *The Content of the Form: Narrative Discourse and Historical Representation*. Baltimore: Johns Hopkins University Press, 1987.

Whitney, Caspar "The History of Musk-ox Domestication." *Polar Record* 17, 106 (1974): 13-22.

–. *On Snow-Shoes to the Barren Grounds: Twenty-Eight Hundred Miles after Musk-Oxen and Wood-Bison*. New York: Harper and Brothers, 1896.

Williamson, F.H.H. "Game Preservation in Dominion Parks." In *Proceedings of the Committee on Fisheries, Game and Fur-Bearing Animals, Commission of Conservation, November 1-2, 1915*, 125-40. Toronto: Methodist Book and Publishing House, 1916.

Worster, Donald. *Nature's Economy: A History of Ecological Ideas.* 2nd ed. Cambridge: Cambridge University Press, 1994.

Wright, J.G. "Economic Wildlife of Canada's Eastern Arctic." *Canadian Geographical Journal* (October 1944)1 184 95.

Zaslow, Morris. *The Northward Expansion of Canada, 1914-1967.* Toronto: McClelland and Stewart, 1988.

–. *The Opening of the Canadian North, 1870-1914.* Toronto: McClelland and Stewart, 1971.

Zeller, Suzanne. *Inventing Canada: Early Victorian Science and the Idea of a Transcontinental Nation.* Toronto: University of Toronto Press, 1987.

Index

Harper, Francis, 57, 203
Hay Camp Abattoir, 94, 96-97, 99, 100
Hay River, 70-71, 82
Hearne, Samuel, xi, 26
Helm, June, 242
Heming, Arthur, 12
Henik Lake, 226-28
Henshaw, H.W., 155
Herchmer, Laurence W., 26-27
Herschel Island, 124, 125, 154
Hewitt, C. Gordon, 10, 119, 120, 233
  caribou regulations, drafting of 155-57
  on cross-breeding bison, 11, 59
  on domestication of caribou, 145, 160
  on muskox domestication, 111-12, 234
  plea for protection of muskox, 111-13
Hoare, W.H.B., 113, 125, 130-32, 134, 135,
  168-70, 176
Hornaday, Willian T., 56, 60, 112, 121
Hornby, John, 42, 126, 127, 129, 134, 149,
  164, 171, 175
Houston, James, 212
Hrobjartson, T., 175
Hudson Bay, xiii, xiv, 113, 118, 120, 121, 130,
  141, 146, 162, 220, 224, 227, 239
Hudson's Bay Company, xiii, 81, 85, 96, 114,
  141, 152, 170-71, 172, 182, 190, 224, 225
Hume, H.E., 75

Indian Affairs, Department of, 13, 61, 181,
  185, 196, 200, 208, 209, 210-11, 238
  and preservation of hunting and
    trapping economy, 44, 180
  wildlife conservation, objections to,
    39-40, 117-18, 157, 208, 237
  Wood Buffalo National Park, objections
    to, 40-41, 43, 45, 48, 53
Indian Affairs Branch, 32, 76, 81, 84, 88,
  94, 96, 101, 194, 214, 223, 224
International Treaty for the Protection of
  Migratory Birds. See Migratory Birds
  Treaty
Inuit, xvi, 8, 114, 121, 133, 138, 179, 197,
  201, 206, 207, 208, 210, 232, 236, 238
  caribou hunting practices, criticisms of,
    143-44, 149-55, 163, 165, 167-77, 189-
    91, 199, 211-12, 218, 224-25

conservation, opposition to, 8, 217, 212,
  242-43
fishing, 184-85, 214, 216-18, 239
hunting practices, 15-16, 151-54
importance of caribou to, 15-16, 216
muskox hunting, 112, 117, 122-6, 134
provision of alternative resources (to
  caribou) for, 17, 19, 167, 169, 172-73,
  183, 191-92, 210-11, 214-18, 219-20,
  230, 238-39
relocation of, 19, 124, 196, 220-30, 239,
  242
and social assistance, 214, 216, 223
Stefansson's description of, 116
starvation of, 180, 203, 217-18, 225,
sub-groups, 15
use of firearms, 150, 154
wage employment for 196, 218-20, 227,
  229-30, 239, 303n102
See also Baffin Island
Inukjuak, 220
Ireland, De Courcy, 70
Itavia, 227

Jacoby, Karl, 74
Jarvis, Inspector A.M. 28, 30-32, 37, 238
Jean Marie River, 242
Jérémie, Nicholas, 118
Johnson, Oscar, 174
Jones, Buffalo. See Buffalo Jones
Jones, E.G., 133-34
Joussard Célestine, 61, 62

Keewatin Reestablishment Project, 227,
  228
Kelly, M.T., 127
Kelngenberg, Charles, 126, 171
Kelsall, John, 93, 196, 201-5, 224
Kennedy, R.L., 227
Kikkik, 226
Kirkby, I.F., 200
Kitto, F.H., 41-43, 46, 158
Klondike Gold Rush, xiii, 29
Knox, A.J., 130, 131
Kooloola, 190
Krech, Shepard, 19-20, 152
Kridluk, 190-91

Printed and bound in Canada by Friesens

Set in Adobe Garamond by Robert Kroeger

Copy editor: Sarah Wight

Proofreader: James Leahy

Cartographer: Rajiv Rawat and Seth Loader